Literature versus Theatre

Britische und Irische Studien
zur deutschen Sprache und Literatur

Etudes parues en Grande-Bretagne et en Irlande
concernant la philologie et la littérature allemandes

British and Irish Studies
in German Language and Literature

herausgegeben von H.S. Reiss
und W.E. Yates

Band 14

PETER LANG
Bern · Berlin · Frankfurt /M. · New York · Paris · Wien

David Barnett

Literature versus Theatre

Textual problems and theatrical realization
in the later plays of Heiner Müller

PETER LANG
Bern · Berlin · Frankfurt /M. · New York · Paris · Wien

Die Deutsche Bibliothek – CIP-Einheitsaufnahme

Barnett, Cavid:
Literature versus theatre : textual problems and theatrical realization
in the later plays of Heiner Müller / David Barnett. – Bern ; Berlin ;
Frankfurt/M. ; New York ; Paris ; Wien : Lang, 1998
(British and Irish studies in German language and literature ; Bd. 14)
ISBN 3-906760-56-1

ISSN 0171-6662
ISBN 3-906760-56-1
US-ISBN 0-8204-4203-8

Spiegel: Und Sie glauben, daß das ein Theaterbesucher kapiert?

Müller: Das ist nicht mein Problem.
Das ist das Problem der Inszenierung.

Der Spiegel, 9-5-83, p. 196

Acknowledgements

First and foremost: thanks are due to my supervisor, Tom Kuhn, for his constant attentiveness, his willing helpfulness and his relentless ruthlessness. I also thank him for drawing my attention to the source of the motto of this book. Gill Hughes, the librarian for the German section at the Taylor Institution, also deserves much gratitude for her ever-keen bibliographic eye.

Three archives also merit a special mention. The 'Deutsches Presse-Archiv' in Dortmund was kind enough to send me several very full dossiers of newspaper reviews in the original which have proved indispensable. Second, the 'Zentrum für Theaterdokumentation und -information' in Berlin provided essential materials for my research on the GDR productions of Müller's plays. Their thorough documentations (a selection of videos, interviews, set designs and summaries of the rehearsal process, which are unparalleled to my knowledge) saved many of my descriptions from becoming mere footnotes. Special thanks go to Frau Doktor Toni Engelmann who was always on hand and very helpful. Third, the Henschel Verlag's archive of theatre programmes and other ephemera deserves my gratitude. Again, it was an archive that was always open for me, and for that I should like to thank the archivist, Harry Auschner, and the co-ordinator, Maria Tragelehn.

My thoughts go to the memory of Heiner Müller, who permitted me an extensive interview but six months before his death. I offer my sincerest condolences to his widow, Brigitte Mayer-Müller, and to his daughter, Anna.

I am also very grateful to the theatre people who gave up their time to allow me to interview them. Best wishes go to Sabine Andreas (freelance director), Regina Fabian (freelance actress), Gabriele Groenewold (Schauspielhaus Bochum), Marianne Janietz (Kammerspiele Magdeburg), Christoph Schroth (Staatstheater Cottbus), Wolfgang Schuch (head of the Henschel Verlag) and B. K. Tragelehn (freelance director).

In addition, there are several dramaturges, administrative workers and other theatre people who have supplied me with material and information, without which this book would have been much the lighter. Before I go on to list the various names, there is one man whom I would like to thank in particular. Herr Stecker of the Schauspiel Leipzig spent many hours reconstructing the prompt book of *Wolokolamsker Chaussee* for my benefit and for this I am most grateful. Many thanks also to: Christiane Burgsmüller (Thalia Theater), Matthias Caffier (Schauspiel Leipzig), Margrit Carstensen (actress, Münchner Kammerspiele), Frau Engels (Deutsches Theater, Berlin), Frau Dr Regina Fitl (Burgtheater, Vienna), Heiner Goebbels (composer and director), Dr Dieter Hadamczik (Mykenae Verlag), Brigitte Kabel (Kleist Theater, Frankfurt/Oder), Brigitte Käding (Schauspielhaus

Bochum), Dr Herwig Kaiser (Saarländisches Staatstheater), Ulrike Köhler (Kölner Schauspiel), Frau Koß (Maxim-Gorki-Theater, Berlin), Andreas Krock (Reiss-Museum, Mannheim), Hannah Kuhnert (Schwerin), Klaus Laskowski (Schiller-Theater, Berlin), Margrit Lenk (neues theater, Halle), Andreas Linne (Theater und Philharmonie, Essen), Monika Lück (Deutsches Theatermuseum, Munich), Herr Dr Neumann (Stadtarchiv Bochum), Dr Ben Morgan (Emmanuel College, Cambridge), Frau Dr Hedwig Müller (Theaterwissenschaftliche Sammlung, Cologne), Beate Mutschler (Münchner Kammerspiele), Barbara Norminton (Münchner Kammerspiele), Herr Philipps (Hans-Otto-Theater, Potsdam), Klaus Pierwoß (Maxim-Gorki-Theater, Berlin), M. Rühl (Schauspiel, Frankfurt), Kristina Ruppal (Wuppertaler Bühnen), Giesele Schlößer (Berliner Ensemble), Dr Gerd Schmidt (Theater der Freien Volksbühne, Berlin), Prof. Hans-Dietrich Schmidt (Ruhrfestspiele, Recklinghausen), Brigitte Spiegel (Volksbühne, Berlin), Sabine Steinhage (Zentrum für Theaterforschung, Hamburg), Werner Walkner (Schauspielhaus, Vienna) and Ursula Zangerle (Dumont-Lindemann-Archiv, Düsseldorf). Thanks also go to the anonymous sender of material from the Staatstheater Stuttgart.

Table of Contents

Chapter III: Plot and Structural Coherence

List of Abbreviations

The following Heiner Müller texts in the standard Rotbuch carry abbreviated titles in the chapters that follow.

Germania Tod in Berlin, Texte 5 (Berlin: Rotbuch, 1977) = G

Geschichten aus der Produktion 1, Texte 1 (Berlin: Rotbuch, 1974) = GP1

Geschichten aus der Produktion 2, Texte 2 (Berlin: Rotbuch, 1974) = GP2

Herzstück, Texte 7 (Berlin: Rotbuch, 1983) = H

Mauser, Texte 6 (Berlin: Rotbuch, 1978) = M

Shakespeare Factory 1, Texte 8 (Berlin: Rotbuch, 1985) = SF1

Shakespeare Factory 2, Texte 9 (Berlin: Rotbuch, 1989) = SF2

Introduction

1   Aims and Method

The following much-quoted line from Genia Schulz's monograph on Heiner Müller is still a fair summation of his stature as a writer. She describes him as 'der sprachmächtigste und politisch wie theoretisch strengste und anspruchsvollste Dramatiker im deutschsprachigen Raum'.[1] The interrelationships of language, politics, history and dramatic form within his work have occupied scholars and critics for the last twenty years. The emphasis on the different areas, however, has been highly disparate.

As texts, the dramas are highly provocative. Devices are employed which undermine our ideas of what a play can be. In *Zement* we find two sections of text without any mention of a speaker. *Traktor* combines episodes from a 'Fabel' with anonymous commentaries. *Bildbeschreibung* seemingly presents itself as a piece of prose.[2] The movement into a dramaturgy which does not conform to our expectations is signalled in the quotation that inspired the title of this book: 'Literatur ist dazu da, dem Theater Widerstand zu leisten'.[3] The line offers an interesting angle on Müller's ideas in 1975 on the function of the dramatic text within the theatrical context.[4] (It is also one that harks back to Brecht, who once asserted 'Theater theatert

---

1   Genia Schulz, *Heiner Müller* (Stuttgart: Metzler, 1980), p. 15.

2   Its status as a play has no formal basis. The note that follows the text and Müller's comment, 'es ist ein Theatertext, da ich ihn geschrieben habe und dazu erklärt habe' (quoted in Heinz Klunker, 'Vom parasitären Umgang mit einem Gegenwartsstück. Heiner Müllers *Wolokolamsker Chaussee* auf der Bühne', in Paul Gerhard Klussmann and Heinrich Mohr (eds.), *Jahrbuch zur Literatur der DDR*, vol. 7, Bonn: Bouvier, 1990, p. 29), are the only indications.

3   'Literatur muß dem Theater Widerstand leisten', in Heiner Müller, *Gesammelte Irrtümer* (Frankfurt/Main: Verlag der Autoren, 1986), p. 18.

4   The view cannot be interpreted as programmatic as such. Müller contradicts himself time and again in the many volumes of interviews that have been published. I am not consequently trying to assert that he ever wrote with such a defining principle in mind. I do believe, though, that this opinion can provide us with an important line of inquiry, within the context of the later output especially, whether Müller meant it or not.
(We know from the quotation on the dust jacket of *Gesammelte Irrtümer* that Müller considered interviews theatrical, performances, and this is how they should be seen in all subsequent interview quotations cited in this book.)

alles ein, also muß man ständig dem Theater etwas in den Rachen schieben, was das Theater nicht verdauen kann'.[5] In order to give the theatre 'indigestion', a play has to be made of strong stuff.) Müller's position is one that exploits the difference between text and performance, and seeks, rather than to harmonize or unify, to rend the two apart. The text must become so problematic that each staging confronts (theatrical) issues that have not been solved beforehand in the text. The sentiment is that the theatre system should not be able to appropriate the text with any degree of ease. The vitality of the theatre, as constructed in the quotation, is generated by the continual expansion of its possibilities. A dramaturgy must be created in which familiar concepts are pushed to breaking point. The more conventional way of dealing with a play in production is deciding what to do with the characters or the conflicts. Production becomes a question of emphasis or interpretation. The portrayal of certain figures provides the starting point. If, however, the very issues of character and plot are at stake, then realization is, to some degree, to be founded upon the theatre's solution to *dramaturgical* problems.

The aim of this thesis is to see whether Müller's programme can be fulfilled. How can the author make such basic features of the drama problematic? Is it possible to construct texts which are so demanding? Can a text resist the imposition of a style or a tradition when it becomes a part of the canon? These questions are integral to our understanding of the mechanics of Müller's later output. Texts will thus be investigated from a formal standpoint in a bid to 'anatomize' their workings. Our central interest lies in the conceptual development of character and plot within the dramas. We shall observe how they diverge from more conventional models and try to assess how 'durable' they are in the face of the institution of the theatre.

There would be little point in investigating the dynamics of the plays if we were not to contextualize our findings. The real performance in a theatre is our measure of the resistance a dramatic text can give to its practical realization. Additionally, the fascination of Müller's plays is, in part, the unimaginability of their performance. A reading of *Verkommenes Ufer Medeamaterial Landschaft mit Argonauten*, for example, is a baffling experience. Its three ostensibly unrelated sections (two of which carry no character attribution) and its extreme brevity confound our expectations of what a drama actually is. Each play under consideration will, then, be discussed in its theatrical context. On the whole, I have selected very diff-

5   Quoted by Müller in 'Am Anfang war...', in Heiner Müller, *Gesammelte Irrtümer 2* (Frankfurt/Main: Verlag der Autoren, 1990), p. 47.

erent productions of each play in order to demonstrate a range of potential differences in performance.

This method of formal investigation and theatrical contextualization raises two major problems. First, which plays should we investigate? Second, how do we reconstruct real performances?

A refusal to periodize Müller's work (cf. the discussion of Andreas Keller's book in the next section) allows one considerable scope to examine plays on their individual dramaturgical merits. However, a survey of single plays proves repetitive. The *Wolokolamsker Chaussee* cycle, for example, is unusual as a drama for various reasons. It challenges our understanding of conventional character because there is no division into roles in the five sections. The relationship between these five disparate parts is also of interest. If we then investigate *Leben Gundlings Friedrich von Preußen Lessings Schlaf Traum Schrei* we find an overlap of our interest in the organization of the parts. In order to avoid potential repetition we need to identify broad problematic areas. They can then be discussed in the light of plays that exemplify the different problems most strikingly.

The first problem area that presents itself is perhaps the most basic. A play cannot be staged without actors. A variety of approaches to acting have emerged this century and in Chapter I, I shall investigate how they might deal with the problematic 'textures' of the speeches. Acting style provides a way into, simultaneously, character and production style. It is a relatively limited and defined way of approaching a problem (of text and performance) which could otherwise become boundless. Once we have an idea of how Müller's understanding of character affects the stage, we can move on, more specifically, in Chapter II to the problematic texts that actors have to deliver. The speeches themselves are not always that straightforward. Several of the plays include text which is not attributed to a character at all. The actors and the director must therefore resolve the problem by bringing their own ideas to the unnamed passages. In Chapter III I widen shall my lens to the dramaturgy of certain plays as a whole. The organization of the differing scenes is a central problem that Müller's 'synthetic fragments' pose. We must ask how productive (a word I shall return to presently) the disparate elements can be and how different textual organizations of the fragments affect our understanding of character and incongruence as categories in drama.

These, of course, are not the only ways of approaching the issues, and other matters, such as the status of stage directions and the role of choruses, are dealt with along the way. The division into chapters is pragmatic rather than essential. It enables one to move on, in each case, to new textual examples, which again are not the only examples, but which are appropriate and useful ones.

The plays discussed in each chapter are taken exclusively from Müller's later output. A brief comparison of the form of the dramas shows that the degree of technical complexity increases over time. It is therefore sensible to concentrate on the most challenging works.

My choice of play for the first chapter is *Der Auftrag*. The text displays many features in its treatment of character which recur in the other plays under discussion later in this book. We find an oscillation between realistic and more metaphorical language and a conception of character as collectively remembered construct on stage. The choice of plays for the following two chapters is more self-evident. *Die Hamletmaschine* provides a particularly difficult set of attributions, and *Wolokolamsker Chaussee*, as noted above, has no character attribution at all. For the chapter on plot and structural coherence, three models suggest themselves. *Germania Tod in Berlin* plays, almost exclusively, with a concept of progressing paired scenes. *Leben Gundlings* is a collection of groups of scenes whereby disparate episodes form unstable wholes. *Verkommenes Ufer* presents us with three parts which are seemingly unrelated.

There is, of course, a problem with certain other later works which have been left out for reasons of space. The most conspicuous is the highly elliptical *Bildbeschreibung*. Others of note include *Anatomie Titus Fall of Rome* and *Quartett*. An advantage of my book's method, at least in part, is that it can make up for these deficiencies by covering dramaturgical issues common to these texts in the relevant chapters.

One additional extra problem which I have not dealt with explicitly is that of brevity. The shortness of much of the later work is, as with texts by Beckett, a very concrete theatrical problem. I shall, however, touch upon this indirectly in the discussions of *Die Hamletmaschine* and *Verkommenes Ufer*, both of which fail to reach double figures in terms of printed pages. My descriptions of real productions also take up other qualities of the texts under discussion which are not overtly addressed in the chapters' titles.

The business of reconstructing staged productions is riddled with problems of the subjective perceptions of the reconstructor. The polyphony of the theatrical sign (which will be discussed below) destabilizes any attempt at a re-presentation of the real event. The totality of the theatrical event also means that every description is a partial one. For example, without illustrated foot mappings one can never reproduce the position of the actor in space, not to mention the gestures. An interpretation of the speaking voice is just as difficult. One has no means to narrate the nuances that are to be found in a single line of dialogue with any high degree of faithfulness. Any description is therefore restricted by the plentitude of the theatrical event and the limitations of language or any other sign system.

There is also a problem with the materials at our disposal for such a set of reconstructions. I have attended very few of the productions under discussion. The productions have been put together at second hand. A mixture of videos, prompt books, photographs, interviews with the practitioners involved in the productions, newspaper reviews and programmes has been used as the basis for the descriptions. Video is clearly one of the most useful media, yet its importance should not be overestimated. Although it seemingly presents us with images 'as if we were there', we must not forget that we were not. The tension between performer and spectator can never be simulated, and a darkened room with a television is no substitute for the experience of the theatre. Besides, the fixed video camera adopts an inflexible and very distanced point of view. This is quite different from the roving and multi-focussed perspective of the spectator (physically fixed in a seat, of course, but mentally agile). Each description should be regarded as an attempt at a description rather than a faithful reproduction of a series of real events.

These caveats might make the task of a reconstruction sound like a vain endeavour. However, this imperfect method is all that is available. Müller's plays do present very real problems to the theatre (and to the reader). We would be foolish to pass up the opportunity of examining the practical ramifications of the provocative texts.

Another question that arises is precisely which productions deserve consideration. For plays such as *Der Auftrag* or *Die Hamletmaschine*, there are many, many productions to choose from. For a start, only professional stagings have been considered. One does not want to track the strategies of the production to practical trivialities, financial constraints or technical failings. The second exclusion is that every production has to be in the original language of the texts. The additional problem of translation is beyond the scope of this dissertation. Unfortunately this excludes the world premières of both *Die Hamletmaschine* and *Wolokolamsker Chaussee* (although the former is touched on below in Chapter II).

On the subject of productions that do qualify, one of the most obvious criteria for the descriptions is the availability of materials. If one is unable, even tentatively, to reconstruct a production, then there is little point in a speculative attempt based on a few reviews. With this in mind, various other criteria present themselves. Clearly the initial realizations of the texts, the 'Uraufführungen', will tell us much about the first attempt to deal with the various problems. The division of Germany doubled the opportunity to investigate this feature because either 'west-' or 'ostdeutsche Erstaufführungen' give us different angles on the initial reception of the work in question. Another factor is the perceived importance of a production. Over the years, certain interpretations have been celebrated as yardsticks in either newspaper reviews or in academic criticism. Their privileging means that we are, for the most part, unable to ignore them, even if the investigation is merely to relativize their importance. A further category is diversity. In the chapter on acting, for example, we do not want to hear about similar ways of dealing with the role of the actor. We are interested in the merits or drawbacks of various and particular styles.

The many criteria cannot be met with equal success. In some chapters, 'important' productions were sacrificed in the name of variety. Elsewhere, obscure productions were favoured for their interesting perspectives. Obscurity perhaps provides a little more space for the director who is no longer pressurized by the demands of the major venues of the German theatre scene (cf. section 5 of this introduction). I have attempted to strike a sensible balance in order to highlight the range and divergences in the realization process. At times I have been unable to discuss premières in any detail due to a lack of material. Where possible I have tried to note interesting points from them without attempting a rounded description or interpretation. Elsewhere I have tried to include details from as many productions as possible in order to present a larger cross-section.

2   The Secondary Literature

The recently published Heiner Müller bibliography contains approximately 2,300 entries of secondary literature (although many are newspaper reviews).[6] The playwright has generated much interest in both the formal and the thematic aspects of his plays. Major areas of attention have developed and the critical literature has produced, as is the case with every author, many advances and much dead wood. Much has been written on Müller's conception of history and his reception of various dramaturgical and philosophical traditions. Less attention has been paid to his own practices as playwright.

Secondary literature on the dramaturgy of Müller's plays has not dealt explicitly with the major challenges of the works and their innovative techniques. It is generally accepted that Müller is the most accomplished and

---

6   Ingo Schmidt and Florian Vaßen, *Bibliographie Heiner Müller* (Bielefeld: Aisthesis, 1993).

adept of Bertolt Brecht's successors.[7] However, no study as yet has defined either what is meant by 'Brechtian dramaturgy' or what Müller's modification or transformation of it might be.[8] For the most part the dramaturgy provides only a fleeting point of reference. Such treatment leads to both hopeless exaggeration and a sense of trivialization. Andreas Keller, for example, calls Müller's analysis 'illusionslos' whilst Georg Wieghaus maintains that Müller breaks with every traditional form in *Die Hamletmaschine*.[9] Werner Schulze-Reimpell, on the other hand, is more guarded and exploits the contradictory nature of the dramas when he writes of the 'Heiner Müller, der schon früh mit allen Traditionen brach und sie doch in sein Werk hineinholte, sich vielfältigen Einflüssen öffnete'.[10] Klaus Teichmann makes the point, 'die Tendenz zur Unspielbarkeit ist dabei wohl ein Teil seiner [ie. Müller's] Intention und muß als Provokation zur Erneuerung des Theaters und seiner Mittel gesehen werden'.[11] Theo Buck comments with similar astuteness that

ohnehin kann man bei den Texten neueren Datums von einer Dramaturgie des subjektiven Bewußtseins sprechen, muß

7   Critics have, however, been keen to spot Müller's affinities with many precursors. For example: 'Für manche ist er der konsequenteste und begabteste Nachfolger Brechts, andere halten ihn für einen deutschen Majakowski. Einige vergleichen seine Stücke mit Antonin Artauds "Theater der Grausamkeit", wieder andere glauben in ihnen die todessüchtigen Endspiele eines sozialistischen Beckett erkennen zu können' (Uwe Wittstock, 'Die schnellen Wirkungen sind nicht die neuen', in Heinz Ludwig Arnold [ed.], *Heiner Müller: Text und Kritik*, vol. 73, Munich: Text und Kritik, 1982, p. 11).

8   This includes the promisingly titled *Developments in Post-Brechtian Political Theater: The Plays of Heiner Müller* by Sue Ellen Case (Ann Arbor: University Microfilms International, 1991).

9   Andreas Keller, *Drama und Dramaturgie Heiner Müllers zwischen 1956-1988* (Frankfurt/Main: Peter Lang, 1992), p. 90; and Georg Wieghaus, *Zwischen Auftrag und Verrat. Werk und Ästhetik Heiner Müllers* (Frankfurt/Main: Peter Lang, 1984), p. 268.

10   Werner Schulze-Reimpell, 'Theater als Laboratorium der sozialen Phantasie: Heiner Müller, Volker Braun, Christoph Hein', in Wilfried Floeck (ed.), *Tendenzen des Gegenwartstheaters* (Tübingen: Franke, 1988), p. 179.

11   Klaus Teichmann, *Der verwundete Körper. Zu Texten Heiner Müllers* (Freiburg: Burg, 1986), p. 3.

allerdings hinzufügen: eines sich kollektiv verstehenden Subjekts. Fremdes Leben wird über den individuellen Erfahrungsrahmen mitgedacht.[12]

The final three quotations, which are representative of many other perceptive insights into Müller's dramatic style, remain passing comments. In each case, the quotations target salient points very accurately. Their problem is that there is little subsequent development or no consequent study.

The critical literature is, on the whole, prepared to treat the very basis of Müller's dramas, the form, as a subordinate to the content. A glaring example of this is the recent book by Richard Herzinger.[13] Herzinger is one of the few critics openly to attack Müller. He criticizes the anti-Western, anti-individualist strain which he identifies in Müller and links its thought to several conservative thinkers in the German tradition. For more than half the book scant regard is paid to the dramas. Interviews and essays form the main points of reference for his one-sided assault on the morals of Müller the writer. Herzinger tries to manufacture a manichaeism in Müller which posits oppositional relationships. The final sections apply this position to selected later plays without a mention of the dramaturgical structures which might make such an argument questionable. Herzinger's relationship to Müller's texts fails to take account of the various devices that undermine clear interpretation. His deductions about the author from metaphor-ridden essays and ironic interviews are as suspect as those from the plays.[14] We cannot take the plays (or the essays and interviews) at some 'face value'.

---

12   Theo Buck, 'Von der fortschreitenden Dialektisierung des Dramas. Anmerkung zur Dramaturgie bei Bertolt Brecht und Heiner Müller', *Forum Modernes Theater*, 1/89, p. 26.

13   Richard Herzinger, *Masken der Lebensrevolution: vitalistische Zivilisations- und Humanismuskritik in Texten Heiner Müllers* (Munich: Wilhelm Fink, 1992).

14   The relationship between author and work is difficult (and possibly superfluous anyway) at the best of times. With Müller the attempt at connecting the two seems all the more hopeless. His works actively frustrate reductive biographical readings. Thus a mapping of a supposed persona onto complex and contradictory texts comes across as none too helpful. Collecting motifs from Müller's life and examining their deployment in the plays (as Raddatz does in his book on Müller) would seem to yield more insight.

Too often, critics ignore difficulties in the texts. Interpretations are offered without regard for the sand upon which they are built.[15]

One major exception is the first chapter of Norbert Otto Eke's study of Müller.[16] Eke prepares the way for his close readings of the later work with a large chapter on his understanding of an open drama. There is much useful and general comment on the aesthetics and the dramaturgy. Eke devotes much space to a survey of Müller's later style as a whole without concentrating on any one drama in particular. He constantly reminds us of the provisional nature of the texts and how they should be viewed as associative triggers for their recipients. He concludes that the plays share a common link with Brecht's concept of a 'große Pädagogik' because the intense activity demanded of the spectator turns him or her into an essential player in the theatrical process.[17] Another critic who has made a significant contribution to our understanding of Müller's dramaturgy is Bernhard Greiner. Later (in Chapter II) I shall examine his thoughts on *Die Hamletmaschine*. Here, however, we can consider an emphasis constant in his work. Greiner continually draws our attention to the note at the end of *Zement* (GP2 p. 133) which is also the title of his article.[18] He takes the comment as paradigmatic of the split between text and performance. 'Vorgang' (events on stage) is not the doubling of 'Beschreibung' (the text). The two should remain discrete yct simultaneous on stage.[19] He argues that Müller's drama must be understood in this way if it is to be effective in performance. Like Eke, he also stresses the 'unfinished' nature of the texts, that they require active input in order to be realized for either the reader or spectator.

15   Later we shall see, for example, how the characters 'Hamlet' and 'Ophelia' are referred to without any caveats in many articles despite their dubious ontological status in scenes 1 and 2 of *Die Hamletmaschine*. Similar assertions are to be found in criticism of other plays, too.

16   Norbert Otto Eke, *Heiner Müller: Apokalypse und Utopie* (Paderborn: Ferdinand Schöningh, 1989).

17   Ibid., p. 60.

18   Bernhard Greiner, '"Einheit (Gleichzeitigkeit) von Beschreibung und Vorgang": Versuch über Heiner Müllers Theater', in Paul Gerhard Klussmann and Heinrich Mohr (eds.), *Jahrbuch zur Literatur in der DDR*, vol. 7 (Bonn: Bouvier, 1990), pp. 69-81.

19   Greiner, p. 80.

Practically no work has been done on Müller's plays in performance. Criticism of Robert Wilson's *Die Hamletmaschine* has been mainly concerned with Wilson's practices rather than Müller's (cf. Chapter II). *Der Lohndrücker* (under Müller's direction at the Deutsches Theater, première 29 January 1988) is the only production that has received any serious academic criticism apart from that.[20] In part this was to do with the montage of different fragments employed (*Der Horatier* and 'Kentauren' were both integrated) which had enlivened the contemporary GDR stage. Elsewhere there are one or two articles on the staging of this play or that. In each case, there is little interest in the process of transforming the text into performance. For the most part, the articles are interpretations of the director's work.

A full analysis of Müller's dramatic technique is frustrated rather than enacted in Keller's book, *Drama und Dramaturgie Heiner Müllers zwischen 1956 - 1988*, mentioned above. Marc Silbermann's conclusion to his 'Forschungsbericht' of 1980 warned against all reductivism in the treatment of Müller's highly heterogeneous plays.[21] This is unfortunately the practice of Keller. He reduces the wide and varied output of the playwright to three chronological periods. The first phase, 'Produktions- und Lehrstücke', runs from *Der Lohndrücker* to *Zement*, the second, 'Textmontagen und Collagen', from *Germania Tod in Berlin* to *Die Hamletmaschine*, and the third, 'Provokation und Grenzüberschreitung', from *Der Auftrag* to *Bildbeschreibung*.[22] The phases themselves are highly problematic. It is difficult to understand why *Die Hamletmaschine* is a phase two play and not in the next category. Also, the breadth of the categories includes huge divergences in the texts; it seems impractical to ally, for example, *Die Korrektur* with *Mauser*. The main argument of an article by Marianne Streisand is that Müller's plurality

---

20 For example, Gottfried Fischborn, Frank Hörnigk, Marianne Streisand and Renate Ullrich, '*Der Lohndrücker* von Heiner Müller (Für und Wider)', *Weimarer Beiträge*, 7/88, pp. 1180-1194; or Hugh Rorrison, 'Küchenschabe und Kanalisation: Montage als Selbstinterpretation bei Heiner Müller', in John Flood (ed.), *Kurz bevor der Vorhang fiel. Zum Theater der DDR. Londoner Symposium* (Amsterdam: Rodopi, 1990), pp. 81-90.

21 Marc Silbermann, *Heiner Müller* (Amsterdam: Rodopi, 1980).

22 Keller, p. 43.

of forms is, in part, closely related to his writing practice.[23] In the period 1963-4 she notes that the *Der Bau*, *Philoktet*, 'Winterschlacht 63' (a poem), *Herakles 5* and *Der Tod ist kein Geschäft* (an unpublished radio drama, written under the engaging pseudonym Max Messer) were all in some state of production. Whether Streisand is correct or not does not detract from the charge against Keller who consigns these to a single phase. There is also a further problem in that *Wolokolamsker Chaussee* is not assimilated into the tripartite structure although it is clearly within the book's scope as defined by its title. Is the cycle a 'Lehrstück', a 'Textmontage' or a 'Grenzüberschreitung'? The later analysis in Chapter II will show that it comes under each heading, just like many of the other plays. Keller defends the phase model with weak arguments. He criticizes Eke's refusal to periodize by asserting that this leads to an imputed continuity in Müller's dramaturgical practice. He fails to see that each play might be considered in its own right, an approach which guarantees diversity. Keller's method is also reductive. It assumes that for each phase, a 'typical' play might be selected for further inspection. *Die Umsiedlerin* is supposed to exemplify the first phase, *Germania Tod in Berlin* the second and *Bildbeschreibung* the third. Although Keller makes valid and interesting points on the individual dramas, it is impossible to assert that the dramaturgy of any one of these examples is a helpful index for either the others in the group or for Müller's *oeuvre* as a whole.

Müller's plays defy periodization, although we can accept a broad notion of 'development'. The variety of dramaturgical styles can only be unjustifiably obscured by a grouping of the plays. In Keller's case, we see that major stylistic differences are ignored by his chronological method. Chronology is a major problem in Müller's work. The time-lags between starting and completing projects (described more fully in the discussions of the plays themselves) make the business of dating them problematic. Yet even if one tries an organization by themes, it would be hard to unify the differing dramatic structures. If we think of his reworking of plays from antiquity, the plays on the theme of revolution, or on the theme of history, each category presents the investigator with a vast range of structural features which cannot be dealt with in terms of formal generalizations. Even the themes themselves overlap. Would we call *Der Auftrag* a play about

23 Marianne Streisand, '"Mein Platz, wenn mein Drama noch stattfinden würde, wäre auf beiden Seiten der Front, zwischen den Fronten, darüber". Über das Arbeits-prinzip der Gleichzeitigkeit bei Heiner Müller', *Weimarer Beiträge*, 4/91, pp. 485-508.

revolution or history? Clearly it deals with both, just as *Zement* treats of revolution and develops motifs from antiquity.

One can conclude from this short survey that even though useful nuggets are to be found in the critical works on Müller, there is no comprehensive study of the mechanics of the dramaturgy. The more incisive criticism has only managed to describe broad, generalizing features of the corpus as a whole. It has focussed on aesthetic questions without illustrating results in practice. An investigation of the innovative devices in the texts themselves and their practical ramifications has not been attempted. Müller as a writer for the stage has almost totally been ignored.

3   'Blinde Praxis', the Aesthetics of the Dream and 'Material'

Before I examine the plays of Heiner Müller in detail, we should try to understand their status as texts for performance. If they are to challenge the theatre's apparatus, they must satisfy certain prerequisites that make them resistant to the standardizing process.

A concept that Müller returns to again and again is 'blinde Praxis'. In the 'Gesprächsprotokoll' of 1981, 'Mich interessiert der Fall Althusser', we find the lines, 'ich habe seit Jahren überhaupt keine analytischen Impulse mehr. [...] In gewisser Weise ist ja Kunst eine blinde Praxis'.[24] The sentiments here are defined more clearly in the essay 'Fatzer ± Keuner':

> Zwischen den Zeilen Benjamins steht die Frage, ob nicht Kafkas Parabel geräumiger ist, mehr Realität aufnehmen kann (und mehr hergibt) als die Parabel Brechts. Und das nicht obwohl, sondern weil sie Gesten ohne Bezugssystem beschreibt /darstellt, nicht orientiert auf eine Bewegung (Praxis), auf eine Bedeutung nicht reduzierbar, eher fremd als verfremdend, ohne Moral. [...] Die Blindheit von Kafkas Erfahrung ist der Ausweis ihrer Authentizität. (Kafkas Blick als Blick in die Sonne. Die Unfähigkeit der Geschichte ins Weiße im Auge zu sehen als Grundlage der Politik.)[25]

24   'Mich interessiert der Fall Althusser', in Frank Hörnigk (ed.), *Heiner Müller Material* (Göttingen: Steidl, 1989), p. 28.

25   'Fatzer ± Keuner', ibid., p. 30-1.

Müller proposes a writing practice which does not use ideas in the conventional sense. Somehow they have to be liberated from systems of reference and ideology. They must be able to question their contexts. In the assertion, 'ich hab ja gar keine Ideen. Ich habe nie Ideen gehabt', the obviously coquettish words belie a more programmatic sense.[26] In this context ideas define and limit. Clearly, Müller does not write without themes or motifs in his head. It is also difficult to see him in a 'naïve' light: the network of (modified) quotations in his work is taken from an extensive knowledge of historical and cultural reference points. It is the development of ideas and influences, however, which is allowed free reign. His use of language attests to its uncontrollable strength ('die Metaphern sind klüger als der Autor').[27] The intertexts that provide the germ for the far greater part of Müller's output are allowed to grow in the metaphorical spaces of the text. Writing without aims or purposes is praised later in the 'Fatzer' essay when Müller describes the writing practice of Brecht at what Müller considers to be his best: 'Der Schreibgestus ist der des Forschers, nicht der des Gelehrten, der Forschungsergebnisse interpretiert, oder des Lehrers, der sie weitergibt'.[28] The author has no responsibility to be the constructor of meaningful texts. S/he is not the seat of knowledge.

Herzinger has criticized the concept of 'blinde Praxis'. He maintains that it marks a return to intuitionism and the 'Geniekult' of the 'Sturm und Drang' movement.[29] The reproach is that Müller is celebrating an organic claim to truth through the mystical and mystifying practice of his writing. Müller's potential rejoinder is witty and concise: 'ich bin kein Weltgeist an der Schreibmaschine'.[30] He dissociates himself from Hegel's all-knowing world-spirit and relativizes the mysticism implied in Herzinger's critique. Müller plays with eventualities and possibilities which arise from the engage-

26   'Ich scheiße auf die Ordnung der Welt', in *Gesammelte Irrtümer*, p. 127.

27   'Fatzer ± Keuner', ibid.

28   Ibid., pp. 35-6.

29   Herzinger, p. 33 and p. 69. He also criticizes Müller's writing style as a whole as 'eine Verrätselung' (p. 53). The charge that the author deliberately obfuscates meaning by playing elaborate word games is also somewhat reductive. Müller has often argued that if we could understand art, there would be no point in having it (for example, cf. *Gesammelte Irrtümer 2*, p. 100).

30   'Ein Gespräch zwischen Wolfgang Heise und Heiner Müller', in Heiner Müller, *Gesammelte Irrtümer 2* (Frankfurt/Main: Verlag der Autoren, 1990), p. 65.

ment with the intertexts and the world around him. He makes no claim to absolute truth, rather his main business is to create works which free themselves from narrowness. In the words of Oscar Wilde, 'there is no such thing as a moral or an immoral book. Books are well written, or badly written. That is all'.[31] The emphasis on a writing technique which shuns the individual values of a society and/or an ideology triumphs over writing practices which defer to them.

A means to achieve this is the appropriation of the aesthetics of the dream. In an interview, Müller talks about the dream as an ideal and the vast problems involved in capturing it on paper: 'die eigenen Träume sind immer besser als das, was man daraus machen kann. Als Träumender ist man ein Genie. Die ganze Arbeit besteht darin, sich dem so weit anzunähern, wie es geht'.[32]

One may take issue with various interpretative aspects of Sigmund Freud's epoch-making study, *Die Traumdeutung* (1900), yet a reading of his notes on the qualities and characteristics of dreams reveals many common features with Müller's later output. For Freud the dream's first qualities are density and displacement, 'Verdichtung' and 'Verschiebung'. He notes: 'nicht nur die Elemente des Traums sind durch die Traumgedanken mehrfach determiniert, sondern die einzelnen Traumgedanken sind auch im Traum durch mehrere Elemente vertreten'.[33] Dreams are also composed of highly associative material. Connections not usually made on a conscious level become 'nachlässig und zwangslos' to the dreamer. The associations are then turned into visual representations of ideas so that even abstract concepts can be presented as images.[34] The moral neutrality of (or the dreamer's subjective indifference to) these images is determined by the prevalence of the

31 Oscar Wilde, The Preface to *The Picture of Dorian Gray* (London: Penguin, 1985), p. 21. Wilde's claim is clearly one that, in his day, was tied to aestheticism and 'l'art pour l'art'. Müller is an author whom we would be pushed *not* to call a 'political playwright'. The question thus raised of commitment will be considered in the conclusion to this book.

32 'Fünf Minuten Schwarzfilm', *Gesammelte Irrtümer 2*, p. 142.

33 Sigmund Freud, *Die Traumdeutung* (Frankfurt/Main: Fischer, 1991), p. 285 and p. 290.

34 Ibid, p. 74 and p. 65.

logical operator 'gleichwie' which confers a simultaneity upon contradictory elements. Opposites are presented with special predilection as a unity.[35]

The raw material of the dream is also presented in a way that reminds us of Müller's own fondness for the use of many and varied intertexts. Freud calls the dream's fuel the 'ihm zur Bearbeitung vorliegender Text'. The assertion is supported by the claim that dreams are full of 'Witzworte, Zitate, Lieder und Sprichwörter' which are found either in their original or in a modified form. At one point he posits the thesis that *all* speech in dreams is quotation.[36]

The result of the dream work is 'Erleben statt Denken'. Various problems arise as a consequence. Freud finds that the resultant difficulties for the analyst can be couched in the following formulation:

> Es ist im allgemeinen bei der Deutung eines jeden Traumelements zweifelhaft, ob es:
> a)   im positiven oder negativen Sinne genommen werden soll (Gegensatzrelation);
> b)   historisch zu deuten ist (als Reminiszenz);
> c)   symbolisch, oder ob
> d)   seine Verwertung vom Wortlaute ausgehen soll.[37]

The 'moral neutrality' of the dream's content which allows such large room for interpretation is one of *the* qualities Müller seems to be striving for in his literature.

Dream psychology has long influenced the dramatic arts, so it might prove interesting to discuss briefly the limitations of a famous example, Strindberg's *A Dream Play* (1901-2), in order to understand Müller better. The proliferation of characters, the bizarre transformation of scenes and the illogical, irrational texture of the play lend it a superficial relationship to the features of a dream described above. Yet in many ways the play does not exploit the full range of possibilities. There is something self-conscious about many of the characters. Their symbolic and sententious utterances seem to aim at meaning, albeit one that is at odds with the claims of reason. We are aware that they are signifying a dream-like state. This inherent consciousness implies an intention which is lacking in the description of Freud's architec-

---

35   Ibid., p. 323 and p. 322.

36   Ibid., p. 318, p. 348 and p. 317.

37   Ibid., p. 66 and p. 344.

ture of the dream. By the end of the play values have been constructed so that we are left with the impression that humans are miserable or pitiful slaves to the laws of the 'righteous', as Strindberg calls them. Elsewhere, well-executed dream associations, where incongruous images present themselves as harmonious stable-mates, are succeeded by explanation on the part of one character or another. The constant imposition of interpretation again restricts the possibilities generated by the potentially powerful compositions. The play also seems to deal with the dream world as if it were an allegory of the real world. The play fails to gain autonomy from other sources of value. Although there is much to be said in favour of *A Dream Play*, it is far more dream-like than like a dream. If Müller's later texts really are dream texts (a thesis which will in part provide a subtext for the discussion of the actor's relationship to the script), then their aim is to divorce the signifier from a concrete mapping onto a signified.

In an interview with Müller, he told me that he had read most of Freud's major works early on (between the ages of sixteen and seventeen), 'später eigentlich weniger', in a bid to resist a programmatic appropriation of the texts. The texts have perhaps remained in his unconscious mind, which would seem the best place for them in Müller's scheme of things. Conscious sources present a problem to the writer who strove to attain an art free of authority. Müller's own experiences in the theatre also presented a potentially inhibiting factor to his writing. Because he was at that time a director as well as a playwright, he was more familiar with the practical exigencies of transforming a text into performance. In the same interview Müller hoped that his role as a director did not influence his writing too much, although he acknowledged that it was possible. His writing ideal was articulated thus: 'wenn man schreibt, ist man immer allein mit der Schreibmaschine'.[38]

Müller's goal was to manufacture texts which functioned as 'Material'. The term implies that what is presented is employable as a catalyst free from the restrictions of a stringent context. He has commented that he used his sources in this way. They become unprivileged parts of a disparate whole: 'I use Marxism as material, in the same way I use a Shakespeare play or a ride on a trolley'.[39] The sources are not employed as programmatic bearers of a message. Their function is rather to dislocate and to challenge

---

38   David Barnett, '"Ich erfinde gerne Zitate": Interview mit Heiner Müller', *GDR Bulletin*, 2/95, p. 12 and p. 9.

39   'Poets have to be Stupid', in Heiner Müller, *Germania*, tr. by Bernard and Caroline Schütze (New York: Semiotext(e), 1990), p. 202.

other nuggets of text. Roland Barthes' prophetic view of a theatre after Brecht points to the independence of its parts:

> Doubtless there would be no difficulty in finding in post-Brecht-
> ian theatre and post-Eisensteinian cinema *mises en scène*
> marked by the dispersion of the tableau, the pulling to pieces of
> the 'composition', the setting in movement of the 'partial organs'
> of the human figure, in short the holding in check of the
> metaphysical meaning of the work - but then also of its political
> meaning; or, at least, the carrying over of this meaning towards
> *another* politics.[40]

The ideal would be an artistic work that was pulled from perspective to perspective by the varying impulses of its text so that a uniform interpretation would be impossible. The work, composed of 'Material', becomes 'Material' itself. Its manifold qualities resist singular appropriation.

The concept of 'Material' is one that is closely allied to that of 'productivity' in Müller's dramaturgical scheme of things. If texts are productive, then they are able to activate those who come into contact with them. Here productivity is the opposite of consumerism. Text as material frustrates attempts to understand it. Directors and actors will therefore have great difficulty in presenting highly associative speeches. If they choose to defer interpretation (by adopting, for example, a neutral style of delivery) then the spectator is activated all the more.[41] If it is not only the texts that provide a difficulty for their realizers but also the dramaturgies, then productivity is generated at a far more fundamental level. No one production will ever be the same if, for example, there is no character assigned to a text. Productivity is the ability of a fixed playscript to generate new interpretations by engaging its realizers and its recipients to the most intensive degree possible with the text.[42] This takes us back to the thesis, that if literature is to challenge the apparatus of the theatre, it must ensure that it cannot be

40   'Diderot, Eisenstein, Brecht', in Roland Barthes, *Image Music Text*, tr. by Stephen
      Heath (London: Fontana, 1977), p. 72.

41   Yet even if a production does try to interpret, there is little chance that the
      spectator will be able to rest easily in his or her seat. There is too much provoca-
      tion in the metaphorical and intertextual speeches to allow an 'interpretation' in
      the conventional theatrical sense.

42   Whether Müller achieves this and to what extent this can be said of *all* plays will
      be discussed in the conclusion.

reduced to fixed meanings. The employment of elements without a concomitant employment of their positive or negative value in a social, political, historical or aesthetic context confers on them a position equal to that of elements in a dream.

4   Text and Performance

The question of the relationship between text and performance has provoked a variety of responses. The central point of the debate is the extent to which the text holds sway over the performance. The problem is concisely summarized by Keir Elam:

> The question that arises, then, is whether a semiotics of theatre *and* drama is conceivable as a bi- or multilateral but nevertheless integrated enterprise, or whether instead there are necessarily two (or more) quite separate disciplines in play.[43]

On the one hand, there are critics who view the text's role as crucial. Herta Schmid maintains 'das Schauspiel muß einerseits werkgetreu sein, andererseits eigene, autonome künstlerische Qualitäten zur Erscheinung bringen'. Consequently 'dramatisches Werk und theatralische Aufführung sind [...] verschiedenartige Ausdrucksformen ein- und desselben Kunstwerks'.[44] The first quotation is interesting because it uses the highly problematic term 'werkgetreu'. If we are to ascribe to the text implicit qualities, we are dealing with an essentialist argument as to the 'real' nature of the text. These may then be transformed by 'autonome, künstlerische Qualitäten', yet they act as appendages to a set of given textual parameters. Richard Hornby presents a similar view of the text based on structuralist concepts of surface and deep structures. He sees the job of performance as bringing out the 'hidden world' of the text by viewing its parts and their relations to each other. 'To alter a playscript, then, is really a contradiction in terms; to do so is to defeat its basic purpose'. The integrity of the play lies in its completeness and its meaning is generated by the essential relationship of each part

---

43   Keir Elam, *The Semiotics of Theatre and Drama* (London: Routledge, 1980), p. 3.

44   Herta Schmid, 'Das dramatische Werk und seine theatralische Konkretisierung im Lichte der Literaturtheorie Roman Ingardens', in Erika Fischer-Lichte (ed.), *Das Drama und seine Inszenierung* (Tübingen: Max Niemeyer, 1985), p. 24 and p. 35.

to the other. The text has a fixed field of meanings and only these may be realized in performance: 'a playscript, like a human being, is a complete entity. Like a human, it has a "personality" that will vary in differing production circumstances but which remains at bottom a unity'.[45] Like Schmid, Hornby allows for a variation based exclusively on the 'innate' qualities of the text.

Richard Sheppard's remarks on the nature of the literary work cast doubt on the limiting nature of the script: 'the signified of any text is not a unifying idea, principle, energy or repertoire, but a meta-textual dialectic out of which that text has been generated and which consists, simultaneously, in a set of problems and a set of responses'.[46] The text can no longer be said to be saying anything. Its complicated relationship with the problems with which it seeks to engage resists resolution. The essentialist argument is undermined by the lack of a fixed set of meanings. Erika Fischer-Lichte augments Sheppard's argument by placing the text and its performance in a cultural-historical context:

> 'Werkgetreu' meint nun nicht mehr in erster Linie die Unantastbarkeit des Dichterwortes, sondern die Vorbildlichkeit einer bestimmten Inszenierungsform, deren in einer spezifischen historischen Situation entwickelte Prinzipien dergestalt als zeitlos gültig postuliert und proklamiert werden.[47]

The paradigms of a 'true' production are the product of privilege. Because particular interpretations have found certain resonances, they have gained a status which denies their historical context and suggests a phoney universality. The 'definitive' production or performance is no longer a concept for us.

The nature of the theatrical sign also causes problems to notions of a 'correct' realization of the text. Elam describes the freedom of the theatrical sign in the introduction to his book on the semiotics of the theatre. He

---

45 Richard Hornby, *Script into Performance. A Structuralist Approach* (New York: Paragon House, 1977), p. 13, p. 99 and p. 109.

46 Richard Sheppard, *Tankred Dorst's "Toller": A Case Study in Reception* (New Alyth: Lochee, 1989), p. 9.

47 Erika Fischer-Lichte, 'Was ist eine "werkgetreue" Inszenierung? Überlegungen zum Prozeß der Transformation eines Dramas in eine Aufführung', in Erika Fischer-Lichte (ed.), *Das Drama und seine Inszenierung*, p. 40.

asserts that everything on the stage is a semiotized version of the object we know from everyday life so that each aspect of performance is torn between a dialectic of connotation and denotation. As a result even an attempt at the illustrative representation of an object undergoes a transformation into a theatrical metaphor. At very bottom, he argues, every object on stage represents both itself and a theatrical prop.[48] The theatrical sign, however, need not stop at a notion of the representational. Elam writes, following Jindřich Honzl, a Czech theorist of the 1940s, that 'any stage vehicle can stand, in principle, for any other signified class of phenomena; there are absolutely no fixed representational relations.'[49] John Rice and Paul Malone contend in the light of such sentiments that 'performance is just an alternative form of language; and it is not just the graphic representation of the written word'.[50] Just like a language, the theatrical signifier can float over possible signifieds, resisting any pressure to denote. The arbitrary nature of the sign means that any conception of 'adequateness' has no foundation any more. The different types of theatrical signs are many and varied. Elam lists them on five pages; they number twenty-nine in his reckoning. He concludes that the process of realizing a text 'cannot be accounted for in terms of a facile determinism'.[51]

It would seem that scholarly theory has arrived at an important impasse. We are unable to evaluate the efficacy of a performance and we have no vocabulary available even if we wanted to. Müller's texts do not help the business of a 'correct' staging: many fundamental givens are no longer accepted as such. The *dramatis personae*, 'unbestritten konstitutiv' of

---

48   This is, however, not necessarily so. We could add that an additional tension is created by the relationship of the free-floating signifier to the *real* events on stage. We can understand this assertion better, for example, from Frank Castorf's montage of *Die Schlacht* and the boulevard farce *Pension Schöller* at the Volksbühne, Berlin, in 1994. Here a live python was brought on by one of the guests at the Pension. We cannot imagine that the experience of the spectator would have been remotely similar if it had been a mere representation of a python. The same is true when human beings perform physically demanding or potentially dangerous feats.

49   Elam, p. 8, p. 11 and p. 13.

50   John Rice and Paul Malone, 'Text or Performance. The Rationalism and Intoxication of Presence in Theatre', in Eitel Timm and Kenneth Mendoza (eds.), *The Poetics of Reading* (Columbia: Camden House, 1993), p. 113.

51   Elam, pp. 57-62 and p. 209.

a drama as Fischer-Lichte puts it, is made problematic in *Die Hamlet-maschine* and cannot be said to exist in *Wolokolamsker Chaussee*.[52] The ontology of character is questionable in these two plays, as well as in the 'Erinnerung' *Der Auftrag*, and the first and third sections of *Verkommenes Ufer*.[53] Even the traditional status of the stage direction is challenged. Whereas it usually gives information as to how we arrange a scene or deliver lines, Müller's nightmarish instructions sometimes ask the impossible and have on occasion become areas of spoken text in performance. Even his notes on staging which precede or follow some of the plays have been incorporated into certain productions. It would seem, in the light of this brief overview, that his texts expose and emphasize the distance between text and performance.

We are thus left with a seemingly imponderable task. If one is to compare Müller's later, formally challenging work with its realizations on stage, one must ask what manner of criteria are available, in order to assess the relative merits or drawbacks of the production in question.

It is difficult to use the appreciation of the audience as a yardstick. First, its response comes to us second-hand via the writers of newspaper reviews. We are therefore uncertain whether the critic has distorted the description of the applause in order to give his or her own report credence, or whether the critic's subjective position in time and space has prevented an accurate reporting of the reception of a play for the run as a whole. Where possible, I shall mention the reported response of the audience, but merely to illustrate tentatively whether the production in question found any sort of popular resonance.

Another option is to use the problems of the texts. Müller continually presents actors and directors with grey areas or insoluble theatrical situations. This study must therefore include an evaluation of how such difficulties are dealt with in the practice of realization. One can ascertain whether a team has tried to solve the problem in hand, has decided to fudge it, or has opted to defer any fixed answer by highlighting the provisional nature of their performed work. (It is also possible that the team has not apparently noticed the problem at all.) Reductionism or the failure to acknowledge or to exploit Müller's textual provocations would, in this scheme, suggest a more negative view of a particular production. The degree to which the challenge is taken up becomes the main criterion. It also allows

52   Erika Fischer-Lichte, *Semiotik des Theaters*, vol. 3 (Tübingen: Gunter Narr, 1983), p. 39.

53   All these contentions are discussed in the relevant chapters.

one to assess how successful Müller is as a writer of texts which should resist the institution of the theatre. When I asked Müller which productions of his plays were his favourites, his reply was an ironic 'eigentlich keine'.[54] His complaint was that no production had, as yet, managed to encompass the wealth of material and the complexity of the works. In the words of Hasselbein in *Der Bau*, it could be a case of 'Praxis, Esserin der Utopien' (GP1 p. 94).

5   The German Theatre System and Müller's Place in It

As already mentioned in section 2, this book is solely concerned with the professional German stage. In order to understand the nature of some of the productions, it is important briefly to note the distinguishing features of the theatre system, with a particular emphasis on its effects on the more experimental stages.[55]

The most important feature of the German theatrical institution is that it is the most highly subsidized in Europe. Theatres are not as constrained by the profit motive, unlike their counterparts in other countries. They can afford to be more experimental and to cultivate a repertoire of more challenging works because of the lessened financial pressure. Of course, many German theatres produce commercial and popular plays just like in any other land. Yet this does not detract from a marked tendency in major cultural centres such as Berlin, Hamburg, Frankfurt or Munich to indulge in more demanding plays or theatrical effects. The results of this financial arrangement are felt in all other areas upon which the theatre impinges.

The internal structure of most German theatres differs greatly from e.g., the British example. At the head of each theatre is the 'Intendant', who takes ultimate responsibility for the house. The 'Intendant' has the power to shape all artistic output and thus define the theatre in the style of his/her choosing. As a result, we shall see in the sections on real productions that certain theatres have repeatedly found space for Müller's plays in their 'Spielplan' over the years. The other position for which there is no generally acknowledged equivalent in the British theatre is the 'Dramaturg' (rendered in English as 'dramaturge').[56] The job of the dramaturge is one that is

54   Barnett, p. 9.

55   There were, of course, two systems, the GDR's and the FRG's. Their basic structures were similar in the way that they diverge from the British system, although I shall discuss their own internal differences below.

34

certainly open to interpretation, although certain strands can be recognized. The dramaturge is mainly responsible for the 'integrity of the text', which might mean that research is carried out to ascertain which costumes or props would be most fitting, or that various contexts or intertexts are investigated. They also adapt or abridge the dramatic text. Other roles see them as versed more broadly in the skills of theatrical production. The dramaturge, when employed in such capacities, forms a dialectical relationship with the director, the 'Regisseur'. Sometimes this can be highly productive: in the sixties, the Peter Stein/Botho Strauss team produced many major theatrical events. At others the dramaturge does little more than produce the programme.[57]

The 'Regisseur' is also a key figure, especially in the FRG 'art-house' theatre scene, more so, for the most part, than the actors. Actors in Germany do not have the same crowd-pulling ability as in Britain for a variety of reasons. The decentralized, nodal distribution of the theatres means that actors find it hard to achieve anything more than regional recognition. The lack of a developed film or television industry also prevents the 'syndication' of the actor. Actors are usually part of an ensemble, so their profiles are not as high. They also tend to be associated with the style of a particular 'Regisseur'. When, for example, Claus Peymann left the Schauspielhaus Bochum for the Burgtheater in Vienna in the mid-eighties, he took a troupe of his favourite actors with him. The variety of acting styles of the 'serious' theatres also dilutes the importance of psychological realism as an acting mode; actors are prevented from stealing shows in the way they do in Britain. The 'Regisseur' becomes a central figure with a characteristic style or preoccupation with certain genres or types of plays. The system indulges the 'Regisseur', and the charge is sometimes raised that productions are too intellectual and abstruse.

56 The OED defines 'dramaturge' as 'a composer of drama', which very is different from the German meaning. However, the use of the word in this book will be merely an English spelling of a German term. 'Dramaturgy' and 'dramaturgical' retain their meanings which are linked to the OED's definition of 'dramaturge'.

57 The importance of the programme should not, however, be underestimated. The German theatre has a long history of loading programmes with articles and associative texts in order to steer the imagination of the spectator. Some of Brecht's 'Lehrstück' theory and Müller's *Die Hamletmaschine* were originally published in programmes. Again the status of the programme is in part made possible by subsidies: high quality tomes, which sometimes run to complete printings of the playscript (together with the theatre's cuts in some cases), are not uncommon.

'Serious' theatre critics also seem to be more influential and intellectually demanding. Some have applied for (and sometimes succeeded in attaining) jobs as 'Intendant'. Their reviews employ terms which we may consider high-brow in a British context. Words like 'Lehrstück', which many drama undergraduates might not understand, are used without any special explication in the German press.

As a result, the German audience can be influenced by a highly developed system of information both within and without the theatre. Its sensibilities can be developed in a more experimental environment. Productions which we might be inclined to consider overly self-conscious or pretentious should be re-considered in this context. The development of non-realist aesthetics has been steady over the century (we should not forget the radical practices of Expressionist performance in the second decade of this century) and the subsidized German theatre system can be seen to play a crucial role in this.

The two Germanies dealt with the common structures in very different ways. The FRG has gratified (and still does gratify) the 'Regisseur' in his or her artistic whims. This condition has produced both innovative and challenging productions, and ludicrous displays of self-indulgence. The director's relative autonomy has also led to a certain autocracy in production in order to re-produce his or her 'hallmark'. More aspects of the realization process, of course, were subject to the rigours of the dominant ideology in the GDR. On the one hand, there was more commitment to collectivity in the workplace, but there was also the constant threat of censorship. For all the financial security of the system, it was far more subject to the arbitrary power of well-placed 'Intendanten' and a network of 'Stasi' informers. The only way to break such strictures was to have 'connections', or a connection to an institution with a good reputation. This could mean the international fame of an artist like Müller, or associations with 'powerful' directors or theatres.

Even within the framework of the German theatre system, authors and plays have to endure cycles of popularity and obscurity. If we look at the following statistics on the production of Müller's works, we can see that he is also subject to such processes.[58]

58   Notes to the statistical tables:
1. All figures are based on the following volumes: *Wer spielte Was?* (Berlin: Henschel, one year after each season) for table 1, *Was spielten die Theater?* (Darmstadt: Mykenae, one year after each season) for table 2, and *Wer spielte Was?* (Darmstadt: Mykenae, one year after each season) for table 3.
2. In each table, ranking refers to the number of performances per playwright. In

Table 1: GDR, 1981-89

Year	No. of Productions	No. of Plays	No. of Perfs	Ranking
1981	12	7	144	(27th)
1982	8	6	98	(49th)
1983	10	7	110	(44th)
1984	6	6	50	(117th)
1985	8	5	85	(65th)
1986	7	4	51	(108th)
1987	15	9	125	21st
1988	20	14	223	-
1989	29	18	241	-

Table 1, this is somewhat misleading. Between the years 1981-86, playwrights were ranked alongside composers and hence only the 1987 statistic shows his position as a dramatist. There is no ranking for GDR years 1988 and 1989. This double volume of data seems, understandably, to have been rushed through the printers. Additionally, Müller did not make it into the top 51 in 1981 (table 2) and into the top 73 in 1992 (table 3) and therefore does not receive a ranking.

Table 2: FRG, Austria and Switzerland, 1981-89

Year	No. of Productions	No. of Plays	No. of Perfs	Ranking
1981	-	-	-	-
1982	15	5	246	43rd
1983	21	11	323	30th
1984	23	11	271	43rd
1985	14	6	190	152nd
1986	18	9	220	56th
1987	22	11	228	50th
1988	23	11	293	39th
1989	25	9	285	41st

Table 3: Re-unified FRG, Austria and Switzerland, 1990-93

Year	No. of Productions	No. of Plays	No. of Perfs	Ranking
1990	26	16	273	58th
1991	24	16	323	52nd
1992	16	11	142	-
1993	20	12	252	64th

As we know, there are 'lies, damn lies and statistics' in the words attributed to Disraeli, and we should not read too much into these tables. Their use lies more in showing tendencies. Although the performances and ranking figures indicate Müller's popularity with audiences, I would suggest that the figures which hold most interest for us are the number of productions. They give us more of an impression as to how popular Müller is with directors and 'Intendanten'.

We notice that in the GDR, the plays, mostly for reasons of censorship on the part of the state and reluctance on the part of the theatres, only receive serious attention in the final years of its existence. Their reception at that time, however, is phenomenal. The interest in Müller develops intensely as the number of productions increases at an astounding rate. The other German-speaking countries, on the other hand, show fluctuations. One year may show a trough whilst another indicates a peak. Support on the whole was moderately constant and only the odd blip interferes with this reading. The post-Wende table indicates a tangible decline. If we add the production figures of all the German-speaking countries for the years 1987, 1988 and 1989, we get the following totals: 37, 43 and 54. A comparison with table 3 demonstrates a huge falling off of interest in the wake of the collapse of the GDR. One can only speculate about the down-turn although this can shed some light on the statistics.

The re-unification of the two German states in 1990 meant a new set of values for GDR citizens and a new economic reality for the FRG. Evaluation and re-evaluation pervaded all aspects of life. Theatres are just as prone to disorientation as other institutions. Müller, the critical voice in a Stalinist regime or the most gifted theatrical voice of dissent, depending upon which stance one chose to take during the Cold War, lost his obvious point of reference, the GDR. Much of his reception, as the discussion of the productions will show, implicitly took this context as a starting point. The theatres simply could not find any purpose in staging Müller in the cultural turmoil that followed the fall of the Wall. The shock affected the status quo to such an extent that readings of his works had to re-adjust to a non-existent 'new state of things'.

This book could be said to chart the first phase of a Müller reception. For the most part, the productions under discussion were staged in the eighties. It was a period when interest in the dramatist was maintaining its popularity, after a breakthrough in the late seventies. Very few post-Wende productions are discussed, yet those which are show some of the attendant tensions of the years immediately succeeding 1989.

In the season 1995-6, various theatres have again shown more interest in Heiner Müller. The year's *Theater heute Jahrbuch* contained several announcements of Müller premières from various theatres over Germany. Many of the directors and theatre practitioners with whom I have spoken in the course of my research see Müller as the key figure in the theatrical 'Vergangenheitsbewältigung' of the GDR. It is ironic that his recent death will also stimulate interest in works left untouched since the 'Wende'. The number of major obituaries across Europe (including, surprisingly, the U.K., which has never shown much interest in Müller) has been phenomenal and this can only raise our consciousness of the playwright. One can envisage a re-assessment of his work beyond a GDR context. A new reception appears to be under way. Perhaps this book could be written again in twenty years' time.

CHAPTER I

The Problem of Acting

1   A Theatre of Memory

The twentieth century has borne witness to a range of techniques and dramatic philosophies which have sought to transform texts by redefining the relationship between the actor and the script. Many have been related to a certain type of text or genre. If the work of Heiner Müller is to provoke the institutions of the theatre, his plays will also pose problems to the orthodoxies of the various acting schools. Our interest in this chapter lies in conceptions of character. An example of a play which switches between various modes of character production is *Der Auftrag*. It was written in 1979 and first produced by Müller himself in association with his then wife, Ginka Tscholakova, at the Volksbühne am Rosa-Luxemburg-Platz, Berlin, in 1980.

There are several reasons why this play is more suitable for analysis than seemingly more opaque and challenging works such as *Die Hamletmaschine* or *Verkommenes Ufer*. They clearly raise the problem of how an actor is to come to terms with texts in which traditional categories such as plot and character are no longer available. However, *Der Auftrag*, as we shall see, combines elements of both conventional drama and the more innovative techniques found in Müller's later work. This mixture suggests that more experimental approaches to acting might have to mix with more traditional ones.

Initial reaction to *Der Auftrag* was tinged with a sense of disappointment. When we read the following comment made by the Frankfurt dramaturge, Horst Laube, Müller's interlocutor in an interview of 1980, we can see the possible problems *Der Auftrag* presents us within Müller's *oeuvre* itself:

> Ich habe hier Urteile von Theaterleuten über den *Auftrag* gehört, die dahin gehen, dieses Stück als formalen Rücktritt hinter Positionen zu betrachten, die du mit der *Hamletmaschine* oder *Leben Gundlings* schon erreicht hast.[1]

---

1   'Kunst ist die Krankheit, mit der wir leben', in Heiner Müller, *Gesammelte Irrtümer* (Frankfurt/Main: Verlag der Autoren, 1986), p. 56.

Precisely what Laube means by a 'formaler Rücktritt' is not clear, but one can qualify it in the light of certain appraisals, from both the world of the academic and the world of the theatre critic.

Secondary literature has been absorbed with questions of psychology, psychoanalysis and history in the construction of the main figure, Victor Debuisson. Frank Hörnigk sees a critique of both Debuisson and the dominant social structures that permit his activities in the play, and Helmut Fuhrmann believes that Müller is fascinated by his social psychology.[2] Fuhrmann goes on to ask the very pertinent question as to why Debuisson is so interesting when he is so easy to condemn in terms of ideology. In the programme to the production at the Landestheater Halle, the dramaturge, Erhard Preuk, writes 'die Schwierigkeit: Debuisson nicht verurteilen. Jeder Mensch will/muß glücklich sein. Diese Möglichkeit ist Debuisson. Aber es ist nur eine individuelle. Sie taugt nicht für die Menschheit'.[3] Preuk's dilemma rests on an understanding of Debuisson as character in the traditional sense, because Debuisson, as already noted by Fuhrmann, seems clear-cut enough simply to be condemned as a villain. The return to an understanding of Müller's speaking figures as characters would seem to challenge our view of the playwright as a theatrical innovator.

Müller himself acknowledges the 'problem', but also shows a possible solution in an interview of 1982 when he discussed *Der Auftrag* with Rolf Rüth and Petra Schmitz. His starting point is the reductive view of certain directors:

> Müller ist Kommunist, also findet er Kapitalisten böse, also müssen die so dargestellt werden. Das sind die sogenannten politischen Inszenierungen, die einfach das ganze Material zerstören, das im Text steckt [...] Es ist eigentlich ein reaktionärer Begriff von Politik, der dahintersteckt.[4]

2   Frank Hörnigk, 'Erinnerungen an Revolutionen. Zu Entwicklungstendenzen in der Dramatik Heiner Müllers, Peter Hacks' und Volker Brauns am Ende der siebziger Jahre', in Hans Kaufmann (ed.), *Tendenzen und Beispiele. Zur DDR-Literatur in den siebziger Jahren* (Leipzig: Reclam, 1981), p. 151; and Helmut Fuhrmann, 'Der Mythos der Revolution: Heiner Müllers *Der Auftrag*', in *Forum Modernes Theater*, 2/90, p. 145 and pp. 148-9.

3   Erhard Preuk, 'Die Menschen machen ihre eigene Geschichte...', *Heiner Müllers 'Der Auftrag'*, programme of the Landestheater production, Halle, 2-2-85.

4   'Ein Grund zum Schreiben ist Schadenfreude', in Heiner Müller, *Gesammelte Irrtümer*, p. 114.

Müller demonstrates how easy it is for naïve or reactionary directors to appropriate the 'character' Debuisson to support their understanding of political theatre. However, he stresses the wealth of 'Material' that informs the text throughout and, as we shall later see, interferes with a traditional approach to the dramatic figure.

Norbert Otto Eke widens the context of the argument by locating the play on three levels: the realistic (the scenes with Antoine, the arrival on Jamaica and the withdrawal of the 'Auftrag'), the surreal (the middle section containing the 'Heimkehr des Verlorenen Sohnes' and the 'Theater der weißen Revolution') and the level of commentary ('Der Mann im Fahr-stuhl').[5] Here it is Eke's 'realistic level' which is of interest. Implied in the term 'realism' is that of traditional character and 'Fabel', which provides us with another link to Laube's 'formaler Rücktritt'.

It is from here that one can turn to the views of the theatre critics who reviewed the productions. Of the reviews, only a tiny proportion omit a plot summary, which talks of how three French revolutionary agents are sent off to Jamaica to organize a slave uprising against the British crown and how they come to grief when 'Frankreich heißt Napoleon' (H p. 62) and the 'Auftrag' is withdrawn. Debuisson, the son of a slave owner, returns to his family, Sasportas, the former slave, proclaims the continuation of the uprising and Galloudec, a peasant from Brittany, joins him.

From the idea that character is once again being used in Müller's dramaturgy and that *Der Auftrag* has some sort of story, one can perhaps comment on the 'formaler Rücktritt' which Laube was criticizing in his comment quoted at the outset. The crux appears to be that Müller has made concessions to a conception of drama which seemed to have been cast off in his previous works. It is precisely for this reason that *Der Auftrag* is an interesting play to examine in terms of character construction and conse-quent acting style(s). Clearly there is more to the play than a simple charac-ter drama: Eke's 'surreal' and 'commentary' levels, as well as the acknowl-edgement of the role of history in character formation in both Hörnigk's and Fuhrmann's articles, point to this. The actor has to come to terms with a variety of dramaturgical influences that act upon the lines s/he is called to speak. The following analysis will investigate the nature of character in *Der Auftrag* by exploring the relationship between psychologically realistic aspects and those impulses one would describe as anti-realist.

---

5   Norbert Otto Eke, *Heiner Müller: Apokalypse und Utopie* (Paderborn: Ferdinand Schöningh, 1989), p. 117.

When we look at what the 'character' actually says, we can view characters as autonomous units which support a continuity of traits or which have a 'psychology'. It is the stuff of much traditional drama on the Western stage and its treatment in terms of acting is closely associated with the work of Stanislavski, whom I shall discuss in section two. Society is the flip-side of the realistic coin. It gives psychology a frame of reference, parameters within which the individual is both permitted to act and restricted in his actions. However, society is one of two external influences that affect the individual in Müller's drama. 'Landschaft' is the other and is one of the key terms in *Der Auftrag*, especially in the last scene where the 'Auftrag' is withdrawn by the authorities in Paris. Müller comments on the term in *Krieg ohne Schlacht*:

> Meine Grunderfahrung in den USA war die Landschaft, zum ersten Mal in meinem Leben hatte ich ein Gefühl für Land-schaft, für den Raum. [...] Das war schon seltsam, dieser Kap-italismus mit Rändern. In Europa hat er keine Ränder mehr, oder es ist da ganz schwer, die Ränder zu sehen. In Amerika [...] sind die Ränder das Lebendige. [...] Landschaften, die nicht domestizierbar sind.[6]

Müller sees that society is not the only non-personal structure to affect the individual. In addition, 'Landschaft', this natural category, has a markedly political character by virtue of its unwieldy expansiveness. The effect on Müller is profound: landscape becomes an image which limits the global aspirations of capitalism, a site of resistance. The critic Klaus Teichmann considers this element crucial to an understanding of the work when he posits a distinction between society and landscape as influences upon the individual. He argues that while society increasingly seeks to fragment and compartmentalize the subject, landscape supplies images of wholeness.[7]

We see that within the realm of character construction, scope for the broadening of individual psychology has been increased. It is the clash between society and landscape that helps to formulate the differing positions taken by Debuisson and Sasportas at the end of the play. Müller endows his characters with 'roundness' through a very conscious use of the outside world. However, to view characters and their stage-world as autonomous is to ignore the other sign systems at work in theatre.

6   Müller, *Krieg ohne Schlacht* (Cologne: Kiepenheuer und Witsch, 1992), p. 284.

7   Klaus Teichmann, *Der verwundete Körper* (Freiburg: Burg, 1986), p. 195.

We can view a character as an impersonal 'figure'. In this interpretation, characters assume representative roles, so that one might consider Debuisson 'The White Intellectual' and Sasportas 'The Oppressed', with Galloudec as a figure caught between them, perhaps as the representative of the critical spectator. This type of analysis, despite attempting objectivity, is also prone to subjectivism, as all the above cases show. One could ask why is Debuisson not 'The Colonist' or 'The Romantic', or why is Galloudec not 'The Proletarian'?

Although this method is problematic, it does confer an extra dimension on the dramatic events. The idea of character on stage as representative has an effect upon the reality of stage action. It effectively breaks theatrical illusion because the spectator is already considering a world outside the one portrayed on stage as thoughts of authorial intention, teleology or allegory disrupt a belief in what is happening before one's eyes.

It seems, however, that the intimate world of psychological character and the impersonal world of character as representative most often exist together, informing each other. In Chekhov, for example, one finds social types intruding upon psychology, whilst a play in the *Everyman* mould has to concede personal characteristics to the allegorical figures. In both examples, one of the two factors is dominant and that can greatly affect the way that a particular theatrical reality is produced. However, the interplay between the two could in fact generate its own way of relating to the acted events by throwing each side into relief. The alternation between the two would mutually highlight their contexts.

There are, of course, other means by which a dramatist can break the realist frame. Acting style, which I shall go on to in the second section, is one such means. Another, which certainly includes acting within its strategic arsenal, is the dramatic device which corresponds to the Brechtian idea of contrasting text (the words spoken on stage) and meta-text (the realities of the theatre).

The 'realism' of a character can be relativized by introducing extra contexts which challenge traditional illusionism. An affinity with a character, created in terms of realist empathy, suggests closeness. Subsequent developments, manufactured in terms of the character as type or through some manner of theatrical frame-breaking, refer the spectator back to the artifice of the performance. With these ideas in mind, we can now proceed with an investigation of how the different devices manifest themselves in the utterances of the characters in *Der Auftrag*.

When looking at the relationship between closeness and distance in terms of what the actors are made to say, we can perhaps start with the sequence of exchanges at the point where the three would-be revolutionaries don their masks. Debuisson is the first:

> Das war ein schlechter Anfang. Nehmen wir unsre Masken vor.
> Ich bin der ich war: Debuisson, Sohn von Sklavenhaltern auf
> Jamaika, mit Erbrecht auf eine Plantage mit vierhundert Skla-
> ven. Heimgekehrt in den Schoß der Familie, um sein Erbe
> anzutreten, aus dem verhangenen Himmel Europas [...] in die
> reine Luft der Kariben.
>
> (H p. 48)

Much is revealed about the character we know as Debuisson. The first lines show that he plays the role of leader within the dynamic of the trio: he both judges the previous exchange and initiates the masking process. He then divulges personal information about his past and his views of the French Revolution in the character he is to assume on Jamaica. His use of deixis ('wir' and 'unser') draws attention to his character as it does to the other two. This makes him, at least in this context, a differentiated conversation partner. Although the lines have an effect upon what we know about Debuisson, they are not mediated in language we would associate with everyday conversation. The details are put across in a style which one might term 'informational'. Clearly opinions are being expressed within the speech, such as when Europe's sky is described as 'verhangen', yet they are couched in distant terms. The language is clipped and there is a minimal use of subordinate clauses. Content becomes 'factual', a report of what Debuisson thinks. In these personal remarks, there is also a lack of modal verbs and particles which could indicate the speaker's relationship to his speech. Similarly, the opinions have not been prompted through conversational catechism. They are presented. They exercise a significatory function. The text *signifies* subjective traits of Debuisson.

Empathy or identification is never quite attainable due to the obfuscating style. The clash of the subjective and the 'reported' manner in which the former is presented becomes a point of rupture in the realistic construction of the 'character'. The most symptomatic line here is 'ich bin der ich war'. Debuisson is donning a mask whose exterior is supposed to signify the slave owner he was before his conversion to the philosophy of the French Revolution. The audience, however, is shown that the mask that he has really donned is that of the revolutionary. The ambivalence of the subjective opinions is maintained by the distancing found in the language of the speech. The audience is thus party to subjectivity and a more questioning frame. Müller mobilizes subjectivity as 'Material'.

46

If we continue, we can see how, if at all, this is affected by direct subjective interruption, as is the case when Galloudec dons the mask:

DEBUISSON: Wer bist du, Galloudec.
GALLOUDEC: Ein Bauer aus der Bretagne, der die Revolution
                hassen gelernt hat im Blutregen der Guillotine, ich
                wollte, der Regen wäre reichlicher gefallen, und
                nicht nur auf Frankreich, treuer Diener des gnäd-
                igen Herrn Debuisson, und glaube an die heilige
                Ordnung der Monarchie und der Kirche. Ich hoffe,
                ich werde das nicht zu oft beten müssen.
DEBUISSON: Du bist zweimal aus der Rolle gefallen, Galloudec.
                Wer bist du.

(H p. 49)

Here we see the unmediated intervention of subjectivism when spontaneous personal opinion overrides the role Galloudec is supposed to play. He employs modal verbs and the 'ich' form, yet one must note that direct subjectivism is only present in the two deviations from his 'script'. We should not jump to the conclusion that Galloudec has suddenly 'found himself'. His subjectivity, too, is signified within the context of a broader speech and therefore denoted rather than expressed. The frame problematizes the subjective utterances and refuses to allow a realist exegesis.

We can see the intrusion of subjectivism at a later stage as well. In the following example, where Galloudec gives his reaction to Debuisson's rejection of the 'Auftrag'. The 'informational' style which predominated in the previous quotation is absent. In the wake of Debuisson's betrayal, Galloudec's language again presents psychological traits typical of what Brecht called the Aristotelian theatre:

Ich habe meinen Hals riskiert ein Jahr und länger [...] alles für
diese faule Menge von schwarzem Fleisch, das sich nicht be-
wegen will außer unterm Stiefel, und was geht mich die Sklaverei auf Jamaika an, bei Licht besehn, ich bin Franzose, warte,
Sasportas, aber ich will auf der Stelle schwarz werden, wenn ich
begreife, warum das alles nicht mehr wahr sein soll und aus-
gestrichen und für nichts, kein Auftrag mehr, weil in Paris einen
General der Hafer sticht. Er ist noch nicht einmal Franzose.

(H p. 63)

The mask is down. The informational style which relativized the role-play of the previous scenes is no longer required to communicate ambivalence. This speech no longer demands the dramatic irony which the distanced language implied. What is perhaps more important is that subjectivism is no longer signified. There is nothing that interferes with or distances our impressions of Galloudec, apart from our previous knowledge of his speeches.

However, even when a character speaks as a 'character', information is not imparted through interrogation (although most of the speeches are prompted by what has preceded them). This suggests that the figures are still employed to a certain degree as representatives which signals the presence of an author to the spectator and thus foregrounds the artifice of the lines. If we expand our focus to other speeches in the immediate wake of the news from Paris, we see that this style briefly dominates. Access is granted to each member of the trio before representative positions are taken up again.

Mediated information and direct subjectivism are not the only styles at work in *Der Auftrag*. An excess of metaphorical language is another linguistic strategy that disturbs a sense of empathy. This excess is couched within the 'informational' style described above and lends the speeches quoted below the status of sententia. Although the use of metaphors in everyday language is not unusual, the manner in which they are structured here suggests that positions are being taken and that emphasis is being placed upon the representative function of the figures. This is most prominently evoked in the final scene when the trio reacts to the news from the Paris of Napoleon. Debuisson's assessment of the situation is a torrent of images that accentuate the difference between the character and its status as representative:

> Die Revolution hat keine Heimat mehr, das ist nicht neu unter dieser Sonne, die eine neue Erde vielleicht nie bescheinen wird, die Sklaverei hat viele Gesichter, ihr letztes haben wir noch nicht gesehen [...] und vielleicht war, was wir für das Morgenrot der Freiheit hielten, nur die Maske einer neuen schrecklicheren Sklaverei.

(H p. 65)

The metaphors explode the idea that the speaker has spoken spontaneously, yet they still refer to the 'characteristics' of the speaker, giving him simultaneously immediacy and distance. Sasportas waxes eloquent in a similar fashion only a few pages later when he identifies himself as nature, landscape:

Der Aufstand der Toten wird der Krieg der Landschaften sein,
unsre Waffen die Wälder, die Berge, die Meere, die Wüsten der
Welt. Ich werde Wald sein, Berg, Meer, Wüste. Ich, das ist
Afrika. Ich, das ist Asien. Die beiden Amerika bin ich.

(H p. 69)

In the first quotation, we see that Debuisson's personal views are informed
by certain social and historical sources placed beyond his individual psychology. His philosophy is pessimistic, his attitude resigned. It aims at timeless-
ness and could have been written as much about the GDR as about Jamaica. In the second, Sasportas as individual reacts to different external
stimuli (including Debuisson's question 'oder willst du lieber ein Berg sein.
Oder eine Wüste', H p. 67) and articulates himself using different images.
However, both speeches employ the same 'informational' style: both are
clipped, lacking in subordinate clauses and put personal opinions into
grander contexts. The tenses of the speeches are also significant in this
respect. Debuisson remains in the present, positing an eternal slavery.
Sasportas is more portentous, placing his 'Krieg der Landschaften' in the
future. Both comment on a historical level and communicate a delimited
picture of the world. Their programmatic subject matter also helps to break
the frame in terms of a character's usual manner of speaking.

Müller has other means of distancing when, for example, a character's
personal opinion requires a more critical response from the audience.
Without some manner of disruption, a prolonged identification between
actor and character or between audience and character could ensue and
signal a reversion to the poetics of empathy. One of the most striking
examples of this is ErsteLiebe's monologue. It starts with the personalized
informational style which we have already seen, whereby opinion is objecti-
fied by a drier more sober linguistic style: 'Der kleine Victor [...] kehrt [...]
heim in den Schoß der Familie. Heim zu Papa mit der wurmstichigen
Hirnschale. Heim zu Mama mit ihrem Geruch von verfaulten Blumen' (H
p. 51). Sometimes, however, the personal reflections which seem to be
presented as universal facts are relativized by the introduction of stage
directions. They break the intensity and passion that is being created on
stage through a recourse to the grotesque or the exaggerated. Having
already retold an anecdote which seemingly proves that blacks are only
happy when they are slaves, ErsteLiebe (a representative name) then tries
to extend this to the human race as a whole. Her tone is modified by the
illustrative action which the text demands:

Und weißt du, was sie [the freed slaves] wollten. Zurück in die Geborgenheit der Sklaverei. Das ist der Mensch: seine erste Heimat ist die Mutter, ein Gefängnis.
Sklaven heben der Mutter im Schrank die Röcke über den Kopf.

(H p. 52)

The same occurs a few lines later when ErsteLiebe seems to be moving too close to the personal when she describes her physical relationship with Debuisson. Here stage direction transfigures intimate memories by creating transformations on ErsteLiebe's body. Her mouth, nipples and heart are painted on by a female slave. Her intensity remains, yet its articulation reminds the audience that she is also speaking the language of the theatre. (Stage direction fulfils a similar purpose when Antoine is instructed by the text to pour red wine over his head when imparting his opinions on what should be happening in France, H p. 46.)

We have seen that there are several devices that leave the traditional concept of character in need of redefinition. The spoken text now *represents* the character for the most part, it does not *reflect* him/her. Psychology informs the utterance, yet it does not define it. Consequently, the speaker is caught between character as personal, fashioned by the individual's interaction with the world, and character as impersonal, where the character stands for sign systems which extend beyond the illusions of the theatre. This tension is heightened by the two further dramatic considerations: how action is motivated and who is being addressed in the speeches.

In *Der Auftrag* events follow each other in a loose chain. A certain logic links the different speeches, after all, each speech is not entirely cut off from the previous one. Yet the effect is that of a loose causality: it is rare that something will happen that is unexpected, yet what does happen does not take a directly causal lead from the preceding speeches. Nuggets gleaned from certain lines are acted upon. If we, for example, chart the movement of the arrival on Jamaica, we see that it begins in unity with the 'wir waren auf Jamaika angekommen' speech (H p. 47). This shortly dissolves as the three figures define themselves against each other when they state their views on the manner in which their task is to be fulfilled. The failure to agree on this leads Debuisson to initiate the donning of the masks which follows a ritualistic pattern. Sasportas is then given an object lesson in how to be a slave, which is augmented by the unprompted appearance of the Debuisson family's oldest slave. The lack of an overt causality within the text (which would normally be demanded by either the pressure of external events or the interaction of characters) turns the events into representative events. Whereas this may be accounted for as a method of introducing a

50

drama in its first scene, the same manner of linking individual speeches persists throughout the play. Something must have brought them forth, and the only possible agent is an author.[8] Awareness of an author reminds the audience of the interaction between the actors as personalities and the actors as types.

The question of the 'addressed-ness' of the speeches is partly inscribed in the question of motivation. If the scenes function, at least partly, as representative events, then the actors are not necessarily speaking only to each other, they are also speaking to the audience. This dimension is accentuated by the language in which the speeches are presented.

In the following exchange, the position of the spectator is challenged through a play of identification and distance:

SASPORTAS: Was geht diese Männer [the slaves they have been inciting to revolt] Paris an [...] Von eurem General, ich habe seinen Namen schon vergessen, wird keine Rede mehr sein, wenn der Name des Befreiers von Haiti in allen Schulbüchern steht.
Debuisson lacht
SASPORTAS: Du lachst.
DEBUISSON: Ich lache, Sasportas. Frag mich warum.
SASPORTAS: Kann sein, ich habe dich schon wieder nicht verstanden.

(H p. 64)

One assumes by this stage of the play that the spectator finds some sympathy in Sasportas's call for the continuation of the struggle despite the formal withdrawal of the 'Auftrag' from distant Paris. However, one cannot help being forced into Debuisson's shoes when he mocks the naïvety of Sasportas' historical prognosis. Debuisson's bitter laughter is parallel with our own. Although our laughter is provoked by a knowledge of the course of history, whereas Debuisson's is the result of cynicism, the co-incidence of the laughter forces the audience to examine its affinities with Debuisson. We have to examine why we know little about the Haitian revolution today, whereas the

---

8   Naturally, the author of 'realist' drama is responsible for everything that occurs but in this case, his or her agency is disguised by textual coherence.

name Napoleon figures in many people's historical consciousness. We are also called to question why we laugh at all.[9]

The same ambivalence about who is being addressed is found in other forms during the play. When Debuisson declares 'unser Schauspiel ist zu Ende' (H p. 63), tells Galloudec 'du bist zweimal aus der Rolle gefallen' (H p. 49) or refers to the 'Theater der Gesellschaft' (H p. 66), we are left to wonder in which way the text is operating. Debuisson is clearly demonstrating personal traits - that his 'Weltanschauung' is nihilistic, that he sees life as a series of inconsequential roles - but one cannot escape the fact that spectators are directly involved in the process about which he is speaking. The nature of theatre is also questioned when Debuisson foregrounds it and its language in his speeches.

The problems of 'addressed-ness' do not, however, stop with the spectators. The shifting of addressee is as much a problem for the actor as it is for the audience, as s/he is also forced to make the split between the Stanislavskian 'inner life' and the effects of theatrical devices which relativize it.

In the light of the ambivalence that pervades the play, there seem to be two different (although not mutually exclusive) illuminations of the problems of character suggested in the text itself. These are to be found in the form of the scene 'Das Theater der weißen Revolution' and the extensive monologue 'Der Mann im Fahrstuhl'.

'Das Theater der weißen Revolution' is given a privileged place within the drama: it is a play-within-a-play. It allows the spectator to watch spectators watching actors. The actors are conscious actors, something which is

---

9   Berhard Greiner, '"Jetzt will ich sitzen wo gelacht wird": Über das Lachen bei Heiner Müller', in Paul Gerhard Klussmann and Heinrich Mohr (eds.), *Jahrbuch zur Literatur in der DDR*, vol. 5 (Bonn: Bouvier, 1986), pp. 29-63; and Horst Domdey, 'Ich lache über den Neger', in Paul Gerhard Klussmann and Heinrich Mohr (eds.), *Jahrbuch zur Literatur in der DDR*, vol. 6 (Bonn: Bouvier, 1987), pp. 220-34, have both discussed the role of laughter in *Der Auftrag*. Domdey identifies the main role of laughter as the differentiator of positions. He maintains that laughter is 'Schadenfreude'. In order to exploit this type of humour, Debuisson must acknowledge (and thus differentiate) inequality and inhumanity, the 'Schaden', to enjoy the 'Freude'. The laughter is also productive for the victim. The victor rubs salt into his wounds and highlights demarcation. Greiner's argument is that laughter is a means of coming to terms with death. Comedy represses our fears. This existential slant is of interest; yet when considering the role of the audience as the receiver of humour, it would seem that Domdey is closer to the theatrical function of laughter in *Der Auftrag*.

made clear both in their character attribution (SasportasRobespierre and GalloudecDanton) and in the directions to the other real actors who are referred to as *'das Publikum'* (H p. 53). The dialogue is carefully tailored to a structure of alternating utterances of comparable lengths. The actors are talking both to the audience and to each other. They mark the precariousness of this position by the ironic use of their opening lines: the Robespierre figure tells Danton 'geh auf deinen Platz' (H p. 54), which is then split by a vocative, and which is then turned against the theatrical sense of the first half of the line with the addition of 'am Pranger der Geschichte' (ibid.). The Danton figure begins his long speech with 'jetzt bin ich dran' (H p. 55), a signal to the audience as much as to himself. For the most part, they are little more than historical caricatures, presenting parodies of French Revolutionary rhetoric. Yet there is much reference to personal exchanges that have already taken place and this occurs around the points of deixis. They retain a distorted semblance of personal history. So, to a certain extent, they present a highly self-conscious version of the characters we have already seen. Additionally, grotesque pantomime, presented earlier as a relativizing theatrical device, is in evidence. It becomes clear that what is taking place here is precisely what is taking place for the rest of the play, only here we are able to view ourselves in the actors playing the audience (with all that this might entail). We thus have a window of sorts on the events that happen before our eyes. This scene also signals a thematic function. Sigrid Weigel comments, 'sein Theater der weißen Revolution bezieht sich aber nicht nur auf das bekannte Personal und die bekannten Bilder der Revolutionsgeschichten, sondern auch auf den Theater-Charakter der Revolution selbst'.[10] The revolution is nothing more than a show, heavy on rhetoric and performance. Its major figures are actors. The play-within-a-play comments on both the form and the content of the rest of the play. The scene draws our attention to the relationship between history, politics, the theatre and its actors. However, we are still left with the problem of what is informing the play as a whole, of why the characters are pitched in the middle distance.

The language of the 'Der Mann im Fahrstuhl' monologue deviates from the style which dominates the rest of the dialogues. The subjective presence is far more pronounced insofar as a consciousness is suggested rather than the distanced subjectivity (and its occasional release) that is found in the other exchanges. However, rather than thinking of the monologue as direct access into 'a human psyche', there are devices that relativize

10   Sigrid Weigel, 'Das Theater der weißen Revolution', in Inge Stephan/Sigrid Weigel, *Die Marseillaise der Weiber* (Hamburg: Argument, 1989), p. 169.

any such view of the speaker. The lines 'ich bin gekleidet wie ein Ange-
stellter oder wie ein Arbeiter am Feiertag' (H p. 57) and 'verzweifelter
Traum im Traum' (H p. 59) both point to the constructed nature of the
experience.

The monologue, the 'Traumprotokoll' as Müller calls it in *Krieg ohne
Schlacht*,[11] suggests an interesting insight into the problem of proximity and
distance in the play. 'Der Mann im Fahrstuhl' is the confrontation with a
memory, put across in terms of present tense immediacy, which is the status
of the play as a whole. As critics have suggested (and indeed certain theatre
directors have made evident in their productions), Antoine is the medium
through which the 'Erinnerung an eine Revolution', as the play is subtitled,
is attained.[12] This, of course, produces logical problems, as he obviously was
not in Jamaica at the time of the failed revolt. Yet this no longer becomes
an issue when one compares it to the signalled dream construction, 'Der
Mann im Fahrstuhl'. As the monologue continues we are faced with all
manner of unusual occurrences, perhaps the most surprising being the
transfer of geographical position from a European lift to a village in Peru.
What is of interest is that when we are told of this, there is absolutely
nothing in the text that reflects our surprise:

> Ich verlasse den Fahrstuhl beim nächsten Halt [...] auf einer
> Dorfstraße in Peru. Trockener Schlamm mit Fahrspuren. Auf
> beiden Seiten der Straße greift eine kahle Ebene mit seltenen
> Grasnarben und Flecken von grauem Gebüsch undeutlich nach
> dem Horizont, über dem ein Gebirge im Dunst schwimmt.
>
> (H p. 60)

As with the other astonishing events which preceded this one, such as the
sudden ruptures of the normal space-time continuum, descriptive narrative
is the main mode of communication. It is allied, to a lesser extent, with
subjectivity in the form of emotional response or the use of particular
adjectives or particles. The world is an object to the 'Mann'. His style of
describing it has echoes of Antoine's own memories of the events on

11   Müller, *Krieg ohne Schlacht*, p. 297.

12   Eke, p. 177; Fuhrmann, p. 140; Teichmann p. 184; Arlene Akiko Teraoka, *The
     Silence of Entropy or Universal Discourse. The Postmodernist Poetics of Heiner
     Müller* (Frankfurt/Main: Peter Lang, 1985), pp. 136-7; and Georg Wieghaus,
     Zwischen Auftrag und Verrat (Frankfurt/Main: Peter Lang, 1984), pp. 283-4,
     amongst others.

Jamaica. But yet again we are left with a problem: why is Antoine's speech very much in the same style as that of the memories he evokes? If we widen our focus, the problem leads back to an author, dredging up the figure of Antoine (as well as the 'Mann') as part of a memory. Eke moots that the memory is not that of an individual but that of the collective. He sees this signalled by a 'Chorspiel', the 'wir waren auf Jamaika angekommen' speech (H p. 47).[13]

Characters therefore form part of the memory of an author (as manifested in his creative output), a dimension which is governed by the past, not some timeless void where the writer seeks the autonomy of art. The figures in *Der Auftrag* are not 'human' in terms of their speech although traces of their subjectivity are in a constant flux with their manifestation on stage. They are depersonalized whilst retaining personal traits. We can, again, take recourse to Müller who sets this up in his own idiom in his notes that follow *Verkommenes Ufer*:

> Wie *Mauser* eine Gesellschaft der Grenzenüberschreitung, in der ein zum Tod Verurteilter seinen wirklichen Tod auf der Bühne zur kollektiven Erfahrung machen kann, setzt *Landschaft mit Argonauten* die Katastrophen voraus, an denen die Menschheit arbeitet. [...] Wie in jeder Landschaft ist das Ich in diesem Textteil kollektiv.
>
> (H p. 101)

Having investigated the character dynamics of *Der Auftrag*, one can surely extend Müller's concept beyond *Verkommenes Ufer*. The collective figure in a landscape can be seen as paradigmatic in the context of Müller's later plays. Landscapes, as has already been noted, are the scene of resistance, too large to colonize with ideas or dogma. They therefore provide the playwright with the ideal setting for a dream-like dramaturgy. All the supposed 'characters' assume very much a 'dead' role.[14] They are a modification of the figures one meets in dreams: full of qualities yet not fully justified as human beings. The landscape they are situated in is that of memory, which forms a collective framework insofar as memory is a historical as well as a personal category. The vast expanse forms a reservoir of experiences and impressions from which certain ones stand out and go on to structure

---

13 Eke, ibid. and p. 118.

14 A clue to this is presented at the outset. At this stage we know that Sasportas has been hanged and that Galloudec has succumbed to gangrene.

the plays. The unconscious, driven by a logic which the conscious mind is never completely allowed to access, is the backdrop that constructs the text.

2   Remembering How to Act

The great theorists of acting on the Western stage in the twentieth century have never worked in a vacuum. There has always been a close link between the dramatic text and the theory that followed. This process can be seen in the plays that have driven the three greatest figures in this field: the Russian director Constantin Stanislavski, the theatrical innovator in both theory and practice Bertolt Brecht, and the Polish theatre 'scientist' Jerzy Grotowski. Stanislavski's work takes its lead from the naturalist/realist movement of the late nineteenth and early twentieth centuries with which one associates names such as Ibsen, the early Strindberg, Hauptmann and Chekhov. Brecht was his own theorist, using his own work as his example. Grotowski's actors were directed in plays where the theme of individual sacrifice in the name of purifying others reflected the physical sacrifice he demanded of his actors. The question that confronts us is what style of acting Müller inspires. Having already discussed Müller's modification of the traditional character, we might find it useful to examine how close the 'characters' in *Der Auftrag* come to the ideas of the theorists mentioned above.

The following appraisal of Stanislavski, Brecht and Grotowski is intended as an exposition of the three major strains in European acting theory in the twentieth century. There are, of course, many others who have contributed to this field. It is, however, beyond the scope of this section to discuss them in as great a detail and they are thus left on the periphery.

Stanislavski, whose thoughts have dominated the realist stage (and nowadays, after the reading of Lee Strasberg, much of the output of Hollywood), would perhaps seem a peculiar point of departure. We would not expect to find realist acting techniques in Müller. However, we are unable to ignore the bursts of subjectivity that do make their way into the play's text and these seem to have something to do with an 'inner life' of the character. 'Inner life' is a phrase that occurs several times in Stanislavski's work and its reconstruction is the ideal striven for in the process of building a character. One would expect, however, that if the actor were able to identify with the 'personal' aspects of the text, this would not produce the same effect as identifying with the text as a whole. The 'inner life' reflected would be an obvious construction due to the counterpoints found in the rest of the spoken text. Yet it is here that Stanislavski's conception of realism may have to be reassessed. The received view of his artistic ideal, one of hyper-realism or naturalism, is clearly contradicted by the following passage:

> Those who thought we sought naturalism on the stage are mistaken. We never leaned toward such a principle... we sought inner truth, the truth of feeling and experience. [...] We wanted to show the real *muzhik* and not only the costume but also the inner physique of his soul. But... we had not reached the stage where we could interpret [the spiritual side]. In order to fill the void... we exaggerated the external side. [...] This resulted in naked naturalism. And the nearer it was to reality... the worse it was.[15]

Stanislavski makes a distinction between a surface realism and one which operates from the inside outwards. Stanislavski's realism, as defined in the quotation, is a transformed naturalism, one that acknowledges the weakness of superficial realism and which suggests a special reality which only the stage is able to provide. One might add that his realism is an emotional or spiritual one, rather than one that favours a reconstruction of material, outward appearance. This distinction sows the seeds of an acting style that differentiates itself from a recreation of everyday life on the stage. This form may well be contextualized within Stanislavski's other key terms such as 'the magic "if"' which justifies the fake realism on stage or the 'super-objective' which is supposed to act as a focus for the actor's efforts. Yet one cannot emphasize too much the concession made to the reality of the theatre as opposed to the reality of life. Thus, the subjective moments in *Der Auftrag* may communicate an actor's affinity with his or her role without necessarily having to expand this to the part as a whole. With this in mind, one can see how Stanislavskian techniques might form a part of the actor's preparation.

Stanislavski is also significant in another area, that of a particular rehearsal technique. One of the most important discoveries made by the Russian director was the somatic approach to acting. Here a physical, external, corporeal relationship to the text can lead inside to the 'inner life' or 'emotional memory' of the character. 'There are no physical actions divorced from some desire, some effort in some direction, some objective, without one's feeling inwardly a justification for them', he observes and this

---

15 Constantin Stanislavski, *An Actor's Handbook*, tr. by Elizabeth Reynolds Hapgood (London: Methuen, 1990), pp. 100-1.

technique may indeed prove useful for the subjective impulses which are framed within the text.[16]

Yet the somatic approach goes beyond merely realist parameters. Müller talks of the sensual approach to literature which he claims overrides an intellectual one:

> Wenn ich einen Text, einen poetischen Text, lese, dann will ich zunächst mal nicht verstehen. Ich will irgendwie aufnehmen, aber mehr als eine sinnliche Tätigkeit denn als eine begriffliche. Erst wenn man einen Text sinnlich wahrnehmen kann, kann man ihn später auch verstehen.[17]

Müller is talking about the reader's relationship to the text but it would not seem unfair to extend this to the actor's. In the light of the later plays, the texts wilfully discourage an instant rational exegesis and encourage the actor to engage in a productive process. Because of the impossibility of a more conventional connection between the actor and the script, the sensual appeal, suggested by the body's response to the text, could in fact create new possibilities. The somatic technique can thus be applied to non-realist text, infused with a sensual quality, in the hope that the body's external movements will create an inner world. This inner world, however, will not be the same as that produced by the intellectually coherent character à la Stanislavski.

We can investigate the extension of the somatic approach with reference to the theatre of Bertolt Brecht. Brecht's textual realism takes more account of 'the world' as represented by the conflicts in the text between the individual and the socio-economic machinery of capitalism. This 'intrusion' provides another extension of the somatic approach to acting and is one that informs the ideas discussed above. The Stanislavskian belief in physical action originating from the individual is revised by taking the social effects of the external into account. The aim is to show how the body, too, can be made aware of the influence of society. This is picked up by the post-Brechtian director and theorist of the 'Theatre of the Oppressed', Augusto

16   Stanislavski, p. 8.

17   'Am Anfang war...', in Heiner Müller, *Gesammelte Irrtümer 2* (Frankfurt/Main: Verlag der Autoren, 1990), p. 43.

Boal, in his book of the same name.[18] In his exercises, which are designed for 'spectactors', as he calls them, the first reality to become aware of is that bodily control is partially determined by the employment in which the spectactor is engaged. When a secretary shows how she must hunch over a typewriter or a dustman sees how his body is affected and conditioned by constant manual work, the opportunity for a deeper understanding of corporeal potential is available. The body does not have to be solely subject to these conditions. Such insight leaves the way open to theatrical methods of demonstrating the effect of society upon both 'body and soul'. Overlarge chairs and undersized tables can highlight the pressures upon the secretary, for example. Realism that takes its lead from a psychological perspective fails to acknowledge the constructed nature of body relations. The redirection of Stanislavski through Brecht provides a way of conveying the realistic in terms which are grotesque or exaggerated. These prisms are at work in *Der Auftrag* as well. They are partly placed within the styles of the text and the dream-like status of the scenes, partly within the sparsely distributed stage directions.

The text can also be seen as too unstable to be viewed as a coherent whole. As discussed in the first section, the 'characters' oscillate between subjective utterances and representative speeches: the two elements play off each other. Brecht, the master of the theory of acting at a remove from the text, provides theoretical models which bear a stunning resemblance to those of Stanislavski. In a way, Brecht accepts them only to surpass them with an extra dimension. Brecht's contribution is the level of awareness, that the actor is conscious s/he is acting the role, not that s/he is the role (and that this can be communicated to the audience). Brecht's task was to maintain both the level of realism of character and the level of meta-text with which it was to contrast. The simultaneous grasping of two levels is advocated, and is seen most clearly in the following three exercises from Brecht's 'Übungen für Schauspielschulen':

1) Temperamentsübungen. Situation: Zwei Frauen falten ruhig ihre Wäsche zusammen. Sie täuschen für ihre Männer einen wilden Eifersuchtsstreit vor. Die Männer sind im Nebenzimmer.

18 Augusto Boal, *Theatre of the Oppressed*, tr. by Charles A. and Maria-Odilia Leal-McBride (London: Pluto, 1979), pp. 125-8.

m)   Sie geraten beim schweigenden Wäschefalten in eine Balgerei.
n)   Aus Spiel (l) wird Ernst.[19]

The critic Shomit Mitter provides an excellent commentary on what is happening in the exercises. The first, he says, deals with the concurrent holding of two levels of reality where 'we know that they are merely *feigning* the quarrel'. The second stage, he continues, shows that 'the actors are thus introduced somatically to the elements of both inversion and simultaneity in alienation'. The third stage is the real test: 'the "roles" they are playing slowly assume the status of "reality", two "truths" emerge in a manner whereby neither takes obvious precedence over the other'. This posits an interesting modification of the somatic approach which formerly could have supplied a useful means of tapping into Müller's text on the first level only. Through the exercises we see that 'on the one hand a fiction has become reality', which we have seen to be the case with Stanislavski, however, 'on the other hand, that fiction continues to be merely a fiction'.[20] The play of the two levels mediates both proximity and distance, although Brecht's dialogues usually provide demarcated areas: realistic dialogue is placed within an epic framework. The mixing of proximity and distance *within* the speeches themselves of, say, *Der Auftrag*, may not be as susceptible to the identification of the two levels from the outset. Whereas, for example, a singer announces acted events in *Der kaukasische Kreidekreis* which take the form of 'realistic' exchanges, the two differentiated areas become a blurred textual mass in Müller.

So we are left asking how far Brechtian 'epic acting' can be applied to Müller. The pitching of the texts *between* the personal and the impersonal suggests that both the somatic approach (in whatever form it might take) and the distancing of Brecht do not account adequately for Müller's text. A way of progressing is to consider the contribution made to acting theory by Jerzy Grotowski. His is a theatre sometimes considered the realization of Artaud's 'Theatre of Cruelty', which is itself an irrationalist institution.

The body is the centre-point of Grotowski's theatre, demonstrated most clearly in the two chapters on the training of actors in the seminal

---

19   'Übungen für Schauspielschulen', in Bertolt Brecht, *Große kommentierte Berliner und Frankfurter Ausgabe*, ed. by Werner Hecht, Jan Knopf, Werner Mittenzwei and Klaus-Detlef Müller, *Schriften 2*, vol. 22 (Berlin, Weimar and Frankfurt/Main: Suhrkamp, 1991-3), p. 615.

20   Shomit Mitter, *Systems of Rehearsal* (London: Routledge, 1992), all p. 59.

collection and reporting of his thoughts, *Towards a Poor Theatre*.[21] Pushing
the body to previously undefined limits is the subject matter of both chapters. Impossible tasks are set in order to attain an inspired and liberated
sense of one's own corporeality. For example, Grotowski says, as recorded
by Eugenio Barba, that the actor should 'make [...] the left side of the face
react vivaciously while the right side is sluggish' or that the actor should use
his 'voice to make a hole in the wall, to caress, to push, to wrap up an
object, to sweep the floor'.[22] The actor is pushed towards an inspirational
relationship with his audience, performing feats that defy the usual categories into which we place our knowledge of the body.

An important part of Grotowski's acting philosophy is that the actor
is never fully ready for performance. In the reporting of Grotowski's words
by Franz Marijnen, there is a passage, emphasized by Marijnen, which draws
our attention to this point:

> *The peak of a climax can never be rehearsed. You must only
> exercise the preparatory stages of the process that leads to the
> heights of that climax. A climax cannot be reached without prac-
> tice. The climax itself can never be reproduced.*[23]

This is a new departure. The models of Stanislavski and the Brecht of the
later years (of course, with the understanding that performances differ from
night to night) imply that character is constructed and then ready for the
stage. Both Stanislavski and Brecht rely upon the actor making sense of the
lines in rehearsal. By the end of the rehearsal period, an *interpreted* production is waiting to be seen. Grotowski gives back the unknown to the actor.
In order to perform the feats demanded, there can be no comprehensive
system that replaces the real experience of playing before an audience. This
is the first irrational way of dealing with the problems of the actor and one
which might seem well suited to the texts produced by Müller. The actor is
dealing with unknown territory, hovering between the subjective and the
stylized. There can never be a point when the actor can say that s/he knows
what is required of him/her: the text is not that accessible. When Grotowski

---

21   Jerzy Grotowski, *Towards a Poor Theatre*, tr. by various translators (London:
     Methuen, 1975), pp. 101-172.

22   Ibid., p. 114 and p. 134.

23   Ibid., p. 172.

makes the rehearsal period one of preparation only, not of perfection, he concedes that the actor is not greater than the text.[24]

We see a link here between text and body: both are only knowable after extensive periods of study. Yet even these periods do not guarantee total knowledge. Grotowski argues that 'the "arsenal" or store [of acting methods, artifices and tricks] may be nothing but a collection of clichés'.[25] An actor's self-knowledge may be an accumulation of self-delusions. He demands that his actors induce rather than deduce their parts. The former implies an immanent style of tackling the exigencies of the text, the latter an analytical mode of applying 'prejudices' or tools which suggests *a priori* knowledge.

The theatre of Jerzy Grotowski enables the actor to extend the body's awareness of itself. Grotowski's purpose, however, was to provide the audience with an example. In the plays discussed in *Towards a Poor Theatre*, the central character is always the one who sacrifices himself for the good of the collective, just as the actor sacrifices himself to the audience. This messianic figure was to function partly as an inspiration to the audience to indicate that the vast wealth of physical authenticity was also available to the spectator. However, one is quite able to see how this could also act as alienation, confronting the spectators with the perceived talentlessness of their own selves.

In Grotowski's understanding, the power of the individual is of prime importance. Peter Brook describes Grotowski's practice in an article on Artaud in the following terms: 'Grotowski's work leads him deeper and deeper into the actor's inner world, to the point where the actor ceases to be actor and becomes essential man'.[26] The actor is no longer seen transforming the role but transforming him- or herself. The irrational appeal of Grotowski's approach seems to have gone beyond itself, leaving text in favour of actor. This is a position which does not bode well for the theatricality we associate with Müller. If we are to apply Grotowski to Müller, we have to understand how the collective can take up the mantle of Grotowski's individual.

24   The Grotowskian director functions in a similar way. The director is merely the catalyst, outlining techniques, not interpretations.

25   Grotowski, p. 34.

26   'Artaud and the Great Puzzle', in Peter Brook, *The Shifting Point* (London: Methuen, 1989), p. 41.

It is at this juncture that one can find illumination in a short article by Peter Brook, the English director who has adopted all the three major theorists' stances in his time. He confronts the problems posed by a text such as *Der Auftrag* in terms of his own encounters with adapted myth.

The article in which these thoughts are expounded deals with Brook's notes on Seneca's *Oedipus* (reworked by Ted Hughes in this version), which he directed in the late sixties. The mere three pages, entitled 'A Lost Art', discuss the problems involved in Brooks' inability to locate a 'personality' within an attributed character, as is the case, he claims, in acting the drama of classical mythology.[27] It is impossible to say that Oedipus would have done this or that because he is the creation of a collective memory:

> *Oedipus* was never "invented": before the Greek dramatists were the legends - the Roman writer reworked the material - Shakespeare often reworked Seneca - and now Ted Hughes reworks Seneca and through him reaches the myth. [...] In serving a preexisting pattern, it is not himself and his own meaning that the dramatist is trying to impose - it is something he is seeking to transmit.

That these writers rework and do not invent has much to do with the subject matter. This idea is one close to Müller's writing practice: *Die Hamletmaschine* draws on *Hamlet*, *Verkommenes Ufer* on the *Medea* plays and Eliot's *The Wasteland*, *Der Auftrag* on Anna Seghers' *Das Licht auf dem Galgen* and Brecht's *Die Maßnahme*. With these intertexts as the 'preexisting pattern', we see how Müller's texts fulfil Brook's axiom. He goes on:

> Yet to transmit properly he [the dramatist] realizes that all of him - from his skills, his associations, to the deepest secrets of his subconscious - has to be potentially ready to leap into play, into rhythmic order, to act as carrier. The poet is a carrier, the words are carriers. So a meaning is caught in a net. [...] he gets to a form which is his own and not his own.[28]

The mixture of objective (the intertext) and subjective (the author's contribution) in one work seems to be an accurate summation of the texture of

27   'A Lost Art', Brook, pp. 64-6.

28   Ibid., p. 65 and pp. 65-6.

Müller's work. The writer submits to his 'material' and allows it to activate all that resides within and without him. Although this art is very much alive and well in the drama we have inherited from the ancients, it is the 'lost art' of acting in this style of drama that Brook moves on to discuss.

Once again, Brook's remarks pinpoint the seemingly schizophrenic position for the actor of communicating identification (as seen in the discussion of Stanislavski and partly in that of Brecht) and distance (Grotowski and partly Brecht again). Identification is impossible, yet dehumanization is also to be abjured as it is 'mechanical, using the willpower of the intellect as a sort of Pentagon holding rebel forces at bay'. The proffered solution is one of understanding the two positions on the part of the actor: 'the way opens when he [the actor] sees that presence is not opposed to distance. Distance is a commitment to total meaning: presence is a total commitment to the living moment'.[29] Its corollary in acting terms is a call to eclecticism. Directors are encouraged by Brook to use a range of exercises in order to strike the correct balance. By attacking the text from as many angles as possible, a more conscious interaction may be achieved that combines the supposed opposites, which have already been questioned in the discussion of the three main acting theorists. Brook's solution is still couched in terms of the actor becoming more in touch with 'the original theme' of the work, which is not of much use in the context of Müller's *oeuvre*: his criticism of 'politische Inszenierungen', which was quoted in the first section of this chapter, demonstrates how the varied impulses of the play's 'Material' resists a Stanislavskian 'super-objective'. However, even with this small caveat, the article still contributes positively to the problem of dealing with a text that demands many seemingly contradictory positions from the actor. However, if the actor is not to penetrate the play's 'original theme', then what is to be achieved?

When we read that Müller provocatively contends 'Theater ist nicht möglich in Deutschland, außer als Krieg gegen das Publikum', we have perhaps a justification for his use of eclecticism without the goal of understanding or communicating the 'meaning' of the text.[30] An eclectic approach presents perspectives which emphasize the differentiated texture of the plays. The audience is confronted with a patchwork of potential meanings. We have already found that meaning in any conventional sense is not

29 Ibid.

30 'Das Wiederbefinden der Biographien nach dem Faschismus', in Heiner Müller, *Gesammelte Irrtümer 2*, p. 20.

presented to the actor or spectator on a plate; it is (only possibly) attained after submersion in the material of the text. What is not to be excluded is the actor's relationship to the text, something which does not necessarily have to convey his understanding in order to be theatrically effective. Here Müller suggests another alternative to the techniques described above, one which is derived from his collaboration with the American director, Robert Wilson:

> Was mich interessiert bei Wilson [...] ist, daß er den Bestand-
> teilen, den Elementen von Theater die Freiheit läßt. Er würde
> nie einen Text interpretieren, [...] ein guter Text braucht nicht
> die Interpretation durch einen Regisseur oder durch einen
> Schauspieler. [...] Die Interpretation ist die Arbeit des Zu-
> schauers. [...] Dem Zuschauer darf diese Arbeit nicht abgenom-
> men werden. Das ist Konsumismus.[31]

The actor is no longer allowed to make a contribution to interpretation as such. S/he becomes the articulator of the text, and this is where the process stops. Identification, distancing and a corporeal reaction to the text, the three points of entry that we have already examined, are jettisoned in the name of 'audience democracy' where the spectator's power is supposedly supreme. Müller elaborates on the 'neutral' style of delivery: 'mein Text ist ein Telefonbuch, und so muß er vorgetragen werden, dann versteht ihn jeder. Denn dann ist es eine Erfahrung, die man mit einem fremden Material macht'.[32] This may seem an interesting twist in acting history but it is one that, on closer inspection, can be seen as somewhat disingenuous. The very idea of 'neutral' productions is open to as much criticism as 'ideology-free' art. Müller himself exposes this when discussing the treatment of a certain line from Wilson's English language version of *Die Hamlet-maschine*:

> Eine Frau sagt den Text, dieses 'butchered a peasant' ganz
> neutral, ohne irgendeine Interpretation oder Bedeutung, und
> drei Frauen nehmen die letzte Zeile auf, dieses 'butchered a

---

31 'Die Form entsteht aus dem Maskieren', in Heiner Müller, *Gesammelte Irrtümer*, p. 153.

32 'Ich scheiße auf die Ordnung der Welt', in *Gesammelte Irrtümer*, p. 119.

peasant', und verzerren sie: Das geht von... bis... (*verzerrte Laute*).[33]

The 'neutrality' of the first articulation is modified by the subsequent treatment of the line. The actors may well have no relationship to the text but the director certainly has. The neutrality becomes spurious. In effect, production is interpretation and this is seen in such areas as position on stage of the characters, costume, set design and all the other signifiers of the theatre. We return to a director's theatre. The 'neutral' style of acting may well be seen as a possibility open to a production, yet it does not seem to avoid the interpretation it sought to eschew: this process is merely deferred from the actor to the director.

The analysis of *Der Auftrag* in the first section, as well as Peter Brook's comments to his *Oedipus*, show that the construction of the text has much to do with an individual memory which is fused with a literary and a historical collective consciousness. For the actor to tap into this complex, s/he must integrate him- or herself into the vast system of associations that the text accrues. This can mean that there is a real affinity to certain areas of the text which require creation of an 'inner life' whilst the informational style puts a pressure on the actor to demonstrate the distance implied in the impersonal sentences. Alternatively, fusing the Grotowskian body with the text as a whole (using the full range of exercises detailed in *Towards a Poor Theatre*) could promote a very physical reading of the play which would not be constrained by the 'interpreted' style of training regime. What is likely is that acting is only possible when the actor relates to the text as if it were part of his/her own memory.

3   The Collective Meets the Collective

The question that arises from the two analyses above is how text and theory translate onto the real stage. My discussion of *Der Auftrag* will centre on four very different approaches to acting and will attempt to assess the strengths and weaknesses of each.

Müller's début as a director coincided with the 'Uraufführung' of *Der Auftrag* when it was premièred on 13 November 1980. The author co-directed with his wife, as she was at that time, Ginka Tscholakova, at the Volksbühne am Rosa-Luxemburg-Platz in East Berlin. The play was Müller's

---

33   'Am Anfang war...', in *Gesammelte Irrtümer 2*, p. 42.

first since *Die Bauern* (première 30 May 1976) to receive its world première in the GDR. In an interview he told me that the authorities were so relieved that the play differed so greatly from *Die Hamletmaschine* that *Der Auftrag* was allowed to be performed without further ado.[34] As a result, the ensemble had to make do with the 'Theater im dritten Stock', the Volksbühne's studio-theatre. The shock of the instant permission from the SED to perform meant that there were few vacant stages in Berlin.

Lily Leder records in the dossier compiled from her own experiences of the rehearsal period and from interviews with the directors that the initial idea was to produce the play as a 'Befreiung der Vergangenheit' by means of mask, costume and set.[35] It was also decided that certain linguistic clichés should be challenged, including 'Revolution' itself. These considerations, whose points of reference are theatrical and socio-political, were then played off against the more visceral, sado-masochisistic elements of the play.

Müller's and Tscholakova's use of the limited space was highly economical. Drapes were employed to suggest both space and intimacy. They were changed from scene to scene. Sparseness was also a feature in the acting style. If we examine the complex of Antoine and Debuisson (played here by the same actor), we can understand better the condensed and subtle technique employed to combine the social and the sensual. We first saw the bald actor in a dark corner of a bare room, bewigged and dressed in black to complement the shadows in which he was cowering. His social 'Gestus' was immediately signalled as one of concealment. The disguise showed us that he was 'not himself' whilst the text elaborated the political circumstances which had led to this state of affairs. As the scene went on, the veneer seemingly peeled away and he revealed himself to the audience. However, this intimacy was destroyed during the speech of the 'Engel der Verzweiflung'. Antoine climbed a stairway towards the back of the seating stands where the corpses of Sasportas and Galloudec came to life and pulled off Antoine's disguise. Antoine's opinions and direct addressing to the audience were thus relativized by a contradiction between his words and his actions. The black garb was torn away to reveal the radiant white outfit of Debuisson. A broad-brimmed hat was added and he returned down the stairs to undergo a peculiar rite of passage back to Jamaica. Sheets created a linen box-set of sorts: a white tunnel presented itself to the audience. A

34 David Barnett, '"Ich erfinde gerne Zitate": Interview mit Heiner Müller', *GDR Bulletin*, 2/95, p. 11.

35 Lily Leder, *Dokumentation zu 'Der Auftrag'* (unpublished documentation held in the Zentrum für Theaterdokumentation und -information: Berlin, 1981), p. 5.

bright light at its furthest point teased Debuisson back. The stage lights that initially guided him into this womb-like set dimmed and he was left with the single beacon. He adjusted himself to the new condition and made himself ready for the next scene.

From this description we see how Antoine was revealed as a seemingly credible character, only to have his identity called into question by his transformation into Debuisson. We then learned more about this body, this figure, from his wordless interplay with the light and dark in his passage home to Jamaica. Characterization was constructed through a series of shifts of perspective, brought about by contradiction. Concealment gave way to apparent openness which in turn gave way to a sensual sketch of the character. From this process we see how important the term 'Maske' was in informing the conception of character in this production. Masks were worn by Sasportas and Galloudec (black and white respectively) in all scenes prior to the final one, and ErsteLiebe donned a tiger mask at the end of her monologue. The actors thus remained on a knife-edge: their stage identities were never rigid. They were never fully able to empathize with their roles yet never fully able to play them with complete distance. The dropping of the masks as a consequence of the coup in Paris was the only moment when the faces were revealed but even then, the various roles played previously affected our view of the supposedly 'natural' voices.

The acting style could also be seen as one that promoted associations in the auditorium through its refusal to settle on any one meaning. Müller and Tscholakova's associative acting style was concerned with grasping the text as a generator of meanings. Association begins where rational message-reading ends. When ErsteLiebe acted through a variety of ages from that of a young girl to that of an old woman, we were forced to surrender a psychological view of character in favour of an associative collage. Naturalism was certainly nowhere to be seen. Even at moments of high emotional charge either mask, costume or set worked against illusionism. A carefully executed stylization ensured that there was always at least one sign system that prevented audience empathy.

Role-playing was much in evidence in 'Das Theater der weißen Revolution'. Overlarge death's heads were worn backwards (that is, the actors wore the masks on the back of their heads, so that their backs were acting). The declamatory and ironic style commented on the masks we had already seen. The thanatos imagery also referred both to the death obsession of the French Revolution and to the dead figures on stage. 'Der Mann im Fahrstuhl', however, was delivered far more soberly. Jürgen Holtz, the actor of Antoine and Debuisson, advanced slowly from behind a black curtain. Only as the speech indicated the arrival in Peru did he emerge in a dark suit. A beam of white light then framed and pinned him and he was unable to move any further. His style was narrative and distanced. He created the neutrality of the dream, and his own subjective remarks were relativized by the regular tone. The clash of styles in the two scenes demonstrated two important acting strands that pervaded the production. On the one hand, we were presented with the hollow grandiloquence of political discourse, on the other, the phenomenological confrontation with the impossible events of a dream. Both took up the idea of the mask: even the 'Mann', for all his distance, had been seen previously in the production in two different roles.

The critical response to the staging was mainly positive. The combination of sensuality, politics and memory was praised by Andrzei Wirth, whose perceptive comments also detected the 'Lehrstück' structure of the play.[36] Ingrid Seyfahrt, although impressed by the production on the whole and the 'große Schauspielerleistungen', criticized the orgiastic nature of the the scene 'Heimkehr des Verlorenen Sohnes'.[37] She maintained that a more 'rational' (which I interpret as more distanced) approach would have been preferable. It would seem, however, that she had missed the division of body and voice implicit to the scene. Although the bodies of the actors were engaged in sexual tensions, the voices managed to retain a certain distance, thus driving a contradictory wedge through the proceedings. Andreas Roßmann saw what he considered the laboured acting style as the communication of the texts as memories.[38] He claimed that every syllable had been trawled for meaning, although this could be construed as an opening up of the text for the audience. Müller himself was not entirely happy with the production. The theatrical room was too small and intimate for the landscapes found in the text.[39]

36 Andrzei Wirth, 'Erinnerung an eine Revolution: sado-masochistisch', *Theater heute*, 2/81, pp. 6-8.

37 Ingrid Seyfarth, '*Der Auftrag*', *Sonntag*, 7-12-80.

38 Andreas Rossmann, 'Das Scheitern von Hoffnungen', *Deutsches Allgemeines Sonntagsblatt*, 23-11-80.

39 He was later to direct *Der Auftrag* again in Bochum (première 13 February 1982) where the space of the Schauspielhaus was available to him. We should not deduce that the distanced yet corporeal style at the Volksbühne was a reaction to the intimacy of the playing area. In Bochum, the distant acting style was heightened by a triangular gauze screen which restricted the view of the stage. Each spectator became a very conscious voyeur.

Anklam, a small town on the Peene in what is now Mecklenburg-Vorpommern, might seem a strange place to tackle the problem of acting. Yet it was there that the director Frank Castorf staged *Der Auftrag* (première 2 February 1983). Today Castorf is the radical and controversial 'Intendant' of the Volksbühne, whose credo could be an inversion of the title of this thesis: 'Theater ist dazu da, der Literatur Widerstand zu leisten'. In 1983 he was still cutting his teeth and only became well known in the GDR after his treatment of *Der Bau* in Karl-Marx-Stadt in 1986. In order to understand better the methods he uses, I shall partly refer to the documentation of the performance drawn up by Siegfried Wilzopolski.[40]

Wilzopolski outlines Castorf's dramaturgy as one centred upon subjective experience. This he tapped by engaging everyone associated with the production, which included not only the actors but the crew as well. Castorf directed against what he considers Müller's intellectualization of subjective textual areas. The 'didacticism' (the authorial intervention he calls 'Müllers Moralisieren') of 'Das Theater der weißen Revolution' or the abstract musing of the 'Engel der Verzweiflung' disturb the subjective flow found elsewhere in the text. He dismissed a reading of the characters as representatives. The dramatic concept was summed up in Castorf's terms as 'die Psychologisierung der Geschichte'. This involved integrating the body into the historical process without the individual losing his/her subjectivity. The way to bypass the constraints of the more sententious moments was to reactivate Stanislavski in the light of Grotowski.

Castorf laid down certain rules within which his actors may function and then let them get on with the task of transferring the ensemble's collective experiences to their characters. What was demanded was that each character had to have a real story, a real history. The character had to be 'attraktiv', Castorf's cipher for 'rounded'.[41] Yet the inner life that this suggests was then taken up by the ensemble and redirected externally. The character was no longer permitted to reflect inwardly but rather to project, to activate the body as the extension of emotion. The externalization of feeling produced a double effect: one of optical resonance in the visual spectacle and one of associative resonance in the consciousness of the audience.

40 Siegfried Wilzopolski, *Das Associative im Theaterspiel* (unpublished documentation held in the Zentrum für Theaterdokumentation und -information: Berlin, 1985)

41 Wilzopolski, p. 4 and p. 16.

The translation of this style into concrete production showed a variety of interesting modifications that essentially rewrote the play. Castorf's insistence on the literal in terms of the text meant that the 'allegorical' figures such as the Vater, Robespierre and Danton were jettisoned, and that the Mutter, the Engel der Verzweiflung and ErsteLiebe were 'humanized' in a bid to accentuate their personalities. Under the same imperative, attacks were also mounted upon the monologic structure of the major speeches. This can be seen in the example of the scene 'Heimkehr des Verlorenen Sohnes'. In the following transcript, which formed part of the archival documentation, D denotes Debuisson, M the Mutter, 1 and 2 the two incarnations of ErsteLiebe.

1:      Ach Debuisson. Ich habe es dir gesagt, sie ist nur eine Hure [referring to 2], die du betrogen hast mit der Revolution, deiner blutbeschmierten zweiten. Mit der du dich in der Gosse gewälzt hast.

M: Hurt er wieder herum.

D: Mutter. Bitte.

M: Mein Herz ist gebrochen, seht ihr.

D: Mutter. Ich bin heimgekehrt in den Schoß der Familie aus dem verhangenen Himmel Europas in die reine Luft der Kariben.

M: Auf die Knie, Kanaille. Bitte deine Mutter um den Segen.

1/2:   Voodoo.

M: Victor!

D: Gut, Mutter.

M: (schlägt ihm ein Ei auf den Kopf) DA DROBEN AUF DEM BERGE/ DA WEHET DER WIND/ DA SCHLACHTET MARIA/ DAS HIMMLISCHE KIND![42]

As we can see, these few lines did not occur thus in the original. What is more, additional dialogue and ideas were added in order to fracture the expansive structures and to exploit and to encourage the actors' associations that were triggered by the original. The concept of voodoo was resonant to the ensemble in the keyword 'Jamaica'. We might find the association clichéd or even offensive, yet its productivity lay in the challenge it made to

---

42   Castorf's version of *Der Auftrag* (unpublished transcript held in the Zentrum für Theaterdokumentation und -information: Berlin, 1985), p. 11.

its audience. Later on in the scene, even the 'Fabel' was modified.[43] The ErsteLiebes unmasked Debuisson as a spy (by reading the 'wir waren auf Jamaika angekommen' speech which was not read on arriving in Jamaica) and humiliated him. The text was clearly just a starting point in Castorf's dramatic process, a point which was subordinated to the directoral principles discussed earlier. The aim was to confront the audience with a version of the play that stressed the collective's confrontation with the text. The techniques conferred a very personal view which was mediated through a collective dynamic. The process of 'Sich-Aufeinander-Einlassen'[44] was extended to the audience by means of the actors' interpretation of the text, through their lines and through their bodies. We could see this in action, for example, in the arrival on Jamaica. When Galloudec was unable to assume his role correctly, Sasportas's body was stricken with agony. We were left to ask whether he was disappointed that Galloudec would blow their cover or reviled at the thought of assuming an unnatural role. Maybe Debuisson's coolness was too much to bear. Textual opacity was translated into a corporeal reaction, unknowable to the intellect, but perhaps more accessible to the unconscious of the audience.

The result was a slightly contradictory one for a production so closely associated with a Stanislavskian perspective: although there was a plethora of 'real' stories at work in this version, there was nonetheless a definite distance created by the un-naturalistic manner of the theatrical communication. Even the demolition of the realistic was played off against the reality of the theatre. The 'Mann', away from his 'Fahrstuhl', actually left the stage through an emergency exit, having finished his monologue. Also, at the end of the play, Debuisson left the stage through this door and drove off in a Volkswagen Beetle, an ironic symbol of the comfortable West. The other two revolutionaries sat on the stage smoking while the door gaped open. The final speech was omitted; Debuisson's treachery was rendered visually instead. The provocation of the real world reminded the audience of the ramifications of the play and polemicized the theatricality of the production at the same time.

Martin Linzer's criticism in the GDR theatre magazine *Theater der Zeit* is the only review available and thus cannot be judged representative.

43 *Heiner Müllers 'Der Auftrag'*, video of the Theater Anklam production, Anklam, 2-7-83 (held in the Zentrum für Theaterdokumentation und -information: Berlin, 1983).

44 Wilzopolski, p. 16.

It is nonetheless of interest. Linzer draws our attention to the 'literal' reading of the text: 'die Inszenierung ist indes nur konsequent in ihrem Bemühen, den Vorgang - ohne ihn mit Bildern zu überladen - als Geschichte eines historischen Versagens aus der "Erinnerung" heraus - und nahe genug an uns selbst heranzuziehen'.[45] The category of memory and a jagged intimacy formed a contradictory whole, whose tensions generated productivity. The ever-changing perspectives of the actors and their bodily expressions followed an eclectic line which complemented the ever-changing impulses of the text.

The production of *Der Auftrag* in Magdeburg (première 22 November 1987) was directed by Wolf Bunge. It did not employ the same degree of sensuality as Müller had at the Volksbühne. What seemed to triumph was a more illustrative mode of acting whereby resonances were more consciously produced than in the externalized and non-verbal, corporeal style of Castorf in Anklam. Here the use of the non-verbal and Grotowskian body work was more understated.[46] The acting style took on qualities reminiscent of the detachment found in Brecht. Bunge combined a more rationalist approach with spatial geometry. The characters' positions on stage acted as hermeneutic tools for the spectator.

The first scene accurately demonstrated Bunge's style.[47] Antoine sat before a television, anaesthetized, while Monteverdi's *Orfeo* played. The Matrose entered, obsessed with getting rid of the letter dictated by Galloudec (which was not read out at the beginning of the play). Soon after, Antoine's wife appeared and delivered all her lines with a tone of mockery and contempt. However, amid this one-dimensional characterization, it was Antoine who was conspicuous for his range of feeling and emotional variety. The figures of the Matrose and Antoine's wife gave Antoine his depth and privileged him as a character. Yet the belief that Antoine was a realistic character was dispelled by the wealth of constructed associations that

---

45   Martin Linzer, 'Variante Drei', *Theater der Zeit*, 9/83, p. 50.

46   Although there was one important exception to this in the form of a pantomime at the end of the arrival on Jamaica. The slave who carries Debuisson in the text (H p. 50), repeated the task over and over again. The more he tired, the harder he was whipped by Galloudec in his role as task-master. As he eventually dropped to the ground, dead we suppose, Sasportas took his place as the ritual was repeated a few more times.

47   *Heiner Müllers 'Der Auftrag'*, video of the Freie Kammerspiele production, Magdeburg, 22-11-87, in-house copy.

surrounded him. Much work went into this scene as the head dramaturge, Marianne Janietz, told me in an interview. The television and the music ('Todesmusik, so schön, daß man damit sterben könnte')[48] were intended to suggest a resigned condition, the 'DDR-Bürger', his ideals in tatters with nothing better to do. The figure was also informed by readings of Canetti's *Masse und Macht* which helped with the construction of a personality that had known what it was like to have wielded power. The scene can thus be seen as far more functional and calculated, an intellectual exposition of associations surrounding a dramatic conflict. And this was indeed the manner in which the play was dealt with as a whole.

The more analytic style was summed up in the following assessment by Janietz of the predominantly Brechtian technique employed: 'wir mußten nicht psychologisieren, sondern die Grundsituationen nehmen'. A process of distillation was called for. While the arrival on Jamaica got under way, for example, the three recited the initial speech in unison as silhouettes. When this narrative ended, the shock of Jamaica was evoked by blinding light and heavy-metal music. Debuisson and Galloudec were sensually overwhelmed. Their adjustment to the new climate came across in the fairly neutral manner of delivering their lines. Having established the impact of Jamaica, dialogue was seen as an exchange of ideas, a treatise, or a series of dialectical progressions. The lines were reflected in the physical presence of the actors, too. Their bodies interpreted the text through positioning on the stage rather than through a Grotowskian projection of feeling. They became part of a geometric arrangement, determined by the 'Grundsituation', rather than a belief in their autonomy.

The shifting of perspective within the context of a conscious theatre presented the spectator with a small arsenal of acting styles at a remove from realism. The 'Heimkehr des Verlorenen Sohnes' took the form of a tableau. The stylized stage space presented an image of colonial exploitation as if we were staring at a real picture whilst the dialogues destroyed any sense of verisimilitude. 'Das Theater der weißen Revolution' employed massive masks which came down to the knees of the two actors. While theatrical bombast echoed around the auditorium, canned applause compounded the constructed nature of the scene.

The lack of naturalism also had much to do with the oneiric 'Grundgestus' founded upon the faculty of memory. Thus, the more problematic areas of the text where poetic hermeticism obscured rational interpretation

---

48 Unpublished interview with Marianne Janietz by the author, 25-5-94. Further references to production details are taken from the same source.

were dealt with by engaging in an emulation of unreal dream. As Janietz explained, 'wir hatten eigentlich keine Probleme, uns in Träume zu begeben'. Consequently 'difficult lines' were marked by a neutral tone which conceded incomprehension. In this way the play proceeded within the broad context of 'memory', of acting at a remove from contingent action. It was this factor that gave the production a certain justification for its more illustrative handling of the text: it was piecing together remembered fragments.

An opposite tactic was employed in the production in Cologne, premièred on 14 March 1992 and directed by Dimiter Gotscheff. The characters were highlighted as characters, something which we have already seen in Anklam. There the emphasis resulted in a cost to the original text but perhaps a gain to the spectator. Space had to be manufactured by taking the original script as a starting point and then developing a rehearsal script through an active engagement with it from the cast and crew. Gotscheff's interpretation left the text intact whilst attempting to convey what one might call a pseudo-Stanislavskian method of character construction. A deep empathy, even with the more allegorical figures, led to a widespread pathos on stage. What Castorf considers Müller's 'Moralisieren' and what Friedrich Dieckmann sees as Müller's romanticism seem to have been accentuated in this production.[49] Gotscheff's manner of dealing with character emphasized the pessimistic whilst ignoring the other impulses. The reductive reading homogenized the action in a way that eliminated the twists and turns of the dramatic text. The informational style discussed in the first section of this chapter seemingly resisted a Stanislavskian interpretation. When this was imposed upon it, a mournful melancholia predominated.

The 'Engel der Verzweiflung' assumed the role of 'guiding light': she read Galloudec's letter, played Antoine's wife and spoke the final 'Verrat' speech. This archetypal representation of ambivalence[50] was transformed into a tragic muse. A highly unreal figure attempted to assume human qualities. The effect of this tactic upon the acting style of the play as a whole was enormous. The ironies and distancing found in the text were

49   'Das Pathos ist sein Feld, daß Witz es begrenzen muß, ist seine Erfahrung, seine Praxis. Mit Witz und Pathos, einem Weltschmerz, der die Wunden des Herzens, der Geschichte hinter einem Schein von Chaosgläubigkeit zu verbergen sucht, ist er ein Romantiker...', Friedrich Dieckmann, 'Zeit-Wege', in Wolfgang Storch (ed.), *Explosion of a Memory* (Berlin: Hentrich, 1988), p. 14.

50   Eke, p. 124.

ignored in the name of a pessimism that the text only partly bears out. The acting stance was concisely summed up in the review of Reinhard Kill when he considered the characters 'Leidensfiguren zu Ikonen stilisiert'.[51] The concluding speech of the performance was accompanied by Bach's *O Haupt voll Blut und Wunden*, which sealed the sentimental tone of the production.[52]

Despite the stylized suffering found elsewhere in the performance, space was nonetheless found for the mock-heroics of the 'Theater der weißen Revolution'. It was brought forward in the running order so that it opened the evening. This positioning led one critic to consider this scene as an 'Alibi' for the rest of the play.[53] Two old cripples in the caps of the Jacobin Club took to the stage and required prompting from a loud-speaker at certain points. In contrast to the main aesthetic of the play, the scene was remarkable for its use of improvization and cabaret-style badinage. Once again, the aim was critical. The failure to follow through was somewhat equivocal. We have to ask ourselves to what extent this 'exposition' informed the rest of the production.

The main corpus of the play was presented in a pessimistic mood and expressed itself through a chiefly realistic acting technique. The 'Theater der weißen Revolution' was presented in different terms but seems to have been articulating the same sentiments. Memories of the revolution had to be prompted and the reasons for this could be that it meant so little to the Danton and Robespierre actors. Their negative summation of the past did not contradict or even challenge the action that followed. The scenes were different ways of expressing similar sentiments. The (fleeting) change of perspective underlined one set of meanings rather than throwing different ones into relief.

51   Reinhard Kill, 'Disput mit den Toten', *Rheinische Post*, 27-3-92.

52   Cf. Müller and Tscholakova's production at the Volksbühne. Here a recording of Maria Callas singing the madness aria from Donizetti's *Lucia di Lamermoor* was played to accompany the final speech. The combination of extreme aesthetic beauty and existential destruction drove Debuisson to tear away his clothing and to run up and down the stage in torment. The seduction of beauty was thematized and acted as a counterpoint to Debuisson's mental state. The physical reaction was not, however, the audience's last impression of the character. A return to a more Brechtian theatre followed. The music stopped and Debuisson sat staring at the audience, challenging them to applaud.

53   Reinhard Tschapke, 'Die Revolution geht in Rente', *Die Welt*, 23-3-92.

For the most part, the importance of the scene seems to have been forgotten in the press reception of the staging. The seriousness which governed eclipsed the comic prologue. Rainer Hartmann's comment that the production was 'allzumenschlich'[54] was echoed in the remarks of other reviewers who highlighted the production's 'Pathos'.[55] One could see this as a new reading of the play, one which embraced a sense of defeat found in the post-Wende Germany of 1992. However, this defeat was always present in the text, which was written in the stagnating, thirty-year-old GDR. The one-sidedness of the reading ignores the wealth of material found elsewhere in the text. Stanislavskian techniques were not able to do justice to the heterogeneity of the script. The play was reduced rather than enriched and became a more simplistic tragedy.

4   Texts that Resist the Reductive

From the four examples discussed above, it would seem that *Der Auftrag* is, not surprisingly, open to different approaches to acting style. At the 'Uraufführung' in East Berlin, a mixture of styles created a fragmented whole. A predominantly Brechtian influence fused in part with the sensuality of Grotowski and played with ideas of a psycho-historical interpretation. At times, however, this style would defer to a cursory naturalism, or to a more neutral tone as in 'Der Mann im Fahrstuhl' scene. Castorf's production in Anklam accentuated the characters' status as collective individuals. Composed associatively and then allowed to express themselves through their bodies, the characters communicated the results of their histories. The emphasis shifted to a highly personalized view of the figures *whilst* preserving them as collective actants. The advantage of this method was that it short-circuited any claim to a rational discourse. As Müller puts it: 'ein Körper ist unverständlich. Ein Körper läßt sich nicht analysieren. [...] Man nimmt ihn wahr. Man braucht ihn also nicht zu übersetzen'.[56] A more

---

54   Rainer Hartmann, 'Denkspiel kommt auf den Laufsteg', *Kölner-Stadt-Anzeiger*, 23-3-92.

55   Marion Löhndorf, 'Schwanengesang der Revolution', *General-Anzeiger*, 31-3-92; Gerhard Preußer, 'Heiliger Heiner', *Die Tageszeitung*, 24-3-92; Andreas Rossmann, 'Auf schmalem Steg in die Gegenwart', *Frankfurter Allgemeine Zeitung*, 25-3-92; and Reinhard Tschapke, 'Die Revolution geht in Rente', *Die Welt*, 23-3-92.

56   'Am Anfang war...', in *Gesammelte Irrtümer 2*, p. 43.

calculating approach was, however, presented in Magdeburg. Actors took a more distanced approach to their characters in order to show the mechanics of the historical process. Their bodies became a part of this, producing meaningful shapes on the stage. Even the occasional brushes with a realist aesthetic were dialectically challenged by consciously constructed frames of reference. The Cologne production was the only one to collapse the historical dimension in favour of a humanized lament. Positive impulses were subsumed by an almost all-encompassing melancholia. The revolution became a redundant concept. Even the guiding light, the Engel der Verzweiflung, could not off-set the pessimistic mood of the production.

The eclecticism suggested by Brook in section two of this chapter was taken up, to varying extents, by all the directors, save by Gotscheff in Cologne. Scenes would play off each other, creating a shifting frame. The figures never remained static, and even in Castorf's highly character-based staging the repertoires of bodily movement and vocal inflection suggested more than a mere group of individuals. Only in Cologne was there the semblance of a character drama in the more conventional sense. The lack of a critical framework manufactured a homogeneity alien to the polyphonous text.

We obviously cannot draw too many conclusions from four productions of a play that ranks alongside *Quartett* and *Die Hamletmaschine* as Müller's most frequently staged work. Yet even from these different examples, an interesting pattern emerges. All four productions shared common traits. The key scenes 'Das Theater der weißen Revolution' and 'Der Mann im Fahrstuhl', and the beginning of the final scene where Debuisson announces that the 'Auftrag' has been withdrawn displayed unexpected convergences. We are left to ask whether the text calls for a pre-programmed eclecticism or whether it is still open to the varying impulses of its performers.

As I have already noted, Castorf's Anklam production omitted the 'Theater der weißen Revolution' on the grounds that it was 'too intellectual', an unnecessary intrusion into the personalized structures already set up. However, when the scene was included in the other productions it seems that despite superficial variances, the underlying thrust was the same: theatrical posturing was demanded by the text. So in Müller's and Tscholakova's East Berlin production we saw that the two actors who played Galloudec and Sasportas donned death's head masks and played the scene with their backs to the audience, adding an extra element of 'Verfremdung'. Grotesque props were also part of Bunge's Magdeburg production. This time the actors wore giant white plastic masks, representations of the faces of the historical Danton and Robespierre, that covered their bodies down to the knee. Once again, swollen voices filled the stage. What is perhaps surprising is that Gotscheff's production in Cologne also followed this pattern.

'Der Mann im Fahrstuhl' also showed similarities in performance. Again there were superficial differences: in both the Müller/Tscholakova and Bunge productions, the scene began in the dark, refusing to offer the audience a visual correlative to the words heard, suggesting a direct line to each spectator's mind or imagination. Once Peru was reached, the lights were gradually turned up to reveal a man dressed in a plain suit, narrating his lines for the most part, inflecting with emotion here and there. Castorf, as before, gave his actor more of an associative personality in terms of foibles (he used, for example, a breath-freshener) yet he was nonetheless lacking in the usual Grotowskian corporeal style that typified the scenes beforehand. Like the previous two 'Fahrstuhl' actors, he tended to narrate the speech drily with occasional digressions into a more naturalist interpretation of some of the lines. The narrative impulse was also to be seen in Gotscheff's Cologne production, where this time the speaker was draped in a sheet from which he eventually emerged when he arrived in Peru. In each case, the speech was left narrated for the most part, conveying its dream-like status, whilst small impulses of feeling permeated it and gave it moments of immediacy.

The withdrawal of the 'Auftrag' created no real dramaturgical breach in either the Castorf or the Gotscheff productions. Their brands of corporeal and emotional acting respectively persisted into this scene. What is interesting is that both the Müller/Tscholakova and the Bunge productions assumed a more character-centred manner as the masks were discarded for the time being. As mentioned in the first section, the beginning of the scene is marked by a textual movement into subjectivity. This was reflected in both of the more Brechtian interpretations. Clearly in a production such as the one in Berlin where the emphasis was placed upon the mask, the 'moment of truth' required a relative reduction of artifice when each character was forced to come to terms with a situation that left him exposed. The rug had been pulled and a re-orientation was demanded. As a result the actors could no longer hide behind a consciously constructed personality and concomitantly adjusted their acting styles to ones closer to the Cologne and Anklam models. We witnessed a far more emotional parting of the ways in Berlin. The black and white masks of Sasportas and Galloudec were dropped as 'character' made a brief appearance. This also happened in Magdeburg: the more distanced analytical style gave way to a more naturalistic manner. We should not forget, however, that as the scene progressed in both Magdeburg and Berlin and positions were eventually redefined, the geometric symbolism of the placement of the actors resumed. A return to a more distant acting style also followed. This tallied with the more sententious conclusion.

The similarities in the three scenes should not be seen as a new type of dramatic inflexibility. The contexts into which the recurring motifs had been placed affect their status within each production. Individual scenes, however convergent, play a role both in themselves and as a part of the experience of the whole play. The declamations of 'Das Theater der weißen Revolution', the pseudo-narration of 'Der Mann im Fahrstuhl' and the emotional outbursts of the final scene interact and interfere with conventions that were already being developed. In Berlin the 'Theater' tapped into the sado-masochistic theme by linking the speakers to the death drive, and 'Fahrstuhl' functioned on a consciously theatrical level too: the speaker was also Antoine and Debuisson. In Magdeburg the 'Theater' and 'Fahrstuhl' formed part of a chain of tableau driven scenes. The panoramic effect enhanced the dream-like quality of the play. Incongruous scenes passed by one after the other confronting the audience with a series of bizarre images.

It would seem that various approaches to acting can highlight the many textual disparities as long as a non-uniform strategy was taken as a pre-requisite. Because Brecht and Grotowski assume the interaction of different influences, their acting styles when used alone or together provided a stimulating and eclectic mode of dealing with the unruly text. Stanislavski was too linear, yet a tactical employment added to the polyphony and encouraged the spectator to examine the mechanisms that had led to the partial manifestation of the 'realistic' character.

Thus far Müller's texts may be seen to propel directors towards the more avant-garde acting techniques and theories. They have not, however, offered any substantially new challenge. If there was 'Widerstand' within the text for the actors, then it could relatively easily be overcome by reference to familiar standards and authorities of the twentieth century European theatre. Even their eclectic combination seems to have been achieved without incident. It would also seem that Müller was not particularly stepping out of line with respect to GDR theatre politics or practices with his texts either. Brecht's legacy of an avant-garde acting theory had been passed on to audiences through a network of directors from the sixties until the demise of the country in 1989. Non-Stanislavskian approaches were features of the theatre scene in all the major GDR cities. Müller's challenge to the FRG was practically nil. The director's theatre of the seventies was awash with non- or anti-realist acting techniques. We must move on to other conventionally constitutive elements of the drama and theatre.

CHAPTER II

Characters, Figures and Voices

1   Actor, Role and Voice

On paper, a drama is conventionally distinguished from other literary genres by, amongst other things, the attribution of a name to a section of text. The linking of name and text manufactures the institution which we have come to know as the character. When produced, an actor then dramatizes the character and a degree of identity is created for the viewing public between speaking body and spoken text. Developments in modern thought, primarily in the spheres of psychology and philosophy, have taken issue with the uniform conception of the human subject. Such developments have become central to what is often described as the 'postmodern'. The representation of human beings on the stage, in a theatrical setting, clearly offers opportunities to explore and exploit these ideas. Janelle Reinelt summarizes:

> If the notion of a unified subject is bankrupt, peculiar questions arise for an art form like theatre whose fundamental elements are the physical presence of a live human being performing actions before other observers.[1]

With this in mind, the identity of body, voice and 'character' can become problematic in performance. Reinelt gives the following 'recognizable aspect of postmodern performance' as 'the recognition of the body of the actor in space as a sign among other signs, not as the privileged representative of meaning, authority, logos, unified subjectivity'. Just how recognizable this is, is problematic because 'it is difficult to separate the notion of a unified discrete subject from the image of a human being performing actions on a stage'. The modern spectator is nonetheless unlikely to reach the liberated state implied by Reinelt's 'recognizable aspect' without some form of *theatrical* signpost.

1   Janelle Reinelt, 'Approaching the Postmodernist Threshold: Samuel Beckett and Bertolt Brecht', in Ronald Roblin (ed.), *The Aesthetics of the Critical Theorists. Studies on Benjamin, Adorno, Marcuse and Habermas* (Lampeter: Edwin Meller, 1990), p. 337. The following three quotations are p. 338.

Much of Müller's later output provides a *textual* marker for the disrupted relationship between the actor, the text and the speaking subject. A refusal to link the three in the traditional sense is announced in an interview in which Müller describes the writer's role in the process:

> Ich merke bei dem Stück, an dem ich zur Zeit arbeite, daß ich immer auf Strukturen komme, bei denen ich Schwierigkeiten habe, zum Beispiel die Besetzung aufzuschreiben. Die Sachen, die ich da sage, will und kann ich nicht mehr an Figuren festmachen. Ich delegiere etwas an Figuren, die ich gar nicht wissen will. Es wird immer beliebiger, wer was sagt oder spielt. [...] Das empfinde ich im Augenblick als sehr angenehm.[2]

The refusal to delegate, to confer authority to a speaking figure, shows that for Müller the text need not be restricted by traditional categories. His 'ignorance' is transferred to the written page.

Examples of Müller's wilful resistance to assigning text to specific actors are plentiful. The *Wolokolamsker Chaussee* cycle, like *Der Horatier* before it, was written in the form of an epic poem, without character attribution of any sort. *Bildbeschreibung* is, at least to an extent, just what the title implies, yet unlike the examples above, there is no narration, just impressions. Elsewhere, Müller selectively plays with attribution by refusing to assign certain sections of text to named figures. There are examples in the two commentaries in *Zement*, 'Die Befreiung des Prometheus' and 'Herakles 2 oder die Hydra', the first and last sections of *Verkommenes Ufer*, the 'Der Mann im Fahrstuhl' passage from *Der Auftrag* and the commentaries to *Anatomie Titus Fall of Rome*.[3] *Die Hamletmaschine*, as we shall see, causes more than one problem with regard to attribution. Even *Quartett*, where each speech is marked as either Merteuil's or Valmont's, proliferates

---

2   'Kunst ist die Krankheit, mit der wir leben', in Heiner Müller, *Gesammelte Irrtümer* (Frankfurt/Main: Verlag der Autoren, 1986), p. 60. The interview was given in 1980. We therefore assume that *Quartett* is the play in question: work on *Verkommenes Ufer* only resumed in 1982.

3   Müller referred to the formal aspects of *Anatomie* as 'eine Vorarbeit zu den Wolokolamskern' (in 'Solange wir an unsere Zukunft glauben, brauchen wir uns vor unserer Vergangenheit nicht zu fürchten', ibid., p. 182). A glance at the programme of the production at the Kölner Schauspiel (première 30 January 1993), which prints the complete script, shows the imaginative divisions of the commentaries. We will find similar practices later in the discussion of *Wolokolamsker Chaussee*.

the voices of the actors so that two (attributed) characters assume the personae of two absent players as well as of each other. It is a 'quartet' for two voices.

In the following sections of this chapter, I shall investigate how the various devices of *Die Hamletmaschine* and the uninterrupted verse of *Wolokolamsker Chaussee* both redefine the relationship between actor, role and voice, and challenge directors and casts to stage such unusual texts.

2   *Die Hamletmaschine*

I   Speaking without Permission

Die Hamletmaschine, a condensation of a planned 200 page version of *Hamlet*, seems one of the most hermetic dramatic works in the modern canon.[4] Its puzzling form and its extreme brevity have caused problems for audiences and critics alike. For the latter, the play has, to a certain degree, become an excuse to indulge in all manner of speculation which pays insufficient attention to textual details that contradict the often loose usages of both 'postmodernist discourse' and more traditional critical concepts. One must proceed with caution when discussing both the play and its interpretations.

The reception of the drama is, on the one hand, typified by the word 'Geschichtspessimismus'. Frank-Michael Raddatz comments that it is 'mit Abstand das negativste Stück Müllers'.[5] The subtitle of Theo Girshausen's edition of the play, 'Heiner Müllers *Endspiel*' gives Raddatz's evaluation a more literary context. Joachim Fiebach goes on to refine Girshausen's idea by contrasting Müller with Beckett in order to assert that *Die Hamletmaschine* is a historical *Endgame*, not an existential one.[6] The case is

---

4   Cf. Heiner Müller, *Krieg ohne Schlacht* (Cologne: Kiepenheuer und Witsch, 1992), pp. 293-4; and Carl Weber, 'Heiner Müller: The Hope and the Despair', *Performing Arts Journal*, 12/80, p. 137. Both references suggest that only sketches for scenes were written which went on to become *Die Hamletmaschine*. The full project remained unrealized. The story was confirmed to me by Müller in '"Ich erfinde gerne Zitate": Interview mit Heiner Müller', *GDR Bulletin*, 2/95, p. 10.

5   Frank-Michael Raddatz, *Dämonen unterm Roten Stern. Zu Geschichtsphilosophie und Ästhetik Heiner Müllers* (Stuttgart: Metzler, 1991), p. 193.

6   Theo Girshausen (ed.), *Die Hamletmaschine: Heiner Müller's Endspiel* (Cologne: Prometh, 1978); and Joachim Fiebach, *Inseln der Unordnung* (Berlin: Henschel,

developed by critics who view the play as a 'postmodern artefact'. Douglas Nash, who contends that postmodern aesthetic production has 'assumed, since the sixties, the role of cultural norm' deduces that the 'sublimity' (his codeword for 'mystifying nature') of the images in the play 'obliterates any clear message whatsoever'.[7] The consequent meaninglessness condemns the spectator to the role of a mere appreciator of an impenetrable aesthetics:

> Sublime images [...] only serve to accentuate the incapacity of the human mind to fathom and give representation to a world made incomprehensible by the immensity of multinational capitalism in its current 'late' form.[8]

The assumptions that art's function is to transmit messages and that capitalism has suddenly made the world unintelligible challenge the validity of Nash's argument. Christa Caravjal follows Nash to a certain degree by emphasizing the 'incomprehensible' images of *Die Hamletmaschine*. She imputes a stasis, especially to the Ophelia scenes, which she believes blunts any form of dynamism in the play.[9] The alleged depthlessness of his images compounds the 'postmodern' argument.

Christian Bertram is one of the few critics who resists this reading. He explodes the idea of stasis implied in the *Endgame* interpretation:

> Aber *Die Hamletmaschine* ist kein *Endspiel*, Hamlet nicht Hamm, Müller nicht Beckett. Sondern eher die Lust am Chaos, die Freude am Exzeß; die Entfesselung des Wahnsinns und des

1990), p. 19.

7   Douglas Nash, 'The Commodification of Opposition: Notes on the Postmodern Image in Heiner Müller's *Die Hamletmaschine*', *Monatshefte*, 3/1989, p. 299 and p. 305 respectively.

8   Ibid, p. 300. The use of the word 'late' leads back to the theorist from whom Nash takes his lead, Fredric Jameson.

9   Christa Caravjal, '*Die Hamletmaschine* on two stages: Heiner Müller's allegories and the problem of translation', in Karelisa V. Hartigan (ed.), *Text and Presentation*, vol. 9 (Lanham: University Press of America, 1989), p. 16 and p.20.

Irrationalen; die Findung einer neuen Waffe des Nicht-Wissens, um das kranke Wissen in die Selbstkritik zu führen.[10]

The very productivity of *Die Hamletmaschine* lies in the density of the text. It provides numerous paths rather than an unapproachable incomprehensibility. Heinrich Vormweg turns Nash's and Caravjal's argument on its head by reintegrating the role of language into the reception of the images: 'nach mehrmaligem Lesen ist das Potential an Bildern nicht verbraucht, [es] bleibt immer noch Unerkanntes'.[11] Vormweg, like Bertram, emphasizes the energies found in the incommensurable text rather than its ability merely to baffle.

The clash between the two camps seems to have much to do with the many and disparate impulses that pervade *Die Hamletmaschine*. One of the most revealing accounts of the play's intricate texture is given by Bernhard Greiner, who takes the *Hamlet* intertext as his starting point. He relates Hamlet's treatment of 'The Murder of Gonzaga' to the transformed and performed text 'The Mousetrap'. In order to ensnare the usurper and regicide Claudius, Hamlet adds an unknown number of lines to 'The Murder of Gonzaga'. Their nature and location remain mysteriously elusive. Greiner sees Müller's appropriation of *Hamlet* in *Die Hamletmaschine* as essentially similar and points to two important moments:

1. Der zweite Text ist im ersten nicht materiell zu fassen, er ist gewissermaßen 'explodiert', um so ein unabschließbares Spiel von Zeichenverweisungen in Gang zu setzen.
2. Von Interesse ist nicht die Handlung des bearbeiteten Stückes, sondern das Verweisungsspiel der Zeichen auf der Ebene des dramatischen Diskurses.

The main function of the problematic overlap of differing dramatic and literary sources is to create a 'Spiel von Interferenzen'.[12] That Greiner

---

10   Christian Bertram, 'Machine Morte oder Der entfesselte Wahnsinn. Heiner Müllers *Die Hamletmaschine*', *Spectaculum 33*, 1980, p. 309.

11   Heinrich Vormweg, 'Sprache - die Heimat der Bilder', in Heinz Ludwig Arnold (ed.), *Heiner Müller: Text und Kritik*, vol. 73 (Munich: Text und Kritik, 1982), p. 21.

stresses the play of theatrical signs refers us back to Reinelt's point that in postmodern theatre the body is only to be viewed as one of many signs, not as a privileged one. Coming from a slightly different direction, Burkhard Schmiester argues that the style of the writing as a whole is dominated by a need to abstract (ie. make metaphorical) because concrete language cannot be related word for word to reality.[13] Either way, the unconventional language of the play can be seen as a means of challenging the dominance of the rational speaking subject. The play of the original text and its 're-write' provokes so many unknowns that the speaker, the normally assumed actor, is obliged to betray uncertainty in performance.

Much of the 'Endzeit' criticism ignores the jagged nature of the content: the speeches become a senseless babble to this school, rather than the site of contradictory impulses. An examination of the play's form also reveals provocative aspects that complement the variety of the text and open up *theatrical* possibilities. The central problem of the play's dramaturgy is that of character attribution:

> The first scene is totally lacking in attribution, the second presents a surfeit of attribution, the fourth contains a denial after ten spoken lines and the fifth begins with a transformation. The conventional starting point [of dramatic analysis] is clearly not one available to the reader of *Die Hamletmaschine*.[14]

Many critics ignore this essential point and continue to comment on the figures of Hamlet or Ophelia without due qualification.[15] Hugh Rorrison

12   Bernhard Greiner, 'Explosion einer Erinnerung in einer abgestorbenen dramatischen Struktur: Heiner Müllers *Shakespeare Factory*', *Jahrbuch der deutschen Shakespeare Gesellschaft 1989* (Bochum: Ferdinand Kamp, 1989), p. 90.

13   Theo Girshausen, Burkhard Schmiester, Richard Weber, 'Kommunismus oder Barbarei', (a discussion), in Theo Girshausen (ed.), *Die Hamletmaschine: Heiner Müllers Endspiel* (Cologne: Prometh, 1978), p. 31.

14   David Barnett, 'Some Notes on the Difficulties of Operating Heiner Müller's *Die Hamletmaschine*', *German Life and Letters*, 1/95, p. 75.

15   Cf. Thomas Eckhardt, *Der Herold der Toten: Geschichte und Politik bei Heiner Müller* (Frankfurt/Main: Peter Lang, 1992), pp. 153-4; Erika Fischer-Lichte, 'Zwischen Differenz und Indifferenz. Funktionalisierungen des Montage-Verfahrens bei Heiner Müller', in Erika Fischer-Lichte and Klaus Schwind (eds.), *Avantgarde und Postmoderne* (Tübingen: Stauffenburg, 1991),p. 237 and pp. 244-5; Georg

does draw attention to the problem of the unattributed first scene but fails to pick up on the potential of the absent speaker when he writes that 'internal evidence suggests that it is Hamlet or the Hamlet-player who is speaking, yet the voice is also that of Heiner Müller'.[16] We may assume that the 'evidence' is derived from the refunctioned *Hamlet* story of the 'Familienalbum'. This seems to be a somewhat literal treatment of a very metaphorical work. Rorrison's deduction goes against the metaphorical nature of the play and closes possibilities on a theatrical level which the absence of attribution leaves open - as we shall see when I discuss the speaker(s) of the scenes below.

The 'surfeit of attribution' of the second scene, 'Das Europa der Frau', is denoted by the direction 'OPHELIA [CHOR/HAMLET]' (M p. 91). Norbert Eke sees the bracketed Hamlet as a signal that Ophelia is his projection.[17] Once again, an attempt to rationalize becomes reductive. Although the projection thesis may be plausible, there is no reason to believe that the square bracket exclusively symbolizes this function. The problem of the chorus is also left unaddressed. Eke's 'explanation' deals with Hamlet and Ophelia as if they were unproblematic characters in the traditional sense of the word. He fails to tackle the issue on a dramatic level. This attribution highlights the rehearsed nature of the speech and banishes the idea that the utterances are what Ophelia, Hamlet or the chorus *really* think. If the characters are no longer operating within the psychological realm, we must

Guntermann, 'Heiner Müller: *Die Hamletmaschine*', in Lothar Pikulik, Hajo Kurzenberger and Georg Guntermann (eds.), *Deutsche Gegenwartsdramatik*, vol. 1 (Göttingen: Vandenhoeck and Ruprecht, 1987), p. 42; Nash, p. 301; Doris Perl, '"A study in Madness". Zu Heiner Müllers Umdeutung der klassischen Charaktere in der *Hamletmaschine*', *Shakespeare Jahrbuch 1992* (Weimar: Hermann Böhlaus Nachfolger, 1992), p. 160 and p. 163, and Arlene Akiko Teraoka, *The Silence of Entropy or Universal Discourse* (Frankfurt/Main: Peter Lang, 1985), p. 88 and p. 113, amongst others.

16   Hugh Rorrison, 'Heiner Müller and Shakespeare', in John Flood (ed.), *Common Currency? Aspects of Anglo-German Literary Relations since 1945. London Symposium* (Stuttgart: Hans-Dieter Heinz, 1991), p. 152. Even Eva Elisabeth Brenner, who has written a lengthy thesis on productions of *Die Hamletmaschine* calls the speaker of scene 1 the Hamlet-player (Eva Elisabeth Brenner, *'Hamletmachine' Onstage: a Critical Analysis of Heiner Müller's Play in Production*, unpublished PhD thesis, New York University, 1994, p. 73).

17   Norbert Eke, *Heiner Müller: Apokalypse und Utopie* (Paderborn: Ferdinand Schöningh, 1989), p. 89.

try to understand precisely what type of theatrical space they do inhabit. The problem is compounded by the following three scenes.

The third scene, the 'Scherzo', is a highly troublesome scene for two reasons. First, we note a return to attributed dialogue. Although it is fair to summarize the scene as a 'burlesque nightmare of multiple and exchanged identities', the character enigmas of the two previous scenes are missing.[18] Both Hamlet and Ophelia, as well as the 'Stimme(n) aus dem Sarg' (M p. 92), which act chorally, are given lines to speak. Despite the role-play and the role reversal, the figures are distinctly named and more closely resemble characters of traditional farce. Second, it is questionable whether the scene can actually be staged as written. Müller comments:

> Die Regieanweisungen waren ja schon damals eher ein Kopf-
> theater, also ein geträumtes Theater, weil ich keins hatte oder
> keine Aussicht hatte, gespielt zu werden, dann baut man sich im
> Kopf ein Theater auf. [...] Das ist absolut lächerlich, das [the
> 'Scherzo'] auf der Bühne zeigen zu wollen. Das gehört in den
> Kopf des Zuschauers.[19]

Although we might question Müller's alleged motivation for writing the scene as he maintains, there can be little doubt that it confronts directors with seemingly impossible demands. The phantasmagoric nature of the scene suggests that a precise repetition of the events described (and the dialogue lines they surround) would present considerable problems. However, literalism, as we have already seen, is not an approach that necessarily lends itself to the plays of Heiner Müller in general (and to this one in particular).

'Pest in Buda Schlacht um Grönland', the fourth scene, takes the theme of the change of identity a stage further. Whereas the 'Scherzo' played with characters, 'Pest in Buda' does away with the character Hamlet and we are left with his actor. At the point where Hamlet *legt Maske und Kostüm ab*' (M p. 93) the play's texture starts to normalize, that is, the stream of consciousness style that has pervaded the text up until then is temporarily halted. The use of 'quotation, misquotation, pseudo-quotation, metaphors without referends, anachronism, ambiguity, syntactic obstruction,

18   Teraoka, p. 114.

19   Heiner Müller, 'Kopftheater', in Martin Linzer and Peter Ullrich (eds.), *Regie: Heiner Müller* (Berlin: 1993, Zentrum für Theaterdokumentation und -information), p. 108.

tense shifts and metatheatrical discourse',[20] which typified the earlier text is almost eschewed in the initial narrative which mainly plays on allusions to the Hungarian uprising of 1956. The actor is seemingly no longer Hamlet. It does not take long, though, before the description of an uprising slips into a description of the speaker. As the subjective element becomes more pronounced, metaphors of schizophrenia signal a return to the textual practices of the previous scenes. The actor eventually comes full circle both theatrically and thematically when he re-dons his costume amid a sea of non-realistic literary devices.

The final scene also involves another change of identity, yet this time it remains a literary one: Ophelia (as denoted by a direct attribution, M p. 97) announces that she is now Electra. Critics have argued that the final speech is qualitatively different from those of scenes 1 and 4, and therefore gives Ophelia an edge lacking in Hamlet.[21] An inspection of the speech, however, reveals various allusions and quotations.[22] It is therefore difficult to evaluate a qualitative distinction when such knowledge is available. Ophelia is just as prone to the words of others as Hamlet is - the only difference seems to be that Ophelia hides her quotations better.

Our notions about the nature of character are questioned by all the dramaturgical devices listed above. In the analysis of *Der Auftrag* we saw that the characters found themselves somewhere between realistic dialogue speakers and anti-realistic channels for streams of consciousness. All the same, this was a problem for the single actor to surmount - attribution was consistent throughout. Even the unattributed text that signals the arrival on Jamaica had an obvious collective function, insofar as the trio are named in its first sentence and as the text denotes their initial cohesion as the united voice of revolutionary France. *Die Hamletmaschine* has a similar texture, yet it takes its cue from the monologue rather than from the dialogue. We must therefore try to reconcile the texture of the speeches with the predominantly monological form in order to understand the effect they have on the speaker(s).

20   Barnett, p. 80.

21   Cf. Fischer-Lichte, p. 244-5, who calls it 'scheinbar bruchlos'; Perl, p. 163; and Teraoka, p. 91.

22   The title is a direct quotation from a later fragment of Hölderlin. We also find references to and quotations from Luxemburg, Foucault, Euripides, Conrad, Sartre, Fanon, Heiner Müller, Artaud, the Falangists, and Susan Atkins, who, as Squeaky Fromme, was a member of the Manson Family.

'"Ich war Hamlet" (M p. 89) poses an insuperable problem for both the actor and the audience [...]. The imperfect tense refuses to divorce the "ich" from the past whilst failing to affirm a present identity'.[23] We can never know who speaks the first scene, although its openness presents us with a series of alternatives. The two basic options for the director are the employment of the single voice or of multiple voices.

There is no reason to exclude Hamlet from the contenders, after all, in scene 4 the Hamlet-player flatly denies his role before finally re-assuming it (a mirror of the line 'ich war Hamlet'). The main problem with this solution is that it takes a literal reading of the speech. If the Hamlet (/player) is the speaker of the lines, as Rorrison deduces, one must ask why the simple addition of a word (or two) in small capitals at the top of the text was omitted. The single Ophelia figure is also a possibility. Scene 2, which marks a break in the existences of Ophelia, Hamlet and the choral voice, could certainly be read as a response to scene 1.[24] An anonymous voice could also speak this opening scene. Through this it would gain the status of a disinterested introduction or exposition, devoid of a relationship to figures that only appear later. These three possibilities maintain the pattern of one actor to one part. The monologue remains the form for the solitary speaker.

However, the amount of role-play that the speech contains and the fragmentary construction principles it employs might suggest that a single actor is not the appropriate theatrical means for an exploration of the highly problematic text. If the 'unified subject is bankrupt' (Reinelt) and the theatre is the possible site of non-realistic representation, then perhaps we can expand the options open to the director by including several voices for the first scene. The singular figures could be represented by more than one actor. The diversity of the utterances would become the different impulses permeating the speaking subject. Several representatives of Hamlet or Ophelia would be able to communicate the fractured whole(s). The two 'characters' could also divide and/or share the lines creating an uncertain definition of themselves. It is also quite possible that the chorus named as one of the speakers of scene 2 could negotiate the speech. At the extremes,

23   Barnett, p. 77.

24   When Müller directed a radio version of *Die Hamletmaschine* in 1978 for Süddeutscher Rundfunk in Baden-Baden, the first scene was exclusively spoken by Ophelia. I am not aware of any other production where such a practice recurred.

either all the voices deliver the text uniformly or they are totally fragmented into a network of discrete units. The former option emphasizes a collective interpretation of the text. Here, the differing moments mediate a larger picture that goes beyond the individuals of the chorus. Precisely how ironic or mannered such a solution would prove is, of course, a matter for the production. The latter allows the voices to emerge from the collective without losing its cohesion. The monologue is taken apart and lines are distributed among a theatrical community. A middle position is also not to be ignored. One could imagine, for instance, that the voices of the chorus would sometimes converge only to become fragments once again. The group solutions are the ones that most effectively convey the lack of attribution. The author no longer controls the action and has to defer to the will of the ensemble.

In the analysis of *Die Hamletmaschine* in performance we shall see how, in most cases, the treatment of the voice in the first scene influences the rest of the production. If, however, we adhere to the attribution of 'Das Europa der Frau' ('OPHELIA [CHOR/HAMLET]', M p. 91), we note that this almost corresponds to the final configuration of the voices described at the end of the last paragraph. Yet the second scene has a different quality to that of the first. The mystery of precisely who speaks the first scene is replaced by a definition which foregrounds Ophelia whilst insisting upon the inclusion of Hamlet and the chorus. The autonomy of the Ophelia figure is undermined in this scene to a degree that is uncertain from the attribution. The square brackets problematize the role of the voices they encase, so that the reader is unsure of the degree to which Hamlet and the chorus speak. We do not know whether they follow Ophelia word for word as an echo, or pick up on words or phrases that resonate for them. Either way, the scene once again attacks the unified character and suggests a mode of theatrical communication that actively dispels the psychologism of traditional Western drama.

The 'Scherzo', like 'Die Schule der Nation' in *Leben Gundlings* or 'Nachtstück' in *Germania*, is a scene where stage directions dominate.[25] The dialogue (the first and only in the play) is unproblematic from the readers' and actors' point of view. It follows the mechanical style of the scene. The

---

25 The term 'stage direction' is very problematic in Müller, as indicated in the intro-
    duction to this book. Müller's remarks on 'Kopftheater', which were quoted
    earlier, do not necessarily suggest a total break with the convention, as we shall
    see in the section discussing *Die Hamletmaschine* in production.

voice is consequently left intact in this nightmarish 'Spiel im Spiel'.[26] I shall return to the question of whether the scene is actually stageable later.

The first two scenes of *Die Hamletmaschine* play with a theatrical provocation: in both it is possible to stage two monologues with several voices. The fourth scene resists this format by clearly attributing the first part of the speech to 'HAMLET' and the rest to the 'HAMLETDARSTELLER' (both M p. 93). As we have already noted, the text and not the attribution suggests that many impulses are working on the speaker. The fifth scene, 'Wildharrend / In der furchtbaren Rüstung / Jahrtausende', runs parallel in this respect. A single attributed speaker transforms a role (from Ophelia into Electra) and we are left to see how the varying impulses of the speech are dealt with. The dramaturgy of the final two scenes concentrates exclusively on the single speaker. The dramatic texture of the scenes is, however, highly unstable. The play of attributed role and resistance to it within the single speaker is what the re-appearance of character names indicates in the play's concluding scenes.

The pattern that emerges from this formal analysis is most interesting with respect to the drama as a whole. Critics have picked up on Müller's own statement, 'Sie können den Text der *Hamletmaschine* als fünfaktiges Stück lesen',[27] in terms of content insofar as the first two scenes act as an exposition, the 'Scherzo' as a peripeteia of sorts and the final two as the dénouement.[28] The dramaturgical reading also establishes this structure. We can read the first two scenes as expositions of what we previously considered 'character'. The huge variety of influences that pervade the speeches are highlighted by the problematic attribution of the first two scenes. The dialogue of the 'Scherzo' confronts two of the voices with each other and we are left to view the aftermath in the two scenes that follow, armed with the knowledge that the two characters of scenes 4 and 5 are only distillations of figures seen and heard in scenes 1 and 2. This reading, that Hamlet and

26 Guntermann, p. 46, suggests that the use of motifs and images from the previous two scenes confer this status to the scene. One could add that the lack of communication that is symptomatic of the other scenes, along with the bizarre imagery, lend this one a decidedly different status from that of the others. The dialogic form of the 'Scherzo' also makes it a highly ironic utopia where communication now seems possible.

27 'Ein Grund für Schreiben ist Schadenfreude', in Müller, *Gesammelte Irrtümer*, p. 113.

28 Guntermann, p. 42; and Perl, pp. 159-60.

Ophelia emerge from the first scenes, carries over the dramaturgical theme of contingency: the speakers of the last scenes are merely possibilities, extracted from the many voices that introduced the play.

III   Picking Up the Pieces

The problems that *Die Hamletmaschine* poses to the actor are also reflected in cast lists and in the play's production history. Both bear witness to the peculiarities we have noted above.

Cast lists are, to a degree, a record of a production and help us to understand the director's and/or dramaturge's view of the roles the actors played. If we take a brief look at a random selection of programmes, we see how some theatres have tried to attribute whilst others remain vague. In the Theater im Bunker, Aachen,[29] actors filled the parts of the Hamletdarsteller, Ophelia, 'Chor der toten Frauen' and a 'Schauspielerin'. In Schwerin (première 8 October 1993) a similar cast listing was given, except that the 'Schauspielerin' was replaced by Claudius (who also doubled as Horatio). On the other hand, the Theater Angelus Novus in Vienna (première 2 May 1984) listed six 'Schauspieler',[30] the Deutsches Theater, Berlin (première 24 March 1990) had nine actors' names, the Landestheater Dessau, which called the production 'ein theatralisches Konzert' (première 18 May 1990), had twelve 'Mitwirkende' (a term also appropriated by the Theaterstudio in Löberhof, near Gießen, première 10 April 1992). The Stadttheater Würzburg listed six 'Darsteller' and the Podewil, Berlin (première 29 April 1995) divided the five-person cast into 'Schauspiel' (two actresses) and 'Gesang' (three singers).[31] The Thalia Theater, Hamburg, the site of Robert Wilson's production which will be discussed below, listed the actors according to some element of their onstage function so, for example, we find 'Frau

29   *Heiner Müllers 'Die Hamletmaschine'*, programme of the Theater im Bunker production, Aachen, 18 November, no year given.

30   The collective dynamic at work in this production meant that each actor learned the whole script and was free to speak whichever lines s/he wanted to. The only 'rule' imposed by the director, Josef Szeiler, was that for each scene the complete text had to be spoken at least once. (Brenner p. 337 and p. 351.)

31   Even these terms are misleading. The three singers went on to perform 'The Mousetrap' from *Hamlet*, in costume, at the juncture in scene 4 when the Hamletdarsteller denied his Hamlet role.

stehend', 'Mann mit Buch am Tisch' and 'Mann hinter der Frau' in the cast list. 'Hamlet' and 'Ophelia' are conspicuous by their absence. The conflict between those productions that named their characters and those that remained unclear highlights the difficulty that the text presents on even this most basic of levels.

The performance history of the play also illustrates a peculiar phenomenon not as yet encountered in other works by Müller. The abortive 'Uraufführung' in the Schauspiel Köln is documented in Theo Girshausen's edition of *Die Hamletmaschine*.[32] Volker Geissler, the director of that ill-fated production, was not the last to fail in the attempt to realize the text. Rainer Werner Fassbinder, the internationally renowned director of both stage and screen, whose 'anti-teater' [sic] had rocked Munich in the late sixties, was unable to stage *Die Hamletmaschine* in Frankfurt. There was similar failure in Zürich.

Müller folklore asserts that theatre-goers had to wait until 1979, and even then had to travel to Paris, to witness the 'Uraufführung' of the play at the Théâtre Gérard Phillippe Saint Denis (première 30 January 1979), together with *Mauser*. This is factually inaccurate. The world première actually took place in a small theatre in Brussels on 7 November 1978.[33] A few months later, the German-speaking public was granted its first experience of the play in the Casa Nova, Essen (première 28 April 1979) which received a modestly positive response from the theatre critics.[34] What followed was an explosion: there were at least fourteen productions between the 'Deutsche Erstaufführung' and the Wilson production of 1986. As the programme summary above also reveals, the play, unlike much of Müller's later work, has been performed several times since the fall of the Berlin Wall. It has also been staged many times outside the German-speaking world. The combination of false starts and a long series of (inter)national stagings suggests perhaps that after initial hesitations and bafflement, the

32   Theo Girshausen (ed.), pp. 46-78.

33   Brenner puts the record straight in her doctoral thesis when she discusses the production in her first chapter. She accounts for the production's omission from the theatre history of *Die Hamletmaschine* as being due to the small size of the theatre's reputation and the low-key staging. *Theater heute* did not review it, neither did any other large newspaper.

34   Lack of documentation makes it impractical to discuss this production. I am thus forced to mention it only in passing.

play became known for the myriad possibilities that it could bring to the stage.[35]

Mystery surrounds the Freies Theater production, Munich, in 1981. Martin Laske lists the première as March 1981 and the production is accredited to George Froscher and Kurt Bildstein in *Explosion of a Memory*.[36] That a video of the production has come into the possession of the Freie Universität, Berlin, is also puzzling, although it may have formed part of the 'Heiner Müller Werkschau' festival which took place when Berlin was the European City of Culture in 1988. The production that it documents is an exciting and surprisingly close reading of the play and for these reasons deserves our attention.

Although much was adhered to (in terms of stage directions), there were actually cuts made to the short text. The scene's title, 'Familienalbum', was not announced and this may signal the absence of the sections dealing with the family. The cuts to scene 4, on the other hand, trimmed part of its meta-dramatic frame. The denial of the Hamlet role was intimated by the dropping of the actor's cloak (which was later re-donned for the final sequence). The omission of the lines on the actor's 'Drama' also took away the self-conscious tone of the 'Hamletdarsteller'. It is hard to account for the absence of the parody of the Lord's Prayer: the revulsion at the consumer society may have been sacrificed in order to intensify the actor's revulsion at himself, which follows.

---

35 For this reason, I must admit that this section is the one that is the most limited. A discussion of eight productions might have done justice to the breadth of ideas brought to the text since its publication in 1977. However, this chapter does document a great degree of variety and I hope that this conveys the wider picture I am unable to present.

36 Martin Laska, 'Inszenierungstabelle der Stücke Heiner Müllers', in Heinz Ludwig Arnold (ed.), *Heiner Müller: Text und Kritik*, vol. 73 (Munich: Text und Kritik, 1982), p. 87; and Storch (ed.), p. 76, respectively. Neither the Henschel Verlag with its array of programmes nor the Theatermuseum in Munich were able to provide me with information or a programme and consequently I am unable to say where it was put on or who took any of the roles. The company was listed in the *Deutsches Bühnenjahrbuch* from 1980 (when it opened with a production in July of that year) until 1983 after which it has failed to appear. *Leben Gundlings* was staged by the Freies Theater, Munich, in 1993, and the same two directors were named in the première section in *Theater heute*. However, the group is still neither listed in the *Bühnenjahrbuch* nor the Munich telephone directory.

Of all the productions discussed in this section, this is the one that comes closest to Sue Ellen Case's description of *Die Hamletmaschine* as a 'theater of terrorism'.[37] Admittedly, she uses the term in connection with a literary terrorism of Shakespeare's *Hamlet*, but it does not seem unfair to extend this to the realm of performance.

'Familienalbum' took place in the corridor outside the theatre space proper.[38] A figure in black tarpaulin rushed down the stairs just before the corridor. He was then dragged off into the main theatre space by two hooded men, leaving the spectators out in the cold. The first line was then spoken from within and only then did Hamlet, wearing a biker's jacket, emerge and continue the speech.[39] (As we shall see from scene 2, the actor returned to provide the attributed Hamlet voice. Thus one can assert that the actor was also playing Hamlet in scene 1.) The actor's tone was far from uniform when he paced up and down the corridor. Much repetition of lines and shouting was offset by a more contemplative enunciation of the lines in capitals (for example, 'WER IST DIE LEICH' etc., or 'FLEISCH UND FLEISCH GESELLT SICH GERN', both M p. 89). For the first section of quotations he brought out a radio cassette player which played the lines so that he could react to them. Hamlet was quoting (as the text suggested). The lines 'DU KOMMST ZU SPÄT' etc. (M p. 90) saw the entrance of a Horatio figure who repeated certain words of the line. This created a minimal sense of dialogue. The mention of Ophelia that followed was accompanied by the sound of a female voice singing. A sheet of glass was produced and held between the two by Hamlet at the line 'Dänemark ist ein Gefängnis' (M p. 91). At the end of the monologue, Hamlet exited up the stairs. The audience was then led into the main theatre space.

The space occupied two levels: the much larger upper level was used for most of the acting whilst a small pit below, connected by a ladder and visible through a smallish square hole in the upper level, housed the two-man chorus and Hamlet in scene 2. Seating was not provided; the audience was free to sit or stand where it wished in this scene and in the 'Scherzo'. The attribution 'OPHELIA [CHOR/HAMLET]' was interestingly negotiated:

37   Sue Ellen Case, *Developments in Post-Brechtian Political Theater: The Plays of Heiner Müller* (Ann Arbor: University Microfilms International, 1991), p. 59.

38   *Heiner Müllers 'Die Hamletmaschine'*, video of the Freies Theater production, Munich, 3-81 (held in the video archive of the Theaterinstitut, Freie Universität, Berlin).

39   A picture of this scene is to be found in Storch (ed.), p. 77.

Hamlet declaimed the first line several times before Ophelia struggled for and eventually gained the line for herself. During the speech, the chorus acted as an ironic echo to Ophelia from below. Whether they were mocking her lines or deflating potential pathos was a matter for the spectators. As the speech progressed and Ophelia gained mastery over the lines Hamlet had tried to speak, she began to run around the edge of the larger room, sometimes shouting, sometimes declaiming. Towards its end, Hamlet tried to climb out of the pit while the chorus succeeded in keeping him down. Ophelia remained dominant.

The company then engaged in the most literal attempt at a realization of the 'Scherzo' that I have as yet seen.[40] The scene opened with a man (a new, second Hamlet) enclosed by a large rubber ring who was rolled around the space by an anonymous figure before coming to rest. Then the 'Universität der Toten' was suggested by two figures in white coats who entered on a customized hospital trolley. One lay face down on the trolley reading, under a scaffold of lights mounted on top of the contraption. The other slowly wheeled the vehicle while it weaved in and out of the spectators. After a lengthy tour and an inspection of Hamlet in the rubber ring, they moved off and out of the space. The next entrants were Ophelia in a simple white dress and Claudius in a ruffled, clear plastic garment, a blank white face-mask and glass shoes with lit light bulbs in the large, clear platform soles. Both Hamlet and Ophelia, who were now acting inside the rubber ring, said their lines twice, exchanged clothes and Hamlet received his whore's mask. The voices of Ophelia and Claudius then laughed their lines. Horatio entered with small cardboard wings on his back and wandered around the area, finally stopping at Hamlet. A transparent plastic sedan was then carried in. Its contents were the torso and head of a mannequin. Its chest was full of arrows and after a while it was lit from within. Hamlet was

---

40   In Brussels, the two actors danced a slow tango whilst the Hamlet figure spoke the complete text. Both wore evening dress and the attempt was made to make them look as similar to each other as possible.
      In Essen, one of the two Ophelia actresses, then dressed as a cleaner, stumbled upon the text whilst sweeping the stage. In a broad Cologne accent she proceeded to read the scene in a baffled and mocking tone.
      At the Podewil in Berlin, the text was presented quite literally as a large yet unstable edifice. In scenes 1 and 2, wooden cubes with binary opposites on opposing faces (for example, 'TRAGEDY' and 'COMEDY', 'GUILT' and 'INNOCENCE'), and sections of either the 'Mousetrap' scene (*Hamlet* III ii) or the 'Scherzo' on the other two faces, were moved around the playing area. The cubes were then assembled in scene 3 into a tall structure (approx. 3m high) that displayed the 'Scherzo' text at its front and the *Hamlet* text at its rear.

then rolled out of the playing area by Horatio. Throughout, discordant and disordered music accompanied the (almost) dumb show. Stage directions were neither spoken nor read.

The pillars which created an inner area in the large upper room were used to restrict the spectators in scene 4. Long sheets were wrapped around them and a smaller, narrower area was created. At one end a new Hamlet, shrouded in a cloak with his arms outstretched like a prophet, declaimed the capitalized lines at the beginning of the speech before becoming more narrative for the Zhivago lines. Two televisions were then switched on with blank screens as directed by the text. The description of the revolt was at first spoken in a very matter-of-fact style, yet while the narrative continued, the actor became more and more excited, as if he were there. He then moved into a small room at the side of the restricted playing area where he re-donned his cloak and declaimed the Macbeth/Raskolnikov speech. He changed back to a more 'natural' style for the 'privileges' section that followed and returned to the main area. Surprisingly there was no photo of Müller nor a subsequent tearing (cf. the Wilson production below for a full discussion of its status within both his version and *Hamletmaschine* criticism as a whole). Three naked women each with an overlarge cardboard mask of either Marx, Lenin or Mao then entered to rousing 'socialist' anthems over the PA. They went on to speak their texts as instructed. Hamlet said the lines from 'Zwei Briefe' as if he were reading poetry.[41] Then the lights went out. In the darkness he took a circular saw to the three women who fell down one by one, illuminated by the bright sparks that the saw gave off.

The sheets that surrounded the audience were then taken down. Ophelia stood at one end of the formerly narrower space between two of the pillars. Two thick tapes/bandages criss-crossed from the top of each pillar to the bottom of the other so that Ophelia's face was covered at their intersection. She had been crossed out. Practically unable to move, she shouted the lines of the fifth scene as a declaration. Bright lights illuminated her from behind towards the end of her speech, at which point she laughed. Silence followed and one of the televisions from the previous scene continued to flicker.

This highly mobile, yet very strict production tackled some of the major problems posed to both the actor and the director. Although the first scene only featured the single voice of Hamlet (if we exclude the very minor part played by Horatio), we were confronted with different actors for Hamlet later on in scenes 3 and 4. Hamlet became a succession of voices by taking on different guises. We were presented with various possibilities. The

41   Heiner Müller, 'Zwei Briefe', GP1 pp. 81-2.

variety of inflections and tones throughout (including Ophelia's in scene 2) also matched the many impulses that run through the text. Any suggestion of psychology was avoided and the concept of traditional drama was undermined. Striking unity of character, text and action was only found in the 'manifesto' of scene 5 which repressed the intertextuality discussed above. The Munich production clearly wanted to emphasize a relatively positive ending, signalled both by the strength of the voice and by the confident laughter that concluded the piece. Ophelia was shown to develop, whereas Hamlet remained a reactionary. The production as a whole also took up the challenge of the text's peculiar directions. The interpretation was an attempt to push the scenes to their visual limits by following as much of the stage direction as possible. We should also notice that the narrowing we observed in the 'five-act' reading of the dramaturgy was also found in the spatial arrangements in Munich. The theatre space was enclosed in scene 4 and the audience was forced to concentrate on one area in scene 5. For all the production's inventiveness in realizing the text with a close adherence to its surreal details, it did attempt a conventional distinction between text and stage direction. It cannot be maintained that the actors and directors presented the text 'as it was' but they did take it as a visual challenge. The images created, especially in the 'Scherzo', were imaginative realizations which used the text as a practical starting point.

If the late Ernst Wendt's production of *Germania* in Munich, 1978, brought Müller to the attention of the West German theatre-going public (which we shall see in the next chapter), then it was the Texan director Robert Wilson who made Müller's international reputation. In May of 1986 he staged *Die Hamletmaschine* in New York with students from the drama department of NYU. Later in the year he began rehearsals in Hamburg, again with student actors (only one member of the cast was a professional), and on 4 October the production was premièred in the Thalia Theater's Kunsthalle.[42] Although the two productions differed in certain ways, the basic ideas that underpinned each one seem to have remained the same. Running times were the major difference: the New York version lasted two and a half hours, Hamburg lost half an hour.[43]

---

42   The production also came to the Almeida Theatre, London, with its original US cast in 1987.

43   In the interview 'The Forest', Müller praised the American students' mechanical and dry acting styles (*Gesammelte Irrtümer 2*, p. 112). The Hamburg actors, he asserted, were too human and lacked distance. Consequently he considered the

The production was one marked by a fascinating play of repetition and difference.[44] In order to understand this relationship, we must look at the 'prelude' which preceded the first line of text by fifteen minutes. The stage on which this took place was confined by three screens which formed a trapezium, whose two parallel sides were the back wall and the front of the stage. In this space, a highly choreographed and stylized set of movements was enacted on the command of the clicking of two percussive pieces of wood. At each click a new set of actions would be initiated. As the clicks progressed, the stage gradually filled with the seven female and seven male actors. Each took a specific position. Having taken it, each click demanded a different (yet precisely rehearsed) movement from those actors already on stage. The pantomimes themselves were as hermetic as the texts that followed later in the performance. Although seemingly arbitrary, they followed the relentless clicking and formed discernable patterns within the cycle as a whole. For example, a grey old woman in a fright-wig would swivel on a chair with her mouth wide open for one sequence, and then turn her head through ninety degrees for the next. Other figures included three women in fifties' dresses who sat at a table and whose movements were always in unison, a woman who leant on a bare tree fitted with casters, a man dressed in a black suit, shirt and top hat, whose face was also made up in black. He appeared towards the end of the whole cycle behind a woman in a flowing dress who wandered around the set for a short while. The Peggy Lee song 'Is That All There is?' was played single-fingered on a piano. This ironic musical accompaniment functioned as a teasing question for the duration of the performance. The 'prelude' was concluded by the appearance of the 'Mystery Man'. His arrival occurred once the cycle seemed to be over: the lights, which had been dimmed, came up and the assembled cast proceeded to move the props (the tree on casters, the table and the swivel chair) though ninety degrees clockwise in a consciously rehearsed and ordered manner. Whilst this was happening, the Mystery Man stood at the front of the stage staring into the audience. His presence and the schematized nature

New York production superior.

44   A precise description of the Wilson production is impossible without a 'Regie-buch'. The positions of the actors' bodies in space would require exact diagrams which I am unable to give. The reader must accept the approximate nature of the following description. It should be noted that the video of the production discussed here was a recording specially made for television by the Norddeut-scher Rundfunk (NDR) and broadcast on 21 December 1986. Although this version remains faithful to the original and was filmed in the Kunsthalle, it only lasts for an hour and three quarters.

of the ninety degree turn signalled that this was still part of the performance and not merely a practical scene changing necessity.

What followed was the integration of the *Hamletmaschine* text into the pantomime of the 'prelude'. Each scene used the sequence of movements and varied them according to the demands of the text. At the end of each scene the Mystery Man appeared and the set was once again turned ninety degrees clockwise. The only exception to this scheme was the 'Scherzo'. This took the form of a short film projected onto a screen which was lowered in front of the stage at the end of the second scene. The end of the performance was marked by a tableau of the final sequence of movements which was held for longer than in the previous scenes. While the scene was frozen, the curtains that covered the three screens were opened in turn as a final curtain was then drawn across the stage.

'Familienalbum' began well into the cycle of movements. The woman in the swivel chair, the woman leaning on the tree and the three at the table went through their motions before 'Der Mann über die Wand blickend' entered and began with the 'Ich war Hamlet' speech in a dry, emotionless tone. The capitalized lines were inflected differently: sometimes there were traces of cynicism, other times they were declaimed. After the several clicks that punctuated the speech had passed and the various movements had been executed, another man, 'Mann sitzend', took over the first quotation section of the speech. 'Hier kommt das Gespenst' (M p. 90) introduced another male speaker. During this speech certain phrases (for example, 'Man sollte die Weiber zunähn, eine Welt ohne Mütter' or 'Die Hähne sind geschlachtet', both ibid.) were repeated and screeched by the 'Mann sitzend'. Tones were changed and some of the lines were spoken by several male actors at one time. In the imagined rape of Gertrude almost every word was given to a different male actor, which intensified the lines. By the end of the speech there were still minutes of pantomime to come. The words ceased and the movements, always signalled by the clicks, continued until the time came to rotate the set.

The second scene followed the same pattern: female voices took the text apart as and when they appeared on stage. 'Frau stehend' spoke most of the speech in a clear, dry voice, others formed a chorus. The 'Frau an den Baum lehnend' would chime in with her one line, 'AUF DEN LIPPEN SCHNEE' (M p. 91), throughout the scene. The three women at the table said the 'tote Frauen' lines one at a time, each in a different voice. When the voices announced the destruction of Ophelia's former life, male sobs and cries augmented the words. Repetition gave the speech a fugue-like quality; motifs and themes were developed, challenged or emphasized.

The 'Scherzo' featured no spoken words. The only sound was Schubert's 'Der Zwerg' sung with gusto and passion by the American opera singer, Jessye Norman. The film combined the positioning of the actors on stage and the back projection of images. The various sections of the film were accompanied by projections of the text of the 'Scherzo' which scrolled from right to left. The cast remained relatively static throughout. Changes to the images of the actors were created by superimposition. The men caught fire just before the projected words 'Willst du mein Herz essen, Hamlet' (M p. 92) while the women smiled malevolently. As the scene progressed the women, remaining in position, became gorillas. By the end, all the figures returned to their normal places, uncharred and non-primate. The screen then became computerized: squares of single colours obscured the sitting figures. The image gradually became smaller and smaller while the final text scrolled across the black, empty screen. The images projected behind the cast included blue skies, clouds and a crashing aeroplane's fireball.

Scene 4 saw a mode of line speaking similar to the first two scenes: the lines were shared between the figures who in turn repeated, contorted or declaimed the words allocated to them. What is of particular interest in this scene is the status of the stage directions. For the most part, the directions were spoken by female voices, sometimes drily, sometimes seductively, sometimes as shouts. (The three women at the table followed the direction to speak the line 'ES GILT ALLE VERHÄLTNISSE UMZU-WERFEN' etc., M p. 96, in German, Russian and Chinese.) The one direction that was not spoken but actually executed on stage was the '*Zerreißung der Fotographie des Autors*' (p. 96).[45] In the course of the descrip

---

45   This image, possibly more than any other, is seen in the secondary literature as particularly central to Müller's understanding of the function of the author. Opinions seem to fall into two camps which are, broadly speaking, the reductive and the more open. In the first we find Burkhard Schmiester who sees the gesture merely as Müller's reluctance to identify himself with Hamlet, in Girshausen (ed.), pp. 42-3. Caravjal somewhat surprisingly calls it 'a violent anti-theatrical gesture that bespeaks the will to purity, the will to mastery by the writer who makes his project appear self-sufficient, independent of collaboration', p. 14. The more open readings consider the act as questioning Müller's right to call himself the author of this highly heterogeneous work. Alex Schalk in *Geschichtsmaschinen. Über den Umgang mit der Historie in der Dramatik der technischen Zeitalters. Eine vergleichende Untersuchung* (Heidelberg: Carl Winter, 1989), p. 220; and Bertram, p. 311, both take this view. Eckhardt, pp. 156-7; Perl, p. 162; and Teraoka, p. 102, present the argument that the gesture points to the paradox of modern writing. In Perl's words, 'die Bemühungen des Autors, seine eigenen

tion of the revolt both the 'Mann über die Wand blickend' and the 'Mann sitzend' each very slowly tore a piece of white paper whilst speaking their lines. This action was repeated with the photo of Müller later on in the scene. That this direction was carried out rather than read perhaps points to the importance it had in the production. We shall return to its significance later.

The scheme of reading out stage directions continued into the final scene where again various figures spoke Ophelia's final text within the orchestration of click-induced movements.

Today the Wilson production is celebrated and ascribed cult status. Its reception at the time from theatre critics, however, was more measured.[46] It was mostly favourable and although not gushing in praise, the reviewers realized that they had witnessed a theatrical event which was both challenging and thought provoking. Horst Köpke called it 'eine Symphonie für Worte', Klaus Wagner found the artistic interplay 'simpel wie zugleich raffiniert' and Erika Brenken compared it to the 'Triadisches Ballett' of Oskar Schlemmer at the Bauhaus.[47]

Academic criticism has endeavoured to play down the clash of image and word. Nash sees Wilson's production as an act of commodification which blunted Müller's 'dubious' critical edge. The performance was a typical 'postmodern product'. Nicholas Zurbrugg considers Hamlet merely a 'postmodern figure in crisis' and sums up the production as a whole as 'rather tired, rather European'.[48] Interestingly, none of the theatre critics in Hamburg used the word 'postmodern' or its variations once.

Privilegien zu eliminieren, finden wiederum aus einer privilegierten Situation heraus statt'.

46   This seems to be the case with events which have been awarded a special status only in hindsight. If one compares, for example, the contemporary reception of Monty Python's 'Parrot Sketch' with the somewhat run-of-the-mill laughs that it gets when originally recorded before a studio audience, one sees how nostalgia or cultural privilege can distort our view.

47   Horst Köpke, 'Vor den Ruinen Europas', *Frankfurter Rundschau*, 20-11-86; Klaus Wagner, 'Ein magisches Quadrat aus lauter letzten Bildern', *Frankfurter Allgemeine Zeitung*, 6-10-86; and Erika Brenken, 'Ophelia, auf den schwarzen Lippen Schnee', *Rheinische Post*, 9-10-86.

48   Nash, p. 308; and Nicholas Zurbrugg, 'Postmodernism and the Multimedia Sensibility', *Modern Drama*, 3/88, p. 440 and p. 447.

Wilson himself has been quick to counter the charge that his images were totally divorced from the text. Although he concedes that the images came before the text was allocated to the players,[49] his aim was to provide a visual and an aural dimension for the spectators:

> Bei meiner Inszenierung der *Hamletmaschine* habe ich Bilder gezeigt, von denen viele glauben, daß sie nichts mit dem Text zu tun haben. Das ist nicht so [...]. Durch diese Ebenen [what he later calls the 'Hörspiel' and the 'Stummfilm'] können die parallelen Ereignisse, die parallelen Momente im Text und im Spiel aufeinander einwirken und einander verstärken.[50]

It is here that the tearing of the Müller photo comes into play. One could read its inclusion as an action instead of as a spoken stage direction as a point of contact between Wilson's levels, where the textual and the visual moment become one, as opposed to the other stage directions which very much refer to the textual world of *Die Hamletmaschine*.

Müller is also wont to divorce the images of Wilson's theatre from the text. When he says, 'er hat nie versucht, ihn [the text] zu interpretieren', there seems to be a wilful praise of obscurantism.[51] I would rather suggest that Wilson's production of the play very much emphasized the 'Maschine' aspect of the text whilst coming to grips with the problems of attribution with great astuteness. The dislocation of character into voices and perspectives gave the impression of being inside the consciousness of the speakers: impulses were exchanged and modified in the course of the performance. Clearly Wilson did not follow the subtle changes in attribution discussed above, yet the general sense of expanse found in the dramaturgy of the first scene was pursued in the others. This proved an illuminating experience of a new style of theatre. Like the Munich production, space was created for the audience. It is interesting to notice how one staging tried to keep to the text in order to achieve this while the other sought to break it up to attain the desired effect.

49   Robert Wilson, 'Be Stupid', tr. Guntram Weber, in Storch (ed.), pp. 62-3.

50   Knut Hickethier (ed.), *Heiner Müller Inszenieren. Unterhaltung im Theater* (Berlin: Die Dramaturgische Gesellschaft, 1987), p. 23. No credit is given to a translator of Wilson's words. There is, however, little doubt that he needed one (cf. 'Be Stupid', in Storch (ed.), p. 65).

51   'Ruth Berghaus und Heiner Müller im Gespräch', in *Gesammelte Irrtümer 2*, p. 82.

Of all Müller's plays, *Die Hamletmaschine* is the one that he has directed the most times. The radio version in 1978 (cf. footnote 24) was followed by a production in Gießen (première 8 February 1985). He was also involved in a version of the play recorded for GDR radio by the avantgarde new-wave band, 'Einstürzende Neubauten'. The one for which he is best known, however, is the *Hamlet/Maschine* marathon at the Deutsches Theater, Berlin (première 24 January 1990) which ran to 40 performances before leaving the 'Spielplan' on 18 December 1993. *Die Hamletmaschine* was 'inserted' into an almost uncut *Hamlet* in the Müller translation. With three intervals, each performance lasted eight hours in total.

The documentation of *Hamlet/Maschine* shows interesting developments in the form of the production.[52] The epic was originally planned early in 1988 and was scheduled to run in two-night cycles. On the first night *Die Hamletmaschine* would be performed at the end and would look back on the action, on the second it would open the evening, looking forward to the action that would succeed it. Other variations were also considered. Initially there was a plan to use a different actor for each act of *Hamlet*.[53] In March 1989, way before rehearsals started (29 August 1989), there was even talk of scrapping the whole idea and putting on Müller's translation of *As You Like It* because two of his favourite actors were unavailable.

Rehearsals coincided with the momentous events of November 1989. This naturally made the director's job highly problematic. All of a sudden, measures had to be taken in order to avoid a directly allegorical reading of the production. Müller commented on the pressure in interviews at the beginning and at the end of the run respectively:

> Ein Problem ist sicher, daß man *Die Hamletmaschine* gar nicht mehr brauchen würde in dieser Inszenierung. Als wir das geplant haben, war *Hamletmaschine* in der DDR noch ein verbotenes Stück, und je mehr es aufs Ende zuging, desto historischer wurde der Text. Bloß, es war eine rein moralische Frage, das zu machen.

> Was in *Hamletmaschine* beschrieben ist, fand inzwischen auf der Straße statt. Dadurch wars ganz schwer, das Stück noch zu

---

52 Stephan Suschke, *Dokumentation zu Heiner Müllers 'Die Hamletmaschine'*, Deutsches Theater, Berlin, 24-3-90 (held in the Zentrum für Theaterdokumentation und -information, Berlin, undated).

53 Linzer and Ullrich (eds.), p. 80.

inszenieren, das war dann eher die Verweigerung einer Inszenierung oder eine Minimalisierung der Vorgänge, eher ein Referieren.[54]

Conditions were far from perfect. Müller's production became a forced reaction to the fall of the Wall and the process of the GDR's liquidation.

Die Hamletmaschine was positioned between Hamlet and Horatio's chance meeting with the Norwegian army (IV iv) and Ophelia's madness scene (IV v). Although performed in full, it also made appearances elsewhere in the *Hamlet* text: lines kept seeping into Shakespeare's original.[55]

The set remained the same for the duration of *Die Hamletmaschine* (which lasted approximately forty minutes). The stage was essentially empty. A projection of an abandoned room with a menacing stooped male shadow lit the back wall. A rectangular light above the stage cast its outline upstage right and two grey walls flanked the stage. Video monitors were placed beyond the walls at both sides of the stage. There were no set changes between the scenes and all the actors remained on stage throughout.

As already mentioned above in the programme survey, no roles were attributed to the nine actors involved. The five women assumed a fragmented Ophelia and three of the men implied a Hamlet figure. (The other man read the 'stage directions' and announced the scene titles.) In a way this lent *Die Hamletmaschine* a play-within-a-play status like 'The Murder of Gonzaga' (cf. Greiner's comments above) because actors who played Hamlet, Claudius, the Ghost, Gertrude and Ophelia dissolved into nameless roles.

The performance started with the blistering bass of Jean-Jacques Burnel as *Die Hamletmaschine*'s theme tune, 'No More Heroes' by the Stranglers, blared across the PA.[56] Two male voices began the first section of 'Familienalbum' after a few bars. At the end of the speech all went quiet

54   Ibid., p. 108 and p. 200.

55   In all there were eight intrusions, ranging from single lines (for example,'Exit Polonius', M p. 91, not surprisingly when Hamlet murders the counsellor in III iv) to whole speeches (scene 5 was broadcast over the PA at the play's conclusion).

56   *Heiner Müllers 'Die Hamletmaschine'*, video of the Deutsches Theater production, Berlin, 24-3-90 (held in the Zentrum für Theaterdokumentation und -information, Berlin). As with the Wilson production, it is virtually impossible to give a precise description of all movement on stage.

and the scene was formally announced. The five Ophelias sat mainly stage left, one was in a wheelchair, another had a box of photos (which would be torn up later). Only two of the Hamlets ever spoke: dressed in dinner suits, bow ties and bowler hats, there was something of both Laurel and Hardy, and Magritte about them. The third Hamlet remained silent, dressed in the armour of the Ghost, prowling upstage for the most part of the performance. The speaking Hamlets always formed a pair and their movements were either parallel or opposite. Their voices, however, were not in any harmony. The first scene was spoken in a mixture of cadences and inflections, repetitions and alternation of lines. The Ophelias would also join in from time to time with their own renditions of certain lines (all of the capitalized lines were echoed by at least one of them). At times the Hamlets would pace around the illuminated rectangle. Some of the Ophelias would also write the speeches in chalk on the stage. The line 'Exit Polonius' stopped all action for a short while and the Gertrude speech was addressed to the Ophelia in the wheelchair.

The second scene also started with the scene's title and stage directions, and an almost complete rendition of 'No More Heroes'. While the music was playing, the women congregated in the illuminated rectangle and the two Hamlets mimed a duel with their hands as guns. A fight ensued and the two fell to the ground. There they attempted, in a very conscious and rehearsed manner, to strangle each other (which was possibly also a cheeky pun on the musicians who accompanied them). On the ground they alternated in cold, emotionless voices the lines of the scene without the accompaniment of the Ophelias.

The 'Scherzo' was then announced and the three lines of dialogue followed. Each of the five Ophelias said the first line one after the other, the Hamlets replied in unison as did the Ophelias after them. After a small burst from the Stranglers, the stage directions were read without the dialogue parts. The women returned to their positions in scene 1 and the Stranglers were played again at the text's end.

The fourth scene was once again announced over the PA as the two Hamlets (facing each other) declaimed the Hamlet speech with some echoes from the Ophelias. They wrote the text on the walls while it was being spoken. When the stage direction ('legt Maske und Kostüm ab', M p. 93) was spoken, the Funeral march and the 'ES GILT DIE VERHÄLTNISSE' speech (M p. 96) were heard. One of the Ophelias recited scene 2 with urgency. For the description of the revolt, the Hamlets exchanged lines whilst bicycle pedalling with their backs on the ground. One Hamlet used the other Hamlet's feet as pedals. Thus they 'generated' the speech by charging off each other. Meanwhile some of the Ophelias stroked and

107

caressed the armoured Hamlet whilst stills of the rotting Rosa Luxemburg and the dead Ulrike Meinhof were shown on the monitors at the sides of the proscenium arch. When the revolt speech reached its end, the Hamlets met each other in the middle of the stage and embraced, speaking the 'Mein Drama hat nicht stattgefunden' lines (M p. 95) into each other's faces. The parody of the Lord's Prayer was said over the PA. The Hamlets froze in their embrace and gazed into the audience. The Ophelias spoke the 'Zwei Briefe' lines in different voices taking separate lines. One of the Hamlets then put the other into the now vacant wheelchair and set the mute Hamlet's helmet onto his head. The PA read the final stage directions.

The final scene saw one of the Ophelias pace mechanically around the illuminated rectangle declaiming the text in fits and starts, finishing one line and then starting the next with the last words of the previous one. Then all the Ophelias lined up at the front of the stage and calmly recited the lines and cheerfully sang the madness songs from the scene that would follow in *Hamlet*. The one Hamlet wheeled the other to join the line. The dissolved roles of *Die Hamletmaschine* then started to establish themselves again when Dagmar Manzel (one of the Ophelias and Gertrude) spoke the lines attributed to the Queen and Jörg Gudzuhn (the wheelchair-pushing Hamlet and Claudius) spoke those of the King.

Müller's production was clearly playing with a Wilson conception of theatre in that the visuals did not correspond directly to the text. However, Müller never attained the autonomy of the text over the points of reference within it (and, of course, there is no reason to assume that that was his aim) and thus his style hovered somewhere between Wilson and a more illustrative mode. Some of the images visualized the text whereas others were too far removed and created tension on a more abstract plane. 'Müller macht Theater-Theater' commented Roland H. Wiegenstein, and Benjamin Henrichs called it 'keine Inszenierung, eine Demonstration'.[57] Henrichs, as well as C. Bernd Sucher, considered *Die Hamletmaschine* superfluous, whereas others were more interested in the mystifying mode of the spectacle. Hanna Niederdorfer simply saw the whole evening staged 'in einer neuen Form der Publikumsbeschimpfung'.[58] The very mixed reception seemed to have more to do with the reviewers' endurance than with particu-

57   Roland H. Wiegenstein, 'Eine alte Geschichte, wie zum erstenmal erzählt', *Badische Zeitung*, 28-3-90; and Benjamin Henrichs, 'Acht Stunden sind kein Theater', *Die Zeit*, 30-3-90.

58   Hanna Niederdorfer, 'Alte und neue Macht', *Handelsblatt*, 30/31-3-90.

lar features of the plays. According to their accounts of the audience, much applause was received by both the cast and the director. Müller himself was not pleased with the *Hamletmaschine* section, although he was generally happy with the production as a whole.[59]

As we saw above, Müller had to take flight to a position that refused to comment directly on the contemporary situation. His *Hamletmaschine* thus had more to do with the *Hamlet* text that surrounded it. The play of role and voice became more interesting for this very reason. After the play of the one mute and two vocal Hamlets and the pluralistic resistance from the five Ophelias, the transformation back into the aesthetic frame of *Hamlet* contextualized *Die Hamletmaschine* within a literary tradition. The play communicated with its intertext rather than with the outside world. When the possibilities of *Die Hamletmaschine* reached their conclusion in the fifth scene, the dramatic intermezzo had to defer to the main action and did so in a highly theatrical way. Whereas the Munich version left the audience with a pure and positive manifesto of hate, and Wilson kept his machine ticking over, Müller left the audience with a question mark that played with the realities of the theatre, not of the new Germany.

As our brief survey of the production history showed, *Die Hamletmaschine* has remained popular since the collapse of the GDR. One 'post-Wende' production took place in Schwerin at the Mecklenburgisches Staatstheater (première 8 October 1993) under the direction of Sabine Andreas. Andreas had already staged a successful version of parts I and III in the *Wolokolamsker Chaussee* cycle with students of the Hochschule der Künste, Berlin, in the Summer of 1988, which was highly rated by Müller.[60] In Schwerin, however, Andreas found that this production would have far more to do with the contemporary social climate than she had previously expected.

Rehearsals lasted seven weeks and were plagued with inter-German tensions. The actors, who were all actors from the GDR, felt put upon by the 'Westtante' Andreas. They considered *Die Hamletmaschine* unplayable and insisted that no-one would come and see it. Their participation was only guaranteed by their contracts with the theatre. The dramaturge, Andrea Koschwitz, had to act as go-between on several occasions. It was perhaps this tension that led to the unanticipated success of the play which ran for

59 Unpublished interview with Heiner Müller by the author, 20-6-95.

60 This information and the subsequent description of the performance is the product of a long, unpublished interview with Sabine Andreas by the author, 23-3-95.

seventeen performances. This was a great feat for a text like *Die Hamlet-maschine* in a town without a university.

A relatively bare set was employed. Its focal point was a black back wall with five black doors, each with triangular head pieces, which resembled grave stones. The programme made clear that the actors took roles, so we find a named Hamlet, Ophelia and Claudius (who also doubled as Horatio). This did not mean that the first scene was simplified by merely employing a single voice to fill the void of the unattributed text. 'Familienalbum' was introduced by three minutes of silence. The device had several functions although, it apparently caused the actors' hackles to rise. It called the language that would follow into question, as well as challenging the audience's theatrical expectations. Hamlet then approached a microphone stand and initiated the monologue. The rest of the cast sat behind him and improvized reactions to the text in a playful and ironic manner. Each night different resonances would emerge. Sometimes Ophelia would translate the English lines for the rest of the chorus and as their knowledge of the text grew, so their treatment of it changed. On certain occasions the 'Internationale' was sung when the dialogue with the Spectre began. The interplay with Horatio was also performed in this playful style. Textual and theatrical discourses were constantly in flux.

'Das Europa der Frau' took up the enigmatic attribution of the scene. Hamlet entered alone with his back to the audience and started to recite the speech as if he were writing it. Halfway through Ophelia entered and started again on her own terms. She was then joined by the chorus of dead women while the text was repeated a few more times. The different styles of speaking the text were thus compared during the scene. The women then got stuck in a loop of 'ich's, which became musical as the word was said more and more. This accent pointed to the problem of the subject in this text: how can the individual liberate herself whilst remaining obsessed with the 'ich'?

Andreas attempted to realize the 'Scherzo' in accordance with the stage directions but admitted that she was not completely happy with the half-complete result. The scene opened with Hamlet in the pose of Rodin's classical thinker. Whispers were heard from behind the back wall. The five grave-stone doors, which implied a cemetery atmosphere, sprang open but all was quiet. Before Hamlet had a chance to investigate, they closed again and would not open despite all his efforts. The whole pantomime was then repeated. This time, when the doors opened the other actors 'stoned' Hamlet with books, burying him in the process. By the time he had got up, the chorus of the dead women appeared as statues. After his inspection of them, Ophelia gently undressed him. Claudius then entered in a soldier's uniform and a crown. The two men danced and the scene ended. The treatment of the scene points to the very major difficulties involved in a literal realization. The first part worked fairly well, but as the images built up, the director was unable to convert them into the language of the theatre. A burdening literalism entered which destroyed the dream-like atmosphere of the scene.

The fourth scene began with Hamlet's inability to identify wholeheartedly with the realities of modern Communism. While the Chinese national anthem played, Hamlet tried to raise a clenched fist in support while the rousing yet kitschy tune merged with the sound of tanks. The set was bathed in red light. When he denied his Hamlet role he moved to the microphone. The description of the revolt was spoken as if he were a pedantic history teacher. When his character became more schizophrenic, his delivery got faster and faster until he reached the line 'Mein Drama hat nicht stattgefunden' (M p. 95) where a resigned and cynical air took over. The parody of the Lord's Prayer was clownish and the photo of Müller was replaced by an ironic visual metonym for the author, a bottle of whisky, which was drunk during the speech that followed. The alcohol fired up Hamlet whose final lines sounded like anguished pleas: 'Ich will eine Maschine sein' (M p. 96). 'Zwei Briefe' was read over the PA while Russian Orthodox icons of Marx, Lenin and Mao dropped from the flies. The fortuitous presence of a Chinese member of the theatre staff allowed the classics' lines to be read in the original languages, as designated in the text. By now Hamlet had donned a suit of armour and proceeded to destroy the pictures with an axe.

The final scene ran as the text demanded. Ophelia was bandaged to a wheelchair by members of the stage crew as she repeated her lines 'wie eine Botschaft an die Welt'. Whale sounds, which provided a link with the 'Tiefsee' direction (M p. 97), were heard and got louder and louder until we could only see Ophelia mouthing the lines. She was then wheeled off.

The contradictory nature of the text and its subsequent realization was picked up by Horst Köpke who wrote that it was 'ein rätselhaftes Stück, doch nicht so abseits der Realität, wie wir im Westen gemeint haben'. This 'Eastern' reading was also acknowledged by Dietrich Pätzold who found 'sporadische Erinnerungsbrocken aus DDR-Zeiten assoziativ eingeworfen'.[61]

---

61 Horst Köpke, 'Die Macht, die nicht mehr ist', *Frankfurter Rundschau*, no date supplied; and Dietrich Pätzold, 'Das Zeitalter verendet als starker Theaterabend', no paper title supplied, 11-10-93. All reviews of the Schwerin production were provided by Sabine Andreas. Unfortunately, some bibliographical details were

Andreas seems to have found resonances in her associative, improvized style which were recognized by reviewers and spectators alike. In this way, her production, which still problematized the traditional conception of character, became a way of coming to terms with the GDR past. Association was her bridge to the audience, over which she hoped to communicate through the fragmentary impulses of the text.

The discussion of the four productions has shown that directors have, for the most part, been conscious of the problems presented by the demanding nature of the text and of the attribution in *Die Hamletmaschine*. Yet one must note that in at least one case, these challenges were somewhat steamrollered in the name of 'plot'. In the Münchner Kammerspiele production (première 14 November 1984, directed by Wolf Münzer and Wolf-Siegfried Wagner as the first half of an evening which concluded with *Verkommenes Ufer*) there was only a cast of two. Margit Carstensen, who played Ophelia and represented Horatio and Gertrude, wrote to me that they saw *Die Hamletmaschine* 'als die Gedanken eines Stalinisten' and played it with this reading in mind.[62] Although the critics reported that the acting ebbed and flowed with the textures of the different lines, it is hard to believe that the theatrical element was pushed too far because of the persistence of unchallenged 'characters'. The reviews, however, were not unfavourable. It would seem that the plentiful images and richness of the text carried the evening although an exploration of the possibilities of 'character' was to a certain degree ignored.

IV   The Productivity of the Unstageable

Our incursion into *Die Hamletmaschine* has proved more insightful than our investigation of *Der Auftrag*. The two chapters are, however, both concerned with similar issues, namely, how we understand the 'subject' on the modern stage. In order to get this far it was incumbent to do the necessary spadework. *Die Hamletmaschine* is a more radical and challenging text and extends our understanding of categories dealt with in Chapter I.

The text and the dramaturgy of *Die Hamletmaschine* are both major provocations to the institution of Western theatre. The actor is no longer the master of his/her role because the concept of the role has been so

missing.

62   Unpublished letter from Margit Carstensen to the author, 17-1-95.

thoroughly undermined. We have seen that by adopting unconventional and experimental attitudes to the play, interesting and equally provocative productions have been staged. Each of the four main examples given above, signal a radical change in theatrical communication. The sovereign role of character has deferred to a more exposed understanding of the speaking theatrical figure. Even the use of a named Hamlet figure in Schwerin was relativized by a mocking, playful and ironic chorus. Ophelia, too, had to struggle for possession of scene 2. The category of individualism in the theatre is called into question. The unified character has to give way to a different conception of the speaking figure on stage. In our above examples, directors have engaged in collective processes through which unstable and challenging performances have been generated.[63]

The variety of the impulses in the text creates a dizzying sense of identification and distance. Resonances and foreign matter oscillate before the audience and the actors. We are no longer invited, as is the case with Brecht, to step back from the so called 'natural order' so that we may understand its social construction. The points of distance attained in *Die Hamletmaschine* are ones of incomprehension at the very sites of human consciousness. Yet this is not a manifestation of blissful postmodern ignorance, as posited by Nash or Zurbrugg. The ignorance is not complete. The differing elements are presented in such a way that individual resonances may be absorbed whilst others are left as question marks. The variety of distancing found in our four main examples would seem to bear witness to this phenomenon. The collective playing or delivery of the speeches widens the spectators' focus. It allows them to go beyond the individualism that buffets them everyday through the mass media. The dramaturgy is thus imbued with an ideological thrust which wrenches the receivers of the text (be they actors or spectators) from traditional models of social make-up.

The theatre is also challenged by the bizarre imagery of the piece. The 'unperformable' stage directions have initiated a variety of experiments. The literal and semi-literal treatments in Munich and Schwerin respectively, and the use of spoken text in Hamburg and Berlin illustrate the possibilities

---

63   It is interesting to note that one major reason for the failure of the planned 'Uraufführung' in Cologne was the individualist stance of the Hamlet figure, Gerhard Winter. Winter was a conventionally trained actor whose approach to the role displayed a facile superiority. He considered the play 'ein normales, ein verstehbares, erklärbares, interpretierbares Stück', Girshausen (ed.), p. 56. Contradictions soon emerged when he refused to co-speak scene 2, as directed by the text. By refusing to submit to the polyphonous texture, Winter reached an impasse. Consequently the director had to start afresh with a new concept.

generated by an active commitment to the text. There is no clear-cut manner of realization. These non-verbal sections again function as activators of the collective's associations. Several obstacles trouble the transformation from text to performance. The text demands the imaginative engagement of its realizers. Even in Munich the university of the dead became an associative image: the link of a customized hospital trolley and obsessive reading took the textual image and telescoped it into a visual metaphor. Even if directors take up Müller's argument that the 'Scherzo', for example, was conceived as 'Kopftheater', the varieties of a 'read solution' are plentiful. By treating the images as text, several options are open (as seen in Brussels, Essen, Hamburg, the Deutsches Theater, Berlin, and at the Podewil, Berlin). The text would seem to provoke new solutions in every new production.

We should also not forget the productivity of the play's brevity. If a cast were to deliver the lines as written, it is unlikely that the nine pages of text would take more than twenty minutes. Length becomes a provocation and a challenge. Unlike Beckett's shorter works, which are kept short by elaborate and extensive stage directions, Müller's cry out for input from their realizers (cf. the discussion of *Verkommenes Ufer* in Chapter III for more evidence of this). The associative textures generate theatrical activity. The text becomes but one element in the production, along with the physicality of the actors and audio/visual dimensions. Text loses its authority in order to encourage dynamic engagement from the theatre.

A possible problem for the play is the 'intertextual' nature of the theatre itself. Dramaturges often process previous productions when preparing dossiers for directors and the cast. The temptation either to appropriate or modify existing solutions replaces imaginative impulses with a staidness all too common in the theatre. Our examples have not shown any sign of this practice although four productions do not exclude theatrical pilfering elsewhere.

Die Hamletmaschine is nonetheless a piece for the theatre, regardless of the theatre's inherent limitations. If we take up Reinelt's point from the introduction that the human subject is no longer to be considered the privileged sign in the theatre, we can see how provocative techniques have been employed in the *text* to communicate this. Actors have been asked to show the contingency of each line. Sovereignty over the text is banished. The human subject's part in the process of coming to terms with the machinery of history and the outside world is revealed as dependent on the need to go beyond the limitations of individualism. The theatre has proved itself as a highly suitable forum for the discussion of alternative ways of envisaging the speaking subject.

114

The absence of obvious staging possibilities is the root of the productivity of *Die Hamletmaschine*. The protean text remains productive in the West, the East, and even in a non-university town. The texts cannot be realized without active input on the part of the director and/or the cast. They mix complicated, inexplicable images which are both difficult to comprehend in one's head and to realize on a theatre's stage. The text no longer signals explicit answers. The only way to realize such an unwieldy text is to confront it on the level of theatre practice and to allow the results to come from this activity. *Die Hamletmaschine* formally stands out on its own. The question then arises as to whether the text spawns its own tradition, or creates its own context. The answer unfortunately has to be 'yes and no'. The reason for the diversity in our four highlighted productions has been a willing submission to the different strains of the text. Either the single speaking subject defers to the manifold impulses of the text and/or a chorus of voices splinters it in order to emphasize its heterogeneity. The subjectivity involved in both processes leads to different results in each case. Because the conscious mind is unable to take in all the vicissitudes of the text, a strict regulation of the text is no longer contingent. The speeches and directions make both the director and the cast unknowing. Basic techniques can communicate this ignorance or bafflement, yet these techniques are only the starting point in the process of realizing the text. The end-products remain diverse due to the different stimuli that different ignorance brings forth.

3   Wolokolamsker Chaussee

I   The Mysteries of the 'Lehrstück'

'Russische Eröffnung', 'Wald bei Moskau', 'Das Duell', 'Kentauren' and 'Der Findling', the five plays that make up the *Wolokolamsker Chaussee* cycle, were written between 1984 and 1987. Like much of Müller's work, the plans were sketched many years before a word had been typed. Müller had read Aleksander Bek's novel of the same name, which appeared in the GDR in full translation in 1962,[64] and decided that the material would, at some

---

64   Bek's novel was written in two phases. The original novel came about between 1942-7. It was later extended in 1960. 'Russische Eröffnung' is taken from the chapter 'Angst' from the first phase, 'Wald bei Moskau' from 'Medizinische Hochschulbildung' from the second.

stage, form the basis of a future work.[65] The piecemeal writing and publishing of the cycle confirm Müller's assertion that each can be viewed as an independent play. This was a necessary strategy because he feared the censorship of parts III-IV in the GDR, yet hoped at least that I and II could function alone.[66] As a result we find that the plays were used in a 'parasitär' manner, as the critic Heinz Klunker put it.[67] The première of 'Russische Eröffnung' on 9 May 1985 saw the play as a prologue to Becher's *Winterschlacht* at the Deutsches Theater, Berlin. In its West German début on the following day, it prefaced Kleist's *Robert Guiskard*.[68] 'Wald bei Moskau' received its world première in Potsdam together with 'Russische Eröffnung' on 4 May 1986. Next year the first two were combined with 'Das Duell', which again was given its first performance in Potsdam, on 6 March 1987. 'Kentauren' was premièred jointly at the Deutsches Theater, Berlin (where it formed part of Müller's own production of *Der Lohndrücker*), and at the Großes Haus in Schwerin, under the direction of Christoph Schroth, together with 'Das Duell', on 29 January 1988. The final part was staged for the first time with the four others in the Théâtre de Bobigny in Paris in 1988 and received its first German performance in Potsdam on 4 February 1989. In the meantime the Hochschule der Künste in West Berlin had put on parts I and III (première 26 June 1987), and drama students in Cologne performed 'Russische Eröffnung' in August of that year. This was then

65   David Barnett, '"Ich erfinde gerne Zitate": Interview mit Heiner Müller', *GDR Bulletin*, 2/95, p. 10.

66   Müller, *Krieg ohne Schlacht*, p. 344.

67   Heinz Klunker, 'Vom parasitären Umgang mit einem Gegenwartsstück. Heiner Müllers *Wolokolamsker Chaussee* auf der Bühne', in Paul Gerhard Klussmann and Heinrich Mohr (eds.), *Jahrbuch zur Literatur der DDR*, vol. 7 (Bonn: Bouvier, 1990), pp. 29-44.

68   Both premières occurred close to the fortieth anniversary of the defeat of Germany in World War Two. The choice of plays reflects this important date.
      Becher's *Winterschlacht* presents a German view of Operation Barbarossa. It charts the fortunes of two protagonists: one chooses to desert the Wehrmacht, the other stays. 'Russische Eröffnung' clearly contrasts with the German perspective whilst maintaining a common thread favouring the Soviet cause.
      Kleist's *Robert Guiskard* is also the tale of a military offensive. Guiskard leads an ill-fated siege of eleventh century Constantinople. Plague ravages his men, who plead with him to withdraw. The inevitable catastrophe is then signalled when Guiskard himself contracts the disease. The combination in Bochum of Kleist and Müller again contrasts themes of attack, defence and questions of necessity.

followed by a 'Lehrstück-Workshop' of 'Das Duell' organized by Florian Vaßen in Hanover that November. Professional theatres in Rostock and Frankfurt/Oder had staged parts I-III and Nordhausen put on parts I and III. Once all five had been produced back-to-back in Paris, a flood of productions of the complete cycle swept the two Germanies. The season 89/90 saw the entire *Wolokolamsker Chaussee* (in chronological order of première) at Dresden, Munich, Cologne, Aachen, Leipzig and Berlin. Two further productions occurred in Hamburg and through the Südbayerisches Städtetheater (which covers theatres in Landshut, Passau and Straubing) in the next season. Müller also inserted 'Der Findling' into his *Mauser* montage at the Deutsches Theater, Berlin, in 1991, and re-used that part and 'Das Duell' in *Duell Traktor Fatzer* at the Berliner Ensemble in 1993.

We see from the above sketch that the five parts are highly adaptable. Their suitability for independent function is emphasized by their frequent use outside of the cycle's five-part context. Although the new contexts were primarily Müllerian, this was not always the case. It would seem (from newspaper reviews) that when combined with plays of different types or genres, the individual elements functioned well as contrasts or rogue elements.

The brief production history of the plays shows something we have not as yet noted in the context of Müller's *oeuvre*: immediate resonance. Although *Die Hamletmaschine* has become something of a popular favourite, we observed that it took a while before directors understood the wealth and potential of the text. *Wolokolamsker Chaussee*, on the other hand, scored an instant hit. Textual accessibility would seem to account for this, although, as we shall see, the freedom of the form did not make the cycle any less problematic than *Die Hamletmaschine*.

In 1986 Müller commented on the relationship between the writing of the texts and the historical moment:

> Natürlich sind diese Texte *Wolokolamsker* provoziert durch eine aktuelle Situation [the Gorbachev era], und ich bin daran interessiert, dazu etwas zu sagen. Möglichst darauf Einfluß zu nehmen, soweit das mit Theaterstücken geht. Das bedeutet, daß solch ein Stück für mehr Leute begreifbar sein muß, vor allem schneller begreifbar sein muß, als ein Text wie *Bildbeschreibung*.[69]

---

69 'Solange wir an unsere Zukunft glauben, brauchen wir uns vor unserer Vergangenheit nicht zu fürchten', in Müller, *Gesammelte Irrtümer*, p. 187.

A quick reading of any of the five texts shows that associative and highly metaphorical language is not as prominent as in the vast majority of his later work. Textual instability is manufactured by a more fundamental theatrical problem: each text is without any manner of character attribution. The same was true of *Bildbeschreibung*. However, in this case, each part is focussed by a narrative 'I' who ostensibly narrates events of the past as opposed to the anonymous present-tense description in *Bildbeschreibung*.

The movements from the narrating present to the events of the past found in *Wolokolamsker Chaussee* signal an appropriation of at least some formal features of the Brechtian 'Lehrstück'. Several critics have mentioned the terms 'Lehrstück' or 'episches Theater' in the context of the narrated cycle.[70] Müller's own thoughts on this term and his own texts betray the slipperiness of his theatrical concepts. On the one hand, he openly admitted the appropriation of the form: '[*Wolokolamsker Chaussee*] hat eine Lehrstückstruktur. Das ist klar. Da ist es geradezu eine Voraussetzung, daß es keine überbordenden Metaphern gibt'.[71] On the other, he was against the definition as an all-encompassing term: 'ich würde sie [the *Wolokolamsker Chaussee* plays] nie "Lehrstück" nennen. [...] Sie haben viel mehr mit außereuropäischen Theaterformen zu tun genauso wie Brechts Lehrstücken'.[72] Müller concedes 'Lehrstück' qualities to the plays without restricting them within the genre as such. Our dramaturgical understanding of the cycle is at least partly dependent upon how the 'Lehrstück' is used and modified in the light of the unattributed verse form.

Rainer Steinweg's ground-breaking book on the 'Lehrstück' provides much material from the Bertolt Brecht Archive in Berlin and gives a good

70   For example, Gottfried Fischborn, '"Poesie aus der Zukunft" und künstlerische Subjektivität heute. An einem Beispiel: Heiner Müllers "Wolokolamsker Chaussee I"', *Zeitschrift für Germanistik*, 4/88, p. 446; Helmut Kreuzer, '"Ostfront" 1941. Ein dramatisches Thema in drei Variationen von Herbert Reinecke, Johannes R. Becher und Heiner Müller', in Hartmut Eggert, Ulrich Profitilich and Klaus R. Scherpe (eds.), *Geschichte als Literatur. Formen und Grenzen der Repräsentation von Vergangenheit* (Stuttgart: Metzler, 1990), p. 343; J. H. Reid, 'Homburg-Maschine. Heiner Müller in the Shadow of Nuclear War', in W.G. Sebald (ed.), *A Radical Stage. Theatre in Germany in the 1970s and 1980s* (Oxford: Berg, 1988), p. 146; or Bernhard Greiner, 'IM SPIEGEL / DAS FEINDBILD: Heiner Müllers Kriegsrede *Wolokolamsker Chaussee I-V*', *Krieg und Literatur. Internationale Beiträge zur Erforschung der Kriegs- und Antikriegsliteratur*, 2/90, p. 67.

71   *Gesammelte Irrtümer*, p. 188.

72   Barnett, '"Ich erfinde gerne Zitate"', p. 11.

idea as to the function and form of the genre. I shall take his book as a starting point and then examine some of the criticisms raised against it.

The term 'Lehrstück' is concisely defined by Brecht: 'diese Bezeichnung gilt nur für die Stücke, die für die *Darstellenden* lehrhaft sind. Sie benötigen kein Publikum'.[73] This basic premise opens up a new conception of theatrical reality, one which requires a style that is for the benefit of the actor and not for the audience. The role of choruses in the plays provides a collective voice to which the individual has to answer or to defer. As Steinweg puts it:

> das Publikum wird *handelnde Person* in dem Sinne, in dem man
> von einem CHOR als 'dramatis personae' sprechen kann, doch
> steht es [...] einem GELERNTEN CHOR gegenüber, übernimmt
> also nicht einfach die Funktion des Chors im klassischen anti-
> ken oder neueren Drama.

The conflict of individual and collective is the central focus. The form and the concept of individuality is modified: 'er, der die einzelnen Muster mittels Nachahmung und Kritik zur Erweiterung und *Gestaltung* seiner *eigenen*, lebenden Person verwendet statt zur ästhetischen *Gestaltung* einer imaginären, ist der "Held" des Lehrstücks'.[74] The actor consequently becomes a character for him/herself in order to undergo situations which nonetheless may be foreign to him/her. Such situations are not necessarily positive for the protagonist. As Brecht comments, for example, in the *Fatzer* fragment, the clean and scientific approach taken to sex education in school is in fact the wrong one. The communication of such information is best taken care of in the sordid speculations of school children where a far more earthy and thus more rounded understanding of the subject can be explored.[75] The acceptance of dogmatic politics that some critics have ascribed to the 'Lehr-

73   Rainer Steinweg, *Das Lehrstück. Brechts Theorie einer politisch-ästhetischen Erziehung*, second, expanded edition (Stuttgart: Metzler, 1976), p. 61.

74   Ibid., p. 88 and p. 154.

75   This example was originally quoted in Rainer Nägele, 'Brecht's Theatre of Cruelty', in Nägele, *Reading After Freud* (New York: Columbia University Press, 1987), p. 118. (It was first published in German in a collection of new interpretations of Brecht's work.) A compilation of the fragments that make up the *Fatzer* text is now available under Müller's editorship. The quotation can be found in Bertolt Brecht, *Der Untergang des Egoisten Johann Fatzer* (Leipzig: Suhrkamp, 1994), p. 79.

stück' is linked to an imputed coldness in the texts which assumes that consent 'just happens'. Brecht was keen to point out that this was not in fact the case: 'als ich für das Theater mit der Einfühlung mit dem besten Willen nichts mehr anfangen konnte, baute ich für die Einfühlung noch das Lehrstück'.[76] The teaching process must accommodate both the intellect and the emotions.

A further formal point was the mechanical nature of the plays, the repetitions that the series of individual scenes evoked. Steinweg maintains '*Zitierbarkeit*, und das heißt Wiederholbarkeit, ist die Voraussetzung dafür, daß die Bedeutung der Gesten, Haltungen und Sätze, ihre Relevanz und [...] *Tragfläche begriffen* werden können'.[77] By piling on similar situations, the actor can compare personal position and the position of the body. Through this s/he might understand better the discrepancies between the individuated self and the figure s/he was creating.

Steinweg's conclusions are fairly harmonized. Despite the necessary evils in the violent episodes of the various 'Lehrstücke', the dialectic has synthesized the conflicts and the actors are ready for another challenge. This view of a synthesis is questioned by Rainer Nägele who is keen to point out that a critical discourse on the methods of education leaves much unanswered. Violence and cruelty persist at the end of each 'Lehrstück' and indeed it is only through them that the 'Lehrstück' can end. The root of Nägele's critique is that teaching is an asymmetrical business: the teacher's authority is always based on safeguards which go beyond a tacit acceptance of authority. The recipient of the lesson is exposed to 'cruelty, terror and pleasure'. These qualities of teaching are also present in the form of the 'Lehrstück'.

Steinweg's belief that 'Zitierbarkeit' is the point of entry to understanding through repetition is inverted in Nägele's reading. The repetition of events and their subtle changes is derived from the Noh theatre of Japan which emphasizes the ritualistic. Nägele asserts that the form resists a simple shift from religious/mystical to secular/political.

Finally, Nägele has some remarks on the acting technique itself. Following on from Brecht's elliptical remark on 'Einfühlung' quoted above, Nägele challenges the traditional claim that the actor cannot identify with the character. Clearly Stanislavskian identification is not possible due to 'a lack of motivation and interiority'. Character in the 'Lehrstück' is 'the un-

76   Steinweg, p. 159.

77   Ibid., p. 143.

folding in the chain of gestural rhetoric'.[78] If the actor is also the spectator (the 'spectactor' of Augusto Boal's post-Brechtian theatre),[79] a contradictory position must be taken wherein the actors identifies and is prevented from identifying simultaneously. This follows the dynamic of the 'Lehrstück' which plays off the interests of the individual and the collective. Brecht's 'Einfühlung' is one which is not able to accept the 'natural' qualities of the realist character but one which requires a modified approach in order to succeed.

Steinweg opened up the discussion of the 'Lehrstück' and pulled it away from its role as the whipping boy of Brecht's *oeuvre*. Yet it is only when we appreciate the full ramifications of his discoveries as highlighted by Nägele that we can view the genre not only as plays that teach but also as discourses on teaching. Nägele shows how the harmonized dialectic of Steinweg is only superficially correct - violence, ritual and divided actors are implicit to the 'Lehrstück'.

II   A Uniform Form?

The 'character-less' texts of *Wolokolamsker Chaussee* are highly problematic for a variety of reasons. A quick comparison with *Der Horatier*, another text without character attribution, reveals points of divergence. That text is clearly choral: voices emerge from and disappear within the mass of actors, as suggested in the note that follows the play. The text itself, however, is impersonal: the narration carries no 'ich' and all is rendered in the past. Direct speech is always signalled by markers such as 'sagte er'. Although the effects are by no means uncomplicated, especially if the cast decides to follow Müller's note (M p. 54), there is little difficulty in demarcating textual blocks. The *Wolokolamsker Chaussee* texts introduce further devices that make even a simple formal description problematic.

An attempt at a typology of the texts reveals the very serious problems that directors and actors, as well as plain readers, face when trying to

78   Nägele, p. 118 and pp. 132-3.

79   Cf. Augusto Boal, *Theatre of the Oppressed*, trans. by Charles A. and Maria-Odilia Leal-McBride (London: Pluto, 1979), pp. 119-190.

understand the texts. If we take, for the sake of example, 'Russische Eröf-fnung', we can see how quickly the text becomes unruly.[80]

In the following scheme, I have tried to show how the texts can hypothetically be divided in performance.[81] Breaks in the texts have been identified as an opportunity for the casting of a different actor. By concentrating on the polyphony of the texts we can understand better the vast possibilities that they offer. The choral ramifications of the form will be discussed later.

The first page of 'Russische Eröffnung' is exemplary in the way that textual vagueness already frustrates a 'straight' reading:

1. Wir lagen zwischen Moskau und Berlin
2. Im Rücken ein Wald ein Fluß vor Augen
   Zweitausend Kilometer weit Berlin
   Einhundertzwanzig Kilometer Moskau
3. In Schützenlöchern aus gefrornem Schlamm
   Und warteten auf den Befehl zum Einsatz
   Und auf den ersten Schnee Und auf die Deutschen
4. [...] Meine
   Soldaten hatten Angst und wenig mehr
5. Angst ist die Mutter des Soldaten und
   Der erste Schnitt geht durch die Nabelschnur
   Und wer den Schnitt verpaßt stirbt an der Mutter
6. Meine Soldaten kamen von der Schule
   Im Kino hatten sie den Krieg gesehen

(SF1 p. 241)

---

80 Although the *Wolokolamsker Chaussee* cycle is available in a single volume (Hei-ner Müller, *Die Schlacht. Wolokolamsker Chaussee*, Frankfurt/Main: Verlag der Autoren, 1988), I have chosen to remain with the standard Rotbuch edition. 'Russische Eröffnung' is to be found in SF1 pp. 241-9, and the other four are in SF2 pp. 231-58. There is one textual drawback to the Rotbuch edition and this is the omission of the line 'Meine Gedanken überschlugen sich' in 'Wald bei Moskau' which comes between 'An der vorbei der Feind nach Moskau greift' and 'Die Sowjetordnung dachte ich wo bleibt sie' (both SF2 p. 237). The line appears both in the Verlag der Autoren edition and in the Henschel Verlag's rehearsal copy of the script.

81 Of course, the texts can be read/narrated/acted by a singly actor remembering past events.

The six sections illustrate the various choices which a text that is semantically simple can present to the theatre. Section one can be read in one of three ways. It is clear that this is a narrative, spoken at distance from the event itself. The speaker, however, creates a problem through the use of 'wir'. From the context it is possible that the Commander, who takes over as a single voice in section six, is speaking and referring to the batallion under his control. Alternatively the collective voices of the soldiers could speak them. A combination of the two speaking simultaneously is also possible.

Section two is more problematic. The lines are without tense markers and thus we have no idea of *when* the lines are spoken. They might follow the time scheme of the narrative that preceded them, yet they could take on a quality of their own. A possible shift to an implicit present tense cannot be ruled out. The immediacy of the present would then act as a rapid switch to the realm of direct experience.[82] Again the speakers of the lines can be chosen from the collective of voices which could have spoken section one, although this time one could add the voices of the deserters, so that all actors on stage could communicate the universal predicament of the Soviet army and people.

Section three continues with the narrative started in section one and interrupted in section two. Section four sees the move from the possibly collective voice to the singular one of the Commander, who continues to narrate in the imperfect.

Section five marks a definite move to the present tense. Yet just as it was possible to read section two as set in the past, the present or both, we are presented with the same options here as well. If the Commander is saying these lines (and we know that he narrates sections four and six), then they could be a way of experiencing his thoughts *as they were* at that time yet while he is narrating, as a theatrical 'erlebte Rede'. Alternatively, the lines could transfer us directly to the events of 1941. In both cases this ambiguity could be exploited to attain the possible simultaneity of section two. Alternatively, the present tense could confer the speeches the status of a narrative aside (such as used, for example, by an omniscient narrator in a nineteenth-century novel). They have the tenor of a saying. In this case, the speaker is able to control the flow of his/her speech. (The consciousness

---

82 Lines three and four also take on another quality, a non-realistic quality, which is manufactured by their repetition. The lines occur a further three times in the text and gain the status of a motif and remind us of the ritualistic aspect of the 'Lehrstück' form. The pair pound away throughout and could be read in both tenses (past and present) *simultaneously*.

involved in direct addresses to the audience is perhaps something that is not well suited to the potentially choral function of the texts, although we are naturally unable to rule it out.) The change of tense also allows the doubling of the Commander role, which is suggested in Müller's note to 'Russiche Eröffnung' (SF1 249-50): one Commander narrates with the benefit of hindsight, whilst the other acts as if he were there. The same play of levels is true for a soldiers' rendition of the speech.

The text, as we can see from the first lines, is exceptionally difficult to apprehend both in terms of speakers and time levels. Hypothetically, the whole section could be spoken by the singular voice of one actor playing the Commander. Alternatively, a dense wall of voices could be employed to indicate the nuances of the piece.

It is important to remember that semantically, the text is relatively unproblematic (especially when compared with the way language is used in *Die Hamletmaschine* or *Der Auftrag*, for example). The umbilical chord metaphor in section five is both introduced and systematically developed for the audience. The metaphor's referents are clearly signalled, which is not common practice for an artist like Müller whose work thrives on the associative potential of poetic langauge.

Wolokolamsker Chaussee also features what one must advisedly call 'dialogue'. A little further in the text we find the following exchange, when a group of deserters reach the camp (the appended numbers are my addition):

> [1] Wo kommt ihr her Genossen
> [2] Aus dem Kessel
> [3]Der Deutsche [4] Habt ihr ihn gesehn [5] Wie kämpft er
> [6] Der Deutsche [7] Habt ihr ihn gesehn [8] Gesehn
> [9] Ein Horizont aus Panzern ist [10] der Deutsche
> [11] Der auf dich zufährt [12] So ein Himmel aus
> Flugzeugen ist [13] der Deutsche [14] Und ein Teppich
> Aus Bomben der sich über Russland legt
> [15] Du wirst ihn selber sehn [16] Und eh du aufwachst
> Vom nächsten Schlaf [17] Und vielleicht wachst du nicht auf
> Vom nächsten Schlaf
> [18] Wohin so eilig [19] Bleibt
> [20] Erholt euch von der Front [21] Erzählt Genossen
> (SF1 pp. 241-2)

The above scheme shows a possible maximum of twenty-one different voices that could speak these lines in order to exploit a huge chorus of actors.

Although this scheme indicates a division at any hint of a break, there is no reason why such an arrangement should not be possible. I have emphasized the words 'der Deutsche' (voices 3, 6, 10, and 13) as independent exclamations because they too occur as a motif throughout the text and thus open themselves up for the same sort of treatment as lines three and four above.[83] A different organization is, of course, available in which the curious voices of the batallion's soldiers (1, 3-6, 18-21) are contrasted with those of the deserters (2 and 7-17). This scheme could mean that the sides would be taken by anything from one voice per side to a more populous solution. Alternatively, we could read the staggered lines in the text (between 1 and 2, and 17 and 18) as brackets, outside of which only the Commander speaks. The staggering is deceptive, this our analysis has already shown, although it should not be disregarded altogether. The final possibility (and hence the reluctance to call the section 'dialogue') is that the whole exchange is a recollection on the part(s) of the Commander and/or a group of soldiers. The 'dialogue' becomes another example of the theatrical 'erlebte Rede' discussed earlier, even though it would still be a *remembered* dialogue.

Elsewhere there are problems with narrated dialogue. In the following example, the Commander is just concluding a block of unmediated 'dialogue' on the fate of the coward[84] who shot himself in the hand to avoid further active combat:

---

83 In an interview, one of Müller's two interlocutors refers to the use of 'der Deutsche' and 'deutsch' as a 'Dauerpaukenschlag' (in 'Warum zünden Sie keine Kaufhäuser an, Heiner Müller?', in *Gesammelte Irrtümer 2*, p. 155). This could also affect the text outlined in the first example (and all subsequent mentions of the Germans) insofar as a different voice or a chorus of voices wrench the motif from its syntactic position in order to emphasize the word.
    Another implication of the continual use of the 'deutsch' constellation is for the actor. The texts were clearly intended for German performance in the first instance. That German actors are forced to regard themselves as non-Germans through their speeches has much to do with the play of identification in the 'Lehrstück' form.

84 It should be pointed out that the soldier in question is *not* a 'junger Rekrut'. This Herziger alleges in a bid, one assumes, to add more pathos to the scene and to depict it as even more inhuman (in *Masken der Lebensrevolution: vitalistische Zivilisations- und Humanismuskritik in Texten Heiner Müllers*, Munich: Wilhelm Fink, 1992, p. 173). The figure is clearly described as a 'Gruppenführer' in the text (SF1 p. 245). His age is not mentioned.

1.   Ich will ihn nicht sehn Und seine Gruppe
       Soll ihn erschießen von dem Bataillon
       In einer Stunde Das ist mein Befehl
2.   Der Leutnant fragte Haben wir das Recht
3.   Ich sagte Mein Befehl wird ausgeführt
       Und war es Unrecht soll man mich erschießen
       Sie schreiben den Bericht Genosse Leutnant

                            (SF1 pp. 246-7)

Section one carries the same problems as the rest of the 'dialogue' discussed above. The second section brings us back to a different situation by re-introducing the frame, the narration. Several speaking permutations arise from this line and from the following one. The choice depends upon the desire to maintain the intensity of the present tense dialogue lines or else to diffuse it through the tactical use of other voices in the narrator's position. If the original dialogue voices of the Commander and the Lieutenant were retained for the narrative particles, they would be 'telling their own stories' and preserving both levels in one voice (cf. our discussion of Brechtian acting styles in Chapter I). Alternatively by splitting the narrator and the dialogue speaker, the frame and the tension between levels are highlighted. A return to complete narration would throw the preceding dialogue (if it were rendered in such a way) into relief and we would find ourselves back in the narrating present, away from the immediacy of present-tense 1941.

    The play of different temporal tiers as seen in the above examples becomes even more complicated when additional levels are added. The scheme in 'Wald bei Moskau' and 'Kentauren' plays with two: a time from which the text is narrated (which could be the present of the theatre or a fictional present as defined by costume or set) and a time at which the events occurred (respectively, the defence of Moscow and a grotesque dreamworld bureaucracy somewhere in the GDR's history). 'Russische Eröffnung' is very similar to 'Wald bei Moskau' save for a short flashback to the Commander's first experience of war (SF1 p. 244).[85] On the other hand, 'Das Duell' opens up an additional three levels, 'Der Findling' trawls through the lives of both main figures, the Son and the Father.

    The narrator of 'Das Duell', a Communist who had been interned as a political prisoner during the war, describes his experience of 17 June 1953.

---

85   We are not told whether this was the First World War or the Russian Civil war. The former would suggest 'the old enemy', the latter fighting for the Red Army.

This involves the confrontation with his Deputy whom the Director had coached through difficult exams against the wishes of a reactionary Professor whom the Director had encountered in 1934.[86] Thus in addition to the real/fictional present from which he is narrating, there are four narrated time levels which are, in reverse order: the events of June 1953, the coaching of the Deputy at a university's 'Arbeiter und Bauern Fakultät' (ABF), his time in 'Zuchthaus Brandenburg' and his clash with the Professor in 1934. Just as the 'two Commanders' allowed for a doubling of actor, so the additional temporal levels telescope this potential device. The Director could be played by five actors and the deputy by two. There are also lines for the figure of the Professor, should a company desire them.

The time scheme of 'Der Findling' is less stratified. We learn much about the pasts of the two protagonists, the Son and the Father, from exchanges of direct speech. We can deduce that the confrontation between the adopted Son and the party functionary Father comes somewhere around 1973, five years after the Son was incarcerated for his opposition to the Russian invasion of Czechoslovakia in 1968. An episode in 1966 is also mentioned: the Father had tried to kill himself after humiliation at a Party meeting. The incidents from the childhood and adolescence of the Son are also sketched, as is the Father's time in a concentration camp. Again, the employment of several actors for one character is available but here this would mean voices would have to enter 'dialogues'.

Our only guide to the formal and structural features is vague: there are areas of first person singular and plural narration, tenseless lines, blocks of unsignalled present tense communication and lines which can pass as dialogue. We must now ask how these five different styles configure themselves within the five texts in order to understand whether overall styles can be differentiated in the five parts before we link the texts to the 'Lehrstück'.

(One option for our interpretation, which is easily discussed, is that all the texts are open to be read/performed by a single voice and in this way there is no distinction between the five texts. *Wolokolamsker Chaussee* becomes nothing more than a set of short stories or a vehicle for the single actor. The act of individual remembrance would seem to contradict the various moments of collectivity sketched above. It would also reduce the

---

86   Anna Chiarloni deduces that if the Director was of 'student age' around 1934 and hence about forty in 1953, then he could be a leading SED member if the narrative took place around the time of writing (1986), Anna Chiarloni, 'Zu Heiner Müllers "Duell"', in Frank Hörnigk (ed.), *Heiner Müller Material* (Göttingen: Steidl, 1989), p. 229. The fictional location of the narrator is thus potentially of high import in this scene.

127

efficacy of the theatrical medium. As yet, no theatre to my knowledge has staged the texts in this way. This possibility, which certainly might have its function, is one that will only be borne in mind in the following discussion in favour of a more imaginative engagement with the texts.)

'Russische Eröffnung' is constructed in a dynamic fashion so that perspectives are continually added to that of the narrating Commander. Throughout, his inner thoughts are peppered with the odd line or two in the present tense. The movement from past to present within the context of the narrative maintains a rhythm and prevents the narrative from becoming overly subjective. In addition, the three mood-setting dialogues that precede the 'action' help to describe the situation in a style that goes beyond the singular narrator. The immediacy of the dialogues after the feigned attack complements the reflective and descriptive passages. They give way to the direct experience of practice. The aftermath of the decision to execute the coward has some present tense interjection although, for the most part, small lines of external dialogue break up the recollection. The final thirteen lines are all in the present and confront the audience with a concerted blast of immediacy: the results of the court martial cannot be erased and the Commander continues to carry them with him. The final speech presents an open wound which seems to be aimed squarely at the audience. The opportunity of engaging in a collective reading of the text is also available. The potential of the narration in the 'wir' form and the repetition of certain lines and motifs that occur either in the present or which are without tense markers persist and suggest a constant pressure on both the company and its Commander.

'Wald bei Moskau' is far less of a collective piece, insofar as the Commander's consciousness seems to be the main site of the action. Dialogue is less pronounced and there are none of the expository exchanges that we found in the first half of 'Russische Eröffnung'. The exchanges with Captain Belenkow are also sharp, laconic affairs. Larger areas of text are in the present tense (cf. SF2 p. 235, p. 236 and p. 237) as if the Commander were playing out arguments with a doubting self before the audience. The voices of others, however, also find their way into the text in the form of challenges to the Commander. Nagging doubts as to the capability of his leadership and the legitimacy of his decision to take the law into his own hands manifest themselves as present-tense voices. Whether these are spoken by the Commander and/or soldiers (including Belenkow) remains a production decision. The widespread use of present-tense reflection and the dynamic doubting voices once again present the audience with a more direct form of address. This helps to turn potential solipsism into active confrontation. The decision-making process becomes an open challenge to the

128

audience to come to its own position on the issue. The tension is at its peak before the final speech to Belenkow, which comes across as something of a formality. This formality might have more to do with the audience than with the action: by the end of the inner/collective anguish, we know that the Commander will repeat his demotion order, given earlier (SF2 p. 234). The sobriety of its tone and the regained confidence of its speaker suggest the smirk of the victor. Having been put through the process, the audience is presented with the result. This is not a 'happy ending', though, signalling a triumph; it leaves several questions open. The possible inadequacy of the conclusion is emphasized by some of the rhetoric employed: the 'sowjetische Insel [...] im deutschen Meer' and the repeated use of 'Wald' (both SF2 pp. 237-8) echo previous images used to justify the decision to demote Belenkow. The Commander has come through a series of *idées fixes* similar to the recurrent motifs of 'Russische Eröffnung' but, whereas 'there is no question that the Commander had to act as he did' in that case, there is eminently more ambivalence in this notion of disobeying rules in order to uphold them.[87] In the first *Wolokolamsker Chaussee* text we share the pain involved in making an impossible decision, in the second we are confronted with it and challenged by it.

'Das Duell', 'ziemlich im Zentrum' as Günter Heeg maintains, concentrates many of the problems of the whole *Wolokolamsker Chaussee* cycle.[88] As a result, perhaps, this section has also come in for more specific critical attention. Alfred Bergstedt and Kerstin Morling view the text as articulating the chief problems of the committed individual in the GDR.[89] The Director is no longer able to distinguish class division and longs for his days in Brandenburg when enemies were enemies. Chiarloni expands the effects on the Director and interprets the play in a wider context. Five problems are identified: the death of Rosa Luxemburg (and its effects on the Communist movement), the vacuum of the Nazi period, the revolution from above in the GDR, the isolation of the GDR from the rest of the world, and the post-war economic problems that the country faced.[90]

87   J. H. Reid, p. 148.

88   Günter Heeg, 'Der Weg der Panzer. Notizen zu einer geplanten Aufführung von Heiner Müllers *Wolokolamsker Chaussee I-V*', in Wolfgang Storch (ed.), p. 140.

89   Alfred Bergstedt and Kerstin Morling, 'Zu Anna Seghers Erzählung "Das Duell" (1965) und Heiner Müllers "Wolokolamsker Chaussee III: Das Duell" (1986)', *Wissenschaftliche Zeitschrift der brandenburgischen Landeshochschule*, 5/90, p. 700.

90   Chiarloni, pp.233-4.

The narrative opens in the first person plural. The voice of the Director only emerges nine lines into the text. This initial section is most interesting because of the tone it lends to the piece. Once again a collective ritual is evoked ('Das war [...] Im fünften Jahr der Republik Den wir / Gestrichen haben aus unserm Kalender', SF2 p. 239). A collective voice acknowledges the erasure of a historical fact. Then, before the confrontation between the Director and his Deputy has a chance to become the focus of the text, we are brought back to the ABF where the Director assumes a role that mixes authoritarianism and concern for the young member of the working class when he forced him through the course. After another short return to June, a longer remembrance of the past is called forth. This time it sparks off an association with 1934, before returning again to June 1953. In the narratives that frame the direct speech for each section there is a surprising lack of the present-tense immediacy found in the other two parts: we are almost exclusively presented with remembered dialogue. After another swift exchange, the Director once again remembers the ABF but is struck by an image of a bricklayer, a veteran of the Spanish Civil War, promoted to Minister in the GDR. For the first time, the description is presented without tense marker in a flood of memory. The indeterminacy of when the Director remembers this figure (ie. in the present while narrating or during the uprising in June) confers it a powerful status in his recollection. The shock of this remembrance jolts the speaker and consequently the audience. After the inital shock, the memory of the bricklayer is filed back into the past-tense narrative: the Director regains control. Only after a short section of stichomythia does the Director ponder the return of the tanks in the present tense. Even this is mediated by a 'dachte ich' (SF2 p. 242). The tanks' arrival after a short narrative brings us to the truly immediate moment of the text, the climax. In an unintroduced present-tense speech of fifteen lines, a ritualized liturgy is sung to the oncoming tanks.[91] The speech begins and ends in the 'wir' form, although there are lines in the middle ('Und ich / Ich hätt es wissen müssen Ich zuerst' and 'Hab ich gesagt Stalin ist tot Heil Stalin', both SF2 p. 243) where the Deputy is forced to bow his head in an act of contrition (again, a pseudo-religious motif). What follows is another ritualized formality, the signed act of self-criticism. After a short narrative on the acceptance of the chit and the wish to be back in prison, the 'wir' form returns for the final three lines. The content of the lines, however, is an interesting show of division. Both the Director and the Deputy wipe their hands after the customary handshake.

91   In the following analyses of productions, this important speech will be referred to as the 'Tanks speech'.

Interior decision making is replaced by the play of history in 'Das Duell'. The individual narrator becomes a store of images: he projects crucial moments of his life as a Communist. The greater role of changing temporal perspective bestows a cinematic quality to the text: 'scenes' switch with great rapidity. The constant scene changes help to reduce the proximity we were permitted in the first two parts. The individual becomes, to a certain extent, a site to be viewed rather than a point of indentification. Müller's note at the end of the piece emphasizes the pivotal figure of the narrating Director: '*Die Textaufteilung hängt von der angenommenen Bericht-zeit ab (vor oder nach welchem Ereignis, vor oder nach dem Tod)*' (SF2, p. 244). The collective function of the ritualized introduction and dénouement is contrasted with both the perspectives of the past and the external dissent of the Deputy, who is nonetheless forced to 'take the oath' of the tanks. The overtly open ending plays with the contradiction of a collective that is not collective any more.

'Kentauren' is formally the simplest text of the quintet. Its epigraph and the mention of a Saxon Gregor Samsa in the subtitle are the only two devices that give it a degree of complexity, and we shall return to this later. The nightmare of a Stasi Chief which is introduced by the two-line narrative at the beginning of the text divides very easily into two voices, those of a Chief and of an Underling. Once the latter is sent off to cross a busy traffic junction in uniform when the light is on red, the elated Chief briefly nar-rates the successful outcome of the grotesque order. The Underling returns to report his 'triumph' and the Chief briefly relates the Underling's winged departure to heaven when he realizes that he has become one with the symbol of his bureaucratic life, his writing desk. The sovereign human subject has been relativized. At the point of realization, the Chief moves into a present-tense speech that lasts for two pages and concludes the text with a germ of subversion: 'Was knackt / In unserm Holz He Ist der Wurm drin Hilfe' (SF2 p. 250). The present-tense monologue remains a nightmare.

The text offers practically no point of contact between the audience and the speaker(s). The shift of tense in the final two pages opens the Chief up to ridicule when his realization forces him to deal with his ludicrous condition in the present. Even a concept of collectivity is parodied in the final section ('Der Kommunardentraum Vom Ich zum Wir', SF2 p. 249) when the words 'wir' and 'unser' are related to the union of the individual and the state. The text is lonely. It also distances the spectator through its use of humour.[92] Elements of everyday political cliché are held up to ridicule through such formulations as 'Gefallen an der Front der Dialektik', 'Die Dialektik wiederhergestellt', 'Denkmal des unbekannten Ordnungshüters' (all SF2 p. 248) or 'Der Schreibtisch ist volkseigen Was bin ich' (SF2 p. 249). The text would seem to be a well-written skit, a set piece that amuses in the somewhat grotesque manner of much of today's Goons/Python inspired comedy. Dramaturgically, the text is also more accessible (or less problematic) than the previous three. The predominance of dialogue effectively reduces the casting problems found elsewhere. Even the possibility of two Chiefs seems a little pointless. The oneiric context blurs a distinction between the someone looking back and the someone who performed the actions looked back upon, especially because the narrative does not end in this way.

The audience is challenged by the texts at the beginning of the scene. The reference to Gregor Samsa, the protagonist of Kafka's *Die Verwandlung*, as a native of Saxony is puzzling. The parallel between a travelling salesman who turns into a giant insect and a top official who becomes a bureaucratic centaur is clear. We are also aware from the Chief's 'erlebte Rede' that he calls himself 'alter Preuße' (ibid.). Prussia, as the 'Friedrich der Große' scene in *Leben Gundlings* is all too keen to show, is the seat of German bureaucracy. Geographically, the GDR was essentially made up of two halves: the northern Prussian areas and the southern Saxon ones. How are we thus to link this critique to a text written 'originally' in Saxon by Samsa? If this is intended to be read as a cautionary tale, then its Saxon dialect is a warning against Prussian practices. Saxony becomes a site of resistance and acts as a frame for the whole text.[93] The *Tempest* quotation is also a means of framing the text politically. Here the cautionary tone is more evident: the youthful and sheltered Miranda is delighted by the strange and the new. Prospero relativizes her enthusiasm and criticizes it at the same

92 Clearly the West and the East German spectator would differ here. To the West German, the distance could merely involve laughing at a ridiculous system. The relationship of the GDR citizen might have been more dialectical. S/he would be closer to the vicissitudes of the parodied Stasi. Although the scene might have caused much laughter, there would have always been a degree of intimate recognition of the situation which relativized the mirth. Again we note the play of identification typical of the 'Lehrstück'.

93 My research is unfortunately unable to reveal whether the text has ever been spoken either in a Saxon accent or 'translated' into Saxon on stage. One would expect that the productions in Dresden and Leipzig would have been better prepared for such an eventuality.

time. That someone could find the 'brave new world' of the GDR *apparat* exciting is surprising, yet the will to conform to such structures is more the subject of critique here. The younger cadres were still entering the system. The subtitle and the epigraph confer extra, subversive contexts to a text which might otherwise have remained a somewhat flat satire.

'Der Findling' is the only text not to be narrated from a Communist's perspective. It is also highly complex. Hans-Christian Stillmark points out that it has 'eine nicht leicht zu überschauende Fabel' because 'die problematischen Stationen sozialistischer Geschichte verdichten und vermengen sich im Dialog'.[94] A disaffected son of an SED functionary is the voice that opens the text. While he recounts his two 'changes of address' (the first to the GDR's prison for political prisoners in Bautzen, the second to his new home in West Berlin), the present tense is used ('Glas fressen oder Klingen kaun zum Beispiel / Setzt die Gefängnisordnung außer Kraft', SF2 p. 251). We find the same tense shortly after for an extended description of West Berlin. The first seems like a gambit: the Son shows the audience his defiance at first hand, whereas the grizzly description of Berlin is impersonal, a pocket panorama, which could be spoken by either figure. Three lines of narrative then introduce a long section of dialogue between the Son and the Father which is only mediated twice: firstly with 'Er fragte nicht Wer und Was für ein Flugblatt' (SF2 p. 252), secondly, half a page later, one word of the Father's is followed by 'sagte er' (SF2 p. 253). Long passages are spoken by both the Son and the Father in which details from their biographies emerge. But whereas lines such as 'Wie redet man mit einem Leitartikel' and 'Und wie umarmt man ein Parteiprogramm' (both SF2 p. 254) would have caused laughter in 'Kentauren', they now provoke a sense of tragedy.[95] A similar structure to that of 'Russische Eröffnung' is then employed: the Son narrates a section about how he visited his dying adoptive mother. The text is revealed to be a projection, just like the Commander's reprieve of the Squad Leader. The reality of the situation only comes after a most peculiar speech. At the end of the projection the Son describes his putative Father, a Nazi, without a tense marker. His last two lines before what seems to be a breakdown are, one assumes, a quotation

94   Hans-Christian Stillmark, 'Entscheidungen um und bei Heiner Müller. Bemerkungen zu "Wolokolamsker Chaussee III-V"', in Werner Biechele (ed.), *Germanistisches Jahrbuch DDR - UVR*, 9/90, p. 58 and p. 59 respectively.

95   As Müller puts it in the note on *Wolokolamsker Chaussee* as a whole, 'das Satyrspiel KENTAUREN beschreibt die Tragödie als Farce' (SF2 p. 259).

from the Father ('Dreh dich nicht um Dein Vater ist ein Schlächter', SF2 p. 255, the pun is dark) and a framed desire which echoes the 'Hamlet-darsteller' in *Die Hamletmaschine* ('Ich sagte Ich will eine Tochter sein', ibid.). What follows is a completely impersonal present-tense flood of memories.[96] The absence of personal pronouns or possessive adjectives makes the speech troublesome. It could easily be spoken by the Son: its catalogue of defeats would suggest the ideological tortures of the Son and his ruined idealism. Alternatively the lines could belong to the Father. They would expose his *mauvaise foi* as an official. A choral rendition is another possibility. This time the audience would be confronted with the ruins of the GDR in contrast with the choral struggles (in the Russian texts) or the quest for identity within the GDR (in 'Das Duell'). The text's leitmotif ('VER-GESSEN UND VERGESSEN UND VERGESSEN'), a phrase which occurs nine times in total, is found in three of the fifteen lines. Its lack of tense marker allows it to detach itself from the individual time levels of the text in order to inhabit them all. A short narrative then reveals that the Son did not visit the Mother. It is followed by more extended sections of dia-logue in which more accusations and counter-accusations fly. The descrip-tion of the night of the Father's attempted suicide is also recounted. The sober exchanges of the previous scenes of *Wolokolamsker Chaussee* give way to bitterness and mordant scorn. The inclusion of the unmarked 'VER-GESSEN UND VERGESSEN UND VERGESSEN' lines does offer the possibility of dividing the direct speeches, if a choral voice is chosen for them or if the interlocutor speaks them. The text ends unresolved. The Father's voice is heard ('Erschießen solln sie dich du Nazibastard / Er-schießen solln sie dich wie einen Hund', SF2 p. 258) either in the Son's mind or straight from the Father's mouth. It confirms that no settlement has been reached. (The language of the scene is also more complex. In certain places, Müller's more characteristically allusive style of writing makes a brief return.)

The fleeting narration of the scene does not especially attach us to the narrator. There is no longer any hint of a 'wir' or an 'unser' in the the short passages. The loneliness of the 'Kentauren' is carried on to 'Der Findling'. The one potential point of a coming together, the 'Thälmannlied' speech, is laced with defeat and disappointment. We are left standing between two figures, neither especially sympathetic, neither especially repellent. There is no sign of interiority when the two protagonists spew out their hatred.

96 Because of its importance in the production section of this chapter, I shall call it the 'Thälmannlied' speech.

Although the situation is similar to the confrontation in 'Das Duell', there is a qualitative difference between the ritual of this part and the 'godless' remains of 'Der Findling'. The only liturgy is the collective passage.

The question remains how the idea of the 'Lehrstück', discussed earlier, applies to the *Wolokolamsker Chaussee* cycle. Although the basic rule[97] of the genre, that there is no more division between actor and spectator, has not, to my knowledge, been observed in any production, it is interesting to note that Müller saw the texts as useful within the context of acting schools:

> Vielleicht sollte man mit den beiden *Wolokolamsker* Texten überhaupt eher in Schauspielschulen arbeiten als in den professionellen Theatern. [...] Ich glaube, Erfahrungen kann man nur kollektiv machen. [...] Aber da Kollektive meistens so organisiert sind, daß Erfahrungen sofort wieder verdrängt werden, geht es darum, diesen Verdrängungsprozeß zu verhindern oder zu stören. Das ist das Hauptziel.[98]

Although Müller states a preference for 'unossified' student actors, the overall form of the cycle (the unattributed texts) does call for an active engagement with the texts as a collective.[99] The very basis for speaking a solitary line is made problematic and so the texts may encourage a theatre that relies on a group dynamic. Even if the texts are divided up by a director

---

97 Brecht's 'basic rule' was the prerequisite for the 'Lehrstück' as a model for a theatre of the future. Its practical application in theatres of the present is, of course, highly unlikely. However, Brecht's experiments in the late twenties and the early thirties with workers' choral societies and schools do show the possibility of realizing the project.

98 *Gesammelte Irrtümer*, p. 190. The interview took place in 1986, hence the mention of only two *Wolokolamsker Chaussee* texts.

99 Erika Stephan observed the preparations for the Potsdam production of parts I and II (première 4 May 1986). She confirms that in this case the actors were active 'Koproduzenten': 'Gespräche über den Probenprozeß bestätigen immer wieder, daß weder konzeptionell-analytisch vorweggenommene "Lesarten" realisert noch Regieanweisungen aufgeführt werden sollten. Wichtigste Erfahrung war die Kollektivität. [...] An der Stelle der im gewohnten Theaterbetrieb üblich gewordenen Vereinzelung trat ein Ensembleprinzip', Erika Stephan, 'Erprobung von Spielmodellen. Heiner Müllers *Bau* in Karl-Marx-Stadt und "Wolokolamsker Chaussee I und II" in Potsdam', in Siegfried Rönisch (ed.), *DDR-Literatur '86 im Gespräch* (Berlin and Weimar: Aufbau, 1987), p. 298 and p. 313.

or a production team, the form of the scripts allows actors an opportunity to criticize or to modify their roles. In this way the actors do spectate. There are also points built into at least the first four texts with which the actor would find it difficult to identify. Parts I-III are likely to be beyond the experience of several actors and Part IV is a dream.[100] These scenes would become a way of experiencing the past without direct knowledge. Only 'Der Findling', whose dramaturgy, as already noted, is far more akin to a traditional piece by virtue of its substantial dialogue, uses a less 'foreign' subject matter although it is *the* play of the cycle that so clearly foregrounds the forgetting of the past.

Nägele questioned the validity of the 'Lehrstück' as a *site* of learning and argued that the *process* or *mechanisms* of learning were just as important an element in Brecht's short plays. The violence which was inherent in the teaching also remained and resisted Steinweg's argument of a synthesized dialectic at each play's conclusion. In turn, the ritual form of the 'Lehrstücke' helped to emphasize the persistence of a non-rational discourse.

The form and subject matter of the Brechtian 'Lehrstück' is only part of the first three texts. In each a decisive step is taken after a process of justification. The execution of the Squad Leader, the demotion of Belenkow and the necessity of the tanks are all violent products of the 'Spielmaschinen'.[101] As in Nägele's reading, we find elements of persistence and a lack of resolution. The Commander is haunted by the dead Squad Leader. The rhetoric involved in Belenkow's demotion leaves the legitimacy of the decision open. The enmity of the parting at the conclusion of 'Das Duell' confirms the disharmony that pervaded the piece. In each scene ritual plays an important part in arriving at the conclusion. In these ways each of the plays conforms to Nägele's interpretation. If anything, the plays emphasize

---

100   Daniel Schelletter reports the difficulties faced by drama students in a production of parts I and III in West Berlin (première 26 June 1987). Although 'die Schauspieler sollten eine Annäherung an Situation und Konflikt zeigen, ohne jemals zu behaupten, darüber zu verfügen. [...] Doch was immer blieb, war die Distanz'. (Daniel Schelletter, 'Die erste Erfahrung ist die Distanz. Schauspielstudenten spielen "Wolokolamsker Chaussee I und III"', *Die deutsche Bühne*, 8/87, p. 45.) The youthfulness of the actors presented insuperable problems of identification. This distance was nonetheless appreciated by Müller who very much enjoyed the performance (unpublished interview with Sabine Andreas, the director of this production, by the author, 23-3-95).

101   *Gesammelte Irrtümer*, p. 188.

all that Nägele considers more covert in Brecht's dramaturgy. Yet these three do add to and modify the Brechtian 'Lehrstück'.

The first and most important change of emphasis is the choral one. Gone are Brecht's massed voices which passed comment and/or judgement over the proceedings. Their position is replaced by individuals whose voices never fully merge into a choral collective. In both Russian episodes, the Commander has to reach decisions which are intrinsically linked with both his division and the Soviet Union. The Director does not face such a decision but has to justify his acceptance of the tanks. This is mediated by a historical process by which we view 'evidence' from different points of his past. The role of these figures as a focus for the approval of certain acts makes them far more open to criticism. Their collectivity is always founded upon a historical process, which is also open to the scrutiny of the audience. Yet this collectivity in turn allows the audience to participate in the decisions so that the quality of simultaneous identification and non-identification is offered. If the figures *are* teaching, then they very much foreground the foundations of their 'schools' so that pupils (the audience) are aware of the systems that are at work in the personae of the main figures.

The use of individual and collective memory is also a more subjective form of mediating the very stuff of the dramas (as a whole). The employment of a (possibly fictional) present and one or more pasts creates another challenge to the reliability of the remembered action. In all three the remembering subject is undermined by the process of memory. The unmarked and present-tense explosions in the narratives confirm that some of the information simply cannot be set aside under the heading 'The Past'. The repeated motifs and the recurrent images also call a rational control of the past into question.

Müller's 'Lehrstück', if we can indeed call it that, is a teaching system that highlights its own inadequacies. It brings the subjective element into the collective realm with consequences that make the 'lesson' highly problematic.

'Kentauren' and 'Der Findling' are also narrated, yet the subject matter is altogether different and not at all suitable for a 'teaching purpose' in the style described above. The former tells a story until its final scene becomes too unbearable to be left in the past. The latter is a description of a confrontation which ends in defeat for both sides.

There is very little to learn (in terms of the processes inscribed in the dramaturgy of parts I-III) in 'Kentauren'. The critical standpoints implicit in the subtitle and the epigraph signal points of resistance before the text has started. The 'Fabel' and its figures are so estranged by the comic tone that it is hard to see oneself as a player in the scene. Our analysis has shown that even the immediacy of the final speech intensifies the humour rather than identification. The images and jokes are interesting and amusing but the collective function is essentially missing. 'Der Findling', on the other hand, presents the spectator with a surplus of identification insofar as both the Son and the Father are allowed large passages of text that are themselves suffused with memory. There are only two passages of collective text (in the description of Berlin and in the 'Thälmannlied' speech) but one of the main themes of the scene is the act of remembering itself. Both figures experience the past in the present tense of their dialogues. Neither emerges as any sort of victor because of their remembered pasts. Two hardly tenable positions are presented which makes this final scene perhaps the most open of the cycle. In parts I-III we were presented with figures who had faith in their decisions, however much spoke against them. By this point we are shown that we have reached a nadir. The nadir is a crisis for both. There appears to be no way forward after the strangulation of both the Nagy government in Hungary 1956 and Dubček's Prague Spring of 1968. The past, mediated by memory, presents both figures in a negative light, yet only an acceptance of such truths can lead forward. This stalemate is perhaps a productive one, as Heeg puts it: 'wenn die Panzer kein Ziel mehr haben, können die Einzelteile neu sortiert werden. Das ist die Chance ihrer Emanzipation'.[102] What is certain is that there is very little 'Lehre' left in the final two parts. The teaching impulse is one that comes from the wider dynamics of the two 'hopeless' scenes:

> In diesem Zusammenhang gehört der Begriff Furchtzentrum [...]. Es geht grundsätzlich darum, das Furchtzentrum einer Geschichte zu finden, einer Situation und der Figuren, und dem Publikum das auch zu vermitteln als Furchtzentrum. Nur wenn es ein Furchtzentrum ist, kann es ein Kraftzentrum werden. Aber wenn man das Furchtzentrum verschleiert oder zudeckt, kommt man auch nicht an die Energie heran, die daraus zu beziehen ist.[103]

The pains of the past which could have been learnt from were not remembered and went unused. Only by re-creating the process from the present

---

102   Heeg, p. 141.

103   'Ein Gespräch zwischen Wolfgang Heise und Heiner Müller', in Müller, *Gesammelte Irrtümer* 2, p. 56.

and identifying the 'Furchtzentrum' can there be any hope for a solution to the impasse of 'Der Findling'.

Müller's 'Lehrstück' would seem to contradict the impulses that informed Brecht's original models. The genre brings with it at least remnants of an optimistic Enlightenment project that, for example, people can be taught and that the world is teachable. And yet Müller, despite the charges of 'Geschichtspessimismus' raised against him, would seem to be carrying the tradition onwards, albeit in a much altered form. The teaching impulse is still very much there. This we can see in his belief of transforming a 'Furchtzentrum' into a 'Kraftzentrum' and in the passage quoted earlier in which he maintained that the Gorbachev era was a time ripe for change (ie. learning). The major difference is that inherent weaknesses in the pedagogic process must also be acknowledged in order to circumvent reproaches of naïvety or 'message mongering'. Müller is not trying to convince us that social change is a mere pipe-dream, doomed to founder in the face of reaction. He is more interested in showing how difficult and problematic this aim is.

III   Engaging the Collective Imagination

The *Wolokolamsker Chaussee* texts pose two fundamental problems to the process of realization on stage. The first is clear: how the text is to be divided. The second is a little more subtle. Each spoken line is a line taken from a flux, an unfixed point. Is the production able to communicate this in performance? Can the contingency of the texts be taken into account by the actors or is the spectator unfamiliar with the printed version unaware that parts were not already written in?

The main objective of this section is to deal with the first problem (although the second will be returned to later). This means that the analysis of staged versions will focus on the various prompter's scripts rather than, as in previous sections, the way in which the plays were physically realized.[104]

104 Prompt books have been supplied by the archives of each theatre discussed in this section. This includes the Thalia Theater's production in Hamburg which appears later as a footnote. The only exception is Christoph Schroth's script for the Berliner Ensemble production, which was provided by the director himself. The nature of the descriptions is more textually based in this section. In the unpublished thesis version of this book (which is deposited in the Bodleian Library, Oxford) rigorous reference to the texts was made in order to show the

Although reports of the isolated ('parasitic') use of the individual texts are most interesting, I have decided to examine arrangements of the *Wolokolamsker Chaussee* that used all five of its parts, in order to see how the cycle works as a whole. In this way we can understand how the parts relate to each other and investigate whether specific scenes encourage particular styles within the context of a singular production's aesthetic framework.

Müller's own reading (in the literal sense of the word) offers very few hints for theatre groups.[105] His tone is essentially dry. There is no emotion and little stressing of what we might consider the key words of a sentence. This style conforms very much to his suggestion (quoted in Chapter I) that his texts should be read as if they were 'telephone books'. The only hint of interpretation (if one can call it that) is a slight change of inflection during some of the shorter lines of dialogue. *Very* rarely does Müller increase his tempo for some of the present-tense lines. The renditions are not impassioned nor 'realistic', yet the discrepancy is there: the text has been demarcated. There are also pauses that break up the texts into blocks. Unfortunately, these departures from his reading style indicate nothing more than a swift read through might. We know when the text changes tense, and Müller pauses at expected points throughout. Theatres clearly have to look further than the author's relationship to his work. One could say that Müller is reading his text as one would a poem. He is not realizing it as a drama.

The FRG première of the complete cycle took place in the Münchner Kammerspiele on 20 April 1989, eleven years to the day after Ernst Wendt's West German première of *Germania* at the same venue. This time the director was the former chief dramaturge of the theatre, Hans-Joachim

practice and consequences of textual division. The information was sometimes a little dense (especially in the case of the production in Leipzig) but without such details it would have been difficult to discuss the dynamics involved in each realization. For this book publication I have edited the descriptions in order to give a more general overview.

105 Heiner Müller, *Heiner Müller liest 'Wolokolamsker Chaussee'* (Frankfurt/Main: Verlag der Autoren, 1990), cassette format. The tape is taken from a recording made for and transmitted on GDR radio.

Rückhäberle. The scenes were staged in chronological order with two actors only in each scene.[106] There was no chorus and no lines were cut.

'Russische Eröffnung' saw an initial division along the lines of actor A reading the Commander and actor B reading 'the others'.[107] This meant that B always answered the questions in the three dialogues preceding the faked attack. B also created his own story by including the frame in certain lines (for example, 'Der Deutsche *sagten sie* und lachten nicht mehr', SF1, p. 243, my emphasis). The Commander was no longer the sovereign narrator. The impression was given that A and B were both involved in the process of remembering the past.

Any psychologizing reading of the first two scenes was undermined by an inversion of the actors' roles in 'Wald bei Moskau'. The actor formerly playing the Commander became the voices of the doubting soldiers, the Commander's doubting self and Belenkow.

As Rainer Grübel comments on the first two scenes: 'die Sprecher sind, ganz im Gegensatz zu Bek, in einem beträchtlichen Maße austauschbar'.[108] Their interchangeability was clearly demonstrated by the casting arrangements both within and between the scenes. This emphasized the use

---

106 The question of ordering the scenes is one that brings us forward to issues which will be discussed in the Chapter III. The independence of the parts makes them very suitable for experimentation at the production stage. Yet this has been exploited on very few occasions, as we can see from the following information. In Munich, Landshut, Aachen, Berlin and Hamburg the chronology was maintained. In Cologne the plays followed the sequence I, III, II, V, IV. In Leipzig (to be discussed at greater length later) the order was slightly altered by placing 'Der Findling' first to give: V, I, II, III, IV.
In the unpublished notebooks of Christoph Schroth, the director of the Berlin production, sketches for alternative arrangements were explored (but ultimately not realized). This approach, shown in the following scheme, shows much potential. In one sketch the order III, (I, II, V), IV was considered. This suggested that 'Das Duell', which describes the practice of Stalinism, is the starting point for the whole series. By the end all we can do is laugh and allow ourselves to be provoked by the black comedy.

107 The 'A, B' notation has been adopted as opposed to the continued use of actors' names.

108 Rainer Grübel, 'Metamorphosen und Umwertungen. Heiner Müllers Dramatisierung von Motiven aus Aleksandr Beks Prosatext *Volokolamskoe Šosse*', in Paul Gerhard Klussmann and Heinrich Mohr (eds.), *Jahrbuch zur Literatur in der DDR*, vol. 7 (Bonn: Bouvier, 1990), p. 128.

of the scenes as non-psychological models for the audience. Both actors together (who were men) formed a small but not insubstantial collective.

'Das Duell' saw two new actors taking an A and B division of the text. (New actors were also used each time in the subsequent two scenes.) A played the Director and B spoke the lines of the Deputy both in 1953 and earlier in the ABF, and of the Professor. The division of the speakers in 'Das Duell' showed very clearly the contradictions of the piece. The characters were shown to emerge from a collective (they divided the first speech between them). The collective was never fully wrenched asunder (the 'Tanks' speech was delivered by both), yet it was in a state of extreme jeopardy at the play's bitter conclusion: A emerged to narrate the passage starting 'Und als ich seinen Rücken sah' (SF2 p. 243). B emphasized the acrimony at the end of the scene by speaking the last three lines. The dynamics of a two actor cast pointed to the unresolved dialectic of 17 June 1953.

No epigraph prefaced 'Kentauren'. For the first time, an actress took the stage (and the A voice). The voices A and B were divided very much along the lines of the Chief and the Underling respectively. One peculiarity did arise within the scene: the voice of the Underling was given lines which one might have considered to be the Chief's ('Mein Diensteid sagt Ich selber zeig dich an' to 'Bei Rot über die nächste Kreuzung fährt', both SF2 p. 247). The picture that this created was one of ruthless officiousness on the part of the Underling, who became a mirror of rather than a subordinate to his superior. B also sang a hymn to the logic of the situation ('Wie löst man einen Widerspruch Indem' to 'Oder Prometheus den sein Felsen sprengt', both SF2 p. 248) which although unexpected, was not out of place in the new, somewhat more cynical context.

The final part, 'Der Findling', marked a return to the style of 'Das Duell'. The main difference was that the two very male roles were played by women. A took the lines of the Father, B those of the Son. Before the Son arrived at the Father's door, both read the expository narrative. The divided consciousness was narrating as it had beforehand in part III. The dialogue then proceeded as one would have expected. However, as in 'Kentauren', there was one unexpected deviation. The A voice was given the lines 'Der Plattenspieler war für Budapest' to 'Als Stalin starb Jetzt kann ich nur noch lachen' (both SF2 p. 254). The speech, which one would have considered the buying-off of the Son and his consequent resentment, made the Father a more complex figure. It was the Father's friend who was killed at the Wall in this version. His own inability to deal with the state of the GDR was given extra dimensions. The Son was also revealed as a former SED functionary (not just the damaged son of one). The 'Thälmannlied' speech, which I had identified as the only truly collective passage in this part, was indeed spoken in such a way: every single line was repeated by the other speaker.

The Son's position thus radically differed from the more ambivalent picture, discussed in our analysis of the scene above. The balance we had found was replaced by a far more complex depiction of both figures. Both voices had their share of the 'VERGESSEN UND VERGESSEN UND VERGESSEN' motif although it was never spoken by both at the same time (except in the 'Thälmannlied' speech). The way that the new division affected our perception of the figures was stunning. The collective introduction linked the voices in a way we had not expected. We then saw the reason for this link in the equally unexpected turn in their biographies. The scene became directly comparable with 'Das Duell' because of their imposed similiarity of form, yet the outcome was far more bitter. The lives of the two figures had endured more damage and the picture of division at its conclusion seemed more final in comparison. An exaggerated 'Furchtzentrum' had been created. The question of identification was also made problematic by the casting of two women. Their own distance from the men's texts added more criticism to the destructive speeches they were to speak. The Father/Son conflict became Mother/Daughter. This one could interpret as another cynical view of the GDR. The perception that the GDR gave women (at least constitutionally) equal rights implied that they also had an equal right to bitter disaffection. GDR society as a whole had been liberated so that everyone could take part in the process of betrayal and resentment.

One can conclude that although the decision to furnish each scene with just two voices might have seemed to have run contrary to the collective strains of the *Wolokolamsker Chaussee*, a collectivity based on the divisibility of the narrators of the scenes ('Kentauren' excepted) was manufactured. The advantage of the casting of two actors per scene also played with the concept of dialectics. Their refusal to be synthesized showed the persistent problems in the three 'Lehrstück'-esque scenes as well as in 'Der Findling'. The unexpected line attributions were a little more sinister. The picture of the GDR became one riddled with suspicion and consequently a little one-sided in the latter stages of the cycle. This 'Western' image of the GDR seems to have done little to challenge stereotypes and, if anything, encouraged a demonized view of 'the other Germany'.

Unsurprisingly, the reception in the press did not pick up on the provocative textual divisions, rather it criticized certain aesthetic criteria. The delivery of the lines seems to have been very much in the style of Müller's own on tape. The play was reproached for giving 'spröde Denk-

143

figuren', a 'geschichtsphilosophisches Oberseminar', it was a 'Grübeltheater', 'alt und grimmig' and 'vor allem Sprache'.[109] Hans Göhl did nonetheless point out that the two-person casting gave the texts the feel of a 'ritueller Ringkampf', which evokes Müller's much quoted view of German history as the struggle between brothers. The distance in the acting was only lost once and that was in 'Kentauren'. Here the actress playing the Chief, Jennifer Minetti, was frequently complimented on her comic ability. There were dissenting voices among the critics who saw the cycle as a provocative challenge, and some reported a positive response from the audience. The cerebral nature of the production ('denksportliche Sprech-Duelle' as they were called by Ingrid Seidenfaden)[110] seemed to have alienated many who expected a more visual approach to the plays.[111]

109   kr, 'Sprödes Sprach- und Denktheater', *Bayerische Staatszeitung*, 28-4-89; hk, 'Geschichtsphilosophisches Oberseminar', *Applaus*, 6/89; Hans S. Macher, 'Grübeltheater in fünf Stationen', *Trostberger Tageblatt*, 26/7-4-89; Wolfgang Höbel, 'Das Leerstück als Lehrstück ernstgenommen', *Handelsblatt*, 22/23-4-89; and Hans Göhl, 'Vor allem Sprache', *Bayern Kurier*, 8-5-89, respectively.

110   Ingrid Seidenfaden, 'Im Windschatten von Genosse Lenin', *Abendzeitung*, 22/3-4-89.

111   The divisions (with the exception of the treatment of the Father in 'Der Findling') and the distanced delivery were very similar to the production at the Thalia Theater, Hamburg (première 27 April 1990). The cast was different insofar as five actors took the various voices as roles. The Commander was divided along Müller's lines in 'Russische Eröffnung' but remained solitary in 'Wald bei Moskau' where he articulated his own doubts. The Deputy was split into a 1953 and an ABF voice, and the Professor was given a role too. 'Kentauren' was a (well received) comic monologue and 'Der Findling' was a bitter duet. (Only the Son spoke the 'Thälmannlied' speech.) The collectivity was not to be found in shared lines or speeches, although the pool of five actors manufactured it outside of the individual parts. The press response was fairly positive, yet once again reproached the production for its lack of 'theatre'. The impression was given that the play could have been a 'Hörspiel' or a 'Sprechstück' (by Michael Laages, 'Mehr Bilder braucht das Land', *Hannoversche Allgemeine Zeitung*, 11-5-90; anon., 'Lehrstück zur Vergangenheitsbewältigung', *Milwaukee Deutsche Zeitung*, 15-7-90; Joachim Redetzki, 'Müllers Wortfetzen hinterließen Ratlosigkeit', *Stader Tageblatt*, 30-4-90; Axel M. Sallowsky, 'Thalia-Première: Theater zum Abgewöhnen'; *Bildzeitung*, 30-4-90; and Rolf Suhl, 'Montage-Theater', *Hamburger Rundschau*, 3-5-90). Much of the popularity of the production was attributed to the set, a highly raked staged piled with bricks. Mobility was much hindered by both. The characters could hardly move for the rubble left by the fall of the Wall.

If the production in Munich was a little on the ascetic side in terms of its casting, then the staging later that year in Leipzig was anything but. No fewer than fifteen actors (including four members of the Hans-Otto Drama School, which perhaps points to Müller's interest in student actors for the cycle) were involved, all of whom were on stage for four of the scenes.[112] In addition, four members of the Leipzig 'Opernballett' were engaged in 'Das Duell', a scene which (apart from the dancers) only used four actors. The actors did not necessarily all have very many lines in each section, and pantomime was employed to exploit their presence on stage. The director was Karl Georg Kayser and the choreographer was Dietmar Seyffert. Rehearsal started in August while GDR citizens flocked to the West through the recently opened border between Hungary and Austria. The play had its première on 1 November 1989, at the climax of the weekly mass rallies in Leipzig. As we can see the context was very different from that in Munich.

The evening began with a short prologue. A puppet sat in the auditorium under a palm tree, beckoning the audience to distant climes. The ensemble sang the popular hit, 'Wenn bei Capri'. The desire to be elsewhere and the very domestic issues discussed in the cycle made for uncomfortable bed fellows. The ironic tension between the exotic lures and the more familiar problems of socialist society back home were also highlighted by 'Volkslieder'. They were sung between scenes, and included such titles as 'Kein schöner Land in dieser Zeit'.

As mentioned earlier, 'Der Findling' was the first scene of the evening. Its position thus prefaced the more Brechtian teaching impulses of parts I-III. It posed the question as to how the GDR could arrive at the situation of part V. The provocative answers were then to follow in the subsequent sections.

'Der Findling', as in all the scenes that followed, employed an ensemble dynamic in the construction of each figure. For the most part, D, E and G (two men and a woman) spoke the lines of the Son whilst A and B (two men) took the Father's. The dialogue was spoken (by the collectives taking their own pieces of each speech) as had been predicted above (ie without the Munich deviations). The picture of the Father/Son relationship in Leipzig was considerably different from that in Munich. The collective introduction and the joint participation in the 'Thälmannlied' speech which

---

112 The prompter's script which I was sent uses an alphabetical scheme to denote actors' names. The actors now range from A to O.

bonded the two in order to show how radically they had diverged from an initial union, were rendered here by the Son (the latter together with his distant relations C and F).[113] The picture was far more bleak; division pervaded the whole scene from its outset.

'Russische Eröffnung', the first leap back to the past, had been radically cut. There was no mention of the motif 'Zweitausend Kilometer weit Berlin / Einhundertzwanzig Kilometer Moskau' at all. Amongst the other cuts were several of the Commander's reflective and descriptive lines.

The cutting and attribution of the scene changed the tone of 'Russische Eröffnung' so that reflection of the 'present day Commander' was almost entirely eliminated. The stress was placed upon the exigencies of the incidents recounted. Although the Commander (A and B) dominated the scene, the increased participation of the soldiers (C, F, G, H, I, J, L, M, N) and the Commander's absence from their conversations, provided an interesting relationship between the leader and the led. For this reason *all* voices were involved in the decision to execute the Squad Leader. The voices of the soldiers became a part of the Commander.

'Wald bei Moskau' was also heavily cut. As in 'Russische Eröffnung', reflective passages and reflecting details were omitted in order to give the piece an immediacy and to concentrate on the processes rather than the specific context. The deletions also helped to divorce the action and decisions from any notion of an individual consciousness.

A and B again shared the Commander's words and several soldier voices spoke narrative lines without the personal markers 'ich' or 'mein'. Much 'wir'/'unser' narration was read by alternating groups of soldiers. What we had previously believed an interior battle within the Commander became an active debate between the soldiers and their commanding officer. The final direct speech at the end of the now externalized doubt was spoken by seven different voices.

'Der Kommunardentraum Vom Ich zum Wir' (SF2 p. 249), satirized in 'Kentauren', was realized in this scene. The split personal dynamics of the

---

113 It was the roles of C and F, who joined later, that provided interesting angles. C made appearance as an extra narrator for the line 'Geständnis sagte er Und ich Geständnis' (SF2 p. 253) and then together with F spoke a few lines later 'Mit Panzerketten auf den Leib geschrieben' (ibid.). The voices of the D, E, G trio, C and F individually delivered the collective 'Thälmannlied' speech. It would seem that the C and F lines enlarged upon the possibly narrower perspective of the D, E and G speakers of the Son. The Father's exclusion made him less sympathetic and the C and F lines seemed to give the indictment of the Father more power.

Commander in 'Russiche Eröffnung' gave way to the mass of voices which constituted the soldiers and the Commander. The conspicuous absentee was the unified Belenkow, the uncollectivized individual. The army was presented as an active, decision making group, rather than a faceless mass governed by an officer. The two Russian scenes functioned as a pair to indicate a process of collective understanding. They confirm Reid's view of the dramaturgical intention of the opening two scenes:

> Müller's theatre simulates the destruction of the individual in order that the collective may emerge as the only hope for the survival of the human race. One way in which his plays take account of this anti-individualist insight is the lack of roles in the received sense.[114]

The four main speakers of 'Das Duell' consisted of two women (here A and B) and two men (C and D).[115] Again the action was concentrated by cutting narrative detail and repetition.

The narrative began, as in Munich, with the division of the ritualistic lines between the four speakers. The voice of the Deputy became a mixture of A and C in 1953 and B and C at the ABF. C also took the voice of the Professor. On the whole A and D narrated the Director whilst B and C took the Deputy in certain lines of his direct speech. The 'Tanks' speech was delivered by the quartet collectively as one would have expected. The scene ended with a fairly predictable division of Director and Deputy lines although the final three lines were partially rendered by A, C and D.

The emergence of the two sides from the collective was similar to the style in Munich. The use of split voices highlighted the division more pointedly. The effect was compounded by the arrangement of the two previous scenes. The triumph of the group dynamic in I and II emphasized the defeat implied in the split of the collective in III.

The final part of the Leipzig production, 'Kentauren', saw a return to the fifteen actor ensemble. There was only one minor cut.

All the voices rendered the two line introductory narrative. This was followed by L who spoke the Underling's lines alone (except where the lines were spoken by all the actors). The Chief's words became the property of a collective of voices (A, B, C, D, E, F, G, H, K, N and O) which weaved

114 Reid, pp. 150-1.

115 The four members of the ballett only had one line together: 'Wir sind die Totengräber' (SF2 p. 243)

a number of rhythms throughout the scene. Even L had lines in the final present tense-speech. The division of the Underling's lines and those of the collective Chief's followed the expected pattern. What disrupted this scheme was the interjection of the ensemble's voice *en masse*. Its scope ranged from the Underling's lines, to the Chief's (even in the final section), to what one might call the more sententious parodies of Stasi ideology (for example 'Der Staat ist die Mühle die muß mahlen' and the two lines which follow it, SF2 p. 246, or 'Nicht alles was den Massen dient verstehen / Die Massen Jeden-falls nicht gleich', SF2 p. 248). It would seem that there was no guiding thread to determine when the ensemble would speak. It possibly signalled the re-emergence of the collective, wrenched asunder in 'Das Duell'. Alternatively the explosion of the collective into the dream showed the relationship between GDR society and the nightmare with which it co-existed. Maybe the constant stabs indicated permanent disaffection from the ensemble with the entire subject matter of the scene.

The Leipzig production introduced a more theatrical element to the *Wolokolamsker Chaussee* by employing several voices and pantomime in order to achieve a panoramic vision of a collective paradise lost. The picture of a collective in jeopardy formulated the concerns of a socialist society (and theatre) faced with major historical upheavals. The production functioned as a merciless exercise in collective self-analysis. The use of irony (the 'prologue' and the 'Volkslieder') formed a counterpoint to the more sober scenes in the cycle. The plea for collective action represented a 'GDR slant' on the problems. If the state was to reform itself, it would have to come from within and from 'below'.

The only review at my disposal is that of the *Neues Deutschland* critic, Gerhard Ebert.[116] His reception of the play was surprisingly positive. The title of his review stressed the link between the collectives on the street outside and that on the stage. Clearly the 'SED reviewer' was interested in the critical-reforming impulse of the production. Its line centred on the potentials of a new kind of socialism after the fall of the Wall. The ensemble acting was praised although Ebert was unable to categorize it: 'Formales Ästhetisieren? Radikales Straßentheater? Was schien geboten?' he asked. His reply was similarly vague: 'Agitation kaum. Aber Schärfe. Drängende Ungeduld. [...] Aufarbeiten geschichtlicher Widersprüche wurde zwingender'. He concluded 'beim Publikum schlug die Realität durch. Es applaudierte

---

116 Gerhard Ebert, 'Künstlerische Wahrheit, die sich an unserer Wirklichkeit reibt', *Neues Deutschland*, 14-11-89. The Schauspielhaus Leipzig archive was unable to provide me with any reviews.

mit höchst skeptischer, sage ich mal, Zuversicht'. Ebert's inability to pin the parts down and the interesting evaluation of the public reaction pointed to the unconventional and challenging performances outlined above. His uncertainty reflected the historical situation. Today I have been able to evaluate the production more concretely.

The story was a different one in the Filmpalast am Friedrichshain where the Berliner Ensemble and the Theater im Palast joined forces for a production premièred on 12 December 1989. The director was Christoph Schroth, who had previously directed 'Das Duell' and 'Kentauren' in Schwerin. There the production ended with an hour of FDJ songs, used for their 'Kraft und Utopie'.[117] The same was to have concluded the five-play cycle, yet due to the 'niedere Qualität' of the singers and musicians, the planned epilogue was dropped.[118]

Schroth told me, 'ich habe nach Sinn und Figuren die Texte aufgeteilt', before practical staging began. Little or no modification of the textual divisions took place in the three months of rehearsals before the première. Choruses were used in parts I-III, a device derived from Schroth's extensive experience of directing Greek tragedy. Their anti-individualist character made them interesting in the context of the 'Lehrstück' structures. Schroth also retained the chronology of the cycle.

'Russische Eröffnung' featured two choruses, one for the Commander's soldiers (C1) and one for the deserters (C2). (In addition only one Commander voice was employed although he was characterized in a split manner as 'heute/der Harte' and 'damals/der Weiche'.)[119] Thus the dialogue with the deserters became an exchange between the two choruses before the Commander carried on with the narrative. The reported speech of the deserters was spoken both by their chorus and by the Commander so that narration and the real speech overlapped. The news of the Squad Leader was borne by a general chorus, out of which stepped the solitary voice of the coward.

The scene was thus about appending the Commander's subjective voice through the mediation of the collective. The Commander remained

117 Christoph Schroth, 'Unpublished Notebooks on *Wolokolamsker Chaussee*', property of their author. He also provided his own annotated prompt book: the Berliner Ensemble had no archival material to offer.

118 Unpublished interview with Christoph Schroth by the author, 8-6-95.

119 Schroth, 'Unpublished Notebooks on *Wolokolamsker Chaussee*', n.p.

sovereign in his actions although one was never allowed to forget the collective responsibility he carried with him.

'Wald bei Moskau' doubled the Commander's role and had only one chorus for all the soldiers. Belenkow was consistently spoken by one actor. In the course of the action the voices of the Commander divided. One spoke the doubts and the other tried to answer them. At each defeat of 'the other Commander', the actor was shot, only to rise again with fresh qualms. This happened three times in total before the two voices merged and alternated for the final speech to Belenkow. Belenkow's own lines were almost exclusively spoken together with the narrating Commander, so that once again the split time-levels were highlighted. Elsewhere, the chorus, whose participation was relatively slight, would provide echoes for both Belenkow, the doubting Commander and the more certain one.

The scene was remiscent of the 'Lehrstück' in that the collective was the focus for the audience, beyond the frame of the Commander's struggles with himself. With each move it presented the audience with a different perspective or solution to the conflict. The unrealistic and theatrical portrayal of the internal debate prevented the spectator from viewing it with an excess of empathy. It was those affected by his anarchy, the chorus, that ultimately held sway.

Unfortunately, Schroth's notes in his prompt book for 'Das Duell' were too arcane for a reconstruction of individual line allocation. He did, however, explain the conception for the scene (which was very similar to that in both Munich and Leipzig). Two groups/choruses of six actors each sat opposite each other at tables. The evocation of June 1953 was like a 'Totenbeschwörung': the voices emerged from their collectives. The scene was divided into eleven textual blocks with titles such as 'Erinnern. Hoch-holen', 'Schiedsrichter Telefon' and 'Warten auf Godot' (which were never announced in performance). In rehearsal, they acted as thematic focusses for the actors. In each one different voices from one group would challenge those from the other.

'Kentauren' was organized in 'orthodox' fashion. The two roles were divided for two actors. This part was performed as a clown number. The Chief was the conceited know-all who was hounded around a marked arena by his Underling aggressor. The eventual exit of the Underling and the finale alone demonstrated 'die Vereinzelung des Individuums'.[120]

The end-product of this farcical process was 'Der Findling' which portrayed the 'einsames Individuum, absolut allein', to quote Schroth again.

120 Unpublished interview with Christoph Schroth by the author, 8-6-95.

The chorus was no longer to be seen and the two actors, both male, were left to their own accusations and recriminations. Unlike in Munich, the Father's biography followed the expected course. Both characters followed the scheme outlined in the analysis in the previous section. The 'Thälmannlied' speech was spoken exclusively by the Son, which emphasized his own disillusionment, rather than that of the Father. The Son was also the only one to speak the 'VERGESSEN UND VERGESSEN UND VERGESSEN' lines throughout. The only point of contact in the whole scene was the Father's echo of his own direct speech as the Son narrated the lines 'Erschießen solln sie dich du Nazibastard / Erschießen solln sie dich wie einen Hund' (SF2 p. 258).

Schroth's model of a gradual falling apart was not well received by the critics or by Müller, who had enjoyed the Schwerin production of parts III and IV. The length of the performance (three hours) and the consciously dry, emotionless delivery, left many cold. This academic style, as it was interpreted, led to such comments as 'vieles versinkt [...] in Tiefsinn' and 'allzuoft wird die Handlung reduziert auf schwierige Argumentationen über die Handlung' from Jürgen Beckelmann, and 'langweilend, durch chorische Deklamation' from Paul Kaiser.[121] Another reproach, which emphasized an important distinction between the atmosphere here and in Leipzig, was that the production was simply outdated, overtaken by the events of the previous month.[122] In my interview with Schroth, he countered by arguing that Müller's dramas were anyway not 'aktuell, eher eine Epochenproblematik'. This might well be true of the texts, yet Schroth seems to have closed his eyes to the fact that performance should communicate an extra 'something' that a mere reading does not. His interpretation bracketed the historical context in favour of a formal, Brechtian aesthetic. The cold removes of the production refused to take up a dialogue with events on the streets. Many spectators (as reported in reviews) felt that the blinkered direction was missing the potential of the plays. To produce such 'relevant' plays about GDR history without acknowledging the events of the present struck many

121 Jürgen Beckelmann, 'Die Wolokolamsker Chausee in ganzer Länge', *General-Anzeiger*, 23/24-12-89 and Paul Kaiser, 'Die unbefahrbare Straße', *Die Tageszeitung*, 20-12-89.

122 Beckelmann, Paul Kaiser, as well as Ch. Kaiser, 'Von der Wirklichkeit überholt: Müller-Stück in Ostberlin aufgeführt', *Ruhr-Nachrichten*, 20-12-89; Peter Nöldechen, 'Verkünder der Revolution von der DDR-Wirklichkeit eingeholt', *Westfälische Rundschau*, 19-12-89; and Sibylle Wirsing 'Auf der langen Straße nach Nirgendwo', *Frankfurter Allgemeine Zeitung* 28-12-89 all make this point.

as pure formalism devoid of a relationship with the outside world. We have already seen how the Leipzig production managed to present the audience with provocations that were at once pertinent and distant without compromising the plays in a too exclusively topical style.

Critics of both the Munich and the Hamburg productions, who were not satisfied with the lack of 'Bilder' or 'theatricality', compared the stagings to 'Hörstücke' or 'szenische Lesungen'. This is perhaps a point to digress from an analysis of theatrical productions and to examine the work in question in the radio version by Heiner Goebbels.

The texts of Heiner Müller have frequently been presented in this medium. In the section on *Die Hamletmaschine* I mentioned that Müller had directed the play for the Süddeutscher Rundfunk before its world première in Brussels. In the Chapter III I shall briefly discuss Stefan Johansson's version of *Verkommenes Ufer* for Swedish radio. The avant-garde new-wave band, 'Einstürzende Neubauten', have also added music and sounds to the texts. Their somewhat unimaginative *Die Hamletmaschine* was followed by a more exciting *Bildbeschreibung* (some of the music from the latter was used in Müller's *Hamlet/Maschine* at the Deutsches Theater). They also collaborated on a radio version of Brecht's *Fatzer* in the Müller edition. The big name in this field, however, is Heiner Goebbels. His output has included *Die Befreiung des Prometheus* (which included sections from *Der Auftrag*, *Zement* and *Traktor*, as well as *Prometheus*), *Verkommenes Ufer*, *Landschaft mit Argonauten/Shadowland* and the text passage from *Der Auftrag*, 'Der Mann im Fahrstuhl'. His use of modern musical and studio techniques has brought challenging sounds to accompany the provocative texts. His recordings have also received many awards.[123]

The polyphony of voices normally associated with his settings is not a characteristic of *Wolokolamsker Chaussee*. The five parts present the texts in a format that is both chronological and coherent. The sovereign single voice is the main protagonist. Goebbels defends this change of tack in his notes to the CD:

---

123 *Prometheus* received the Hörspielpreis der Deutschen Kriegsblinden in 1985 as well as the coveted Prix Italia in 1986. *Verkommenes Ufer* took the Karl-Sczula-Preis der Donaueschinger Musiktage in 1984. *Wolokolamsker Chaussee* was awarded the same prize again in 1990 as well as the Preis der Publikumsjury, Akademie der Künste, West-Berlin 1989 and the Prix Futura in 1991 for 'Der Findling'.

Bei der Inszenierung und Vertonung dieser Stücke geht es mir einerseits um die monologische Erzählform und ihre Entsprechung in der Musik und andererseits um die Übersetzbarkeit der politischen Perspektive für uns: diese versuche ich nicht durch kunstvoll collagierte Elaborate, sondern durch rabiate, direkte Übertragungen in kulturelle Bereiche, die hier zu Hause sind, konkret durch die Arbeit mit (musikalischen) Kollektiven in meinem Lebensbereich Frankfurt. Als Komponist trete ich eher zurück.

Damit hoffe ich [...] eine Straße der Erfahrungen zurücklassen zu können, die von den Mitwirkenden gemacht wurden. [...] Mich interessiert eher eine Verunsicherung aus den Differenzen der Teile zueinander und ein dadurch wechselnder Abstand zu diesen.[124]

This explanation runs roughly parallel to Müller's own thoughts on the accessibility of the first texts of the cycle, which were quoted above. Goebbels collaborated with the German rock band 'The Megalomaniax', the 'Kammerchor Horbach' and the rappers 'We Wear the Crown', as well as with Alexander Kluge, the film maker and frequent interviewer of Müller. The voice of Ernst Stötzner narrated four of the parts and played the role of the Underling in 'Kentauren'. Each section was both preceded and followed by the repetition of a short musical phrase from the first movement, the Allegretto, of Shostakovich's *Leningrad Symphony* (No. 7). Its upbeat tempo and its positive yet clipped theme gave an ironic counterpoint to the crises of the cycle's five scenes. It also opened up the problematic relationship between the artist and the state in a totalitarian society. The debate regarding the integrity of Shostakovich's motives when writing the symphony (ie. whether the piece was Stalinist or not) presents a provocative challenge to Müller throughout.

After the announcement of the title, 'Russische Eröffnung' and the sampling of a shell's detonation, Ernst Stötzner begins with a swift-paced narrative. The musical accompaniment by 'The Megalomaniax' is in the style of an upbeat 'rock opera'. Distorted metal guitars, a solid bass and pounding drums produce an unrelenting backbeat reminiscent of the heavier side of rock or the more American reception of punk. The scene is composed of a variety of repetitive phrases which only slow down occasionally to be

---

124 Heiner Goebbels, *Hörstücke. Nach Texten von Heiner Müller* (Munich: ECM records, 1452-54, 1994), CD booklet.

overtaken again by the power of the familiar hook lines. Although the voice is usually that of Stötzner, the band (one assumes) also join in for the 'Zweitausend Kilometer weit Berlin' motifs. Desperate voices from the band also provide the speakers of the soldiers' conversations that pepper the first half of the scene. Stötzner's voice has essentially two modes: a 'singing' register where his voice modulates with the music and a more reflective one where his voice narrates without taking note of the music behind him. The dialogues with the Lieutenant and the Squad Leader in the second half are presented with a fevered realism but are still rendered exclusively by Stötzner. Overall the oscillation between the two styles resists naturalism, although one could certainly not accuse the piece of over-stylization.

'The Megalomaniax' also accompany 'Wald bei Moskau', this time, however, with a change of style. The rapacious, electrified power chords and solos are missing. An undistorted 'soft-rock' style, which one might associate with the quieter tracks from pop-rockers Bon Jovi, is adopted. The voice of Stötzner, like the music, is quieter and more reflective. On the whole the narration is more realistic than in 'Russische Eröffnung' although there is still a hint of mannerism: certain words receive unexpected inflections. A more doubtful tone is employed. The piece does have its moments of structural development. Crescendos are reached around the lines 'Wir torkeln wie Zigeuner durch den Wald' and the two that follow (SF2 p. 233) and for the speech from 'Und jetzt marschieren wir zurück und suchen' to 'Nehmen Sie ihre Rangabzeichen ab' (SF2 p. 234). As the scene progresses and as the Commander becomes more confident, so do the instruments and the arrangement. The Commander's final speech to Belenkow resolves the power build up with a return to the more measured tones of the introductory speeches although the instrumentation is kept in its more developed form. Just as predicted, the final speech is not the climax of the action.

The musical accompaniment for the two scenes is certainly not a particularly complex affair. The dynamism and jaggedness of 'Russische Eröffnung' provides a mirror of sorts for the tension of the war and the high pressure on the Commander. The more relaxed 'Wald bei Moskau' changes the tone to the private worries of the Commander. His development finds a fairly descriptive echo in the music. The tunes are both popular and catchy, which allows the listener easier access to the texts. The play of identification and critical distance, a feature of the 'Lehrstück' genre, is replaced by a somewhat more linear and less problematic texture. The shift of perspective and the use of collective voice are ignored. The Commander remains an individual.

154

'Das Duell' is far more complex and unfixed. Much of this is due to the interaction between the narrating voice (Stötzner again) and the three-part male voice 'Kammerchor Horbach', under the direction of Johannes Eisenberg. The discrete treatment of Stötzner and the choir also provides points of interest. The scene has a provisional, rehearsed feel to it. The opening sounds are those of the choir tuning up. One can hear the piano giving the singers their first notes. Stötzner then reads the title in a style which remains characteristic for most of the rest of the narrative. He speaks either with his voice heavily swathed in echo or else in a large hall in a tentative, uncertain manner, as if reading from a script with which he is either unfamiliar or unreconciled. (His reading of the direct speech is more realistic.) The choir sings the opening, collective lines before Stötzner takes over. (The choral voices also sing the Deputy at the ABF as well as providing phrases from 1934.) At one point where the choir was supposed to sing the Professor's lines 'Die Natur / Macht keine Sprünge' (SF2 p. 241), they make a mistake and one can hear either their leader or Goebbels correcting them before the line is sung as desired. The 'Tanks' speech is delivered by Stötzner in a solemn and undistanced fashion before he reverts to his conscious reading style. The final narration (from 'Und als ich seinen Rücken sah', SF2 p. 243, onwards) also sees a break in his hesitant style. Although it is delivered fairly emotionlessly, it is smoother. The choir hums along, giving it a certain irony, and sings the last line in three voices as if the whole business were over. One can then hear them leaving the room.

Stötzner's voice suggests a subtlety lacking in the first two parts. He could have been a nervous public orator, or a witness/defendant at a show trial. His position is precarious, as suggested by Müller's note on the scene, quoted above. The role of the choir is also problematic. Its over-elaborate and ironically reverent phrasing of the collective speeches and the other voices present a wry comment on the position of the Party in such matters. Its intervention borders on Socialist Realist kitsch. Yet its provisional nature, as seen in its warming up, its mistake and its exit, make it less solid. The interaction of the single voice and the choir provide an engaging insight into the relationship between the reminiscing party member and the Party-/collective. The refusal on Goebbels' part to contextualize the two players lends them their productive and unstable status.

Alexander Kluge takes over as the Chief in 'Kentauren' with Stötzner as his Underling. The division of the two parts provides no surprises. Kluge's voice gives the Chief a calm and gentle tone. His measured superiority conceales smugness, seductiveness and threat. For the most part his voice does not change for the whole scene, including the final speech in the present tense. Stötzner, on the other hand, plays his robotic subordinate. His mechanical delivery is punctuated by pauses in the middle of both lines and words. The musical accompaniment is again provided by the Allegretto movement of Shostakovich's *Leningrad Symphony* which includes the musical phrase that links the five parts. The Allegretto (which runs almost for the complete thirteen minutes of the scene) affords a musical development parallel to the mood of the scene rather than to its internal development. The symphony was written in 1941 during the siege of Leningrad by Nazi forces. The first movement reflects the disturbed peace of the city. Rousing socialist themes and phrases are interrupted and modified by discordant motifs. War had arrived. Thus one can hear in 'Kentauren' how the ideals of GDR socialism clashed with its everyday realities as cymbals crash and the orchestra pounds out stray notes. A nightmarish picture of GDR bureaucracy and paranoia is evoked. Dissonant piano chords are also overdubbed. That Shostakovich later maintained that the symphony was also based on the Psalms of David (especially those dealing with vengence and revenge) confers a different tone to the contradictory score for the scene.

The world of angry youth forms the musical backdrop for 'Der Findling'. The ever versatile Ernst Stötzner returns for a characterization in a rap style, together with the group 'We Wear the Crown'. He produces a highly self-conscious and bombastic delivery and speaks or sings all the lines. Fast anger is mixed with a strict adherence to the drum machine and its high number of beats per minute. At times he becomes more like the realistic narrator of 'Wald bei Moskau' although this lasts for a few phrases before he reverts to the dominant tempo. The 'VERGESSEN UND VERGESSEN UND VERGESSEN' motif becomes one of the few musical phrases to emerge from the mass of words. Its regularity imprints it onto the listener's ear and it is casually sung several more times. The music is also infused with a multitude of samples, vocal echoes and scratching. The samples include some Jimi Hendrix, the words 'Sieg', the line 'Zunge heraus' from *Traktor* and *Verkommenes Ufer*, snatches of socialist songs, the Kammerchor's lines from 'Das Duell', 'FREIHEIT und RUSSEN RAUS', and all manner of other musical soundbites. The musical collage with its range of voices forms a useful alliance with the accusatory style of the singing. The anger and resentment of a disaffected youth is transformed into a panorama of memory and experience.

According to Goebbels, Müller was not at all impressed with the arrangement, whereas he had been with the composer's previous output.[125] One can perhaps deduce that Goebbels' limited exploitation of vocal poss-

---

125 Unpublished letter from Heiner Goebbels to the author, 25-5-95.

ibilities and his extensive use of popular musical forms failed to convince the author that justice had been done to the texts. Goebbels was keen to stress to me the importance of the Russian artists Vitaly Komar and Alexander Melamid to his *Wolokolamsker Chaussee*. The two artists are famous for their use of Stalin and Stalinist imagery in their painting which Peter Wollen describes as 'post-Socialist Realist'. Later in their careers they took to a tableau form which exploited a montage principle whereby

> there is no continuous narrative, but instead a series of dramatic and symbolic scenes from a number of different narratives, whose underlying connections can only be guessed at and probably do not exist in any systematic way. A kind of comic strip patchwork.[126]

By viewing Goebbels' *Wolokolamsker Chaussee* as a whole, the dynamic is clearly more exciting than the sometimes uninspiring parts. The less complicated treatment of the Russian scenes becomes more problematic as the cycle continues. The catchiness of the first two scenes is relativized by the difficulties which are articulated musically later. The rage of the finale acts as a 'look back in bitterness'. Together with Goebbels' statement quoted above on the need to open up the plays to musical collectives, one might conclude that the cycle does have a more subtle depth than the mere examination of its parts would demonstrate. The changes of musical direction rather than vocal agility (in the individual pieces) creates a vibrant shifting of contexts which one could reproach the productions in Munich and Hamburg for ignoring.

IV   Free for All

In each production, a different relationship to the texts has established a fundamentally different aesthetic in performance. The problematic relationship between A and B in Munich took issue with any idea of dialectical resolution. The 'orthodox' division of text within the context of five constant 'rememberers' in Hamburg played with ideas of the individual within the group. In Leipzig the concept of the individual was practically exploded. Schroth in Berlin went for a more cold and ruthless stance in his treatment

---

126 *Komar and Melamid*, catalogue from an exhibition of their work in Edinburgh and Oxford (Edinburgh: The Fruitmarket Gallery, 1985), p. 38 and p. 50.

157

of GDR socialism, and Goebbels attempted a link between the texts and popular musical culture.

Each interpretation centred on the way in which the co-producers of the cycle understood the dynamics involved in the uninterrupted texts. The central question for each production was to work out its own relationship to a very fundamental aspect of drama, character. As readers we can only estimate a character's dimensions. In production possibilities are there to be experimented with.

Teams are no longer presented with the paradigm of one actor, one role. The notion of 'role' is replaced with a question mark. The potential for choral renditions is a provocative counterblast to the single voices of the modern stage. The trigger, found in the 'Lehrstück' structures of the texts, signals possibilities which revive a sense of the collective. Yet the collective chorus is not the same as its Brechtian precursor. The wise judges, the 'Kontrollchor' of *Die Maßnahme* or the 'gelernter Chor' of *Das Badener Lehrstück vom Einverständnis*, are replaced by more contingent collectives. Groups of voices can react to the deeds of the Commander (in both Leipzig and Berlin), add an ironic backdrop to the Director (in Goebbels's radio version), create individuals (in Leipzig again), and form a 'pool of rememberers' (in Hamburg). In each case a non-individualized corpus constructs a tension between the role of the individual and a notion of a 'society'. The production team is potentially able to escape the trappings of the bourgeois theatre and explore a more extensive set of problems because the text does not restrict interpretations of this sort by attributing texts to single characters. The possibility of sketching collective personalities in an age of individualism is both provocative and utopian.

Yet even once the ontological question of how characters are to be formed has been dealt with, the construction of the characters themselves is an open matter. Neither Rückhäberle's treatment of the Father or the Son in 'Der Findling' in Munich nor the complete dissection of the texts in Leipzig can be deemed 'wrong' because the importance of textual authority has been demoted in this style of drama. An amateur production in Battersea, South London, in the summer of 1993 introduced the Mother into 'Der Findling' as the voice that spoke the 'VERGESSEN UND VERGESSEN UND VERGESSEN' lines.

The collective's engagement with the amorphous texts is an act of definition. There is no starting place. The team is confronted with a *tabula rasa*. It is free to create characters, figures or voices. The transformation of 'Wald bei Moskau' in Leipzig from what we had considered a potentially interior scene into one where the decisions were made by the mass of the

158

soldiers was a triumph of the text's unattributed form over a reading of the piece that relied on traditional points of reference. Even their treatment of 'Kentauren', the most straightforward text of the cycle in our analysis, gave the scene qualities left unconsidered (and indeed unforeseeable) in a purely conventional reading.

Formally, however, it is difficult to evaluate whether the different productions were able to communicate the contingent nature of the texts that provided such creative freedom. The severe fragmentation of the characters in Leipzig could have signalled this quality, whereas Goebbels' radio version makes the texts sound, for the most part, like straight mono- logues, just like Heiner Müller's reading. The productions in Munich, Hamburg and Berlin are less quantifiable. Choral speech and the division of the single speech into many speaking parts could be construed by the audience as deliberate divisions in the text. Communicating the open form of the texts need not necessarily mean the saturation of each 'role' as in Leipzig. Yet the reeling off of lines leaves the audience in the dark. Perhaps a delivery style that the texts imply is that of a struggle. The texts belong to nobody and the appropriation by each actor is the result of a violent act of interpretation. It is possible that a realization that takes this into account is the one that does the contingent form of the texts justice. This is, of course, not an imperative. The plays' functions can also be viewed in practical terms. They are there to serve purposes which may not be the exposure of their own dramatic form. One could argue that the non-determined aspect of the texts is not there to be communicated as non-determination *per se*, but to leave space for productions to arrive at their own determinations, appropri- ate to their contexts. There is no one answer to be found in any one realiza- tion. Yet the co-existence of all that we have discussed within a very short space of time itself adds up to a useful statement about the text. It is a feature of the German theatre system, and Müller's place in it at that time, that over this period there were so many productions. They may not have related to each other directly but they created a climate of reception in which not only professional reviewers but even members of the German audience were at least aware of other possibilities.

Wolokolamsker Chaussee is a textual tool for directors and actors. Its initial 'Lehrstück' structures can be accepted or rejected in favour of a different aesthetic scheme. Even so, the collectivity implicit in the texts constructs an atmosphere of experiment which is open to all the co-produc- ers of the texts. The speaking figure is no longer the property of anyone, least of all an author. The dramatic text is no longer the site of authority. The independent parts also provide a flexibility in terms of ordering so that differing effects can be achieved by disturbing or adhering to the chronol-

159

ogy. Each part of the cycle is relegated to the status of a raw material. The concept of the hallowed text is obsolete. It becomes a part of a process, no more, no less. By virtue of both the problematic attribution and the mobility of the parts, one might conclude that Müller has presented the theatre with a five-part cycle which is without character *and* plot. If these two fundamental elements of drama are not yielded by the dramatic text, then the theatre can benefit from the active work involved in realizing both aspects in the cycle. Traditional signposts are not available and a simple reading is obfuscated by the lack of obvious demarcation. Production becomes interpretation in a far more radical sense than normal.

The challenge that the *Wolokolamsker Chaussee* texts pose is not one that has prevented companies from staging the cycle, as was the case with the first few attempts at *Die Hamletmaschine*. The latter resisted realization on two counts: it was both difficult to understand in terms of its language, and it refused to respect certain traditional dramaturgical conventions. The combination of the two made an understanding of character and plot highly problematic. We have already noted that *Wolokolamsker Chaussee* does not employ overly taxing metaphors or other puzzling poetic devices. Its texts are far more comprehensible. On the other hand, it no longer presents us with any characters at all. All the same, this problem has been resolved in the productions discussed earlier: taking up the challenge of the texts has not proved too difficult. They nonetheless impel their realizers into an active avant-garde style engagement. The conscious decisions involved in transforming blocks of text into delineated scripts for actors provokes an inventive reply. Although one can imagine staging the cycle, it is still hard to decide how.

CHAPTER III

Plot and Structural Coherence

1   Montage as a Concept for the Dramatic Arts

Coherence of plot is the (originally Aristotelian) category which is still thought to be fairly essential to drama. This has long since been complicated by ideas of sub-plots, parallel plots and episodic plots, which at times can frustrate coherence very effectively. In much of Müller's later dramaturgy, thematically (and formally) disparate scenes are wilfully juxtaposed in a bid to break open ideas of linearity and cohesion. Elements are mobilized in order to achieve the status of 'Material', a term discussed in the Introduction. Müller applies a montage technique to the overall organization of his scenes (although one could spend another chapter investigating the montage of elements *within* the scenes themselves).

One of the first attempts to suggest the possibilities of juxtaposing elements within a literary whole is Sergei Eisenstein's short article 'Montage der Attraktionen', which first appeared in 1923. The method he put forward was 'die freie Montage von willkürlich ausgewählten, selbständigen (auch außerhalb dieser vorgegebenen Komposition und Handlungslinie funktionierenden) Einwirkungen (Attraktionen), allerdings mit einer genauen Orientierung auf einen bestimmten thematischen Endeffekt'. Unlike the overwhelming majority of Eisenstein's writings, this article was written with the theatre in mind and was derived from his experiences at the Proletkult Theatre in Moscow. Consequently he saw the power of the montage style as a way that could liberate the theatre 'aus der bisher waltenden und ausschlaggebenden Knechtschaft einer unausweichlichen und einzig möglichen "illusionistischen Abbildung" und "Darstellbarkeit"'.[1] Wolfgang Seibel adds a thematic level to Eisenstein's dramaturgical one in his book *Die Formenwelt der Fertigteile*. He sees montage as essentially changing

> Zeiterfahrung und Zeitkonzeption, die sich am auffälligsten in der Dynamisierung und Durchbrechung der irreversiblen und kontinuierlichen Chronologie, der Koinzidenz von Gegensätz-

---

[1]   Sergei Eisenstein, *Das dynamische Quadrat*, trans. by Oksana Bulgakowa and Dietmar Hochmuth (Leipzig: Reclam, 1988), p. 13 and ibid.

lichem und der Simultaneität des räumlich und zeitlich Getrennten manifestiert.[2]

The montage process allows us to go beyond the conventions of literary time and space. Such a departure from Aristotle's unities is a radical one. Accepted digressions from the unities of time or space in traditional Western drama retain their coherence by following a concept of plot.[3] A montage approach no longer 'excuses' such disruptions. It consciously foregrounds temporal and spatial discrepancies for a variety of ends (which I shall discuss later).

The status of the elements which form the basis of the assembly is also of import. In the posthumous collection of his thoughts on montage, Eisenstein considered that the process that is of primary importance for the individual element is that of going from the specific to the general, of taking a realist representation and transforming it into a metaphorical one. Yet we should not see this as a process of abandoning one mode in favour of the other. It is 'not breaking its texture but raising it to the utmost limits of specific generalization (i.e. without drifting off into "cosmic abstractions")'. Eisenstein attempted to retain the element's indeterminate position when he described the bridge it had to create between the realistic and the metaphorical: 'the fragment [...] must also be sufficiently unexpected and unusual to rivet our attention and stimulate our imagination, while at the same time not being so unexpected and unusual as to disturb our normal conception of that phenomenon'.[4] This point is clearly integral to a notion of montage as shock, whereby the unexpected challenges our traditional view of the subject matter in question. However, Eisenstein's position here sounds a little conservative. He is concerned with the intelligibility of the fragment and fears for the loss of its meaning. The object becomes too far removed from the original idea. Seibel and Erika Fischer-Lichte argue,

2   Wolfgang Seibel, *Die Formenwelt der Fertigteile* (Würzburg: Königshausen und Neumann, 1988), pp. 15-16.

3   For example, in *Macbeth* the scenes change from Scotland to England in order to follow the rebels' plot to overthrow the usurper Macbeth, or in Chekhov's *Three Sisters* months are allowed to pass between acts. Both types of disruption which theoretically affect the 'purity' of the suspension of disbelief have nonetheless been accepted into the norm of modern drama and are not considered unusual or challenging.

4   Sergei Eisenstein, *Towards a Theory of Montage*, tr. by Michael Glenny (London: British Film Institute, 1991), p. 130 and p. 150.

however, that the fragment refuses to yield its original meaning completely through its transfer to a new context.[5] Meaning is modified but never fully lost. Only by retaining constituents of its old meaning is a montage element able to compare its old context with the new one.

But montage is clearly a technique that not only requires specially constructed elements; their combination or juxtaposition is just as crucial. Eisenstein was not hesitant to attribute just as much importance to this aspect as to the composition of each fragment: 'the true "image" [Eisenstein's term for the generalizing, metaphorical aim of montage] of the montage statement only *emerges* in the sequential juxtaposition of its constituent frames'.[6] Seibel, writing with the experience of montage as a technique which may not only desire one image to emerge from its labours, quotes Hans-Joachim Schlegel who turns the question of ordering into one of the battle of the individual elements themselves.[7] He argues that montage is 'niemals eine bloße Summe von Teilelementen, sondern immer das dialektische Produkt eines neuen Bedeutungszusammenhangs'. The individual parts are therefore liberated from their original contexts in order to challenge the new context thrown up by the elements that surround and influence them. This type of freedom within the literary whole, which goes against Eisenstein's view of montage as creating a new *entirety*, is something that Seibel traces back to the Surrealists. Their use of real objects 'erlaubt, die verwendeten Einzel-Elemente, sonst einer geschlossenen Gesamtkomposition, [...] in ihrer Eigenform und Eigenbedeutung hervortreten zu lassen und ihre Heterogenität in ästhetische Spannung umzusetzen'.[8]

The effects of montage are wide-ranging yet are broadly covered by two headings: the destructive and the constructive. Both result from the process of juxtaposition - namely that a cohesion is broken and a new ordering is produced. Seibel sees the practice as particularly well suited to 'Ideologiezertrümmerung und die Veränderung des Lebensprozesses des Rezipienten'. The productivity of the technique is heightened, according to

---

5   Seibel, pp. 80-1; and Erika Fischer-Lichte, 'Zwischen Differenz und Indifferenz. Funktionalisierungen des Montage-Verfahrens bei Heiner Müller', in Erika Fischer-Lichte and Klaus Schwind (eds.), *Avantgarde und Postmoderne* (Tübingen: Stauffenburg, 1991), p. 234

6   Eisenstein, ibid, p. 80.

7   Schlegel's article 'Zum Streit in der Montage' originally appeared in the journal *kürbiskern*, 2/74, p. 83.

8   Seibel, p. 82 and p. 39.

Seibel, by the jagged nature of the juxtaposition of the montage fragments which both explode the closure of the work and introduce the category of 'Irritation'.[9] Eisenstein interprets the process in a manner that possibly limits effects we find in Seibel, yet the basic notion is nonetheless interesting as a consequence of its ideological foundation. He believed that the major significance of montage was 'above all a tendentious and socially purposive act, the reconstruction of images of reality in the interest of transforming and refashioning reality itself'.

Productivity is the result of the associative power of montage. Eisenstein sees montage as a producer of information gaps: 'it is [...] obvious that the basic characteristic of a montage sequence is its suggestiveness'.[10] The importance of creating links through the comparison of two or more montage elements is *the* activating factor.

An added aspect, highlighted by Fischer-Lichte, is the prominence of the artifice of the work, due to the breaking of what we might have once thought of as 'the organic plot'.[11] The quality of the artificial is taken up by Seibel in the context of Benjamin's 'Aura'.[12] He argues that the liquidation of the auratic quality of art is to be found *par excellence* in the practice of montage.[13] By this technique, the receiver of the work of art is put into a fundamentally different position. The work is no longer complete and it can only have meaning for the recipient through his or her active engagement with it. The damage done to continuity is the starting point of the activation of the recipient. The work of art no longer casts down meaning from a privileged station; it opens itself up to the recipient's experiences.

Montage, of course, does not have a single manifestation. Selectivity in the arrangement of scenes can serve a variety of functions. Seibel, whose book is mainly a dissertation on montage in drama, furnishes the reader with an interesting typology of what he considers the possibilities of montage

9   Ibid., p. 113 and p. 19.

10   Eisenstein, p. 132 and p. 150.

11   Fischer-Lichte, p. 244.

12   Cf. Walter Benjamin, 'Das Kunstwerk im Zeitalter seiner technischen Repro-
     duzierbarkeit', in Walter Benjamin, *Illuminationen*, selected writings vol. 1, ed. by
     Siegfried Unseld (Frankfurt/Main: Suhrkamp, 1977), pp. 136-69.

13   Seibel, p. 20.

as a organizational device. The 'attributive Szenenmontage'[14] is the adding of extra scenes to a structured dramatic 'Fabel' (in a Brechtian sense) in order to add poignant contrasts or analogies. Such a technique is employed, for example, in the use of documentary counterpoints in Kipphardt's *Bruder Eichmann*, in the anonymous commentaries in Braun's *Die Übergangsgesellschaft* or in the classical commentaries of *Zement*. The 'kombinative Szenenmontage' is Seibel's term for a play made up exclusively of disparate elements which consequently fashion their own 'Fabel': '[sie] dient nicht nur als formales Ordungsprinzip, sondern als Aussageinstrument'.[15] Meaning is created through structuring devices, such as the pairing of scenes or the grouping of scenes into thematic constellations. *Germania Tod in Berlin* is an example of this type of montage. Thirdly, there is the 'additive Szenenmontage', which is similar to the 'kombinative Szenenmontage' insofar as it is exclusively constructed from fragments. It differs, however, in the way that it constructs meaning. In this type there is no 'Fabel' to speak of. The scenes only depend on a central theme and their ordering is thus apparently arbitrary. Seibel suggests Brecht's *Furcht und Elend des Dritten Reichs*, although we could add Kroetz's *Ich bin das Volk* or Hochhuth's *Wessis in Weimar*. Although Seibel's tripartite system seems to deal with the problem of typology in montage, there are certain borderline cases that do not comfortably fit into the rubrics. Seibel suggests *Die Schlacht* as a candidate for the 'additive Szenenmontage'. To a certain extent this is true: as the subtitle makes clear, the episodes are just 'Szenen aus Deutschland'. There is also no ostensible 'Fabel'. However, there *is* a chronology: the play starts with the 'Reichtagsbrand' and ends in the liberation of Berlin by the Soviet army. The scenes between the two also have temporal markers: they all take place during World War Two. Müller relates the experience of the Yugoslavian première, where it was decided that the scenes should be staged in reverse:

> Da ergäbe sich eine viel größere Spannung, auch in der Struktur. [...] Man müßte eine Form finden, die Chronologie zu zerbrechen, um dadurch die Aufführung diskursiver zu machen.

---

14   This, like the other two terms, is to be found on Seibel's contents page (p. 6).

15   Seibel, p. 144.

[...] Wenn man einen Kriminalroman liest, achtet man nicht auf die Sprache: man will wissen, wer es war.[16]

Here we have a mixture of two types of montage. Meaning is correspondingly manufactured in a different way here, as opposed to either of Seibel's types taken separately. The typological problem is one that I shall return to in the discussion of *Verkommenes Ufer*.

In the following sections I shall deal in turn with *Germania*, *Leben Gundlings* and *Verkommenes Ufer* in order to understand better the dramatic possibilities of the combination of disparate elements. In each a case a different process is employed in both the construction of the montage elements and their subsequent juxtaposition.

2   *Germania Tod in Berlin*

I   Disrupting the Flow

Germania was written, as stated in the Rotbuch edition of the play, between 1956 and 1971. According to the director B. K. Tragelehn, who worked with Müller on the controversial 'Uraufführung' of *Die Umsiedlerin oder das Leben auf dem Lande* (première 30 September 1961), the second scene, 'Die Straße 2', was written shortly after the affair, at the end of that year.[17] The intention was to continue the play along the lines of the love story whose beginning is signalled at the end of this scene when the 'Junger Mann' saves 'Hure 1' from the clutches of the 'Betrunkener' (G p. 40). The play was to have its 'Fabel'. Certain historical scenes were to be added, giving the play, in Seibel's scheme, the status of an 'attributive Szenenmontage'. After a long gestation period it was completed in Bulgaria in 1971. We see that in the space of ten years the original conception was radically redefined: the drama became 'kombinativ'; the love story a mere thread in a much larger, panoramic whole.

Eisenstein's call for a series of disparate elements is perhaps the best place to start an anatomy of *Germania*, because the question of continuity

---

16   'Solange wir an unsere Zukunft glaube, brauchen wir uns vor unserer Vergangenheit nicht zu fürchten', in Heiner Müller, *Gesammelte Irrtümer* (Frankfurt/Main: 1986, Verlag der Autoren), p. 183.

17   Unpublished interview with B. K. Tragelehn by the author, 27-3-95.

is of great importance in this play. An initial overview of the thirteen scenes yields the following settings in time and space:

1. Straße 1	Berlin	1918-19
2. Straße 2	East Berlin	1949
3. Brandenburgisches Konzert 1	Circus ring	----------
4. Brandenburgisches Konzert 2	Castle, GDR	c. 1949-51[18]
5. Hommage à Stalin 1	Battlefield (Stalingrad)[19]	Temporally displaced mainly Winter 1943
6. Hommage à Stalin 2	Bar, East Berlin	5 March 1953
7. Die Heilige Familie	Hitler's Bunker	1945
8. Das Arbeiterdenkmal	Building Site, East Berlin	16/17 June 1953[20]
9. Die Brüder 1	(Text by Tacitus)	(16 BC)
10. Die Brüder 2	Prison, GDR	17 June 1953
11. Nachtstück	----------	----------
12. Tod in Berlin 1	(Poem by G. Heym)	(1910)
13. Tod in Berlin 2	Cancer Ward, East Berlin	Two weeks after 'Das Arbeiterdenkmal'

The number of the scenes, thirteen, perhaps evokes an association of bad luck which is found in both the folkloric and Christian traditions. The odd number might also suggest a structural pivot located at scene 7. Although this scene does have a special status with regard to the other 'Vorgeschichte' scenes (ie. it has no signalled pair), it does not owe this to its central position.[21]

18 This approximate date coincides with the 'Helden der Arbeit' movement which honoured workers of high productivity in the early fifties. The important temporal factor in this scene is that it follows the founding of the GDR and precedes the death of Stalin.

19 Stalingrad is never named directly although the 'Kessel' is mentioned twice before the entrance of the Nibelungen.

20 The precise date of this scene is subject to debate. Whether it actually takes place on 17 June or the day before when the strike found sporadic support is uncertain.

21 If one were to single out a scene, it would be 'Nachtstück' which demarcates itself from all the other scenes in two ways: i) it is the only scene without any

Two patterns emerge from this series: with the exception of 'Nacht-stück', all the scenes follow the rule of one scene from pre-GDR history ('Vorgeschichte') and one from the history of the GDR itself. The scenes usually form pairs, indicated by their titles, and the only exception to this is found in scenes 7 and 8. Even here we find arguments in favour of their pairing in the secondary literature.[22]

The second, related pattern is found in the chronology that develops in the GDR scenes. The two character groupings of the 'Huren' and the 'Maurer' provide fairly regular points of reference in these scenes. However, the absence of familiar figures in 'Brandenburgisches Konzert 2' and 'Die Brüder 2' makes the history of the GDR the 'main character'. That time can be foregrounded in this way is a direct result of the disruptive montage principle at work in the play.

The employment of patterns affects the dramaturgical independence of the elements that fall under their influence. The pattern will, to a certain degree, limit associative possibilities because it creates its own ordered points of reference.

If we take the pairing of the scenes as our first example of a pattern, we notice that it is a regularity imposed upon two categories in flux. 'Straße 1 und 2' share geography but contrast the defeat of the working classes in the Spartacist Uprising of 1919 with the establishment of 'DER ERSTE ARBEITERUNDBAUERNSTAAT AUF DEUTSCHEM BODEN' (G p. 38). 'Brandenburgisches Konzert 1 und 2' play off two clowns trying to act out a historical anecdote and the celebration of a Stakhanovite worker. The

hint of a concrete time or place, and ii) it is the only non-verbal scene - the only sound that arises is the scream at its conclusion.

22   Wolfgang Seibel in his *Formenwelt der Fertigteile* (pp. 210-11) agrees that the linking of the scenes is problematic but suggests that both deal with the 'Fehl-entwicklungen' of the two German states. Genia Schulz, in her book *Heiner Müller* (Stuttgart: Metzler, 1980), p. 133, sees them paired under the theme of the effects of reaction. 'Die Heilige Familie' presents the results of this as farce, 'Das Arbeiterdenkmal' as tragedy. Also, Georg Wieghaus in his 'Anmerkungen zu *Germania Tod in Berlin*', *Spectaculum 31* (Frankfurt/Main: Suhrkamp, 1979), p. 164, argues that the scenes are linked by the themes of decisive moments in the histories of the FRG and the GDR. It is interesting to note that in the productions in Bochum, at both the Theater der freien Volksbühne and at the Berliner Ensemble in Berlin, and at the 'Uraufführung' in Munich, an interval followed 'Die Heilige Familie'. The production in Wuppertal was staged without interruption.

'Hommage à Stalin' scenes take us from a multi-layered collage of historical and mythical battles to an East German bar on the day of Stalin's death. The other scenic pairs display similar contrasts of place and time. This regularity is, for the most part, the method by which associations are initially generated. By drawing the audience's attention to the possibility of comparing scenes through the employment of paired titles,[23] the suggestiveness of the montage is foregrounded. The titles also play a second role: they not only draw attention to similarities (between the scenes), some are also agents of difference: both the 'Brandenburgisches Konzert' and the 'Hommage à Stalin' pairs create additional tensions. Here the relationship between title and scene becomes problematic. Both cast an ironic light upon the events they cover, and in this irony we find more room for association.

The second emergent pattern, however, seems as if it should have the opposite effect. The chronological, historical progression unifies the differing GDR scenes through temporal linearity. We can, however, understand this as a dramaturgical trade-off. The play requires continuity in order that the paired scenes can function optimally. The flow of events in the GDR becomes parallel with the surges from history and myth.[24]

The disparities between the pairs manufacture associations, that is clear. We should, however, investigate the picture of the GDR that emerges in *Germania* in order so see how productive this pattern can be. Of course, a survey of each of the six scenes would be repetitious and I shall consequently be more selective.

The first GDR scene, 'Die Straße 2' is defined both by its geographical and its temporal subtitle ('Berlin 1949', G p. 38). The loudspeaker announcement (quoted above) attempts to add a politico-historical dimension to the scene but we observe that this actually provides the starting point for the ensuing dialogues. If we quickly summarize the action of the scene, we can gain an overview as to how the announcement is itself relativized. Roughly speaking, the scene divides into six sections: the immediate challenge to the announcement, the monologue of the 'Alter mit Kind auf dem Rücken', the exchange that takes its cue from the last line of the 'Alter', the

---

23 In performance, the audience, as far as my research has shown, has *always* been made aware of the titles of the scenes. This information has been provided by loudspeaker at the beginning of each scene and/or in the programme.

24 The juxtaposition of events was, in part, an implicit criticism of the official SED line on history, which maintained that its goal had been reached in the non-antagonistic society of the GDR. The seemingly arbitrary parallels explode this dogmatic and linear position.

challenge of the 'Windjacken' from the West and the intervention of the agents of state security, the short speech of 'Herr 1', and the dialogue of the 'Huren'. The historical event is transformed into malleable material. By taking the establishment of the GDR as a starting point, that is, before it had had a chance to become history, we can see the various routes the state *could* have taken. The contrast of the various reactions to the declaration becomes more pointed when compared with the form of the declaration: the foundation of the republic is already a closed matter from the point of view of the anonymous speaker. Its wrenching open is the subject matter of the rest of the scene. Criticism is instant: the retort of the 'Mann' in the first section, 'Der Russenstaat' (G ibid.), sets the ball rolling, and he in turn is challenged (physically as well as verbally) by the 'Andrer'. His escape into the mass leaves the argument open. The 'Alter' also challenges the authoritarian nature of the announcement by returning to the politics of Liebknecht and Luxemburg in his reminiscence of the Spartacist Uprising. He carries hope both in his last line ('Der Präsident [Wilhelm Pieck, who was one of the Spartacists]. Ein Arbeiter wie wir', ibid.) and in the ambivalent image of the child on his back. His idealism is then challenged in the following exchange by the 'Stimmen' and the 'Einarm'. Here we see a certain solidarity: the three men cover for the 'Einarm' in the face of State interference. Yet even State interference is provocatively defended. Western agents attempt to stir up discontent within the new Germany through oral and printed propaganda and are dealt with by the 'Stasi'. 'Herr 1' then returns to the theme of the influence of Russia. The scene concludes with the motif of continuity when representatives of 'the oldest profession' contrast the political discourse of the previous sections with that of everyday existence. The scene actively problematizes each of its constituent elements and takes the montage structure down a level so that the sections gain an independence of sorts within the scene itself.

If we now try to contrast the above technique with a GDR scene where there is no panoramic style and where context is partially given by a 'Fabel', we see just how flexible this latter type of scene can be. The typologized figures and the filmic cuts of 'Straße 2' do not occur in 'Tod in Berlin 2'. Here we are presented with familiar characters: the 'Junger Maurer' comes with 'Hure 1' (who is now denoted as 'Mädchen' in the text)[25] to visit Hilse in hospital. Contrary to our expectation, Hilse is in a

25　According to my research this change in 'title' has never been interpreted as a change in actress. This is in contrast to the figures of the 'Maurer' in 'Brandenburgisches Konzert 2' and the 'Aktivist' in 'Hommage à Stalin 2': both have

cancer ward and is not being treated for the injuries sustained at the hands of the youths in 'Das Arbeiterdenkmal'. Unlike the other GDR scenes, 'Tod in Berlin 2' is not a dialectical engagement with a particular historical event or practice. It is, however, a scene which exploits metaphor in order to comment on issues which are not dictated by the 'Fabel'. The speeches swing between the literal and the metaphorical. The scene becomes a reckoning with the events that have preceded it.

Hilse, the only worker not to join the strike is infested with cancer. 'Wir sind eine Partei, mein Krebs und ich' (G p. 76), he says, and here the double meaning of 'Partei' functions reflectively. Similarly, the 'Junger Maurer' must also come to terms with the tainting of a presumed purity. He learns that the girl he has made pregnant, whose virginity he believed was still intact, is in fact a prostitute. In the final seconds of the scene we see the death of the past (Hilse), the problems of the present (the 'Junger Maurer' and the 'Mädchen') and an as yet unknown future (the unborn child). Whereas the former GDR scenes played an anachronistic game of opening up historical 'facts' with provocative sentiments, 'Tod in Berlin 2' divorces itself from the concrete date of the scene through its allegorical techniques and becomes a provocation to the audience. The other GDR scenes mediate attitudes and opinions, 'Tod in Berlin 2' leaves us with a circumstance, a predicament. Having seen the play of 'Vorgeschichte' and real history we are left at the present. Müller presents us with an ending which formulates a didactic impulse. The final scene pointedly asks Lenin's classic question 'What is to be done?'.

The GDR scenes are relatively unstable despite their chronology and they present themselves, for the most part, as sites of possibility or change in the context of a historical progression. The 'Ideologiezertrümmerung' that results from the scenic pairing is combined with chronology to lend *Germania* a polemical function, addressed to the citizens of both Germanies.[26]

We can see that although the two patterns emerge which might have limited the effects of the montage elements, the associative texture of the

bandaged heads and could easily be the same person. This ambiguity is reflected in performance. Some companies have doubled the role whilst others have used two different actors.

26   Of course, the play is more robust than this and is not limited by the demise of the GDR. Today in a united Germany, the play will no doubt gain a different perspective. One can only speculate about this because the play has not been staged anew at the time of writing since the production at the Theater der Freien Volksbühne just before Reunification.

individual scenes compensates for this to a certain extent. I have not engaged in a discussion of the polyphonous 'Vorgeschichte' scenes: this is mainly because of the self-evidence (with two interesting exceptions) of this assertion. The rhyming couplets and the larger-than-life figures of 'Straße 1', the play of dramatic layers in 'Brandenburgisches Konzert 1', the heaping of war images in 'Hommage à Stalin 1' and the grotesque extravaganza of 'Die Heilige Familie' all present distorted and provocative views of well-known incidents and events. The difference between stage presentation and the traditional image of these periods creates the space required to explode customary notions. However, the texts appropriated as 'Die Brüder 1' and 'Tod in Berlin 1' function differently. Both are unmodified primary texts, yet their titles and their appearance in a cycle of scenes does have the effect of re-functioning them. The scenes become provocative literary prefaces or epigraphs to their partner scenes.

The only scene left to consider is 'Nachtstück'. In addition to its distinctive form in comparison with the other scenes (cf. footnote 21), its position before the 'Tod in Berlin' pair is also crucial to its meaning within the play. The two main interpretations of its position in the flow of events reveal its ambivalent status. Genia Schulz sees the scene in its contiguity to 'Die Brüder 2' as a response to the last line of the 'Kommunist', 'wer bin ich' (G p. 74).[27] Horst Domdey considers it in the light of all the scenes that precede it as the result of a Germany that will not reform itself.[28] For him the scene gains the status of a commentary, although his reading fails to address the scenes that follow. We have already examined 'Tod in Berlin 1 und 2' and understood them structurally and dramaturgically as a reckoning. 'Nachtstück' can perhaps also be read as a prologue to the finale. This would seem to be confirmed by certain critics in their summation of the scene in itself. Seibel sees it as a timeless evocation of an ending and of a beginning, whereas for Wieghaus it is part of the process of becoming: the 'Mensch, der vielleicht eine Puppe ist' is no longer a puppet, but not yet a human being.[29] Both readings interpret the scene as a turning point of sorts. Its detachment from the stability of the pairings confers ambivalence.

27   Schulz, p. 132.

28   Horst Domdey, '"Der Tod eine Funktion des Lebens." Stalinmythos in Texten Heiner Müllers', in Paul Gerhard Klussmann and Heinrich Mohr (eds.), *Jahrbuch zur Literatur in der DDR*, vol 5 (Bonn: Bouvier, 1986), p. 74.

29   Seibel, p. 213; and Wieghaus, p. 265.

'Nachtstück' perhaps exemplifies the montage principle because the scene *cannot* be fixed concretely within any context. One should note, however, that this liberated status is dependent upon the establishment of patterns earlier on in the play.

The main quality of montage is its ability to produce associations between elements that do not necessarily belong together. In Eisenstein's definition of the 'Attraktionen' above, one assumes that he has in mind what one would now call in Seibel's terminology 'additive Szenenmontage'. Every element has a chance of cross-referencing with the others in order to create a dense link of associations around a particular theme. In this respect we should not forget the richness of the leitmotif complexes that pervade the drama. Seibel draws our attention to the repeated motifs of 'Blut' and repressed sexuality.[30] The word 'Hund' and the motif of laughter are emphasized in Gerold Theobalt's notes in the programme of the Wuppertal production.[31] Berlin, death, and the repetition of the line 'viel laßt ihr euch gefallen' and its variations build connections that extend associations beyond the cut-off points of the scenic pairs.

Despite the richness of the associative texture, *Germania* restricts the productivity of its scenes by their careful arrangement. Associations are manufactured according to an underlying set of ideas which are expressed by the overall structure of the play. The ideas have much to do with a conscious criticism of a linear understanding of history. The structure defers to ideas, a situation which is at odds with 'blinde Praxis'. Of course, our first impressions of the order are those of shock. The combination of the scenic pairs is innovative, yet once we have understood that contemporary German history is riddled with bloody motifs from the past, the interesting juxtapositions lose much of their effect. The montage technique serves a purpose. The assembly of the parts highlights comparisons in a schematic manner.

We can conclude that the structure affects the montage elements in a significant way. Various critics are keen to point to the associative power of the montage technique in *Germania* without necessarily discussing the formal cohesion of the play.[32] We now see that certain limits are imposed

30   Seibel, p. 215.

31   *Heiner Müllers 'Germania'*, programme of the Wuppertal production, 2-12-89, p. 11.

32   For example, Moray McGowan, 'Marxist - Postmodernist - German: history and dramatic form in the works of Heiner Müller', in Martin Kane (ed.), *Socialism and the Literary Imagination. Essays on East German Writers* (Oxford: Berg, 1991),

upon associative freedom in order to focus ideas. We can also say that development is due to the chronology of the GDR scenes and that the independence of the montage elements is limited by this. There is a trade-off between the associative freedom of the elements and structural devices that restrict it.

II   The Play of Levels and Dramatic Texture

We have seen that the subject matter of the montage elements is multi-layered and/or multi-facetted. What is of importance in performance, however, is how the figures and the characters function. We must ask whether the characters merely 'populate' the scenes as representatives or play a more integral role as more traditional characters.

Germania presents us with many types of character, yet critical opinion seems to take the play as a panorama and fails to distinguish the differences in texture. Andreas Keller contends that individual characterization is no longer possible due to the concentration and clipped nature of the scenes. Klussmann takes the view that the *dramatis personae* is too broad to be reduced to historical personalities. Jost Hermand does distinguish between the two varieties but sees all the historical characters as caricatures whilst the GDR citizens just remain types.[33] A closer investigation reveals that there are in fact a small array of character types, each with a different dramaturgy.

The type that occurs in both 'Vorgeschichte' and GDR scenes is the 'character without a character', the traditional 'bit part'. Either through the briefness of their appearance and/or the brevity of their utterances, these figures take on more representative functions in the scenes. In this class we find 'Mann' and 'Frau' in 'Straße 1', almost all the figures in 'Straße 2' with the notable exceptions of the 'Alter' and the 'Huren', and the minor figures of 'Die Heilige Familie', to name a few. Even the soldiers, and the historical emperors Caesar and Napoleon in 'Hommage à Stalin 1', fall into this category. Each presents a typologized nugget of dialogue. Each functions like a quotation of a real character, be it a bricklayer or a historical person-

p. 133. He argues that connections are manufactured by association and not by dramatic logic.

33   Keller, p. 191; Klussmann, p. 163; and Jost Hermand, 'Braut, Mutter oder Hure? Heiner Müllers *Germania* und ihre Vorgeschichte', in Jost Hermand, *Sieben Arten an Deutschland zu leiden* (Königstein: Athenäum, 1979), p. 139.

ality. Each character's iconic value is supplemented by complementary lines. Such figures help to lend the play its panoramic qualities.

It is only on the larger scale that the figures start to diverge. In the 'Vorgeschichte' scenes, two types emerge. The first is what Hermand calls the historical caricatures (although one would have to add the category of the mythical). The technique by which Hitler, Goebbels, Germania and the Nibelungen are parodied is a fairly traditional one. Each 'great' historical figure is brought down to earth through the use of exaggerated qualities wc associate more with everyday experiences. We see Hitler acting as a child ('Ich werde sie köpfen. Ich werde sie aufhängen. Ich werde sie vierteilen. [...] Ja. Finger abhacken. Hände. Arme. Beine. Ohre abschneiden. Nase abschneiden. *Kichernd und zappelnd.* Pimmel ausreißen', G p. 59) and as a paranoiac ('Sie maskieren sich. Sie wagen es nicht mehr, uns offen entgegenzutreten. Aber ich durchschaue sie. Ich durchschau alles', ibid.). Germania is demoted from the noblesse of her painted representations and is re-presented as a bourgeois mid-wife. The Nibelungen could be a pack of thugs. This satirical method is common dramatic practice and when used as sparingly as in *Germania*, it retains its freshness.

The Clowns, on the other hand, take the process a stage further. They too debunk well-known historical characters as well as the anecdote that they seem to try to illustrate. Yet the actors are not acting the roles of the characters, they are acting the roles of clowns acting the roles of the characters. The discrepancies that emerge between actor, clown and historical figure allow the scene to comment on the drama of receiving and writing history.

The characters with more lines in the GDR scenes are not presented in this exaggerated vein.[34] For the most part they tread a path between a clipped and essentially realistic language and a more abstract, poetic level. Laconic tightness (which is sometimes communicated in a verse form) dispels a realistic approach to the dialogue. The utterances become distillations of real speech, for example in 'Hommage à Stalin 2':

---

34   Although the 'Schädelverkäufer' may appear grotesque, we see that his language is not ostensibly different from the other GDR characters. It is his 'profession' that is grotesque, although Müller draws him from a factual context. During the early years of the GDR, when mass reconstruction was taking place, special details of workers were engaged in the transfer of graveyards (and their grizzly contents) to make way for new roads and buildings (cf. Heiner Müller, *Krieg ohne Schlacht*, Cologne: Kiepenheuer und Witsch, 1992, p. 91).

BETRUNKENER: Du bist Prolet. Ich bin Prolet. Wir müssen
Zusammen halten gegen den Kapitalismus.
Gegen den Sozialismus auch. Ich war
Im KJV seit 24. Mir macht
Keiner was vor. In Stalingrad im Kessel
Haben sie mich ausgekocht. Das war kein Krieg
mehr.

(G pp. 54-5)

Or in 'Das Arbeiterdenkmal':

STIMME: Kollegen, legt die Arbeit nieder. Streik.
GENERAL
zu Hilse: Ich hab's mir überlegt. Ich gehe vom Bau.
Wirft ihm die Kelle vor die Füße.
STIMME: Kollegen. Auf die Straße. Wir marschieren
Zum Ministerium.
GENERAL: Jetzt wird deutsch geredet
Mit den Genossen.
DICKER MAURER:Die verstehen bloß russisch. *Lacht über seinen Witz.*
GENERAL: Amerikanisch werden sie verstehen.
HILSE: Hier spricht RIAS Berlin.

(G p. 65)

In the speech of the 'Betrunkener' we find a realistic narrative shorn of
unnecessary adornment. The story is a concentration of experiences and
opinions, presented in a concise form. The same is true of the exchange on
the building site. Opinions and responses are reduced yet kept within a
realistic framework (which is also evident from the stage directions). Sometimes, however, the language expands and becomes more poetic and
metaphorical, as in 'Straße 2':

ALTER: Die Kaiserhure [Berlin] war Proletenbraut
Für eine Nacht, nackt im Novemberschnee
Von Hunger aufgeschwemmt, vom Generalstreik
Gerüttelt, mit Proletenblut gewaschen.
Wir standen wieder hier im Januar drauf
Der Nebel stieg, die Hand fror am Gewehr

(G p. 38)

Or in 'Die Brüder 2':

NAZI: Die Reue kommt zu spät. Man stirbt nur einmal
       Und ich habs hinter mir. Ich bin gestorben.
       Als ich aus deiner Tür ging in der Nacht
       Der Langen Messer

                                                        (G p. 72)

In both examples, the speakers mix reality with a metaphorical elaboration of that reality. The most extreme instance of this comes in Hilse's delirious last lines. This type of dialogue confers a symbolic dimension to the speaking character whilst the speaker nonetheless remains a familiar figure to the audience. The discrepancy between the character we know and the utterances we hear resembles the character construction of the grotesques in the 'Vorgeschichte' scenes. In both cases, superficial recognition is only the starting point for the audience's relationship with the characters.

We see that the way in which the individual montage elements, the scenes, can be articulated also provides openings for an associative approach. Metaphors and the grotesque within character construction comment on issues which go beyond the exigencies of the scenes whilst remaining in a meaningful context.[35]

III   History in the Making

It is commonly agreed by theatre critics that the production that put Müller well and truly in the consciousness of the West German theatrical world was the 'Uraufführung' of *Germania* at the Kammerspiele in Munich on 20 April (Hitler's birthday) 1978. The late Ernst Wendt, who effectively introduced the West German public to Müller in 1975 with his staging of *Die Schlacht* (Schauspielhaus Hamburg, 14 November 1975), joined forces with Johannes Schütz, Michael Rüggeberg and Sigrid Herzog for the unveiling of a play which had waited seven years before it was finally performed.

---

35 The only places where this is not applicable are 'Die Brüder 1', 'Tod in Berlin 1' and the 'Nachtstück'. The first two are non-dramatic texts. Their articulation is a question for the director. 'Nachtstück' describes an event. If it is to be mimed, there is no real scope for much of a characterization, due to the strictness of the prescribed actions.

The cast of *Germania* is extremely large. There is a minimum of eighty parts.[36] It is clear that the playing of many parts is an essential part of the realization of the play in most theatres. The apportioning of parts is therefore a device that can create theatrical meaning, and it can work in two ways. The variety of parts played by one actor can emphasize either similarity or difference.[37] In Munich, similarity was maintained by the same actors following through the GDR roles, so that the 'story' retained its cohesion. Thus the 'Maurer' of 'Brandenburgisches Konzert 2' was also the 'Aktivist' of 'Hommage à Stalin 2', and the other characters also remained the same. A link was also made between the '3 Huren' and the 'Heilige 3' of 'Die Heilige Familie': the actresses doubled those roles.[38] Elsewhere the same actor played many and various roles that had seemingly little to do with each other: Manfred Zapatka was both the positive 'Mann' of 'Die Straße 1' and the imprisoned 'Kommunist', as well as Clown 1, Volker and Goebbels. Several other actors covered a similarly disparate set of characters. There were also peculiar divergences from both the above procedures: Edwin Noël, who staunchly followed the 'Junger Maurer' from 'Die Straße 1' where he was only the 'Junger Mann' to the final scene, lost his consistently positive function by playing Gernot. Peter Lühr, however, *only* played Hilse, despite the fact that he first appears in the sixth scene.

The casting of plays of this sort involves a play-off between meanings that are generated by doubling and the economics of financing a large cast. We are not to know which of the two took precedence. Did Noël play Gernot because the 'Junger Maurer' is not altogether positive (he does join the strike out of curiosity), or was there a gap in 'Hommage à Stalin 1' that

36   Some productions also include actors for the lion and the dog in 'Brandenburg-isches Konzert 1', others use more than one voice for 'Die Brüder 1' and 'Tod in Berlin 1'. Other possibilities have also affected the number of roles.

37   The Wuppertal production (Wuppertaler Bühnen, première 2 December 1989) made use of a mere nine actors. As the date of the première implies, the production was rushed onto the stage in order to follow the dramatic events of 9 November. After a rehearsal period of a humbling two weeks, the play was staged in the foyer of the Elberfelder Schauspielhaus due to the lack of a free stage anywhere else. The casting here, as opposed to the other productions to be discussed later, emphasized a cabaret flavour because of the meagre size of the ensemble. Their aim was to turn the play into a 'Deutschland-Revue' and thus the highly differing roles taken by the actors had a knock-on effect on genre too.

38   This analogy was also made in the casting of both the Berliner Ensemble and the Bochum productions.

needed filling? Does Lühr keep Hilse untainted for artistic reasons, or were the other roles already taken by the rest of the ensemble? Reading meaning into Wendt's casting (or indeed any of the other director's choices) is problematic.[39] There is little doubt that Müller was conscious of this at the writing stage: it is impossible to ignore a cast of such proportions. For this reason one may make the following deduction: the confusions that an interpretation of the casting entails is in fact a dramatic device. The potential for the recurrence of certain faces ensures that the continuities between 'Vorgeschichte' and the present day cannot be ignored, that a character that would be fighting for the Spartacists one day would be fighting the Huns the next. Perhaps Hilse does retain his single-mindedness in Munich because he is played by just one actor,[40] yet it is impossible to say this for sure. Another corollary of the large cast and the subsequent role-doubling is the avoidance of any hint of star billing. Müller's presentation of his historical subject matter refuses to privilege one particular figure and thus there is also no concentration on one or two leading actors. The production spreads out the larger parts and forces the cast to act as an ensemble. The audience loses the focal points that star actors provide and has to come to terms with a mass rather than individuals.

Let us now take a closer look at the 'Uraufführung'. The production featured the insertion of an extra scene, one familiar to Wendt: 'Kleinbürgerhochzeit', the third scene of *Die Schlacht*. It became the first scene of the second half and thus preceded 'Das Arbeiterdenkmal'. The scene provided a bridge of sorts because it chronologically followed the death of Hitler (whose last hours in the 'Führerbunker' were charted in 'Die Heilige Familie' just before the interval) and highlighted the petit-bourgeois attitudes that were to follow it. Apart from this there were no other additions. The prompter's script also reveals that cuts to dialogue were minimal.[41] The

39　The style of the production also matters here. If there is extensive use of masks or make-up it may not be apparent that one actor has taken several parts. This is intensified if the actor is allowed to play in very diverse ways.

40　In all other productions I have researched, the Hilse actor plays at least one other role. It is interesting to note that in Wuppertal, Bochum and at the Berliner Ensemble he also plays the positive revolutionary 'Alter mit Kind' in 'Straße 2'. The link is clearly there but we should not forget that in Wuppertal the same actor also played Gunther, in Bochum Hagen, Herr 2 (in 'Die Straße 2') and Germania, and at the BE Clown 1, Gunther and the Nazi.

41　*Heiner Müllers 'Germania Tod in Berlin'*, prompter's script of the Kammerspiele production, Munich, 20-4-78.

only one of note was the removal of the sequence in 'Die Heilige Familie' from where Goebbels lets off his violent fart (G p. 62) to Germania's announcement that the real birth is imminent (G p. 63).[42]

Before the action even began, the audience was confronted with the Poe paraphrase of the early text collection 'ABC', 'DER TERROR VON DEM ICH SCHREIBE KOMMT AUS DEUTSCHLAND' (G p. 8), which was emblazoned on the stage curtain in blood red. The set was vast and open with a fairly large sand pit in the middle. The pit sometimes enclosed the action (for 'Die Straße 2', the beginning of 'Hommage à Stalin 1', the hospital bed in 'Tod in Berlin 2'). For the 'Brandenburgisches Konzert' scenes, the sand was strewn all over the stage and remained there until the interval. Other necessary stage-props were employed when required. For example, a buffet for 'Brandenburgisches Konzert 1', a host of coffins for 'Hommage à Stalin 1', and tables and a bar for 'Hommage à Stalin 2' all graced the stage for the duration of their respective scenes. The only major scene change occurred for 'Die Heilige Familie'. Here the implied building sites, formal receptions and streets made way for a purpose-built setting. The scene evoked a grotesque nativity in keeping with the scene's title. The centrepiece was a typical petit-bourgeois home. The cut-out shape of a house was embellished with a sampler with a motto about 'das traute Heim'. Hitler 'entered' by emerging from a coffin and put on the record player which relayed news of his suicide. Germania later arrived in a Volkswagen Beetle whose bonnet opened at the time of the birth to reveal a red interior and the thalidomide wolf. The guard of honour were Bavarians in traditional costume and the 'Heilige 3' entered in the trenchcoats of the three Western allies. The scene concluded in a tableau: Goebbels stood triumphant on top of the Beetle stage left, the allies in their 'three wise monkeys' pose were downstage right, and Hitler and the Bavarians surrounded the embattled Germania centre-stage with Nazi salutes and beer glasses. The cocktail of contemporary German industrial society, Bavarian folklore, Christianity and Nazism confronted the audience with a powerful series of images which went to the very heart of its regional identity. The Bacchanalian tableau compounded its component parts by demonstrating the mesmerizing allure of the constellation.

The differences between the 'Vorgeschichte' and GDR scenes were pronounced. 'Die Straße 1' used real children, without masks or other

---

42   The reasons for the deletion are unclear, although it is unlikely that it was for reasons of good taste: the masturbation antics of 'Hommage à Stalin 1' were retained.

180

devices, and contrasted them with the larger-than-life figures of the 'Bäcker' and the 'Schildverteiler'. 'Brandenburgisches Konzert 1' also played off the 'real' and the exaggerated by retaining traditional circus costumes (for the Ring Master too) and then contrasting them with the imaginary world of Friedrich and the 'Müller von Potsdam'. 'Hommage à Stalin 1' provided an excellent prelude to 'Die Heilige Familie' by moving from grotesque horror to farce. The scene opened with the three soldiers, mutilated as instructed, sitting in the sandpit. The rest of the stage was littered with coffins. By the time the Nibelungen arrived, the coffins had been filled with their remains. The Nibelungen changed the tone of the scene. They entered in a mixture of ancient and modern dress. They wore the helmets and armour of the mythical figures, yet Hagen also wore a cool pair of late-fifties sun-glasses and the masturbation sequence was carried out by rubbing large plastic penises. The characterization emphasized a 'modern' reading and corresponded to the behaviour of beery louts for the most part. Again, the manifestation of the mythical in a contemporary setting confronted the audience with the legacy of the Nibelung mentality. Their brash appeal and 'laddish' demeanour invited identification in order to challenge the audience. A 'novelty' was presented in 'Die Brüder 1': a film of Müller reading the text was projected onto a screen for the audience. This was in contrast to 'Nachtstück' and 'Tod in Berlin 1' which were read and played through the theatre's speakers by ensemble members Christiane Hammacher and Edwin Noël respectively. The refusal to stage the three scenes squarely transferred the role of interpreter to the audience. There was no visual correlative. That Müller was only available on screen rather than in the theatre may have been construed as a critique of the GDR.

The GDR scenes, on the other hand, were considerably less stylized and contained little of the grotesque that we have seen previously. All costumes in the scenes were realistic or historically accurate (including the Friedrich vampire who emerged from beneath the buffet for his entry). The blocking sometimes led to interesting spatial positions on the stage. As already noted, 'Die Straße 2' took place, if one, of course, ignores entries and exits, exclusively in the sandpit. The cramped space communicated physical restriction and the potential for a siege mentality in the GDR. Movement became quite constrained in the small area of the pit. 'Die Brüder 2' also evoked setting without an elaborate set. A couple of chairs and a large spotlight defined the cell. The sense of spatial restriction echoed the situation of 'Die Straße 2'. The final scene, 'Tod in Berlin 2', was the one that was generally reckoned to have been the weakest. Heinz Beckmann, a critic who typified the reaction to the scene, called it 'sentimental'.[43] That 'Hure 1', now 'Mädchen', had her hair styled as Rosa Luxemburg's did not help to relativize Hilse's delirious speech.[44]

It is hard to see that the montage technique at work in the play had particularly provoked the director and his team. There was a clear differentiation between the two types of scenes. Stylistically, Wendt was able to highlight the wilful disruption of continuity by playing off an idea of life in the GDR with monstrous grotesques. The recurrences of certain actors, which manufactured additional links, did little more, however, than underline the basic *idea* informing the play, that events keep recurring in German history.

Müller reports that he once chatted to Wendt about the production. He told the director that he thought the GDR scenes simply were not 'inszeniert'. Wendt agreed and said that such a task was beyond him. The refusal to engage in a dialogue with the play in full (which Müller had later excused, possibly in deference to the dead man, as 'nobel')[45] would seem to say more about Wendt than the play. The one-sided treatment of *Germania* displayed a reverence from the left-wing director which produced a more simplistic reading of the text. The contrast of the 'good' and the 'bad' made exemplary the positive characters of the GDR scenes without formulating the contradictions implicit in them. Wendt reinforced a sense of coherence in the GDR scenes which ran counter to the diversity found in them in section one of this discussion.

The response of the press was mixed. Some strong voices in favour of the provocative play contrasted with moral outrage and the belief that Wendt was merely providing an alibi for the SED. We must naturally note where the 'Uraufführung' took place. Wendt was, after all, working in the

43   Heinz Beckmann, 'Germania-Ragout', *Rheinischer Merkur/Christ und Welt*, 28-4-78.

44   The pathos of the death and the sententious nature of the closing texts have raised the hackles of critics of all the major productions. The ending can, of course, be read as a prophetic vision. It would seem that this style of 'message-mongering' is at odds with the vicissitudes of the contemporary political scene. Before the fall of the Wall, the GDR was under Stalinist rule. The unproblematic affirmation of a general Marxism was thus considered naïve. The lack of irony often associated with the presentation of the final scene also resists the tone of the rest of *Germania*. The scene becomes one-dimensional. The provocations of the play become compromised by such an ending.

45   Knut Hickethier (ed.), *Heiner Müller Inszenieren. Unterhaltung im Theater* (Berlin: Die Dramaturgische Gesellschaft, 1987), p. 22 and ibid.

182

heartland of the CSU. The right-wing faction, as the governing party of Bavaria, was the main subsidizer of the Kammerspiele. There was thus a loud outcry from certain quarters to Wendt's 'defence' of the GDR through a realistic, understated or uncritical treatment of the relevant scenes. The play became a justification of sorts for the GDR (although not the SED). What was undisputed, however, was the variety of the scenes and the forms employed to create this. The word 'Revue' occurred in several of the pieces[46] and the way in which the production attempted to resist a reductive interpretation precisely because of this is revealing. Rudolf Krämer-Badoni, one of the more disapproving critics, could not deny that more than a simple piece of propaganda was being presented: 'wir haben also ein waschechtes kommunistisches Stück vor uns, eine Art kulinarischen Agitprop, wenn auch kannibalisch-kulinarisch'.[47] Here we see how the grotesque elements both combatted and modified a one-dimensional reception of the play. Similarly, Beckmann, despite his disgust for the play, which he called 'eine Müllschütte voller verbissener Einfälle', could not deny the 'Seitenhiebe auch gegen den ersten "Arbeiter-und-Bauern-Staat auf deutschem Boden"'. Criticism did attack the lack of pace in the second half. Peter von Becker described the process as a sobering-up: 'es darf überraschend viel gelacht werden in den ersten zwei Stunden dieser Aufführung. Dann wird man ernster - auf der Bühne wie im Parkett'.[48] Peter Iden called the second half 'fad-belehrend'.

The production in Bochum (première 8 October 1988) was staged by a director of the '68 generation, Frank-Patrick Steckel. There is little doubt that it followed in the footsteps of the Munich version, insofar as it presented the audience with a host of forms that were applied to the different

46   Klaus Colberg, 'Deutschland - eine Dauerkarambolage', *Westdeutsche Allgemeine Zeitung*, 22-4-78; Karl Ude, 'Eine deutsch-deutsche Politrevue', *Süddeutsche Zeitung*, 20-4-78; Michael Dultz, 'Trauer um deutsche Utopien', *Die deutsche Bühne*, 6/78, p. 22; Peter Iden, 'Schrecken aus Deutschland', *Die Zeit*, 28-4-78; and Dietmar N. Schmidt, 'Brüder, zur Sonne? Zur Schlachtbank!', *Deutsches Allgemeines Sonntagsblatt*, 30-4-78.

47   Rudolf Krämer-Badoni, 'Wenn der Agitprop kannibalisch wird', *Die Welt*, 22-4-78.

48   Peter von Becker, 'Schlachthauspostille und Tanz der deutschen Vampire', *Süddeutsche Zeitung*, 22/23-4-78.

scenes. Rehearsals lasted for ten weeks.[49] Initially each scene was examined for its own merits and experiments were undertaken to see which techniques best suited the differing texts. The distance in time to the historical events led to an aesthetic mode of distancing in performance. The idea was to create the provocative image of 'Lachen auf dem Leichenberg'. Some scenes therefore had to lose the sombre tone. For 'Die Brüder 2', for example, the actors were told in rehearsal to 'die ganze Szene durchlachen' in order to create a less reverent view of the prison scene.

Another aspect was that this was an FRG stage putting on a play essentially about the GDR. In an unpublished letter to the critic Andreas Rossmann, Steckel countered the critic's impression that the production was not altogether pro-GDR:

> Ich möchte gegenüber meinen Freunden in der DDR [...] nicht in den Verdacht geraten, mit Hilfe eines subventionierten westdeutschen Theaters die Ansichten derjenigen bekräftigen, die jede alternative Vorstellung von der Zukunft der Bundes-republik für von vorneherein aussichtslos und beliebig krimin-alisierbar halten.[50]

The implicit respect for the GDR was to find its expression not only in the GDR scenes. Groenewold told me that they felt that 'Die Heilige Familie', the only scene to deal with the FRG, had to show that the West could criticize itself too.

An additional element was an intertextual one. It is important to see this production in the context of Steckel's 'Deutschland-Trilogie' in Bochum. *Germania* was preceded by an abbreviated version of Hebbel's *Die Nibe-lungen* and Johannes R. Becher's *Winterschlacht*, the only play in the German repertoire to deal with Operation Barbarossa from the point of view of the Wehrmacht soldiers. Both productions featured as quotations in 'Hommage à Stalin 1': both the Nibelungen and the Stalingrad soldiers reappear in this radically different context. The figures presented echoes of the two productions whilst re-directing the theatrical images familiar to the Bochum audience. The comic element was played off against an atmosphere

49 This information and the subsequent quotations about the rehearsal process are taken from an unpublished interview with the dramaturge Gabriele Groenewold by the author, 15-11-94.

50 Frank-Patrick Steckel, unpublished letter to Andreas Rossman, 23-1-89 (held in the Schauspielhaus archive, Bochum).

184

of horror: the scene took place in the dark, only a UV light was on to pick out the infra-red contours of the actors.

The text showed few signs of tampering. The first scene of *Die Schlacht*, 'Die Nacht der Langen Messer', was worked into 'Die Brüder 2' at the point where the brothers recognize each other, and it occurred as if it were a part of the scene itself. The only deletion was to be found in 'Brandenburgisches Konzert 1': the lion (and, by extension, the Ring Master) made no appearance. Consequently, the class symbolism of the scene made way for a more focussed treatment of the clowns' attempts at aping the historical characters.

The stage area itself was defined by two red curtains that formed two arcs around the back of the semicircular playing area.[51] On the curtains, written in a white script fading from left to right, was the text of the *Manifest der Kommunistischen Partei*. One could no longer read the text by the end of the right-hand curtain. This formed the backdrop to most of the scenes. Various decorations and props were then added, as the individual scenes demanded.

The dichotomy between 'Vorgeschichte' and GDR scenes that was typical of the Munich production was lacking to a certain degree in Bochum. A greater degree of stylization determined both types of scene.

The GDR characters almost exclusively wore masks that covered the face down to just above the lip, as well as fairly uniform buff/grey suits or work clothes. The children in 'Die Straße 1' also wore the masks. The device clearly put up a barrier between the actors and the audience, but it also created problems. Groenewold saw the masking as 'Ehrlichkeit' on the part of the production: the depiction of the GDR had to remain faceless because of Bochum's politico-geographical position. They were dealing with people they respected but did not know, the East was an unknown category for them. However, as with theatrical signs in general, their lack of fixity leads to a variety of interpretations. Andreas Rossmann understood the masks as a sign of alienated human beings without an identity, 'Entmenschte'.[52] The only time that the GDR characters lost their masks was in 'Tod in Berlin 2'. This 'reckoning' remained maskless, which was perhaps surprising for a scene that overwhelms us with allegory and metaphor. Hilse emerged as a real character, with will and suffering, from the crowd. Its particular scenery

---

51   *Heiner Müllers 'Germania Tod in Berlin'*, video of the Schauspielhaus production, Bochum, 8-10-88, in-house copy.

52   Andreas Rossmann, 'Geschichte ohne Gesichter', *Frankfurter Allgemeine Zeitung*, 14-1-89.

was also rather tendentious: the Berlin Wall stood behind Hilse's bed, lending the scene a polemical tone. When the 'inspired' Hilse finished his monologue and the scene drew to an end, the Müller poem 'MANCHMAL WENN ICH MEINE PRIVILEGIEN GENIESSE' was read out over the PA (SF2 p. 202). This addition highlighted the precarious role of Müller the free-travelling East German author who was becoming more and more popular in the West.

Another running theme was the integration of a 'Death' figure played by a dancer, Agnes Moyses, dressed in a skeleton outfit wielding a scythe. The figure did not appear in every scene. During the first five weeks of the rehearsals she merely observed the process and looked for openings. In performance, Death opened the show, emerging from the gap between the curtains, playfully dancing a short routine. The first line of the play referred directly to the solo: 'das war der Krieg' (G p. 37). The figure was never threatening and always provided an ironic comment on the events. In 'Tod in Berlin 1', Death sat downstage left in a rocking chair, picked out by a single spotlight, happily knitting.

Stage devices also turned the 'real' into the theatrical. When the 'Maurer' of 'Brandenburgisches Konzert 2' said 'das ist der richtige Stuhl für meinen Hintern' (G p. 47), he actually had to climb onto a giant empire chair of four metres. His body shrank once seated and provided an interesting image of incongruity for the audience. The sympathetic treatment in Munich was replaced by a formulation of contradictions in Bochum. Similarly, the scene in the bar, 'Hommage à Stalin 2', proceeded quite conventionally, except for when Death both helped the Landlord serve the guests and also led the 'Huren' and 'Kleinbürger' to the door. The thanatic figure did not only live in the 'Vorgeschichte'.

An imaginative approach to the scenes was the keynote to this production. This was particularly evident in 'Die Brüder 1' and 'Nachtstück'. The former was read by two actors, each standing in one wing against the backdrop of Goya's 'Duel with Clubs'.[53] They tried to read the text together but only partially succeeded as they kept diverging and then regained their synchronization. 'Nachtstück' was, however, a coup-de-Müller-théâtre. To my

---

53 This picture is nowadays something of a Müller cliché. He makes mention of his interest in Goya in the interview 'Fünf Minuten Schwarzfilm' (*Gesammelte Irrtümer 2*, p. 143) and in *Krieg ohne Schlacht* (p. 271, p. 289 and p. 297). The picture was used as the poster for Müller's production of *Der Lohndrücker* at the Deutsches Theater (première 29 January 1988) and is to be seen in Storch's Müller compendium *Explosion of a Memory*, p. 135.

knowledge, the scene has never been realized in accordance with the stage directions and has almost always been read aloud.[54] Bochum managed to realize it with the aid of a choreographer from outside the theatre. The result was breathtaking. The text was followed (almost) to the letter. The body of the dancer Frank Frey slowly lost its limbs. Standing in a trap door and with his arms behind him, picked out by a single spotlight, two arrows coated in black paint slowly approached and covered his eyes. When they withdrew, all that they left were black holes. The cry that finished the routine was augmented with a high-pitched electronic wail. The scene received all-round praise in the press with words such as 'eindrucksvoll' and 'unerhört' (in a positive sense), it was greeted as an 'Ereignis'.[55]

On the whole, one could say that the production was more lavish than the Munich 'Uraufführung'. The greater diversity in terms of set design and form gave the impression that the play had had more time to mature and that the ideas that shocked both the audiences and the critics in 1978 had had more chance to develop. The treatment of the GDR was also more polemical. Contradictions which were overlooked in Munich became more exaggerated in Bochum. Perhaps this was because the director believed that he was acting with a theatrical 'reverence' towards the 'other Germany'.

The understanding of continuities in German history was more pronounced in Bochum than in Munich. The integration of the Death figure created several bridges between past and present. However, the employment of this repeated motif merely signalled a theme which was part of the play's title. On the other hand, the commitment to variety within the production ensured that the inscribed differences of the scenes was emphasized more strongly. By dealing with each scene individually in rehearsal, Steckel presented the audience with a more fragmented whole. Again, unfortunately, the montage structure failed to open up the drama to a radical new reading. In both Munich and Bochum the directors interpreted the text, not a set of dramaturgical enigmas as in *Die Hamletmaschine*, as directors usually do. They found interesting solutions to the problems of the various scenes. As we have already seen, such problems were implicit to the shocking contrasts in the structure anyway.

54 In the programme of the Wuppertal production, Gerold Theobald attempted to justify the substitution of this scene with Benjamin's text on Klee's 'Angelus Novus' by saying that he considered 'Nachtstück''undurchführbar'.

55 Duglore Pizzini, 'Ein blutiger Comic-Strip', *Die Presse*, 31-5-90; Rossmann; and Bernd Berke, 'Manege frei für die blutige Geschichte der Deutschen', *Westfälische Rundschau*, 10-10-88.

Reviews were mainly positive, as opposed to the mixed bag in Munich, and tended to praise both the variety and the artistic integrity of the staging. The production also seemed to have been very popular with the audience.

The GDR 'Erstaufführung' at the Berliner Ensemble in East Berlin (première 20 January 1989) bore very little comparison with the two Western productions discussed above. The play had been criticized for ideological reasons by the deputy Minister for Culture, Klaus Höpcke.[56] Fritz Marquardt was the director who carried the double burden of bringing *Germania* to the East German stage. On the one hand, he had the reputation of a successful Müller 'pioneer' in East Berlin: he was the first to put on *Die Bauern* and *Der Bau* (both at the Volksbühne, premières 30 May 1976 and 3 September 1980, respectively). On the other hand, he had the weight of an eighteen-year-old play on his shoulders, which, unlike the two plays mentioned above, had already been given airings in the West. Marquardt acknowledged this in rehearsal by comparing the 'provokativ' nature of the 1971 text to its 1989 status as a 'Klassik'.[57] The expectations were enormous.

The production was marked by flatness and a very measured delivery that tended towards neutral, cold tones. The set was, once again, in the style of an arena, a circus ring.[58] Very little decoration adorned it while the various scenes came and went. Whereas the Steckel production dealt with the 'Vorgeschichte' and GDR scenes with equal stylization and verve, Marquardt treated both types of scenes with similar asceticism. The imperative not to identify with the characters made the play function as a lifeless

56 Although it was criticized, it was not formally banned. In the wake of the fifties and sixties, banning was seen as a last resort due to the political embarrassment of one day having to lift the ban. That a prominent SED functionary had criticized the play was enough to signal its undesirability. The ban was thus implicit. (Unpublished interview with Wolfgang Schuch, head of the Henschel Verlag, by the author, 30-3-95). Höpcke was against the association of Rosa Luxemburg and a prostitute, and the wholesale notion of a homage to Stalin, however complex the scenes might have been (Barnett, "'Ich erfinde gerne Zitate'", pp. 10-11). Müller's feelings on the subject were that it was also just not possible to show a Communist in a GDR prison (*Krieg ohne Schlacht*, p. 255).

57 Torsten Isreal, *Notate zum Proben und zum Probeprozeß* (unpublished documentation held in the archive of the Berliner Ensemble, undated), entry for 9 September.

58 *Heiner Müllers 'Germania Tod in Berlin'*, video of the Berliner Ensemble production, East Berlin, 20-1-89, in-house copy.

corpse. If we compare 'Die Brüder 2' and 'Hommage à Stalin 1' we see how the approach worked. The prison, as in Munich and Bochum beforehand, was defined by a large spotlight shone onto the darkness of the rest of the stage. The lines were delivered in the neutral style outlined above. Movement was slight, if at all. A similar voice interjected with the stage directions through the PA. Comments such as '*Schweigen*' (G p. 69) and '*der Kommunist will den Brückensprenger niederschlagen*' (G p. 70) received the same treatment as '*Volkslärm wird leiser und entfernt sich schnell. Geräusch von Panzern. Klopfchor aus*' (G p. 74). The style clearly refused to allow the audience any kind of proximity to the characters by describing in words actions that could easily have been shown by the actors in question. 'Hommage à Stalin 1', identified earlier as a scene which mixes the horror of war with the exaggerated loutishness of the Nibelungen, was similarly drawn. The stage directions were followed for the most part in the Stalingrad section. Mutilated soldiers did their worst on their young comrade as they enticed him to their trap-door bunkers in the stage's thrust. To the sounds of Wagner, the stage was filled with corpses. The Nibelungen then arrived and the stage became very dark, partly so that short sequences from Fritz Lang's *Die Nibelungen* could intermittently be shown.[59] Their neutral deliveries were by now par for the course. However, precisely when the text calls for the destruction of Gernot ('*die drei Nibelungen schlagen in einem längeren Kampf den vierten in Stücke*', G p. 50) the loudspeaker took over and continued until the end of the scene in total darkness.

There were a couple of places where the text offered some resistance to the dry approach. Some of Hitler's rants occasionally bristled with emotive rage and the comic play of level in 'Brandenburgisches Konzert 1' also managed at times to free itself from the neutral tone that nonetheless held sway. In this context, the non-dramatic scenes lost the flatness perceived by critics of the Munich production. In fact, they actually showed more life than some of the others. 'Die Brüder 1' featured the three 'Huren'. The reading was totally garbled, each voice struggled for primacy - only in the last few lines was a harmony reached. This was followed by a short sword-fight between two of them. The swords were wooden and instead of

---

59   The inclusion of Wagner and Lang drew the audience to the role of German culture in the rise of fascism. Wagner has long been demonized as Hitler's favourite composer. Lang was also a contentious artist. His *Die Nibelungen* had been banned in certain countries after the Second World War as a proclamation of militant German nationalism. Both intertexts were not judged on stage. Their incorporation into the evening did pose unanswered questions to the audience.

helmets, paper hats were worn. The use of the whores and the representation of a fight between children relativized the scene. The female actors debunked the male 'glory' of the struggle whilst conferring a cash nexus to the proceedings in their roles as prostitutes. 'Tod in Berlin 1' was read by Marquardt over the PA while five women stood in the form of an inverted 'V' and held up spherical lights against the darkness of the stage. The ornate shape gave the text a visual solidity and the lights lent the lines a utopian moment. 'Nachtstück' was a consciously read scene: downstage right sat Renate Ziemer, formerly Müller's personal assistant, alone in an armchair fixed in a spotlight. She read the text silently as Müller's recorded voice ploughed through the text. The audience was being directed to follow Ziemer, and to concentrate on the text.

The finale, so often criticized in previous productions, held, not surprisingly, the same tone as in the scenes that preceded it. Here, however, Marquardt broke from the stage directions: the last lines of the 'Mädchen' were not prompted by her beau. This token of her unknowing role detracted from the potential staginess of the final scene. Her knowledge conveyed a less problematic sense to the ending and emphasized the much-criticized sententiousness of the scene. The couple then left the stage and the Berliner Ensemble's revolving stage was employed for the only time in the evening. Hilse's death bed spun round a few times to reveal the famous picture of the dead and rotting Rosa Luxemburg.

The circular movement and the image of a dead revolutionary suggested stagnation. Perhaps this was also the wilful aim of the dry acting style. The acted scenes displayed such little innovation and such precise and mechanical delivery that the motif of deadlock was hard to avoid. There was no drive to productivity, and it seemed that Marquardt's theatre was one that diagnosed the problem without offering any hint of treatment. The lack of a visceral dimension turned the play into what was perceived as a didactic theatre. The cold analysis was unable to encompass the various strains that run through the text. Consequently, the production became surprisingly coherent. Disparity was reduced by an imposed dryness throughout. The production portrayed German history as a monotonous set of scenes which had so much in common with each other that it was not worth commenting on them.

The reaction to the play was almost universally one of disappointment. Perhaps the most telling comment on both Marquardt's ideas and their reception was made by Müller:

Bei der Inszenierung am Berliner Ensemble [...] hat Marquardt auf die kabarettistische Dimension bewußt verzichtet, gegen die Erwartungen. [...] Marquardts Inszenierung war eine Verweigerung. Aber er war tief erschrocken, als Höpcke sagte, er würde gar nicht mehr verstehen, daß er das Stück damals verboten hat.[60]

The lack of audience reaction was observed by Peter Nöldechen: 'es gab darauf keine erkennbaren Reaktionen, kein Pro oder Kontra, nicht einmal beim dünnen Beifall. Man las das, nahm das Spiel zur Kenntnis und ging nach Hause'.[61] The title of his review also reveals his feelings towards the general style of the production. Jürgen Beckelmann judged it 'partiell etwa gar stalinistisch'.[62] Martin Linzer was one of the few reviewers to find a positive comment: 'der Verzicht auf jegliche "Originalität" hat seinen Preis, der seine Tugend auch ist: der Zuschauer wird zum Hörer gezwungen, zur Konzentration auf den Text.' The evaluation was that this was a 'Geschichtslektion im besten Sinne'.[63] Only one other critic saw the style as aesthetically elevating. Gerhard Ebert, whose opinion could well have been partly determined by the paper he was writing for, commented on Hilse as 'ein unscheinbarer Held, ein Held dennoch von antiker Größe'.[64] Too often, however, the production was reproached for its didactic impulse, which was summed up by Henning Rischbieter in the title of the Berlin section of his review: 'Ost-Berliner Defensive: eine Sprechoper in alter BE-Manier'.[65]

The status of *Germania* as a 'history play' seems to be exemplified by some of its performance dates. Wendt exploited the link with fascism when he opened the Munich production on Hitler's birthday, Holk Freytag saw it as *the* play to put on in Wuppertal when the Wall eventually fell, and B. K.

60   Müller, *Krieg ohne Schlacht*, p. 256.

61   Peter Nöldechen, 'Brisantes über 17. Juni als trockenes Lehrstück', *Westfälische Rundschau*, 25-1-89.

62   Jürgen Beckelmann, 'Lieber kaltes Kotelett als Kaviar', *General-Anzeiger*, 7-2-89.

63   Martin Linzer, 'Geschichtslektion?', *Theater der Zeit*, 4/89, p. 23.

64   Gerhard Ebert, 'Szenen, die zu einem Panorama deutscher Geschichte werden', *Neues Deutschland*, 26-1-89.

65   Henning Rischbieter, 'Zu spät? Zu spät!', *Theater heute*, 3/89, p. 29.

Tragelehn chose to première his version at the Theater der Freien Volks-bühne in West Berlin but three days before the GDR ceased to exist. The opening date, 30 September 1990, preceded German reunification by a hair's breadth. The production may therefore be seen as Tragelehn's appraisal of the republic he lived in but, in its later years, could not work in.

As with the other productions, this one too used one fixed set which could then accommodate various props and decorations.[66] It took the form of two black walls which met at a point perpendicular to each other. In each wall there were two large rectangular entrances which gave the space before the walls a sense of an interior. The fourth entrance remained closed for the majority of the play, but was opened for the final two scenes. The extra sense of space marked the 'Tod in Berlin' scenes as chances for a new start.

As with the set, Tragelehn was also economical with his theatrical means. He did not impress the audience with the variety of Bochum, yet he was also not as one-dimensional as Marquardt at the BE.

The first scene, 'Die Straße 1', began with a child holding a lantern. The only illumination was provided by this source. The action took its course and at the end the child put his hands over his eyes. The scene became a flashback of sorts. A remembrance was being re-enacted, some-thing which we associate more with Müller's work after 1976. The child was, however, unable to banish the bleak memories of the Spartacists' defeat: the laughter of the 'Bäcker' and the 'Schildverteiler' continued to echo in his ears although the scene itself had disappeared. History became a collectively personal trauma.

Most of the scenes that followed used a realistic style of acting that sharply contrasted with the neutral distancing effects of the BE. Stylization was not greatly employed but its economical use was effective. 'Die Heilige Familie', so often the comic extravaganza, showed signs of the cabaret flavour one associates with Munich or Bochum. Goebbels affected a camp demeanour and Hitler was given the freedom to play as the infantile paranoiac. The 'Heilige 3' were also permitted to deliver their lines in heavily accented English, French and American German. Similarly, the clown scene, 'Brandenburgisches Konzert 1', enjoyed the playful freedom offered by the text. Elsewhere, however, playfulness or mannerism was cut short in the name of 'realism'. The Nibelungen never really achieved the potential of their scene and the 'larger-than-life' figures of 'Die Straße 1' failed to take on a truly nightmarish quality.

66   *Heiner Müllers 'Germania Tod in Berlin'*, video of the Theater der Freien Volks-bühne production, West Berlin, 30-9-90, director's copy.

On the other hand, there were moments of subtlety that lent gentle comment to certain scenes. In 'Hommage à Stalin 1' the soldiers sat at the centre of the stage like a hedgehog ('in Igelstellung'), defending against all sides. The three outward-facing rifles formed the Mercedes star, giving a link between war and commerce. The clowns too had a symbolic yet discreet make-up scheme. Clown 2 wore the red nose and mouth of a traditional clown and Clown 1 had dark eyes set against an otherwise white face. The skull-like qualities of Friedrich were thus contrasted with the blood of his 'victim', the 'Müller von Potsdam'. The final scene also contained a quotation from the world of art. Hilse lay in a stretcher on wheels of the type that also featured in Joseph Beuys's 'Bahre' installation. The constructed link between potential pathos and the anarchic aesthetics of Beuys lent the scene a more ironic angle, although this allusion seems to have been lost on the reviewers.

Two of the non-dramatic scenes showed creative directorial intervention. 'Tod in Berlin 1' was sung by two women who did not appear elsewhere in the play. They sang to a composition of the play's musical director, Friedrich Goldmann, which had strains of Schoenberg running through it. The haunting serial melodies reacted very favourably with the text to produce many resonances that the conventional readings of the text did not. 'Nachtstück' was delivered by two actors, each alternating sections of text, from the back of the auditorium. The voices spoke the lines with realistic excitement as if they could see something on the totally dark stage that the audience could not. Tragelehn simulated experience and the audience was able to compare its impressions of the text with those of the actors. 'Die Brüder 1' was projected, unread, onto the curtain.

This none too colourful production had the manner of a requiem of sorts. It produced occasional glimmers of light, yet on the whole the acting took place somewhat slowly and the play as a whole lasted for two and a half hours. In an interview, Tragelehn said that he saw the piece as 'das schöne, traurige Volkslied der DDR' and this is an interpretation that very much characterized the torpid and slightly mournful style of the majority of the scenes.[67] One must note that this was the first production which was free of a controversial treatment of the GDR because the country was about to become history itself. There was no polemical strain either in favour of or against the GDR. The production was a reckoning and was only able to attempt a remembered assessment. Again, diversity was not really on offer.

---

67 Stefan Schnabel, 'Das schöne farbige Volkslied von der DDR', *Die Volkszeitung*, 28-9-90.

A dominant atmosphere of uneasy lament prevailed and reduced the incoherence of the different parts.

Critics were a little disappointed by the lack of pace and they realized that this was not to be the great crowd-puller that the Freie Volksbühne desperately needed to secure its subsidized future.[68] Roland H. Wiegenstein pointed to both the negative and the positive effects of the production: 'es läßt sich sehr langsam und überdeutlich spielen und deklamieren, das Grundtempo ist ein Largo, das an den Nerven zerrt', although this did produce a 'Höchstmaß an Intensität'. Other critics too swung between the discipline of the performance and its consequent effects. One reviewer who saw the weakening of the characterization as a tendency to harmlessness had to concede that it was also important not to get bogged down in a 'Hektik'.[69] Others bemoaned the lack of 'Brisanz'.[70] Only Sibylle Wirsing seems to have come close to Tragelehn's own formulation when she called it 'eine spektakuläre Trauerfeier'.[71]

IV   Incoherence as a Challenge to the Theatre?

Textual analysis reveals that the productivity of *Germania* is founded upon the associative relationships between the scenes. The non-linear view of history is suggested by various movements backwards and forwards in the text. Paired scenes and an episodic picture of the GDR present the reader or spectator with unusual combinations. The question we are faced with is whether the play has challenged the theatre practice that has transformed the text into performance.

In both Munich and Bochum, the existence of the GDR made productions highly polemical. The directors, Wendt and Steckel respectively, felt

68   After reunification, the theatre lost its state subsidy. Today it no longer exists. Its buildings now house the Musical-Theater-Berlin.

69   Roland H. Wiegenstein, 'Falsches Märchen und Trauermarsch', *Frankfurter Rundschau*, 5-10-90; and Rüdiger Schaper, 'Vom Sterben der Sozialisten', *Süddeutsche Zeitung*, 12-10-90.

70   Jürgen Beckelmann, 'Die Ausbeutung der Mitläufer', *Stuttgarter Zeitung*, 10-10-90; and Ingeborg Köhler, 'Heiner Müllers Rückblick auf deutsche Geschichte', *Welt am Sonntag*, 7-10-90.

71   Sibylle Wirsing, 'Von deutscher Revolution', *Frankfurter Allgemeine Zeitung*, 3-10-90.

obliged to bring their views and opinions on relations between East and West to their conceptions. Wendt applied a lopsided aesthetic to his production which stylized the 'Vorgeschichte' scenes whilst leaving those set in the GDR to a somewhat realist interpretation. Although the production produced much debate and interest in the press, we are nonetheless left with a traditional 'Theaterskandal'. A director decided to impose a provocative interpretation onto a piece of drama. Steckel, on the other hand, employed a more theatrical language throughout. All the same, the production became a polemic, just as in Munich, with a bias towards the GDR. In both cases, Western directors have felt it their 'duty' to present a picture of GDR which was influenced by a sense of guilt. They were restricted by the contemporary context.

The East German interpretation of Marquardt was another reaction to the GDR, although this time it came from within. The context was given by a cultural policy that had censured the performance of the text. Only through the intervention of Manfred Wekwerth, the BE 'Intendant' and former Brecht 'Meisterschüler', could the play be premièred. Marquardt chose to frustrate the audience and show how little it was possible to do with the text. He 'refused' to stage it as such and confronted the audience with a cultural artefact that made a mockery of paternalistic SED cultural policy. The only scenes which displayed any directorial verve were the non-dramatic ones. Tragelehn, the East German director active in the West, presented an obituary for the GDR. His production was a stock-taking of sorts. An assessment which no longer depended on the existence of the GDR was offered in the tone of a lament. Slow, mournful direction influenced the proceedings.

What linked the four productions was a defined position from each director. This is not meant as a criticism in any way of their respective stances. In each case the director worked within a context, just as anywhere else, which gave the productions shape. The point of criticism here lies more squarely with the play.

The schematic arrangement of the scenes points to a thematic purpose. We have seen that the motivating ideas of the play are easily understood. The incoherence implicit to the various scenes is made coherent by the structure. Consequently, directors have treated a potentially avant-garde text as a more conventional one. The jigsaw construction of the play has allowed various interpreters to make interesting and provocative comments on both the GDR and German history. One gets the impression, however, that it was not the play's montage dynamic which provided the potential for each production.

If literature is to resist the theatre, it can only do so by making the business of staging or even relating to the scenes problematic. In *Germania* the scenes presented little difficulty in themselves. Although many of the them, particularly the GDR scenes, present complex situations, such as 'Das Arbeiterdenkmal' or 'Die Brüder 2', the director has had little problem in staging them in a more orthodox manner. The only scene in the whole play which remains puzzling is the 'Nachtstück'. Its subject matter is elliptical and its positioning fails to yield a functional answer. It interferes with our cognitive faculties and wrenches itself away from the pairings that precede and follow it. We are left to speculate about both facets.

Incoherence of plot is a powerful device if the incoherence is truly difficult to understand. In the case of *Germania*, this is not the case. The reasons for the montage in *Germania* have become self-evident. We are able to explain away the arrangement with ease. As a result, the cognitive problem of receiving the text in performance is greatly reduced. Here the blame lies with the play itself. Like many 'shocking' plays, its initial power was diminished by the logic that supported the structure. Once the play entered the repertoire of the theatre and consciousness of the theatre-going public, its shock was soon forgotten.

Incoherence, discontinuity and a montage technique are not necessarily outdated devices which are no longer able to challenge the theatre. Yet they do become undemanding if they serve a transparent thematic purpose. I shall continue to investigate these categories in the following sections in order to understand just how disparate a play's form and/or content must be in order to function productively on the modern stage.

3   *Leben Gundlings Friedrich von Preußen Lessings Schlaf Traum Schrei*

I   Prussia Then and Now

It is almost impossible to read secondary literature on *Leben Gundlings* without coming across the word 'triptych'. The division is seen to run along the lines of the tripartite title. If one views the structure in this way, one could reach the somewhat speculative conclusion of Axel Schalk who sees the fifth (and thus mathematically central) scene, 'Lieber Gott mach mich fromm / Weil ich aus der Hölle komm', as the most important 'in Müllers streng komponiertem Stück'.[72] Ernst Grohotolsky is more prepared to admit

---

72   Axel Schalk, *Geschichtsmaschinen* (Heidelberg: Karl Winter, 1989), p. 190.

an extra dimension: in his eyes the play can be read as a symmetrical nine scene construction, but he is quick to point out that the trio of 'Preußische Spiele' scenes and the same formation in the 'Lessing' section can undermine this neat ordering.[73] We clearly have an organizational problem here that requires careful attention. If we take a look at the order of the scenes, we see that in *Leben Gundlings* we are dealing with a very different idea of montage than in *Germania*.

The very first scene, deemed by the followers of the triptych theory to be the first section of a neat three-way structure, presents compositional ambivalence. The title, 'Leben Gundlings', is itself a provocation: Gundling's 'life' is depicted in a mere three and a half pages. What we actually see is his elevation to the office of President and the simultaneous humiliation that this entails in Friedrich Wilhelm's Prussia. However, another character who is also present is the young Friedrich, and so there is no reason to postpone the 'Friedrich von Preußen' section of texts to the next scenes. The first scene can therefore be viewed as coming under the lengthy banner 'Leben Gundlings Friedrich von Preußen'. There can be little doubt that a strong link exists between the breaking of the two characters.

The following trio, 'Preußische Spiele', marks a transition in the play that is reflected in the treatment of Friedrich. The first scene restricts itself to the personal realm and deals with the nascent desires of the young prince and his relationship to his father (who is symbolically murdered at its conclusion). The second signals the destruction of the character created in the two previous scenes when the State actively intervenes in the prince's private life in the form of Friedrich Wilhelm (who is very much alive). The third scene shifts the context away from Friedrich as a psychological character. Friedrich is now the King of Prussia. His misanthropy opens the scene in the form of a direct quotation, his only personal goal is uttered in the line 'ich wollte, ich wäre mein Vater' (H p. 16). The movement away from the personal is parallel to his accession to power.

The scenes that follow broaden the context too. 'Die Schule der Nation' puts Prussia into a European context. The imperial ambitions of England and France are compared with Prussia's colonization of its own people.[74] 'Herzkönig Schwarze Witwe' is both an object lesson in political

---

73   Ernst Grohotolsky, *Ästhetik der Negation - Tendenzen des deutschen Gegenwartsdramas* (Königstein: Anton Hain Meisenheim, 1984), pp. 116-17.

74   Frank-Michael Raddatz, *Dämonen unterm Roten Stern* (Stuttgart: Metzler, 1991), p. 116.

rhetoric and a distilled representation of the animosity between Prussia and Saxony.[75] 'Lieber Gott' extends the interest in Prussia beyond the person of Friedrich into a madhouse. A mixture of cruelty and reason is applied to the bodies of the patients, which calls into question the values of Prussian society. 'Die Inspektion' shows the interaction of ruler, intellectuals, artists and peasants. Oppression and subservience go hand in hand. 'Friedrich der Große' presents Friedrich's legacy: a bureaucratic system overflowing with paper.

These scenes are not of the type we have previously experienced in *Germania*. They do not play off epochs against each other, rather they complement each other in order to create a broad set of experiences that Müller roots in the Prussia of Frederick the Great. Disparate historical material merges to form a whole: the scene is continually changing, whilst certain values and themes remain constant. Arlene Teraoka's summation of these scenes as giving Friedrich's life 'in detail' is clearly too reductive a reading.[76] Our interest in the King's character is replaced by interest in his influence on the character of the State. Here chronology is an important way of creating coherence. However, as in *Die Schlacht*, it is a chronology defined by its borders. There is a beginning (the accession to the throne) and an end (death in Sanssouci), what comes in-between is only guaranteed by the frame. Thus it is not of great importance which war Friedrich is fighting in 'Die Schule der Nation' and one must not pay particular attention to the date of the inspection in the later scene. The scene in the madhouse also enriches the texture of our perceptions of Prussia without especially disturbing the collage.[77] These temporal vagaries, as we shall see later, also give directors more space to make the scenes more topical.

One detail, however, which disrupts the blurred edges of Prussia, is to be found in the short note which precedes the text: 'nach dem Irrenhaus-Bild können Schauspieler in einem improvisierten Schäferspiel eine bessere Welt entwerfen' (H p. 9). To my knowledge, no director has taken Müller

75   Schalk, p. 188.

76   Arlene Akiko Teraoka, *The Silence of Entropy or Universal Discourse* (Frankfurt/Main: 1985, Peter Lang), p. 55.

77   Collage is the term that I have chosen to contrast with montage. Within the specific context of this chapter, I see collage as a method by which disparate elements create a unifying picture, whereas montage suggests a jaggedness that resists reconciliation. Unfortunately, critics have interpreted the two terms in this and the opposite way. The failure to agree on definitions has forced me to impose them myself.

up on this cheeky suggestion.[78] Yet this is not to be read altogether as a short-coming on their part: this one-liner is not only provocative, it also introduces a utopian element which may not even be conceivable on the contemporary stage.[79] Its position is nonetheless of great interest to our investigation of structural coherence. It contrasts well with both what precedes and what succeeds it. After the madhouse scene, one is forced to question the category of the insane. The consequent 'insanity' of a proposed better world is therefore also modified. The scene that follows, the ironic setting of which is Arcadia, compounds yet another facet to this utopian scene, because heaven on Earth is revealed as no less than rural Prussia. So far, the 'Schäferspiel' is the only element that disrupts the panorama of the Prussian state.

The scene that follows 'Friedrich der Große' is also problematic for the view of the play as a triptych. 'Heinrich von Kleist spielt Michael Kohlhaas' takes place after Friedrich's death. It is therefore difficult to put this under the 'Friedrich von Preußen' banner. At the same time it precedes the Lessing scenes, disqualifying it from 'Lessings Schlaf Traum Schrei'. Kleist cannot be appropriated fully by either of the two; he becomes a buffer of sorts. On the one hand, we see the oppressive reason of the Prussian state in Kleist's suicide. He is unable to live under such a regime. On the other, the progressive aspirations of Lessing can be seen in the aggression of the Kleist figure on stage. The position of the scene wrenches it from two possible contexts and presents us with the first true montage element of the play.

The trio of Lessing scenes fail to offer any continuity in characters brought over from the previous scenes. The three short episodes show, as the title suggests, 'Schlaf', 'Traum' and 'Schrei' respectively. Müller, however, suggests that the three scenes should not be played linearly:

> Die Teile des Lessing-Triptychons sollten nach Möglichkeit nicht auf einem Schauplatz nacheinander, sondern überlappend aufgebaut werden: während der Schauspieler zu Lessing geschminkt wird, wird der Autofriedhof aufgebaut; während Emilia Galottis und Nathans Rezitation schütten die Bühnenarbeiter

---

78   There also seems to be little interest in this in the secondary literature: only Grohotolsky (p. 117 and p. 120) makes *any* reference to it.

79   A reference to the note's existence in production (for example, the note could be spoken via the PA) and the present inability to fulfil it would be interesting.

(Theaterbesucher) über dem Spartacus-Torso den Sandhaufen auf.

(H p. 9)

The Lessing section is thus differentiated from the Friedrich section in its dramatic conception. The flowing patchwork of our perceptions of Prussia is contrasted with a simultaneous confrontation with Lessing. Wolfgang Emmerich deduces that, if Müller's suggestion is taken on board, the play in fact has three endings.[80] The refusal even to begin and end the section within the traditional scheme contrasts with the loose chronology that preceded it. Lessing is dramaturgically set apart and consequently we see his positive and negative qualities side by side.

In terms of montage, the Lessing section functions in two ways. On a micro level, three views of Lessing are placed in an order that refuses to privilege any individual part. Unlike the vocal harmonies and the sheer acoustic incomprehensibility of operatic duets, trios or larger groupings, the Lessing triptych merely concentrates on speech in the first part. The recitations of Emilia and Nathan have more an iconic than semantic value for the audience. The discrete elements of the three scenes retain their demarcated intelligibility whilst combining to form a single vision of Lessing, his work and his reception within a context that explodes time through anachronism. The three parts are montage elements by virtue of the radical differences in both time and space between them. Their point of reference is naturally the figure of Lessing. Through this montage arrangement, we are perhaps not struck so much by the manufacture of associations as by the shock that arises in the tension between the three components and it is this shock that redefines the familiar, 'classical' Lessing.

On the macro level, the Lessing section liberates the Prussia collage from just remaining an episodic account. As a whole, the Lessing section becomes the third element (possibly the fourth if we are to grant 'Leben Gundlings' its independence) within the structure as a whole. Three (four) possibilities of realizing Enlightenment ideals are presented to the audience. The elements are distinct and are only linked by that common theme. Even a negative view of Prussia is relativized by the mobilization of the elements: positive moments are still to be located within the historical parameters. Lessing, after all, was a representative of the German Enlightenment and Kleist, depicted with such ambivalence, was a Prussian officer.

---

80   Wolfgang Emmerich, 'Der Alp der Geschichte. "Preußen" in Heiner Müllers *Gundling*', in Paul Gerhard Klussmann and Heinrich Mohr (eds.), *Jahrbuch zur Literatur in der DDR*, vol 2 (Bonn: Bouvier, 1982), p. 151, footnote.

Müller does not stop there, though. In the first part of the note to the text, he suggests a tactical doubling of roles:

> Friedrich II kann von einer Frau dargestellt werden oder als Prinz von einem (jungen) Mann, als König von einer Frau. Im zweiten Fall stellt der Darsteller des Prinzen Friedrich auch den Kleist in der Pantomime dar. Gundling, Psychiater, Schiller, Lessing 1 (Schauspieler, der zu Lessing geschminkt wird) und Lessing 2 (Lessing in Amerika) vom gleichen Darsteller, Lessing 3 (Apotheose) vom Darsteller des Prinzen Friedrich und Kleists.
>
> (H ibid.)

Here a link is clearly made between certain characters. Those who compromise their intellect by making it a slave to the status quo are to be played by one actor, whilst another takes the more positive figures.[81] Although this strategy might strike us as a little black and white, we should, however, consider its impact as a dramatic device. The continuity it creates runs counter to the independence of the three (four) montage sections. We see that the unifying theme of Prussia is augmented by the recurrence of certain actors. We are thus torn between *Leben Gundlings* as montage and collage. Müller himself prefers the latter: 'es ist ein Irrtum, das Stück als Montage zu lesen. Interessant sind die fließenden Übergänge zwischen den disparaten Teilen'.[82] In this way the play runs along similar lines to Genet's *The Balcony*. The author chastizes poor productions in his introductory note 'How to Perform *The Balcony*' in which he describes his understanding of the way that the scenes should work: 'I want the scenes to follow one another, the sets to shift from left to right as if they were going to stack themselves up on top of each other under the eyes of the spectator'.[83] Müller's continuity seems to suit this idea better insofar as the piling up of material refuses to see it as past, rather as something that persists.

Both *Germania* and *Leben Gundlings* deal with a redefinition of received history. In order to get 'inside' history, it is necessary to re-order events so that connections that had been repressed by historians, and, specifically, by the GDR reception of cultural history, can be re-suggested

---

81   Whether this is in fact acted upon in performance will be discussed later.

82   Müller, *Krieg ohne Schlacht*, p. 269.

83   Jean Genet, *The Balcony*, trans. by Barbara Wright and Terry Hands (London: Faber and Faber, 1991), p. xi.

through provocative juxtaposition. *Leben Gundlings*, however, differs from *Germania* in its dramaturgical strategy. In order to explode the Prussian myth, a different sort of proximity to the historical figures is developed.

II   Authoritarianism in the Text

The portrayal of historical characters in *Germania* was mainly a question of caricature - modern traits were assigned to historical personalities in order to demystify and to create a different relationship with these figures. In *Leben Gundlings*, one finds that different techniques are used.

If we examine 'Leben Gundlings' we can start to see the difference in character construction. Friedrich Wilhelm, the Soldier King, is a figure famous for his contempt of intellectuals and for his absolutist rule. In his second long speech, in which he also refers to the bear that has Gundling in a hold, we can see these traits:

> Nehm Ers als ein Exempel, was von den Gelehrten zu halten. Und für die Regierungskunst, die Er lernen muß, wenn ich zu meinem Gott eingehe, wie der Hofprediger sagt, oder in mein Nichts. Dem Volk die Pfoten gekürzt, der Bestie, und die Zähne ausgebrochen. Die Intelligenz zum Narren gemacht, daß die Pöbel nicht auf Ideen kommt. Merk Ers sich, Er Stubenhocker, mit seinem Puderquasten- und Tragödienkram. Ich will, daß er ein Mann wird.

(H p. 12)

The first words already use forms which are no longer current. The imperative is switched to a courtly third person singular instead of the modern second singular. Further minor syntactical devices also help to confer a sense of a bygone age. The sentences themselves are also conspicuous for their fullness; the density that we have come to expect in Müller's writing is absent. Details that reveal information about Friedrich Wilhelm's religious beliefs, his attitudes towards the people and the intelligentsia are all there. In short, there is very little that prevents us from seeing this speech as the standard fare of historical drama. An examination of Gundling reveals similar features. Even his quotation from Hamlet ('O WHAT A NOBLE MIND IS HERE / OVERTHROWN', H ibid.) fails to break frame. Whereas in *Die Hamletmaschine* 'foreign' quotes conjure up a landscape of associations, here the line is justified by Gundling's academic background. The quotation fits his despair and bears witness to his status as an intellectual. The young Friedrich, although given little to say, is also depicted in a convincing manner. He displays the contradictory traits of a young boy: we see his disapproval of his father's wind-breaking, whilst later he is excited by the prospect of Gundling's demise at the hands of the bear.

We have already noted that our interest in Friedrich as a character wanes after 'Preußische Spiele 2'. His interaction with the world becomes the focus henceforth. The question arises whether he is drawn differently, in comparison with the pseudo-realism of the first two scenes.

In 'Herzkönig Schwarze Witwe' we see Friedrich's longest speeches of the play and here would seem a good place to analyse his 'mature' character. The scene is written entirely in verse. Let us examine the following two quotations:

> FRIEDRICH: [...] Sie hat recht: ich darf nicht [ie. kill himself].
> Der Glücklichste unter den Preußen, wenn
> Ein anderer Preußens König wär, wär ich.
> Wie neid ich meinen Opfern ihren Tod
> Sie dürfen sterben, aber ich muß töten.
>
> (H p. 20)

> FRIEDRICH tanzt: Ich bin der Witwenmacher. Weiber
> Zu Witwen machen, Weib, ist mein Beruf.
> Ich leer die Betten und füll die Gräber.
> Lacht, läßt den Schleier fallen.
> Jetzt kann Sie mit sich selbst spielen, Witwe
> Schüttelt sich
> Bis sich ein neuer Bauch auf ihrem Bauch reibt.
>
> (H p. 21)

We see from the first three words that the dated form of address is still being used. The verse helps to compound this effect precisely because we, at least partly, identify prosody with works of the past.[84] The first quotation is an ironic appeal to the Saxon Woman that plays with Friedrich's role as

---

84 *Germania*, on the other hand, uses verse, in part at least, to estrange the present. Contemporary structures and vocabulary are made strange by the form. The verse does not illustrate the historical period. Its clipped style confers extra dimensions and allows the characters to be considered in wider contexts.

'der erste Diener meines Staates'.[85] The language is stilted and grandiloquent, and we can see that the King is playing a role. The flip-side of this role is shown in the second quotation. The dancing King reverts to infancy: he delights in his power and makes crude remarks unbefitting a king. Yet we should also observe that he remains within his regal register. The two poles, of the corrupted prince-become-king and the self-satisfying child, constitute the figure we see on stage. Yet where Hitler was clearly a caricature in *Germania*, it is more difficult to pin this label on Friedrich. The egotism that underlies both of Friedrich's roles gives his character a certain credibility. Whilst Hitler drinks petrol, eats his own soldiers and is comforted by the mother-figure Goebbels, the exaggeration in the depiction of Friedrich is presented more gently. He is no longer written in the pseudorealism of the earlier scenes, yet he is also not drawn in the overbearing dimensions of Hitler. He becomes a figure that falls somewhere between realism and parody. The same mocking technique is also to be found later. The incident in 'Die Inspektion' where Friedrich assures the peasant that his turnip is an orange is not exaggerated enough to turn the scene into, for example, the grotesque mutilation of the young soldier in 'Hommage à Stalin 1'. Throughout these scenes an air of 'realism' is maintained in order to play on the differences between seemingly ludicrous ideas (the Prussian orange, the practices of the Professor in 'Lieber Gott', to name but two) and their acceptance in the reality of the play. In this way, we are left with a not too untraditional conception of character. The free spaces that the text created for the actors in *Germania* have been reduced in the Prussia scenes.

A return to Müller's more familiar textual idiom is only to be found at the end of the play in the Lessing monologue. Here realities are mixed when an Actor is dressed and made up as Lessing. Whereas the words of Friedrich are always attached to the historical character of Friedrich, the Lessing figure is given a freer text to speak. Critics have not been slow in picking up on the similarities between Lessing and Müller: they note that there are biographical affinities and that Lessing starts to speak Müller's own published words when describing suicidal women.[86] Here there is

85 This is a line that occurs frequently in 'Brandenburgisches Konzert 1' for satirical effect but which is conspicuous by its absence from *Leben Gundlings*. The lack of such leitmotifs has much to do with the drawing of Friedrich in the play.

86 Cf Emmerich, p. 125; Schalk p. 202; Wieghaus p. 260; and Theo Buck, 'Zwei Träume vom deutschen Theater. Anmerkungen zu Heiner Müllers Lessing Triptychon', in Georg Stötzel (ed.), *Germanistik. Forschungsstand und Perspektiven. Vorträge des deutschen Germanistentages in Passau 1984* (Berlin: Walter de

definitely the multi-layered style employed in character formation that we have seen before in some characters of the GDR scenes in *Germania*. A poetic strain enters the speech which differs from our conception of the historical Lessing, and this provides the actor with a less restricting task, one in which there is no solid basis for identification.

The drama is not, however, only constrained by its characters. Almost in passing, Genia Schulz writes that *Leben Gundlings* 'ist - theaterpraktisch gesehen - Müllers "autoritärstes" Stück - Mimesis an den Gegenstand, das Thema'.[87] This 'authoritarian' stance is to be found in various aspects of the text, the first of which is the binding of the characters to their historical signifieds, discussed above. Another device, which is rare in Müller's *oeuvre* as a whole, is the stage direction. The degree to which he dictates movements and manners to his actors in this play is unprecedented. There is no scene in which dialogue occurs that escapes this practice. To show just how pronounced this is, I shall run through some of the directions, without including the dialogue, from 'Herzkönig Schwarze Witwe' using the abbreviations 'F' for Friedrich and 'S' for the 'Sächsin':

> F: *springt auf.* S: *ihm auf den Pelz rückend* F: *flieht* S: *verfolgt ihn durch das Zimmer* / *Hand aufs Herz* / *Greift, sich auf die Knie werfend, nach Friedrichs Beinen.* F: *entkommt* S: *Fällt in Ohnmacht.* / *Friedrich umkreist die Ohnmächtige in weiten Bögen.* S: *wacht auf, wirft die Arme hoch* F: *nimmt Abstand* / *Sächsin steht auf, streckt die Arme nach ihm aus.* / *staatsmännisch* / *Das Zimmer abschreitend* S: *weint* F: *singt*
>
> (H pp. 18-19)

These make up the direction to just two of the five pages in the scene. We see that there is not only gestural direction, there is also instruction on how to speak the lines. Even the privileged figure of Lessing is directed to read his lines (H p. 34). Müller is purported to be no fan of such instructions himself. In one interview he says that directions must sometimes be inverted in order to work in the modern theatre:

> Wenn du als Regisseur die Regieanweisungen beachtest und das machst was Schiller anweist, bist du ziemlich verloren. Man muß

Gruyter, 1985), p. 486.

---

87 Genia Schulz, 'Der zersetzte Blick. Sehzwang und Blendung bei Heiner Müller', in Frank Hörnigk (ed.), *Heiner Müller Material* (Göttingen: Steidl, 1989), p. 179.

sehr oft das Gegenteil von dem machen, was er da schreibt, damit es stimmt.[88]

Elsewhere he concentrates on the historical aesthetics of the stage direction: 'die Zeiten, in denen die Regieanweisungen überhand nahmen, waren die Zeiten, wo das Milieu dominant war über die Subjekte'.[89] In both cases his criticism revolves around the problem of restricting the dramatic material. The second of the two quotations, however, seems to be the most revealing: one may deduce that *Leben Gundlings* is more concerned with the Prussian milieu than the frame-breaking anachronisms of *Germania*.

Another restricting feature is the amount of pantomime in the play. The game of blind man's buff and the symbolic confrontation with the Father in 'Preußische Spiele 1', the non-dialogic action of 'Die Inspektion', and the whole contents of 'Die Schule der Nation', 'Friedrich der Große', 'Heinrich von Kleist'and 'Lessing 2 und 3': all are dictated by directions. Let us look at an extract from 'Lessing 2':

> *Autofriedhof. Elektrischer Stuhl, darauf ein Roboter ohne Gesicht. In zwischen* [sic] *unter den Autowracks in verschiedenen Unfallposen klassische Theaterfiguren und Filmstars. Musik* WELCOME MY SON WELCOME TO THE MACHINE (Pink Floyd WISH YOU WERE HERE). *Lessing mit Nathan dem Weisen und Emilia Galotti, Namen auf dem Kostüm.* [...] *Polizeisirene. Emilia und Nathan vertauschen ihre Köpfe, entkleiden umarmen töten einander. Weißes Licht. Tod der Maschine auf dem elektrischen Stuhl. Bühne wird schwarz.*
>
> (H pp. 35-6)

Critical interpretation of this particular episode is broad and interesting. The 'Autofriedhof' is universally viewed as the logical conclusion of instrumental reason. Buck sees the destruction as an example of Müller's 'konstruktiver Defaitismus'.[90] Domdey considers the scene a rewriting of the Dionysus myth that calls for the death of the individual in the name of the rebirth of

---

88 'Ruth Berghaus und Heiner Müller im Gespräch', in *Gesammelte Irrtümer 2*, p. 83.

89 'WOZU?', in Martin Linzer and Peter Ullrich (eds.), *Regie: Heiner Müller* (Berlin: Zentrum für Theaterdokumentation und -information, 1993), p. 203.

90 Buck, p. 487.

the collective.[91] Wolfgang Heise evaluates the mutual destruction of Emilia and Nathan as 'das ungelöste Problem des bürgerlichen Humanismus'.[92] What is unchanging, however, is the object, the scene. There is no room to manoeuvre. What is written will be obeyed and thus one imagines that the various productions may be able to configure different car-cemeteries and robots, but what ultimately remains is the same. The scene does not have the power to evolve through time because it stands so fixed on the page. Like 'Nachtstück' in *Germania*, the pantomime scenes are unwieldy textual blocks which, in themselves, are full of images and actions that very much provoke associations and stimulate the audience into active co-production. Their disadvantage, however, is that they do not challenge the theatre in the manner of Müller's more flexible output.

When I asked Müller why the play was so full of 'textual authoritarianism', he replied 'da gehören die Regieanweisungen zum Text. Das ist ein Text'.[93] His argument points to two interesting aspects. First, the directions and pantomimes are a direct result of 'blinde Praxis'. Their inclusion tallies with a sense of correctness in the writing process. Just as the incomprehensibility of *Die Hamletmaschine* was 'right', then so were the textual strategies employed in *Leben Gundlings*. Second, the stage directions should be regarded as text, not privileged authorial diktats. The director should be as free with the directions as s/he is with the dialogue. (This we have already noticed in the treatment of stage direction in *Die Hamletmaschine*.) Yet both interpretations of Müller's explanation are not quite adequate. Stage directions in *Leben Gundlings* are not as unstageable as other examples found in the later work and their 'obvious' status as text is not so apparent.

Leben Gundlings is therefore a highly untypical work. Its characters lack the polyphonous qualities we have previously seen in *Germania* and *Der Auftrag*. They are also restricted by an unusual amount of direction and many of the scenes follow a pre-given schema. It would seem that the task of the director is seriously curtailed to a more traditional role because of the rigidity of the text's construction. One would possibly assume that this would involve stratagems to bring the action up to date, to show the resonances of Prussia in modern society. Emmerich argues that this aspect is already

91   Domdey, pp. 80-1.

92   Wolfgang Heise, 'Beispiel einer Lessing-Rezeption: Heiner Müller', in Wolfgang Storch (ed.), *Explosion of a Memory*, p. 88.

93   David Barnett, '"Ich erfinde gerne Zitate": Interview mit Heiner Müller', *GDR Bulletin*, 2/95, p. 11.

inscribed in the text. 'Leben Gundlings' shows the power of the State over both the bourgeois intellectual and the people; 'Die Schule der Nation' depicts soldiers as Müller has before and thus provides a link with the Wehrmacht; the students in 'Lieber Gott' who suggest castration and amputation (H p. 26) remind us of the Nazis' health policy; 'Die Inspektion' is linked to GDR agriculture; and 'Heinrich von Kleist' finds his counterpart in FRG terrorist groups.[94] These echoes, sometimes a little fanciful or obscure from the textual point of view, are possible routes into a topical realization of the play. We are left to ask how else production can give the play a vitality that is any different from that of former versions.

III   History Repeating Itself

Originally the Schauspielhaus in Hamburg was pencilled in for the honour of being the first theatre to stage *Leben Gundlings*. However, internal disputes concerning problems with Manfred Karge's and Matthias Langhoff's versions of Kleist's *Prinz Friedrich von Homburg* and the Müller version of Brecht's *Fatzer* put an end to that idea. The 'Uraufführung' took place in the Schauspielhaus Frankfurt on 26 January 1979 which pipped the production at Bochum by a mere two months. The irony of this is that the Frankfurt première was an emergency measure taken by the dramaturge Horst Laube when unexpected complications entered the plans for that season. Müller was initially 'booked' to direct *Germania* there. The GDR authorities had other plans and refused him a visa, leaving a gap in the programme. Laube's intervention may not have been a blessing for the box-office, but it certainly produced an interesting version, the like of which has not as yet, to my knowledge, been repeated.

Laube, together with his set designer Jörg Frank, responded imaginatively to the demands of the text. The first striking feature of the production was that the various sections were unified to a certain extent by the playing area. The stage was mostly covered by a huge and shallow pool. It was filled with water so that the actors could not perform without wading across the stage. Two taps upstage kept the water flowing for the full two hours, although their function was more metaphorical because the water level hardly rose from its original ankle depth. The reviewer Hans Jansen saw this giant bath as the trigger for various associations, such as 'Reinigungswahn, Blutbad, ewig rinnender Kreislauf der Gewalt'.[95] The added theatrical

94   Emmerich, p. 128, p. 137, p. 144, p. 147 and p. 149 respectively.

dimension was that it also slowed down the action: actors simply could not stride off or move in a natural manner. What the audience saw was a treatment of history in slow-motion. The other permanent feature of the set was a large radio telescope that blinked happily to itself for the duration of the performance. Its only 'active' participation occurred in the final scene when the Robot/President ascended it. The continued presence of the telescope kept the theme of the Enlightenment's technological legacy in the minds of the spectators. The Robot's ascent gave the image the quality of a refuge. Instead of functioning as a leader, the President retreated to the safety of the machine.

The introduction of a Müller-approved prologue set the tone for the ensuing action. The scene acted as an introduction to the tensions which were to pervade the rest of the play. The young Friedrich gazed at himself in a mirror whilst the Actor/Lessing recited sections of the monologue in 'Lessing 1'. An extra figure was added in the shape of a Black Angel who was given texts from Lautréamont's *Maldoror* which began with the lines 'vielleicht ist es dein Wille, daß ich zu Beginn den Haß anrufe!'. This was said concurrently with the Lessing speech. The constellation provided a dense prelude to the action as a whole.

Laube did pay passing attention to the casting suggestions offered by Müller in the note at the beginning of the printed text. A young male actor, René Peier, was cast as both the young Friedrich and Kleist. He did not play Lessing 3 because there was only one Lessing for the final scene (as opposed to the two suggested by Müller). A woman took the role of 'Friedrich der Große'. Peier reappeared at the end of 'Die Schule der Nation' as one of the sailors, as a student in 'Lieber Gott' and as one of Lessing's friends in 'Lessing 1'. This additional casting may not have compromised his position as the corrupted intellectual. It is possible that he was only used as a faceless 'spare body' in the other scenes.

The acting style itself was presented in a fairly dry, declamatory mode which drew disapproval from certain quarters. The critic P. I. (presumably Peter Iden) surmized that the actors were 'mit wenigen Ausnahmen [...] nur Requisiten der Bilder'.[96] The wholesale doubling of roles also struck Gerhard Stadelmaier as ineffectual: 'die Verstörung durch Tausch, durch die Umkehrbarkeit der Geschlechter ist [...] bloß eine Sache der Garderob-

95   Hans Jansen, 'Aus Preußens Tollhaus', *Westdeutsche Allgemeine Zeitung*, 29-1-79.

96   P.I., 'Spekulationen über Preußen', *Frankfurter Rundschau*, 29-1-79.

iere'.[97] The only character that received both praise and criticism for standing out was Verena Buss who played the older Friedrich.

Laube cannot be accused of shying away from the problematic areas of the text. He did engage himself with the tricky business of the Ghost Ship at the end of 'Die Schule der Nation' (H p. 17): actors playing sailors nailed and unnailed their captain to the mast as directed. The Kleist scene was also adhered to. The most interesting moment came in the final section when Laube came closer than any other production to the simultaneity of the Lessing triptych. As already mentioned, there was only one Lessing so the full confrontation with three figures did not occur. The main way of piling up the material from the three scenes was mediated by the set in a style reminiscent of Genet. The *stage* accumulated various parts of the scenes. By the end of the play the spectator was confronted with the Lessing figure encased in a bust surrounded by other busts, whilst the President remained in the telescope's dish, the film and theatre characters lay dead and a Volkswagen Beetle stood abandoned upstage right. Some of Lessing's friends looked on resigned as meat-hooks that hung above the Beetle began to swing. The Black Angel from the Prologue stood in front of the telescope, doubled over, motionless. Elements were merely presented. The variety of images forced an active engagement on the part of the audience.

The performance drew more criticism for its opaque imagery than for its offence to Prussia. The polemical was replaced by the search for visual complements, which met with a mixed reception. The reviewer of the *Rheinischer Merkur* called it 'neblig begreifbar' and Michael Ben saw the staging as full of 'geheimnisvoll Angedeutetes [...] mangels festerer Kost'.[98] Laube possibly played the clever intellectual a little too well: certain scenes seemed deliberately abstruse. The most notable was 'Preußische Spiele 3' where a film showed Friedrich on a wooden rocking horse, flaying his troops into battle. The line 'Hunde. Wollt ihr ewig leben' (H p. 16) was merely mouthed, assuming an implicit knowledge on the part of the audience. One cannot, however, deny Laube's sense of provocation which was an interesting reaction to a text that could be seen as staging itself. The difficulty we, as readers, have with the various sections was transferred to the stage in a production which resisted easy solutions.

97   Gerhard Stadelmaier, 'Irgendwie daran vorbei', *Stuttgarter Zeitung*, 29-1-79.

98   Anon., 'Haß auf Preußens Gloria', *Rheinischer Merkur/Christ und Welt*, 2-2-79; and Michael Ben, 'Ich weiß schon, was soll es bedeuten', *Deutsche Volkszeitung*, 8-2-79 respectively.

The visceral power of the text was unleashed four years later in the Schiller-Theater, West Berlin. The theatre itself was (until its closure after the 'Wende') known for its grand stagings of the classics. The institution was a reverent one which was not accustomed to the provocations of Müller's dramaturgy. The production, the only one since Frankfurt and Bochum in 1979, was premièred on 2 December 1983 and is generally regarded as the most violent and shocking *Leben Gundlings* to date.[99] The director, Klaus Emmerich, did provide an oblique warning to his audience in the shape of the prologue to *Philoktet* (M p.7). The invitation to leave the auditorium was taken up 'with hindsight' when spectators left the previews during the interval. The exodus was so drastic that the interval was cut for the première to prevent a recurrence.

The shock effects owed a good deal of their forcefulness to the acting style employed and to the manner of staging. One could say that the predominant aesthetic was one of an exaggerated realism. The costumes throughout provided a highly realistic basis and historical details were not missed. It all took place against a dark, open stage, which would sometimes be furnished with elaborate props. A grotesque dimension would then emerge. For example, 'Leben Gundlings' featured officers wearing party masks for the humiliation of the President of the Academy, and in 'Lieber Gott' the professor wore futuristic glasses. The exaggeration also came in the form of the violence done by and to the various characters. Both Friedrich (in 'Preußische Spiele 3') and Voltaire (in 'Die Inspektion') actually vomited (that is, they used 'stage vomit' instead of merely feigning the act with chokes and gestures). The soldiers of 'Die Schule der Nation', dressed in World War II Wehrmacht uniforms, marched through a fiery hoop into a vat of blood. Each emerged as a gory cripple. The violence called for in other scenes was also carried out with realistic sounds and vigour.

Aside from the realism of the violence, the production did manage to stylize in some places. Unlike the Frankfurt version, the devices were more active in creating meaning rather than obscuring it. Thus in 'Preußische Spiele 2', the young Friedrich was 'relieved' of her acting duties by the older incarnation, emphasizing the breaking of the playful adolescent. When Friedrich died in 'Friedrich der Große' he was reunited with his former self and both looked into the audience with regret. Some continuity was estab-

99 Evidence of this is to be found in reviews of subsequent productions that frequently use the Schiller-Theater production as the yardstick for the violence of the reaction that the play can produce.

lished in the casting of the compromised intellectuals. Hilmar Thate (who received much praise for his performances) took Gundling, the Professor and Lessing. The 'positive' line, however, remained fragmented because each role was played by a different actress, although the casting of women in these male roles did establish a subversive pattern.

The Kleist scene was subject to a freer interpretation than dictated by the printed version. The text was first read over the PA. The actress Angelica Domröse then entered, dressed in Prussian uniform and started painting graffiti on a black iron wall. A heart was the first daubing, followed by the word 'ich' at its centre. The heart was then surrounded by crosses and the dates of Kleist's birth and death. The last word to be written was 'Wannsee' which was accompanied by the fifties hit 'Pack die Badehose ein' and evocations of the 1942 conference which finally decided the fate of the Jews in the Third Reich. The associative texture of the scene bombarded the audience without any direction from the stage.

Contemporary references were also to be found in the Professor's donning of a red 'Volksgerichtshof' robe in 'Lieber Gott' and in a parody of the Statue of Liberty in 'Lessing 2' when an actress dressed as Marilyn Monroe with Mickey Mouse ears stood proud at the edge of the stage. The critique of the rationalist tradition was made topical without being overly spelt out for the spectators.

A theatre scandal was touted by some critics who were there for the first night when several members of the audience demonstratively left the auditorium. Yet this was not an entirely true picture of the audience's subsequent reactions. Having calmed down after the initial shocks, the theatre was packed with enthusiastic spectators who perhaps replaced the more conventional Schiller-Theater crowd. The production showed a very active engagement with the critique of Prussia as a system of domination. Emmerich was not, however, using a 'Theatre of Cruelty' style which one associates with Artaud. The staging was still quite didactic: Prussia was *shown* to be an infernal machine. Irrationalism was exposed in a conscious way; the actors were never 'inspired' or allowed to indulge themselves. The power of the violence was equal to the power of the critique.

The pointedness of Müller's criticism of Prussia was the main object of the reviewers' criticism of the production. Amongst this clamour came but few positive remarks in favour of either the play or its dramaturgy. Andreas Rossmann praised the diversity of the scenes and Roland H. Wiegenstein talked of a cabaret-like quality, which might make us think of *Germania*.[100] He also assessed the success of the approach to the acting. Some of the speeches overstretched the actors, in his view, and made for poor delivery. The production seems to have been more of a hit with the audience than with the critics. Even so, the positive emphasis on diversity without a unifying theme helped to present the audience with a fractured vision. The only attempt to connect the scenes was through casting - there was no 'excuse' made to justify the conglomeration of images.

   Leben Gundlings, like *Germania*, arrived late in the GDR. A joint effort from Helmut Straßburger and Ernstgeorg (sic) Hering brought the play to the Volksbühne, East Berlin, and it was premièred on 4 December 1988. According to the anonymous writer who described the rehearsal process, the scenes, which were rehearsed at first individually without reference to the others, quickly developed 'auf der Basis der Gemeinsamkeit' to assume the collage effect noted above.[101] Little cutting was involved and the two major additions to the textual corpus were the insertion of *Herzstück* (H p.7) and a choral rendition of the Ghost Ship episode at the end of 'Die Schule der Nation'. *Herzstück* was placed between 'Friedrich der Große' and 'Heinrich von Kleist' and was originally intended as a play between the Crown Prince and his father. This transparency of the idea gave way to the casting of a beggar and a policeman in the roles of 'Eins' and 'Zwei'. When the beggar finally lost his heart in deference to the authoritarian figure, he moved on to become Kleist for the next scene. The Ghost Ship, on the other hand, used a completely new text which divided the actors into three groups, each with their own narrative.[102] They tell the story of how a pirate ship took a dervish on board. He confronts the captain with the truth of his wickedness and thus invokes his anger. The dervish is murdered but before he dies he curses the ship and its crew, that they shall never live and never die. The crew takes its revenge on the captain by nailing him to the mast and then they take him down again. This goes on

---

100   Andreas Rossmann, 'Preußischer Lokal-Termin', *Rheinische Post*, 17-12-83; and Roland H. Wiegenstein, 'Preußen allewege', *Frankfurter Rundschau*, 10-12-83.

101   Anon., *Der Probenprozeß 2* (unpublished documentation held in the archive of the Volksbühne, undated).

102   The provenance of this text is as yet unknown to me. Its ballad mode and subject matter reminds us of a song of the sea, yet its lack of regular rhythm and rhyme would suggest that this is not the case. The actor and poet Jörg-Michael Koerbl was on the cast list as 'Regie-Mitarbeit' and is thus a possible candidate.

for fifty years. The narrative was told once through with each of the three groups telling one part. It was then recounted twice more with the three groups saying their own texts simultaneously, and this was followed by the choral repetition of the third section (the lament and the wish for death) by all three groups several more times.

The casting did not follow the suggestions of Müller and only one Lessing figure was included. The production itself was less brutal than the one at the Schiller-Theater and seems to have run a fairly conventional course. Possibly the pressures that had affected Fritz Marquardt and his production of *Germania* at the Berliner Ensemble were less apparent. This can probably be put down to a constellation of circumstances. First, that *Leben Gundlings* had less of an overt relationship to the GDR and did not present the directors with such a cultural-political hot potato. Its late appearance on the GDR stage owed more to the violent imagery and to the form (although Müller cites opposition to the reference in the Lessing speech to history riding 'auf toten Gäulen', H p. 34).[103] Second, that the Volksbühne did not have the same high profile as the Berliner Ensemble. Third, that the Volksbühne had already partially premièred the play in the form of an evening entitled 'Preußische Spiele' which took five scenes from the original.[104]

What is interesting is the resonance that the production found with its East German audience. The context of the GDR bracketed the production as a whole. The play began with footage of visitors and tourists in and around the palace at Sanssouci and ended with contemporary film of the Christian Rauch statue of Friedrich Unter den Linden, the 'Palast der Republik' and the 'Marx-Engels Platz'. This aside, however, the audience was quick to identify the parallels that became evident between their current conditions and those acted before them in Prussia. One of these was quite accidental: Gundling's first speech provoked chuckles in view of the GDR ban of the progressive, pro-Gorbachev periodical *Sputnik*. Elsewhere the self-importance of the monarch and his inspection of the countryside traced the path from the eighteenth century to the present day. Whereas the Schiller-Theater production took contemporary Western images which were not FRG-specific, the Volksbühne concentrated on the affinities of Prussia and the GDR. In West Berlin the emphasis was on a broad sense of human-

---

103 Unpublished interviews with Wolfgang Schuch (30-3-95) and Barnett, "'Ich erfinde gerne Zitate'", p. 11.

104 'Leben Gundlings', 'Herzkönig Schwarze Witwe', 'Lieber Gott', 'Die Inspektion' and 'Friedrich der Große'. Ironically, 'Preußische Spiele' was missing.

ist outrage, locating the problem as one of barbarism in the past and the present. In East Berlin, the critique became more political. Violence stemmed from the effects of a style of government which found resonances in the SED.

The staging was economical with its set suggesting scenes rather than depicting them. Eighteenth-century Prussian costume, as in all the other productions, was worn throughout. The grotesque and the associative were also exploited. The resultant complex texture of the production met mostly with praise from the critics. Gerhard Ebert seemed to sum up the general reaction with the following two comments in which he emphasized both unity and diversity. He saw in the production 'drastische szenische Kürzel, lose zusammengefügt zu einem theatralischen Mosaik über einen Stoff' which 'sympathisiert mit sarkastischen Naturalismen, abstrusen Symbolen und possenreißerischen Vulgarismen'.[105] The ensemble playing also provoked the typical remarks about this play's reduction of characters to types although the associative power of the scenes still retained their allure.[106]

The Maxim-Gorki-Theater provided perhaps the most relevant setting for *Leben Gundlings* when B. K. Tragelehn directed the play there (première 19 December 1991). But a stone's throw away from the Rauch statue of Friedrich,[107] the State Opera and the New Palace ('die Kommode'), which were both built during his reign, stands the theatre. The production was undertaken at short notice because a gap arose in the house's plan for the season and this is evident in the final product.[108] The production, however,

105 Gerhard Ebert, 'Wie Theater sich in Metaphern auflöst', *Neues Deutschland*, 8-12-88.

106 Anon., 'Greuelmärchen und anderes', *Neue Züricher Zeitung (Fernausgabe)*, 10-1-89; and Jürgen Beckelmann, 'Tradition der Herrscher - Tradition der Untertanen?', *Frankfurter Rundschau*, 17-12-88.

107 The publicity poster and the programme both draw attention to this detail by showing the statue from the rear. The intellectuals find their place on the frieze beneath the mounted king at the horse's backside. Lessing and Kant are the most noteworthy among them although, as the text around the poster maintains, Kant never visited Berlin and Lessing was driven out.

108 Rehearsal details and a discussion of the performance were obtained in an unpublished interview with Tragelehn by the author, 27-3-95. Extra details were supplied by *Heiner Müllers 'Leben Gundlings'*, video of the Maxim-Gorki-Theater production, Berlin, 19-12-91, in-house copy.

was neither amateurish nor riddled with easy solutions. Some of the actors who were Tragelehn's first choice for some of the key roles had already committed themselves to other productions at the theatre, so the cast was not at its most effective. Of all the productions discussed, it was in fact the truest to the text, yet this, as shall be seen below, was the critics' major line of attack.

The text was hardly abbreviated and nothing was added to it. Only the Ghost Ship episode was missing and this was replaced by extensive footage of the bombed-out German capital taken from an aeroplane soon after the capitulation of the High Command. The plan to realize this episode fell victim to the short rehearsal period. The simultaneity of the Lessing triptych was also not staged but this was more a restriction imposed by the dimensions of the Gorki-Theater itself. The proscenium arch and the relative narrowness of the stage inhibited the stacking of the three elements of the scene and a linearity was imposed. Of course, there could have been ways around this, but again one must remember the pressure of time. A virtue was nonetheless made out of the architectural 'necessity' and almost all the scenes played on the motif of voyeurism. Only 'Die Inspektion' broke this pattern and integrated the audience. The scene was the first after the interval and began with the 'harvesting' of the turnips from the front row. Friedrich and Voltaire entered from the aisle and faced the audience. Friedrich's megaphone boomed at both the peasants and the spectators. The voice of the despot found many addressees.

Tragelehn also followed the casting instructions laid down in Müller's note to the text to the letter. Thus we saw a flowing unity between the stifled figures of the young Friedrich, Kleist and Lessing 3, and between Gundling, the Professor, Schiller and Lessing 1 and 2. The scenic titles also drew the differing moments together: each was projected onto a gauze in front of the stage and each film slowly showed the writing of the title in 'Sütterlin' script. The slowness of the writing (which, again, Tragelehn was unable to speed up due to lack of time to edit the videos) was analogous to the slowness of the play as a whole. The three hour duration did not go down at all well.

Stylization was limited and extra input from the director was not, on the whole, in evidence. One of the few that made it to the stage was a series of projected police record pictures, taken from the traditional three sides, of the actors who played the patients in 'Lieber Gott'.

We are reminded of Tragelehn's *Germania* in which he resisted a polemical urge in order to focus on a fairly 'straight' realization of the texts. There were no shock tactics or didacticism. The presentation of the scenes as real stories for the interpretation of the audience was the primary thrust of the staging. The acting style lacked colour and was criticized for its apparent naturalism. Martin Linzer believed that Tragelehn 'machte dann auch nicht den Versuch, das Publikum zu manipulieren oder belehren zu wollen, aber er insistierte, und das sehr nachdrücklich und oft bis zur Schmerzgrenze, auf den Realismus der Geschichte'.[109] The titles of Rüdiger Schaper's and Susanne Heyden's reviews highlight the disapprobation of the critics in general.[110] The respect for the text was met with almost universal disdain. The audience followed suit, at least on the opening night, when they greeted both Tragelehn and Müller with boos. This reaction to the production is most interesting. The moderate route of the director neither left radical gaps in the play, nor did he err on the side of creative over-indulgence. He merely stuck to the text. It would seem that the lack of innovation was considered wholly inappropriate within the context of the modern German theatre and/or of Müller's *oeuvre*.

IV   More of the Same

Germania and *Leben Gundlings* present two different types of montage structure. The paired progression of the former is replaced by the clustering of fragments in the latter. *Leben Gundlings* also differs from *Germania* in that the clusters are supposed to accumulate material rather than just presenting it scene after scene. The Lessing triptych at the play's conclusion most obviously draws our attention to this dramaturgy of hoarding. Müller asks in his note for a production mode that can turn individual scenes into an unfinished stockpile, a Prussian wreckage. The challenge lies in the organization and accrual of material.

Leben Gundlings is a proscriptive text. The elements of the montage are more clearly and correspondingly more inflexibly defined. The almost traditional characters also seem to submit to a traditional dramaturgy. Complexes develop within the broad categories of Friedrich and Lessing. Kleist remains a figure who is unable to be placed firmly under the umbrella

109   Martin Linzer, 'Abgesessen?', *Theater der Zeit*, 2/92, p. 27.

110   'Naturalismus auf der ganzen Linie', *Süddeutsche Zeitung*, 28/29-12-91; and 'Den Text wie eine Ikone behandelt', *Rheinische Post*, 24-12-91.

of either. The historical personalities are not collective individuals.[111] Rather they are ciphers for different strains within Prussian society. Friedrich's life remains a chronological progression from his youth through his accession to his death. Lessing is presented in a more challenging manner: the simultaneity of his triptych bombards the audience with the explosive potential of the Enlightenment dramatist. The definition of the historical figures, uncollective and differentiated as they are, helps to keep them as jagged entities within the dramaturgy of accrual. We are presented with a mélange, and in order to identify its elements, however distorted, they have to be drawn with a more defined stroke.

In performance, only the Laube production in Frankfurt managed to tackle the peculiar techniques at work in the play. The constant frame provided by the watery set and the attempt at the simultaneous ending showed that Müller was not overly playing the coquette when penning his provocative note to the play. Linearity is the enemy of this drama. Without an appreciation of the dynamic, productions remain episodic. The reception in the Schiller-Theater and at the Volksbühne demonstrates that the power of the images and the iconoclastic scenes can be highly effective, yet the text demands more than that. The simplistic weaving of motifs reduces the overall potential of the play.

The director has to become the organizer of the text's elements. We have found that for the most part he has only sought to contemporize the scenes or to highlight their violent power. The texts have not provoked an unstable or experimental production process and the employment of attributed character and vignette do not make the business of realization more problematic. *Leben Gundlings* takes its challenging cue from a combination of textual construction and Müller's note. There is nothing in the text itself that explicitly resists the processes of the theatre. As a result, the play has been subject to a more superficial production history. It *is*, however, a challenging text, although its challenge, it would seem, has not been properly recognized. Realizations have presented the disparate elements in fitting ways, but they have not either been able to identify the dramaturgy of hoarding or to exploit it.

111 Even the three Lessings communicate three possibilities for one figure. At no point is he constructed in the same way as the anonymous speaker(s) of 'Familienalbum' in *Die Hamletmaschine* or as the five 'ich's of the *Wolokolamsker Chaussee*.

I   Loose Connections

The construction of *Verkommenes Ufer* is one of the few complete stories we have of Müller's montage work. Whereas *Germania* presents us with writing dates from 1956 to 1971, *Die Schlacht* from 1951 to 1974 or *Traktor* from 1955 to 1961, compiled in 1974, the history of *Verkommenes Ufer* is both alluded to in interviews and is documented in *Krieg ohne Schlacht*:

> Das Stück besteht aus Teilen verschiedener Bauart, zu verschiedenen Zeiten geschrieben, der älteste Text: 'Sie hocken in den Zügen, Gesichter aus Tagblatt und Speichel...' noch in Sachsen. So unverstellt konnte man die Großstadt nur aus der Provinz sehen, als gelegentlicher Besucher.[112] Das war 1949. [...] Jahre später war ich mit einer Frau an einem See bei Strausberg, wo das Ufer aussah, wie im Stück beschrieben. Bei Strausberg hat die letzte große Panzerschlacht des Zweiten Weltkriegs stattgefunden. [...] Der Dialogteil von 'Medeamaterial' ist fast das Stenogramm eines Ehestreits im letzten Stadium oder in der Krise einer Beziehung. Das habe ich in Lehnitz geschrieben [in 1955]. Den Monologteil zwei Jahrzehnte später in Bochum, [...] das war 1982.[113]

The sporadic manufacture of the play is reflected in the end-product. The three sections, 'Verkommenes Ufer', 'Medeamaterial' and 'Landschaft mit Argonauten', take three very different forms: the first a phantasmagoria of impressions, the second a dramatic dialogue, and the third a first person monologue.

Before *Verkommenes Ufer* was published in the form with which we are now familiar,[114] an earlier draft appeared in the programme of the Bochum production of *Der Auftrag* (première 13 February 1982).[115] This

---

112 Müller had written these lines after his first fleeting visits to Berlin.

113 Müller, *Krieg ohne Schlacht*, pp. 319-20.

114 The play was originally published in *Alternative*, 145/46, 1982, pp. 178-85. All quotations, however, follow the Rotbuch edition.

115 *Heiner Müllers 'Der Auftrag'*, programme of the Bochum production, 13-2-82, pp. 44-52.

version, which for purposes of brevity I shall refer to as the *Urmedea*, presents the first section in a different order from the later 'standard' version and matches the typescript that is published in *Explosion of a Memory*.[116] The differences between the two are almost exclusively those of textual division: the only change of wording is the distinction between 'Das im Baum hängt Hangar und Kotplatz der Geier im Wartestand' (H p. 91) and 'Das im Baum hängt Hangar und Kotplatz der wartenden Geier'.[117] Norbert Eke, one of the few critics to have discussed the play in detail, offers a breakdown of the orthodox 'Verkommenes Ufer' which will help us to discern the discrepancies between the two texts. Eke divides the text into five sections corresponding to the following lines in the Rotbuch edition: 1-2 ('See bei Straußberg Verkommenes Ufer Spur / Flachstirnige Argonauten'), 3-14 ('DIESER BAUM WIRD MICH NICHT ÜBERWACHSEN' to 'STOSS MICH KOMM SÜSSER'), 15-26 ('Bis ihm die Argo' to 'In den Leichenhallen'), 27-31 ('Die Toten starren nicht ins Fenster' to 'VOR DEM BAUCH DAS SCHILD') and 32-4 ('Auf dem Grund aber' to 'Der Gifte').[118] For the most part the division matches the blank lines in the text itself. The only deviation from this is the division of lines 3-14 and 15-26 which Eke nonetheless traces back to a division found in the *Alternative* text.[119] Not surprisingly, each section has its own interpretation in his scheme, each forming a discrete epistemological unit. The *Urmedea* presents a different division which runs along the following lines of the Rotbuch edition: 1-2, 17-26, 3-14, 15-16, 27-31, 32-4. This version thus introduces an extra section by splitting Eke's third (ll. 15-26) into two (ll. 15-16 and 17-26) and wedging the larger inbetween Eke's first and second divisions. The effect, however, is not unlike that of the Rotbuch edition. The short passages continue to react with each other. The episodes form a collage in the way that Prussia was evoked in the 'Leben Gundlings Friedrich von Preußen' section of *Leben Gundlings*, except that this collage has no overt guiding

---

116 Cf. Storch (ed.), pp. 192-3. In this version, the text section 'Die Toten starren' to 'ICH BIN EIN FEIGLING' appears twice. The first (p. 192) should be ignored and the second (p. 193) included in order to get to the 'Verkommenes Ufer' of the *Urmedea*.

117 *Urmedea*, p. 44.

118 Eke, pp. 195-99.

119 Ibid., p. 194, footnote. He is also not afraid to stress that some versions have no strophic division and that others only have three.

thread. The elements are free to create links and images in the minds of the spectators and in the interpretation of the actor(s). The order is more or less arbitrary. The only section whose position does seem fixed is the final one. It acts as a contrast to the collage. The last three lines both name and emphasize (the use of the particle 'aber', l. 32) a character who stands out from the descriptive patchwork. This character is threatening and larger than an individual; she takes on unknown proportions because of her mythical reference point. A dramatic sequence is initialized and this is contrasted with the impressionistic fragments that preceded it.

'Medeamaterial' is the drama that takes its cue from the end of 'Verkommenes Ufer' and retells the final scenes of Medea and Jason's story. Compared with the *Urmedea*, the Rotbuch version has a beginning, a middle and an end. It starts with the discovery that Jason is planning to marry Glauce, Creon's daughter. Jason is then introduced and sketched very briefly as a character. There then follows a long monologue which traces the build-up to, the manifestation and the consequences of Medea's revenge, her feelings and reasoning behind it. The conclusion of the scene is also the beginning of a new story. Medea's last line, in response to Jason calling her name, has shades of Seneca's *Medea*. In his version Medea replies 'fiam' ('I shall become her'), in Müller's the transformation has already taken place. The past has been destroyed, Medea is left with a future without her husband: 'Amme Kennst du diesen Mann' (H p. 98). The *Urmedea* deviates once again from the final version in its ordering of the events. Here, however, the ordering does affect the interpretation. Müller precedes the Medea/Nurse exchange with that of Medea/Jason. Only the lines, 'MEDEA: Du bist mir einen Bruder schuldig Jason / JASON: Zwei Söhne gab ich dir für deinen Bruder', buffer the last lines with the Nurse and the mono-logue.[120] In this variant a broader picture is painted. The dialogue with Jason that precedes the 'action' sets the scene in an unspecified time where these small battles assume larger proportions. The move to the more narrative form of the Rotbuch edition concentrates the scene, although, as we shall see later, this does not compromise its flexibility as dramatic material.

The final part, 'Landschaft mit Argonauten', differs very slightly from the *Urmedea*, insofar as the latter stops at 'ZWISCHEN DEN SCHENK-ELN HAT / DER TOD EINE HOFFNUNG' (H p. 99) and omits a couple of lines that occur earlier in the text. The monologue, a voyage through a modern landscape of consumerism and alienation, provokes the following

120 *Urmedea*, p. 47.

comments from the critics. Genia Schulz sees it as a scene 'der sich als Versuch Jasons lesen läßt, sich selbst zu (er)kennen', in which the voice becomes collective and diffuse with anonymous impulses.[121] Klaus Teichmann follows suit, seeing it as a musing of the 'Ich' on its own 'Ich-Haftigkeit'.[122] Johannes Birringer perhaps becomes a little bogged down in his terminology when he says that the scene 'is a recognizably postmodern scene of a culture suffused with self-hatred *and* an ecstatic consumption of the technological violence that brings the colonization of the lifeworld to its end'.[123] The question of the scene's 'postmodernism' is thrown into relief both by the echoes of the *modernist* author T. S. Eliot[124] and by ideological themes that suggest older motifs. In this respect our interest is drawn to a remark made by one of Müller's interlocutors in *Krieg ohne Schlacht* rather than to the answer proffered by the dramatist himself:

> *In den Passagen, in denen Du die kapitalistische Überfluß- und Warengesellschaft beschreibst, bist Du erheblich moralischer als in den anderen Textteilen, dann bist Du fast Traditionssozialist.*[125]

One must therefore be careful when discussing the aesthetics of this scene. This 'moral dimension' certainly differentiates 'Landschaft mit Argonauten' from 'Verkommenes Ufer'. The root of this lies in the perspective that is developed: we are no longer presented with the 'nüchtern-objektivierende Bestandsaufnahme der Wirklichkeit in dem Bühnenraum' that Eke sees in 'Verkommenes Ufer';[126] the lyric 'I' takes over from the impersonal first section. The 'I' creates both a link between the describer and the described

121 Genia Schulz, 'Medea. Zu einem Motiv im Werk Heiner Müllers', in Renate Berger and Inge Stephen (eds.), *Weiblichkeit und Tod in der Literatur* (Cologne: Böhlau, 1987), p. 261.

122 Klaus Teichmann, *Der verwundete Körper* (Freiburg: Burg, 1986), p. 207.

123 Johannes Birringer, *Theatre, Theory, Postmodernism* (Bloomington and Indianapolis: Indiana University Press, 1991), p. 54.

124 Cf. Genia Schulz, 'Waste Land/Verkommenes Ufer', in Storch (ed.), pp. 103-4; and Eke, who sees the scene as 'eine Folge düsterer Bilder [...] in einer gelegentlich an T.S. Eliots *The Waste Land* angelehnten Metaphernsprache', p. 216.

125 Heiner Müller, *Krieg ohne Schlacht*, p. 321.

126 Eke, p. 195.

as well as giving the scene more cohesion than the collage effects found in the first scene. The category of time is reintroduced and the monologue assumes a more narrative, consecutive tone.

In *Verkommenes Ufer* Müller presents us with a montage that differs from both *Germania* and *Leben Gundlings*. It is tempting to see the assembly in the totally free context of Seibel's 'additive Szenefolge' (and indeed this is the most accurate description within his schema). Although there is no 'Fabel' to speak of in the traditional sense, the order does follow a certain logic. We are first confronted with a faceless modern mass of images from which the figure of Medea emerges. With this as a prelude to the Medea character, we experience her story. Its aftermath then provides the backdrop for the final section: Jason is left to come to terms with the problem of identity in the society he has created. Unlike *Leben Gundlings*, *Verkommenes Ufer* does take the form of a triptych. The centre-piece, 'Medeamaterial', is the part which acts as a focus, the part around which all turns. It is augmented by the elements found on either side, rather than being dominated by them. The triptych is, however, slightly lopsided: until now, I have only given the final scene its full title. The two that precede it should have been given their full names as they appear in the Rotbuch edition. The first scene is 'Verkommenes Ufer Medeamaterial Landschaft mit Argonauten' and the second 'Medeamaterial Landschaft mit Argonauten'. We see what Eke calls the play's 'Verengung'.[127] The scenes become distilled as they progress: by the end we are alone with the Argonauts.

II   Unsafe Ground

A direction later omitted in the Rotbuch edition, yet found in the *Urmedea*, attributes the text of 'Verkommenes Ufer' to a 'CHOR'.[128] Although this is no longer a 'requirement' in the text, it does shed some light on the performance of this text. One could compare it to 'Tod in Berlin 1' where a poetic fragment is to be realized on stage. The Heym poem, however, is both shorter and less fragmented than 'Verkommenes Ufer', and perhaps the choral direction mediates the ever-changing perspective of the text better than the unattributed text we find in the standard edition. An example of the effectiveness of this approach can be found in the 'Hörstück' version of

127   Ibid., p. 190.

128   *Urmedea*, p. 44.

this scene which was recorded by Heiner Goebbels. We are given access to the method employed to gather the voices from the booklet that accompanies the CD set:

> Das Bild, das Heiner Müller vom Ufer eines Sees bei Straus-
> berg festhält, können wir heute in unseren Städten wieder-
> finden. Thorsten Becker hat in Berlin über 50 Passanten ge-
> beten - in verschiedenen Kneipen, Flipperhallen, auf der Straße,
> im Bahnhof Zoo, auf U- und S-Bahnhöfen, den ihnen fremden
> Text zu lesen.[129]

The piece is made up exclusively of these 'innocent', uninitiated voices. Rhythms are manufactured by repetition and background drones of slowed-down or speeded-up vocal tones. The collage that the text suggests is realized by the variety of voices recorded in Berlin. There is shock, surprise, distance and amusement in the different interpretations of the lines. Although such spontaneity is not possible in a theatre, the heterogeneity of the text is undoubtedly brought to the fore by the choral collage that Goebbels assembles.

The dialogue section, 'Medeamaterial', presents us with characters not seen in either *Germania* or *Leben Gundlings*. There is neither scenic description nor stage direction. All we have is the three figures. On a purely formal level all the dialogue is set in a fairly strict iambic pentameter. Regardless of the content of the speeches, this has the effect of concentrating the language. It also foregrounds the artifice of the speeches and gives the language rhythms that would be absent in common conversation.

In Medea's monologue, the centre-piece of the scene, devices are used to fragment the speaking figure. These take the form of certain constellations that, on the realistic stage, would mutually exclude each other. The first is the psychological level. The form of the speech very much resembles an interior monologue. Thoughts become words:

---

129 Heiner Goebbels, 'Verkommenes Ufer', on Heiner Goebbels, *Hörstücke. Nach Texten von Heiner Müller* (Munich: ECM records, 1452-54, 1994), CD booklet.

MEDEA: Für dich habe ich getötet und geboren
          Ich deine Hündin deine Hure ich
          Ich Sprosse auf der Leiter deines Ruhms
          Gesalbt mit deinem Kot Blut deiner Feinde
                                                    (H p. 94)

The poetic language such as we have seen in the speeches of some of the GDR characters in *Germania* features again here. However, the function is different: whereas the workers and whores gained extra dimensions that transcended their 'characters', Medea is already a problematic 'individual'. The mythical aspect frustrates a realistic appreciation of the figure. The monologue also maintains this quality, by relating all the important incidents of the Medea story: we learn of Jason's visits to Glauce, Medea's rage, her gift of a bridal gown that magically ignites and burns the young bride, and the murder of the sons.

Yet there is an extra dimension in certain sections that challenges the classical backdrop and introduces modern ideas. The theme of exchange runs throughout the monologue. The values of a brother against two sons, treachery of one's homeland and one's family against the love of a husband are continually weighed up. Medea also uses continued references to the theatre in her reproaches to her children that go beyond a classical view of the stage.

Medea is constituted, broadly speaking, by three categories: the psychological, the mythical and the more contemporary. In addition, all of these are articulated through the pentameters. The actress is therefore presented with a role that cannot simply be reduced to a unifying reading if the material is to be embraced in its entirety. Bettina Gruber comments that Müller's deletion of the chorus from the Euripidean original robs the scene of its 'Öffentlichkeitscharakter'.[130] This is true to a certain extent: the scene no longer takes place on a square before Creon's palace, inviting the commentary of a chorus. However, the voice of Medea attains polyphony and in this way comments on itself by offering continual changes of perspective.

The question thus arises as to how an actress is to play Medea.[131] Both Eke and Birringer favour a distanced approach: the former thinks that the role should be 'vorgestellt' rather than 'gespielt', the latter sees the

---

130 Bettina Gruber, *Mythen in den Dramen Heiner Müllers. Zu ihrem Funktionswandel in den Jahren 1958-1982* (Essen: Die Blaue Eule, 1989), p. 136.

131 To my knowledge the role has never been played by a man.

speech as 'all the more powerful if the actress can indeed stand outside of the emotional images she wants to disown'.[132] Matthias Langhoff, who co-directed the Bochum 'Uraufführung', comments in an interview, '"Medea-material" ist nicht als reale Geschichte zu verstehen, sondern als Projektion aus der Gegenwart - als Wunsch einer Frau, zur Medea zu werden'.[133] This trio of remarks emphasizes the need to resist the temptation of identifying with the character as if she were real. It would seem that either a Brechtian or a Grotowskian approach (cf. Chapter I) would prove most useful. The actress Regina Fabian, who played Medea in a version that only included 'Medeamaterial', took a different route into the character.[134] In the two weeks of intensive rehearsals that preceded the performance, the role was initially read drily, without emotion in order to understand the ebbs and flows of the text. It was only in the final stages of rehearsal that emotions were introduced which then consumed the character.[135] Medea gained an emotional intensity which became primal at times. The projected emotions were only relativized by the occasional distanced repetition of certain lines by the Nurse.

The final section 'Landschaft mit Argonauten', like 'Verkommenes Ufer', is now without the character attribution it carried in the *Urmedea*, where the text is directly assigned to 'JASON'.[136] As discussed earlier, the textual fabric of this monologue is quite different from that of 'Ver-kommenes Ufer' in that it takes a unified lead from the lyric 'I' despite the various impulses that pervade the narrative. The figure falls somewhere between the Hamlet-actor in *Die Hamletmaschine* and the figure of 'Der Mann im Fahrstuhl' in *Der Auftrag*. The free verse breaks the strictures of the pentameters that preceded it and we inhabit the fragmented discourse of the speaker.

It is interesting to note the possibilities that arise from the unknown identity of this figure. In his notes on staging the works of Heiner Müller,

---

132 Eke, p. 191; and Birringer, p. 70.

133 Ilka Platzek and Udo Ernst, 'Subjektivität und Phantasie', *guckloch*, 5/83.

134 The performance, 'Medeamaterial', was premièred in the Famagusta studio thea-tre, Berlin, 18-2-95, and was directed by Blanche Kommerell.

135 Unpublished interview with Regina Fabian by the author, 18-2-95.

136 *Urmedea*, p. 51.

Stefan Johannson, a Swedish director, talks of the 'mistake' he made when recording his version of *Verkommenes Ufer* for Swedish radio:

MISSVERSTÄNDNISSE BEI HEINER MÜLLER sind manchmal sehr produktiv. In der Medea-Trilogie habe ich aus Versehen den dritten Teil [...] von einer Frau spielen lassen, die 'dritte' Medea. Wir wußten nicht, daß das ein männlicher, ein Jason-Text ist. Beim Abhören der Aufnahme hat Müller nicht darauf reagiert (oder es nicht bemerkt?). Kleine Fehler sind furchtbar, große Mißverständnisse *fruchtbar*? [...] Eine reife Medea, etwas verwirrt, lange nach den Kindern und dem Drachenwagen, suchte am Ufer allein (?) übriggeblieben einen neuen-alten Zusammenhang...?[137]

The idea is certainly challenging and reveals the extra dimensions opened by freeing the attribution of the monologue.

As a montage for the stage, the elements all seem relatively free for interpretation. An extra factor which affects a production, and one which is also a part of *Die Hamletmaschine*, *Die Schlacht* and *Traktor*, is the brevity of the text. In theatrical terms, this is an open call for creativity. The shortness of the texts means that a production without 'extras' would barely last half an hour. To extend the texts to a full hour already requires an active engagement with non-textual aspects that may arise from the suggestive scenes. The short texts are a provocation and because there is no hint of a solution to the problem, the director must trawl his or her imagination in order to bring these plays to the stage.

Müller does not, however, leave the play in this state of relative freedom. As with *Leben Gundlings*, he appends a note that is once again conspicuous in its irony:[138]

Der Text braucht den Naturalismus der Szene. VERKOMMENES UFER *kann bei laufendem Betrieb in einer Peepshow gezeigt werden,* MEDEAMATERIAL *an einem See bei Straußberg, der ein verschlammter Swimmingpool in Beverly Hills oder die Bade-*

---

137 Stefan Johannson, 'Schweigen und Tanzen', in Storch (ed.), p. 83.

138 Müller told me in the interview footnoted earlier that the notes to his plays were 'eher Provokationen'. In the case of *Leben Gundlings* and *Verkommenes Ufer* we can see this status clearly. In *Wolokolamsker Chaussee*, and *Zement* to a certain extent, this assessment seems less tenable.

anstalt einer Nervenklinik ist. Wie MAUSER *eine Gesellschaft der Grenzüberschreitung, in der ein zum Tod Verurteilter seinen wirklichen Tod auf der Bühne zur kollektiven Erfahrung machen kann, setzt* LANDSCHAFT MIT ARGONAUTEN *die Katastrophen voraus, an denen die Menschheit arbeitet. [...] Wie in jeder Landschaft ist das Ich in diesem Textteil kollektiv. Die Gleichzeitigkeit der drei Textteile kann beliebig dargestellt werden.*

(H p. 101)

Teichmann, in an unusual show of literalism, doubts that any peepshow owner would let a theatre troupe occupy his premises. He thus sees the gloss as a comment, 'die eine Spielbarkeit des Stückes, wenn nicht ausschließt, so doch immerhin jedweden Inszenierungsversuch mit dem Vorwurf der Inadäquatät konfrontiert'.[139] (He does also rate the note as a useful way of seeing the play in a modern light.) It would, however, seem more fitting to understand the metaphorical significance of the suggestions. The peepshow implies a voyeurism that is also found in the ever-changing perspectives of 'Verkommenes Ufer'. The decadence of the luxurious but muddied pool or the bathing rooms of the sanatorium point, as Teichmann agrees, to a contemporary context for the scenes. The most interesting part of the note is to be found at its conclusion. The simultaneity goes against the progressions suggested both by the content of the scenes and by the gradual reduction of the scenic titles. Yet this line is less fixed than the instruction at the end of *Leben Gundlings* that describes the simultaneity of the Lessing scenes. It is also unconditional, like all the remarks: the *'kann'* only shows us the potential of the suggestions. It is the director's task to take Müller up on them.

III   Assembly of the Parts

The early eighties was a period of close association between Heiner Müller and the Schauspielhaus Bochum. The theatre not only allowed him to stage *Der Auftrag* (première 13 February 1982) but was also allowed by him to present the 'Uraufführungen' of several important late works. *Quartett* (première 7 April 1982) and *Anatomie Titus Fall of Rome* (14 February 1985) framed the world première of *Verkommenes Ufer* on 22 April 1983. The production was directed by Manfred Karge and Matthias Langhoff.

139   Teichmann, p. 198.

228

Karge himself took the role of Jason and he was complemented by Kirsten Dene as Medea.

Help in understanding the text came in two forms. The programme itself (all 492 pages of it!) contained a lexicon of references and several Müller adaptations from antiquity, as well as Apollonius Rhodius's *The Argonauts*. Spectators were also greeted with what the critic from *Theater heute* called an 'ARGONAUTENMUSEUM'.[140] In the foyer of the Kammerspiele stood illustrations of numerous sections of the text. For example, one would have seen a pack of condoms with the sign 'FROMMS ACT', a map of Germany with a lake to the East of Berlin coloured in red, the 'SEE BEI STRAUSSBERG', or a broken-off chair-leg with the legend 'STUHL-BEIN EIN HUND'. However, despite the introductory aids, the performance itself still managed to retain the elliptical style of the writing.

The set, designed by Langhoff, did not change throughout the 75-minute performance. The actors played against a crescent-shaped backdrop of dark violet foil. The stage itself was strewn with tin cans without labels, anonymous tokens of consumer waste. An aeroplane propeller mounted on a smooth sheet of steel dominated just to the right of centre stage. Again, it signalled a disembodied relationship to modern technological progress. (At times the propeller would rotate, suggesting dynamism without any sense of movement.) It was flanked by a basin plumbed into the wall, a token of domesticity. Jason had a chair between the basin and the propeller, the Nurse's was stage left and Medea's stage right. An overlarge lightbulb, which would occasionally glow, dangled from the ceiling between Medea's chair and the propeller. The bow of an ancient vessel emerged from out of the tin cans in front of the propeller. It provided an association between the classical material and the emblem of modern transport behind it. Both betokened an ideological force which exploits means of communication as a means of colonization. The set also reached back into the auditorium: wreckage of the Argo was suspended above the heads of the spectators 'wie das Damokles-Schwert', as a couple of reviewers noted.[141] The costumes, too, remained unchanged for the duration and had an associative tone. Jason wore a leather jacket, no shirt, trousers and a bald latex mask that covered his whole head. Facial expression was impossible; the only move-

---

140 Michael Erdmann, 'Theatralische Texttransport-Maschine', *Theater heute*, 6/83, p. 38.

141 Sonia Luyken, 'Der Rest ist Lyrik', *Rhein-Neckar-Zeitung*, 30-4/1-5-83; and Thomas Wiltberger, 'Endzeitsstimmung und antike Tragödie: Müller Premiere in Bochum', *Ruhr-Nachrichten*, 25-4-83.

ment that was barely perceptible was that of the mouth and the eyes. The baldness of the head and the blankness of the mien robbed the audience of both identification and a conventional way of approaching the figure. Medea's mask, on the other hand, was the conscious 'uglification' of the make-up artist Ursula Renzenbrink. The make-up was not grotesque, it merely accented Medea's age and the loss of her looks in an artificial way. Correspondingly, the acting style did not come close to realism in any form.

The scenes were announced over the PA in their full form in a neutral manner.[142] The words 'Verkommenes Ufer Medeamaterial Landschaft mit Argonauten' were repeated four times before the scene actually began. The text was mainly presented to the audience by Karge's taped voice. Sometimes Jason would join the distanced voice. This was most noticeable at the 'EINIGE HINGEN AN LICHTMASTEN' lines (H p. 92) which were repeated four times in an increasingly desperate tone. Music added associative dimensions. Both Cherubini's *Medea*, here an aria sung by Maria Callas, and popular music of the post-war years accompanied certain parts of the text.

'Medeamaterial' was heralded by the covering of the propeller with a sheet by the Nurse and the aforementioned scene announcement. The first sequence was initiated by Medea who mimed vomiting into the basin before the Nurse tried to serve her with breakfast. The gesture, like many in the production, was unfixable. We ask ourselves whether the vomiting was a reference to bulimia or a theatrical sign for Medea's condition. When Medea contemplated herself in the mirror, the howl of 'recognition' ('Das ist nicht Medea', H p. 93) set the tone for her monologue. Dene's rendition of the speech employed a plethora of styles and gave a panoramic picture of suffering, cynicism, calculation and revenge. The language became externalized and the acting style was broadly Grotowskian. It seemed that every muscle was mobilized in order to convey the flow of energy through the actress' veins. The text itself was divided into blocks and the cries and howls that 'filled the gaps' functioned as a non-verbal codicil to the texts. It was as if each block had to be dealt with before Dene could proceed with the next one. Sometimes she would return to a more measured and distant tone, only to radicalize it in a subsequent line. The bridal gown she gave to Glauce was her own dress, which revealed a slip underneath it. The sons were represented by two cans of corned beef, another reference to the consumer society, which were opened at the moment of the murder - their

142 *Heiner Müllers 'Verkommenes Ufer'*, video of the Schauspielhaus production, Bochum, 22-4-83, in-house copy.

contents squashed in the hands of the wilful Medea. Jason, on the other hand, kept his distance. His appearance after Medea's exchanges with the Nurse was measured and neutral. He carried a bunch of flowers which remained a pathetic symbol that contrasted with the blankness of his mask. He pecked Medea on the cheek when receiving the bridal gown and reacted with similar 'emotional neutrality' at the scene's conclusion. Only at one point did he directly respond to Medea's words when he symbolically strangled and raped her around the leitmotif 'Du bist mir einen Bruder schuldig Jason' (H p. 96). Yet even here she was calmly helped up to her feet by the Nurse: the action remained on a non-realistic level. By the end of the scene, the sheet was removed from the propeller, which began to turn slowly. The motionless dynamism was to re-start after the mythical time of 'Medeamaterial'.

A faster rotation accompanied 'Landschaft mit Argonauten'. Both the Nurse and Medea sat dead in their chairs, the latter strangled by her pearls, her tongue out, creating an echo of 'Verkommenes Ufer'. Jason recited the speech in the neutral, distanced style that marked his previous appearances. The verse metres received their due and the speech as a whole was delivered while Jason jogged on the spot. Again, progress was questioned by the 'static movement'. A repetitive punctuation of the text was achieved by synthesized musical phrases. At one point Jason started to whistle along with the sailor song 'La Paloma Ohé' (from which the line 'SEEMANNSBRAUT IST DIE SEE', H p. 98, is taken). The conclusion of the speech was marked by the acceleration of the musical interjections and the introduction of projected footage of an aeroplane looping the loop and icebergs. The circularity of the aeroplane's manoeuvre and the unwieldy size of the natural objects presented the audience with a sobering comparison. The line 'IN DEN RÜCKEN DAS SCHWEIN' (H p. 101) was repeated four times and the sound of a typewriter was heard. The scene ended in a tableau with the rotating propeller while Müller's note to the play was calmly delivered over the PA. Rolf Hochhuth's criticism of the 'krass gegen die Bühnenanweisungen des Autors hergestellte Inszenierung' seems to have missed the tension created by the final PA announcement.[143]

The production explored themes of progress and stasis. The feeling was very much that of an 'Endzeit'. Visual images contrasted the role of technology with its repercussions (colonization and existential emptiness). The 'Medeamaterial' took place in its own 'timeless' space. The propeller

---

143 Rolf Hochhuth, 'Wie in einem blinden Spiegel', *Die Weltwoche*, 4-5-83.

was covered and we were invited to witness a picture of suffering and hatred which took place everywhere and nowhere. The corporeal images suggested by Medea refused to correspond to any single system of reference and transcended the accelerated time of the scenes that surrounded it.

Criticism was highly favourable. It both emphasized the huge pool of associations and praised the acting accomplishment of Kirsten Dene. A mere selection of the reviews demonstrates the relativization of a purely psychological rendition. The reviewer of the *Neue Züricher Zeitung* called her 'ein fleischgewordenes Klagelied' and Wiltberger said she had the played the role 'mit beängstigter Vitalität'.[144] Jason also won praise yet this was understandably more understated, although Erdmann summed up, 'die Figur wird weder sympathisch noch unsympathisch gemacht, sie bleibt in einer halb spielerischen, halb fatalistischen Neutralität, Undeutbarkeit'.[145] The combination of Grotowskian acting and a set with its implied metaphors of stagnation seems to have found many resonances with both reviewers and their reports of the audience's reaction. The imagination required to transform the short text into a theatrical event without presenting any concrete interpretations marked the performance as one of the most memorable in the production history of *Verkommenes Ufer*.

A lack of detailed material prevents me from discussing two productions that followed the Bochum 'Uraufführung' in great depth. They are, however, of interest for both their reception of the material and their subsequent redirection of it. Hansgünther Heyme together with Wolf Münzer and Paul Schalich put on *Verkommenes Ufer* in the Kammertheater of the Staatstheater, Stuttgart (première 8 December 1983). Münzer then went on to join forces with Wolf-Siegfried Wagner in the Münchner Kammerspiele, Munich, to première the play almost a year later on 14 November 1984. Both productions reduced the independence of the three scenes by subordinating them to a unifying 'Fabel' of sorts.

An associate of Heyme, Prof. Hanns-Dietrich Schmidt, wrote: 'die damalige Inszenierung versetzte das Stück in die unmittelbare Nachkriegszeit in Deutschland (1945/46). Der ganze Text wurde von einer Schauspielerin, die in alle Rollen schlüpfte, gespielt, ein *Monolog* mit verschiedenen Ebenen'.[146] Heyme's wife, Helga David, took on this role, with the aid of

---

144 Anon., 'Katastrophen und Tändeleien', *Neue Züricher Zeitung (Fernausgabe)*, 1-5-83; and Thomas Wiltberger, 'Endzeitsstimmung und antike Tragödie: Müller Premiere in Bochum', 25-4-83.

145 Erdmann, p. 42.

the dwarf actor, Gotthard Dietrich, whose physical attributes provided a direct debunking of the Jason myth. The performance started in the foyer. Heyme reminisced to the audience about his post-war experiences, about how he had believed that the US army was the saviour of Germany and how quickly that had evaporated. The audience was then led into the auditorium which was set out as a cheap cinema (which took up Müller's 'peep-show' suggestion). Inside, GIs sat as spectators, rubbing large strapped-on, plastic penises while a pornographic film was shown. Medea then took the centre-stage with Jason at her feet dressed as a torero, and crudely performed 'Verkommenes Ufer' to the soldiers. All the events of 'Medeamaterial' were quoted rather enacted, with Jason providing a couple of dolls to act as the sons. Medea then strapped on her own dildo for 'Landschaft mit Argonauten' and the GIs demonstratively opened Coke cans and smoked Camels. The main tension was created by the interplay between the soldiers and the actress. The critique of the consumer society and its excesses in Bochum was replaced by the theme of colonization and its repercussions. Medea became commodified by her audience which parasitically consumed her cultural products. By the end, she resembled her audience and we were left to ponder whether she had been subsumed or she was being subversive.

Critics were torn between the associative strength of the text and the limiting context of the production. The production became a *pièce-à-clef*. Gerhard Stadelmaier complained about the search for allegories that the production seemed to provoke, whilst condemning the didactic aspect: 'In Stuttgart war man "gelehrt" und dumpf. Aus dem toten Stern ward ein historisches Seminar. Müllers Stücke sind [...] für Oberlehrer nichts'.[147] A similar story was told by Martin Koch: 'an manchen Stellen wirkt Heymes Polit-Idee zu akademisch'.[148]

In Munich, *Verkommenes Ufer* followed *Die Hamletmaschine* and each play featured only two actors. Manfred Zapatka played Hamlet and Jason, Margit Carstensen played Ophelia and Medea. Carstensen told me, 'in dem *Verkommenen Ufer* haben wir versucht, das Schicksal einer Frau aus dem sozialistischen Osten im kapitalistischen Westen zu beschreiben'.[149] The

---

146 Unpublished letter from Hanns-Dietrich Schmidt to the author, 14-1-95.

147 Gerhard Stadelmaier, 'Verkommene Show mit Germania: Schmerzensjodler', *Stuttgarter Zeitung*, 10-12-83.

148 Martin Th. Koch, 'Das Glück der Schamlippen', *Uni Journal*, 1/84.

context, again, was given by the icon of the US soldier. Jason now became an officer, the sons two GIs. The bridal gown presented to Jason was the Red Flag and Medea carried a concentration camp tattoo on her arm and SS runes on her thighs. One of the directors said in an interview, 'wir inszenieren aber keine Endzeitsituation, sondern die Situation eines Imperialisten, die sich immer wiederholt'.[150] The production expressly renounced the Bochum style in order create a 'Fabel'. The possible fatalism of the 'Endzeit' was replaced by a reading that linked the play to a cyclical concept of history which was waiting to be broken. The multiple levels that the text created were not collapsed, as in Stuttgart, and Armin Eichholz commented on the variety given to the role by Carstensen, who played 'von einer Tragödin zu Seeräuber Jenny'.[151] Likewise, the finale, 'Landschaft mit Argonauten' was complimented by Ute Fischbach for the way Jason 'macht seinen Tod zum allgemeinen Ereignis'.[152] The Munich production managed to integrate a collective approach to the acting style and a broad historical context in a way in which each complemented the other. Neither aspect dominated and so the director's concept was able to exist together with the collectivity of the text.

The 'DDR-Erstaufführung' took place at the Berliner Ensemble on 29 November 1987 under the direction of Peter Konwitschny. As with *Leben Gundlings* before it, the play had been partially premièred before: extracts were read by Müller at the Volksbühne, East Berlin, on 10 November 1986 and others were performed in the context of a 'Medea-Projekt' in Rostock, 21 June 1987. Although advertised as a 'Gastspiel', the production was only such because both the director and actress were non-BE personnel - it had not been put on at another theatre beforehand. There were also no overt cultural-political reasons behind its late appearance. I was assured by Wolfgang Schuch of the Henschelverlag that by that time in the history of the GDR, 'Geschichtspessimismus' was no longer a valid ground for refusing

149 Unpublished letter from Margit Carstensen to the author, 17-1-95.

150 In Charlotte Nennecke, 'Klassische Figuren in neuer Umgebung', *SZ*, 14-11-84.

151 Armin Eichholz, 'Das Abgründige in Hamlet und Medea', *Münchner Morgenzeitung*, 16-11-84.

152 Ute Fischbach, 'Hamlet zertrümmert den Kopf von Marx', *Münchner Morgenzeitung*, 14-11-84.

permission to stage plays.[153] Its late première does initially call Schuch's assessment into question but he also contended that resistance to 'dangerous' authors like Müller was also evident in the structures of the theatres themselves. Certain 'Intendanten' would torpedo young directors' plans before they ever reached the dramaturges. Others were too scared of invoking the SED's wrath by staging the work of 'undesirables'. The only forums for Müller were in the big cities where more heavyweight support was available.

According to the documentation of the play, Konwitschny had wanted to put it on for some time, finding it both necessary to stage Müller in the GDR and challenging for the theatre *per se*.[154] He wanted an older, more motherly actress to take on Medea so that the impression could be given that she was now looking back and taking stock. This he found in the sixty-one year old Hanneliese Shantin from Rostock. Discussions of the text then began in early 1987 and rehearsals of 'Medeamaterial' started that April. Having gained the approval of both the BE 'Intendant' Manfred Wekwerth and Heiner Müller, the production was put on in the 'Probebühne' at the end of November.

The custom-built set, erected by the BE, suggested an unknown disaster in a recording studio.[155] A charred mixing desk, damaged loud speakers and a tree made out of frayed cables provided the single set against which Shantin acted. The image of 'technology gone too far' accompanied the production throughout. The actress, however, started on top of the lighting gantry that stood over the set and delivered 'Verkommenes Ufer' from there. Dressed in an army raincoat with a clown's nose, she pushed over a life-size effigy of Müller before laughing her way through the first few lines. This ironic gesture of defiance towards the author constructed the performance as one of irreverence, although her red nose undermined any clear interpretation of the action. Only the 'Weiber von Kolchis' (H p. 91) made her stop and re-think her delivery. Another run through of the

153 Unpublished interview with Wolfgang Schuch by the author, 30-3-95.

154 'Arbeitsbericht', in Eva Qualmann, *Dokumentation zu Heiner Müllers 'Verkommenes Ufer'* (held in the Zentrum für Theaterdokumentation- und Information, Berlin).

155 This description follows the extensive photo-documentation in the Zentrum für Theaterdokumentation- und Information and *Heiner Müllers 'Verkommenes Ufer'*, audio tape of the Berliner Ensemble production, East Berlin, 29-11-87 (also held in the Zentrum für Theaterdokumentation und -Information, Berlin).

speech showed more understanding. Then a telephone, positioned on the gantry, rang and the actress' voice was heard at the other end of the line reciting the 'sie hocken in den Zügen' lines (H ibid.) with more seriousness. A dialogue developed between the two voices. Just as the telephone voice reached the line 'auf dem Grund aber Me...' (H p. 92) the phone went dead and the actress tried, in vain, to re-connect. She then climbed down onto the stage, delivering the scene from the top with more understanding and insight. Music and sounds were also played on tape to accompany the memories. The first movement of Beethoven's '*Spring*' *Sonata* was combined with an air-raid siren, an easy listening tune by Roger Whitaker and the deafening noise of the S-Bahn created an aural backdrop. Each sound evoked an aspect of big city life creating an aural collage. The last (Medea) lines were spoken with irony and cunning. They were then repeated on tape, built up word by word.[156] The actress then took off her coat and clown's nose to reveal a black dress with gold diagonal stripes. She also put on a turban. The exotic costume suggested Medea's 'foreignness' to the audience and defined her as an uprooted bride.

The exchanges between Medea and the Nurse, and Medea and Jason presented an interesting 'Verfemdungseffekt'. Medea found a microphone dangling from the studio and, after some acoustic experiments, summoned up the courage to use the technology in order to play the extra roles through it. The fairly realistic Medea was contrasted with the sterner, more distant voices of the other two, which echoed slightly. The microphone was then hung on a stand downstage right and the monologue began. The verse form was used to emphasize the artifice at certain points as Medea banged out the pentameters with her feet. A variety of means was used to convey the speaking figure, although these did not overly resemble the more Grotowskian style of Bochum. A measured, eclectic style of acting swung from self-hatred to revenge, from considered thought to emotional pain. All extra props were provided by the set: the two sons were walkmans (their deaths signified by their unplugging), the mirror a piece of foil from the cable-tree, the bridal gown a sheet of plastic found on the floor. The acting was also very efficient in its use of the limited space. When Medea told the sons of her 'Schauspiel', she left the stage with them to assume the role of a spectator. The final lines were then repeated both slowly and quickly on tape while Medea prepared the stage for the next scene.

'Landschaft mit Argonauten' saw a desk brought onto the stage with a cardboard box full of hats next to it. Medea donned a collar and tie

---

156   That is: 'Auf', 'Auf dem', 'Auf dem Grund', etc.

leaving the dress on view underneath. She then tested the microphone, now on the desk, with the aid of a stage technician before starting. Up until 'der Jugoslawische Traum' (H p. 99), she tried on the various hats to see which would best fit the speaker of the lines. The hats trawled through history. A contemporary 'Vopo' helmet preceded a topper, a pith helmet and Brecht's famous cap, to name but four. The initial part of the monologue became highly comical. Shantin was both searching for the speaker of the lines as well as showing how each of the personae could have spoken them. The declamatory style gave way to cynicism when the actress drank schnapps, smoked a cigarette and sang along to the song 'La Paloma Ohé'. The voice became more desperate, directly addressing the audience at some points. The speech then gained more irony when she donned a pair of glasses and brought on a typewriter. Typing the lines from 'Wortschlamm aus meinem' (H p. 100) until the end of the scene, she assumed, at first, the manner of a writer. Müller was implicated in her parody, after all they were the words of a male author. As the typing got quicker, the simultaneity suggested in Müller's note to the text became evident. Recordings of the first two scenes started to compete with the actress. By the end all three were on tape in a cacophony of sounds. The actress then put on the trench coat and the nose again and heard the final lines from the first row. She clapped enthusiastically and then tried to get the audience to do the same. Resigned she got up, and dragged out the Müller effigy.

On the whole, the performance achieved a binding of the scenes through the casting of a single actress whilst the scenes themselves were constructed in very different styles. The playfulness of the production went on to undermine the image of Müller as an inaccessible and difficult writer. The problematic relationship of the author to the text was made explicit by the use of the effigy. The problem of the author's role was highlighted in the visualized question of whether we can throw him away as Shantin did at the play's commencement. Her own relationship with 'Verkommenes Ufer' mirrored our own initial impressions of the text. At first she tried to laugh off the seemingly ridiculous lines. Only experiencing them in a more open-minded way could she find elements within them that had meaning for her. Technically, the alienation effects that ran throughout opened up the text and allowed the flow of associations from actress to audience. The exposure of the artifice allowed a subjective reading of the play whilst presenting it as one of many. The comic context resisted the hopelessness of Bochum and subverted the seriousness of Stuttgart. Medea the victim chose a new set of weapons which included irony.

It is hard to judge the reception from the handful of reviews, but the overwhelming response was that of admiration for the variety brought to such a small stage by just one actress. The GDR critics also praised Kon-witschny for actually staging *Verkommenes Ufer* without compromising the text.

At the end of the eighties, B. K. Tragelehn staged the play in the Kleines Haus of the Schauspielhaus in Düsseldorf (première 3 June 1989). Rehearsals lasted for a good three months and allowed the production all the time it needed. Its duration of roughly two hours made it the longest performance of the work of the five productions discussed in this section. This was partly due to the half hour spent on the first scene, although 'Medeamaterial' did run to an hour itself.

One of the most interesting features of this production was the structuring and the integration of the audience. Tickets were sold with either a 'W' (for 'weiblich') or an 'M' (for 'männlich') on them. As the spectators arrived they were ushered through one of two doors, depending on their respective genders. 'Es war wie im Schwimmbad oder in anderen öffent-lichen Einrichtungen' reported Frank Busch.[157] The audience was divided: the sexes sat opposite each other in small grandstands, the playing area was in the middle. We see that before the performance had even begun, the question of gender was clearly emphasized. Each sex was able to watch both the two actors and the reactions of the other sex. Spectators were allowed to mix the theatrical with the 'real' and to observe how the two interacted with each other.

The stage itself was controlled by hydraulics so that it could be raised or lowered. This was used to good effect. The stage sat parallel to the first row in 'Verkommenes Ufer', which helped include the audience, as we shall see. For 'Medeamaterial' it was raised to highlight the text's status as a theatrical dialogue to be watched and to concentrate the spectator on the staged actions rather than the audience opposite. The stage sunk for 'Land-schaft mit Argonauten': Jason became a trapped rat in an arena. At one end of the playing area, which was just beyond the two grandstands, sat the Nurse at a school teacher's desk, a blackboard behind her and a bag of books and other props by her side. For each scene she would write the title on the board, then go back to her chair and knit.

Tragelehn picked up on the choral function found in the attribution of 'Verkommenes Ufer' in the *Urmedea*.[158] Barbara Nüsse and Peter Loh-

---

157 Frank Busch, 'Teilsieg im Krieg der Geschlechter', *Süddeutsche Zeitung*, 6-7-89.

158 The following description is based on a video of the performance, but it should not be taken as representative: Tragelehn told me in an unpublished interview

meyer, as denoted in the programme, were not yet Medea and Jason: for this scene they were just 'Frau' and 'Mann'. Each sat in the front row of their gender's grandstand. With the house lights up, the two started to articulate the lines, gradually forming words and phrases alternately. An acoustic battle of sorts developed between the two when the actors left their places to confront each other. The Woman took the word 'Keksschachteln' and the Man took the following word 'Kothaufen' (both H p. 91) and began to chant them against each other. With beckoning gestures each chorus leader encouraged his/her chorus to join the fray, which they did. Having 'defined' the two gender positions, the use of the words as weapons continued. Short pantomimes developed when certain lines resonated more for the Woman, certain more for the Man. Repetition of simulated coitus around the lines 'STOSS MICH KOMM SÜSSER' (H ibid.) was followed by a more narrative description by the Woman of the lines 'Bis ihm die Argo den Schädel zertrümmert' (H ibid.). The four lines which start with 'Sie hocken in den Zügen' (H ibid.) were then said in unison by both choruses (the two leaders gestured to the text printed in the programmes). Towards the end of the speech, the Man turned on a record player that evoked the popular music of the post-war years and both leaders encouraged members of the opposite sex to dance with them on the common ground of the playing area. The associative elements were played for all they were worth. The lines 'Traum von einem ungeheuerlichen / Beischlaf in Chicago' (H ibid.) raised a smile while several couples from the audience danced their way around the stage. The dancers then returned to their seats and left the Man and Woman to say the last few lines. The memory of the hanged 'cowards' made the Woman laugh, then cough, then simulate vomiting. The Medea lines, said twice by the Woman, shocked the Man who spat out the drink he was then consuming. 'Verkommenes Ufer' became a 'Lehrstück' of sorts. The audiences were encouraged to enter as actors. The common speaking of lines attempted to give the audience first-hand experience of the texts whilst maintaining a division of the sexes. The audiences were 'rehearsing' their relationships to each other.

The stage was raised and the houselights went down. Two chairs, previously unused, stood at the opposite end of the stage to the Nurse and signified thrones. Jason returned to the male grandstand to watch the first exchanges. Each line addressed to the Nurse, who still sat knitting at her desk, took a long slow walk from Medea from one end of the stage to the

(27-3-95) that audience reactions varied from night to night and that the effects recorded on the video were particularly successful.

other before she could deliver them. The verse measures were adhered to and it was only when Jason entered that they started to be neglected by the actress's increase in pace. Jason's delivery was mainly calm, only one outburst brought him out of this and thus he remained fairly 'natural'. The monologue naturally produced many changes in cadence with swings from the declamatory, to the narrative, to the emotional. When the sons were addressed, Medea brought on two dolls with cutaway stomachs that showed internal organs (the type used in biology lessons). The children were addressed from Medea's throne while Jason sat in his. The bridal gown was then brought out of a suitcase that Medea fetched from the Nurse and was draped over Jason. A final kiss and embrace took place under its veil. Jason returned to the male audience. Medea donned a white doctor's coat and photographed members of the female audience with a Polaroid camera. After a sober rendition of more of the monologue she then moved to where she had left the children and built, whilst speaking, a house of cards with the pictures. This was then set on fire, leaving charred remains. The precarious past had been destroyed. At the point where Medea accuses the children of treachery, she gently arranged the dolls' organs around them in a circle to the sound of Mozart's 'Maurische Trauermusik', which communicated the contradictory elements of murder and tragedy. The reckoning with Jason was quite cool and once the last line had been delivered, the voice of Eric Clapton was heard over the PA thanking a live audience before starting on the song 'Wonderful Tonight'.

That signalled the quick change to 'Landschaft mit Argonauten'. Medea looked on from the Nurse's desk while the stage sank and a small canvas wall was raised around the playing area to enclose Jason. Surveying the audience from his new position, he donned a World War II tin helmet. The militarist theme had been initiated. Up until the line 'SEEMANNS BRAUT IST DIE SEE' (H p. 98) Jason was forced to fight the Clapton song which punctuated his verses and chased him around the enclosed space. The declamatory tone continued a little longer. Jason then read out an Argonaut's roll call which included the real argonauts and figures from more modern times. These included Joseph Conrad, Rudyard Kipling, Adolf Hitler and Wolf Biermann. The context was broad and male. In terms of value judgements, the figures differed greatly. Tragelehn was nonetheless drawing our attention to the theme of the male and the results of his mobility. Cynicism then started to replace the coldness of the delivery, and a desperation then set in. Jason started to disrobe and run around the pen. Pinned in a corner, Jason was forced to come to terms with the lines, repeating some of them (for example, 'ODER DIE GLÜCKLOSE LAND-

UNG', H p. 100, thrice, 'DO YOU REMEMBER DO YOU NO I DONT', H p. 101, six times, getting higher each time). After that he slowly moved into the centre of the area and got dressed again. The barrier fell and there was a total blackout. The intensity of the performance left us with a void at the end: there was nowhere further to go. After the great expenditure of energy, Jason could only acquiesce.

The sparseness of the means emphasized the textual aspects of the play and allowed the audience to understand the associative nature of the lines. This was achieved with skill through the 'activation' of the spectators in 'Verkommenes Ufer'. The subsequent changes in stage level also proved economical theatrical devices. The raising of the stage communicated the 'dramatic' nature of 'Medeamaterial' and its lowering turned Jason's monologue into a battle between the defendant and two very different types of jury. The central importance of the theatrical space defined some of the problems treated of in the production. The clash of the sexes dominated. The socio-critical or historical readings of the productions discussed earlier took second place. The lack of elaborate setting and the emphasis on the actors led Andreas Rossmann to write: 'die Regie [...] findet einfache, doch eindrücklich neue Bilder'.[159] Although there was praise for both the main actors, it was more the style of the staging that proved to have made the strongest impression.

IV More than Montage

The montage technique of *Verkommenes Ufer* confers an independence upon its elements, not seen in the other two examples. The thematic connections between the three parts are loose and allow for a broad range of possible associations. Unlike *Germania* and *Leben Gundlings*, there is no guiding thread. The description of a dilapidated river bank, Medea's reckoning with Jason and a journey through a modern landscape take motifs from different times and reference points. Consequently, one cannot 'read off' a context and develop realizations on this basis.

In each production, certain thematic elements were taken up. The sterility of the consumer society, American imperialism, the playful subversion of the text, and gender issues all took their cue from the subject matter of the scenes. The linking of seemingly incongruous texts has created a vast wealth of readings which has made each production diffuse with associative

159 Andreas Rossmann, 'Heiliger Heiner', *Frankfurter Allgemeine Zeitung*, 24-6-89.

material. Some credit for this lies with the construction of the scenes themselves.

'Verkommenes Ufer' and 'Landschaft mit Argonauten' are open to the collective realization of the texts. The various ways with which the scenes have been dealt exposes a highly subjective and multi-layered approach. At the BE, the actress communicated a sense of incomprehension at the first scene before she got under its skin and began to understand the fractured lines. In Düsseldorf, two collectives were activated in order to confront them with the text. Extra dimensions have been bestowed on the productions because of the active participation required to put them on the stage. Units of semic information have to be mediated in some manner and when the director and his cast face this problem the texts' full productivity is engaged. The Medea figure in the middle section also explodes the definition of the Friedrich character in *Leben Gundlings* or the 'Maurer' in *Germania*. The mass of impulses destroys linearity and one can imagine that the Medea role could be cast with several actresses.

The plurality of interpretation of *Verkommenes Ufer* would seem to rest on two factors. First, the thematic independence of the montage elements resists an obvious reading that unifies them. The themes of cyclical history or the GDR in *Germania*, or the Prussia complex or the critique of rationalism in *Leben Gundlings* provide a frame in the mind of the recipient. The disjunctive sections of text in *Verkommenes Ufer* resist such categories. Second, the problem of determining a 'Fabel' in any sense of the word (possibly except in the 'Medeamaterial') disturbs a direct cognitive effect. The suffusion of impulses in all the texts also destroys a linear conception of character. In each section there is a radical questioning of the speaking subject. The production team is forced to experiment with the different styles of associative material. Each scene functions in a wholly different way from the others. It would, for example, be difficult to envisage a successful production which applied the same technique to 'Verkommenes Ufer' and to 'Landschaft mit Argonauten'. For the first time in the three montages under discussion (with the possible exception of the figure in 'Nachtstück') we are faced with the collective construction of figures on stage. The mediation of the various resonances demands an eclectic approach which again has no clear destination in terms of the eventual performance. This obfuscation is then combined with the unattributed status of the first and third scenes which confronts its realizers with problems that require their active input.

The call for simultaneity is also a provocative gesture. As with *Leben Gundlings*, one notes that this dimension is the product of a note appended to the text. Simultaneity was only ever hinted at in the Bochum production with its images of constant stasis, and in Berlin when the three scenes were all played over the PA at the end. It was the indeterminacy of the texts which inspired the plurality of the readings, rather than Müller's codicil. *Leben Gundlings*, as concluded in the discussion above, is a challenging work, although it is one whose challenge is signalled to a great extent by an appended note. The dramaturgy of *Verkommenes Ufer*, on the other hand, is provocative from the outset. The note becomes something of a superfluity. Its suggestions seem to restrict the material, rather than to uncover nuances in the dramaturgy. The suggested simultaneity becomes an option rather than an imperative.

Verkommenes Ufer breaks away from the montage technique that allies itself with thematic concerns. The text becomes 'Material' in a way that *Germania* and *Leben Gundlings* do not. Theatres are not presented with short, polemical scenes. Instead they are confronted with far more open and opaque ones. Both character and plot are highly problematized. The realization process itself is the site where the text starts to yield its potential.

We are left to ask whether the montage technique can still challenge the processes of the theatre. *Germania* and *Leben Gundlings* both present us with difficulties in terms of plot coherence. With the exception of the 'Nachtstück', all the scenes in *Germania* are provocative in terms of their subject matter, whilst remaining relatively easy to understand for an audience or a director. *Leben Gundlings* uses more pantomime scenes. It is correspondingly more difficult to digest cognitively. All the same, our interpretative problems are aided by thematic complexes which are signalled throughout. Both techniques of plot construction can be accounted for with relative ease (even if we are unable to surmise which associations are triggered by the juxtaposition of two or more disparate elements). My investigations have shown that these types of scenic combination have been accommodated into the contemporary theatrical *apparat* with few problems. Theatres *present* scenes without a commitment to explain them. Theatrical ignorance is no longer considered a shortcoming. *Verkommenes Ufer* is more resistant. Its lack of obvious points of reference has more to do with a sense of incomprehension *within* the scenes. When these are then juxtaposed with each other, we realize that we are dealing with three incommensurable elements. The theatre has little trouble (and perhaps even delights) in presenting differently defined scenes one after the other. Once the definition has become problematic, the theatre is forced to engage with the text in ways which demand interpretation on a more fundamental level.

Disrupting the coherence of a plot no longer shocks us. The contemporary scene is one which has accepted its own ignorance and feels few qualms in delegating it to contemporary audiences. Montage has only retained its associative suggestiveness in a climate which has grown accustomed to gaps and ruptures in the texture of artistic output. The true challenge now lies in making the act of presentation problematic. From the trio of texts, only *Verkommenes Ufer* achieves this. Such an assertion is borne out by the great variety of staged interpretations.

Conclusion

1   The First Reception

In the introduction to this book (section 5), I suggested that we were to understand the practical treatment in the theatre of Müller's later work as a first phase of a reception. This was based upon the politico-historical and geographical contexts of his biography. After the fall of the Berlin Wall and the liquidation of the GDR, production statistics showed a decline in interest in the East German dramatist. If we review the texts under discussion, we can see to what extent the GDR informed their production histories.

Germania Tod in Berlin and *Wolokolamsker Chaussee* explicitly deal with the GDR in several scenes. The pre-'Wende' treatment of both texts was suffused with polemical strains which focused on the role of the GDR in the context of the two Germanies. The existence of the GDR was a prerequisite for the stagings. After 1989, the defunct state became more a subject for historical analysis, in the case of both texts. In Berlin in 1990 the production of *Germania* had the quality of a bitter-sweet lament. In Hamburg in the same year, *Wolokolamsker Chaussee* was presented as a struggle to come to terms with the GDR. Bricks were piled high on a raked stage so that it was impossible to move freely without encountering resistance. Little or nothing has been done with either play since 1990.

Der Auftrag and *Die Hamletmaschine* take up the themes of revolution and failure. The dissection of the intellectual as a collective entity within broad historical frameworks was already a provocative subject in the context of a socialist state on German soil. The suggestion that a European revolution was bankrupt could still be considered tendentious in a Europe torn between free-market capitalism and a nominally socialist system. Without an Eastern bloc, the challenge of the subject matter becomes more abstract. The Cologne production of *Der Auftrag* in 1992 took a highly pessimistic attitude to the whole matter. The result was a bleak reading, pervaded by pathos. Our relationship to revolution (amongst other things) is still very much captured by the texts, although the collapse of the GDR has changed our attitudes towards it considerably. Both plays have continued to enjoy productions after 1989.

Leben Gundlings Friedrich von Preußen Lessings Schlaf Traum Schrei and *Verkommenes Ufer Medeamaterial Landschaft mit Argonauten* hardly refer to the GDR at all. Only the setting, 'See bei Straußberg', is mentioned in both. The two have functioned as critiques (of both the Prussian mentality, and modern-day consumerism and imperialism, respectively) and have been appropriated by both Germanies. *Leben Gundlings* at the Schiller-

Theater and the Volksbühne linked the pasts of each state with the pernicious workings of Prussia. *Verkommenes Ufer* never explicitly referred to either country in the productions that have been documented here. Neither has been particularly popular in the last few years.

Quartett, Bildbeschreibung, Macbeth and *Philoktet* have been the most performed works in the post-Wende period. Their non-specific settings and not overtly political subject matter seem to have resisted the demise of the GDR. *Bildbeschreibung* (and only to a certain extent *Quartett*) presents us with the formal challenges discussed in this thesis.

Müller's later output is broad. It does not concentrate on any one subject. At times, the GDR and the history of European socialism are at the centre. The treatment of these plays as texts for production has much to do with our relationship to history at specific moments. The subject of socialism has become perceived as 'irrelevant' and Müller has been shunned for his association with it, however problematic this is. This could account for why *Leben Gundlings* and *Verkommenes Ufer* have not been staged very much in the last few years, despite their 'non-GDR' content. At other times, Müller's critical eye trawls history for themes which recur over and over again. As with any text in this category, staging possibilities are broader and this is reflected in the recent production history of Müller's texts. It would seem, however, that Müller is being performed as a 'great dramatic poet' for the most part, rather than as a political dramatist. It is difficult to say whether the German theatre scene has become more conservative since the 'Wende' or whether it, like the rest of the newly reunified German society, is still trying to find its (political) feet again.

The question of a new reception hinges more on the plays which deal with the GDR and the politics of revolution than those which do not. The texts must be able to make the transition from polemical works to more general treatments of problems. The analyses of the texts have pointed to their robust nature. They are, for the most part, not as 'over-determined' as the output of other GDR authors. Consequently there is more opportunity for experiment within the realms of character and plot (both of which have been extensively problematized in Müller's *oeuvre* as a whole). New interpretations need not depend upon the material existence of an Eastern bloc. The movement away from a polemical stance also lends the texts more power as 'Material' in Müller's own sense. A didactic impulse is no longer called for because the subject matter has become historical.

The recent, untimely death of the dramatist on 30 December 1995 has re-positioned him in the consciousness of the theatre-going public. The lengthy obituaries, reminiscences and evaluations have, for the most part, celebrated Müller as one of the key figures in the drama of the twentieth

246

century. Several 'Prominente' from the worlds of literature and politics attended the funeral at the Dorotheenstädtischer Friedhof, where Brecht is also buried. Journalists report that copies of the playscripts have sold out. Müller is, at the moment, *the* subject of the public's cultural attention. Even if theatres merely present his plays as marks of respect, the processes required to realize much of the later work should produce performances as diverse as they are provocative. Until the East and the West grow together, however, there is likely to be a different reception in each half. Müller's more immanent role as 'therapist' for the East German stage will have to compete with his less productive role as a 'great writer' in the West.

2   Remaining in the Avant-Garde

The resistance of the texts themselves to the processes of the theatre is a dramaturgical problem. As proof of this we merely have to look at contemporary theatre history. Beckett's *Waiting for Godot*, Ionesco's *The Bald Primadonna*, Hochhuth's *Der Stellvertreter* and Handke's *Publikumsbeschimpfung* all generated scandals when they were premièred. In all these cases, the shocking subject matter of the plays proved initially provocative. It did not take long, however, for the institution of the theatre to accommodate them because they did not offer formal resistance to its mechanisms. The same has been true for Müller, too. B. K. Tragelehn reports that in 1971 the playwright had given him the manuscript of *Germania* to read. His reaction was to advise the author to show it to no-one.[1] The subsequent treatment of the play in production shows that after the initial shock, the text was assimilated into the theatre's canon.

Challenging subject matter is, of course, integral for an uncomfortable relationship between literature and theatre. The texts mentioned above are not lacking in that. Yet once they had been assimilated, disentangled or 'understood', their power was reduced. They became instruments of the theatre, parts of the repertoire. The shock of their content certainly broadened the theatre's perspectives, although today we can see that their 'classic' status confirms the fact that they are no longer the explosive products of yore. Shocking content is in no way an index of a play's long-term productivity. More resistant material is to be located in a play's form.

Müller maintains 'das Bleibende ist das Flüchtige'. The oxymoronic motto defines the precarious position of the author who seeks the 'Versch-

1   Unpublished interview with B. K. Tragelehn by the author, 27-3-95.

winden des Autors'.[2] Somehow the writer has to be able to evade the restricting clutches of rational exegeses. The work must not be fully appropriated by any one system of reference or meta-narrative. We should only see glimpses. As long as the theatre is unable to categorize (and consequently neutralize) a play it is still able to create a vibrant and challenging event for the spectators. 'The avant-garde' has always been concerned with methods and techniques which resist the broad category of 'the mainstream'. Texts must be able to re-define themselves in order to avoid the restricting effects of rational comprehension.

The title of the essay from which the two quotations are taken points to another important category in Müller's work, terror. 'Die Rolle des Schreckens, glaub ich, ist nichts anderes als zu erkennen, zu lernen. [...] Der wesentliche Punkt ist die Pädagogik durch Schrecken', he commented in 1981.[3] The script must also shock (by confronting us with the most cruel and visceral aspects of human life) in order to be effective. But Müller's texts, as we have seen, attempt to terrorize the theatre as much as the audience. The theatre must learn that it cannot master and appropriate texts at will. Its own position has to be redefined as the site of uncertainty. Unless this is achieved we are left with the standard problem for the director, formulated in Müller's characteristic manner as 'wie man in einem Bordell noch Erotik darstellen kann'.[4]

We have noted that Müller's dramaturgy can manage to frustrate the all-consuming and neutralizing attacks of the modern theatre, as long as certain criteria are satisfied. If the theatre can deal with dramaturgy with its traditional arsenal of theories and practices, it gains the upper hand and is

2   'Der Schrecken die erste Erscheinung des Neuen. Zu einer Diskussion über Postmodernismus in New York', in Frank Hörnigk (ed.), *Heiner Müller Material* (Göttingen: Steidl, 1989), both quotations p. 23.

3   'Ich muß mich verändern, statt mich zu interpretieren', in *Gesammelte Irrtümer 2*, p. 23.

4   Martin Linzer and Peter Ullrich (eds.), *Regie: Heiner Müller* (Berlin: Zentrum für Theaterdokumentation und -information, 1993), p. 68. The conversation continues with additional comments from the actor Hermann Beyer and the director Thomas Heise:

Beyer: Na gut, ich will eine gute Nutte sein.
Müller: Das will ich ja auch, aber wer kauft wen?
Heise: Das ist wirklich das Problem, wie schafft man, daß die Aufführung nicht zu vermarkten ist?

able to present problematic or shocking drama with ease. If the dramatist is able to subvert or even to explode the conventional mainstays of character and/or plot, then there is a chance for a more turbulent and productive relationship between text and performance in which neither has the chance to dominate. Müller's employment of unattributed character and undermining of plot has attacked the theatre at its most fundamental, without compromise. One is still unable to give a character analysis of *Wolokolamsker Chaussee* or a plot summary of *Verkommenes Ufer*. The incommensurability of the texts confers on them a vitality that hard-hitting yet conventionally written plays often lack. And this is how Müller differentiates himself as a dramatist from all who have gone before him.

One could, of course, argue that every great playwright has produced a huge variety of interpretations (and that that this is a mark of their greatness). We have no way of pinning down Hamlet's character, we do not know whether Antigone or Creon or neither or both are in the right. Great plays examine problems, they do not necessarily solve them. By refusing to judge, they maintain the cleavage between text and performance. Müller, however, rends it asunder. In the drama that preceded his, we could at least ascertain the basics of character or plot. In Müller's later works these features are luxuries. The more fundamental assault on the genre of drama exposes the discrete theatrical units of text, production and performance in order to galvanize the institution of the theatre. Familiar points of reference are subverted and transformed. The director is required to manufacture his/her own. The blistering diversity of the realizations of Müller at his most provocative bear witness to the strength of a dramaturgy that cannot be apprehended. The writing of the plays is not formulaic, there is no dramaturgical key. The resistance to character in *Die Hamletmaschine* is quite different from that in *Wolokolamsker Chaussee* or *Bildbeschreibung*. Similarly, the formal obfuscation of plot in *Verkommenes Ufer* is distinctly demarcated from techniques employed in the above three plays.

Müller does not, however, consistently produce works that stick in the throat of the theatre. *Leben Gundlings* and *Der Auftrag* both feature techniques which function covertly. The dramaturgy of hoarding in the former and the status of the characters as 'remembered' in the latter does not have to be (and at times have not been) taken up in performance. Both plays can be dealt with by ignoring these factors. And if challenges can be ignored, the theatre can appropriate the texts all the more easily. It is not forced to experiment and as a result the texts lose their some of their vital potential.

3   The Model of a Modern Major Dramatist?

In the introduction and in the subsequent chapters it has been impossible to ignore the comparisons between Müller and Brecht in the secondary literature and in newspaper reviews. Müller's own affection for and continued reference to Brecht in interviews, essays and the 'Spielplan' of the Berliner Ensemble, where he was the 'Intendant' until his death, compound the matter. His predilection for the 'Lehrstück' as *the* site of pedagogy in the theatre and his dramaturgy which mirrors Barthes's prognosis for a post-Brechtian theatre (quoted in the introduction) mark him as the most astute successor and modifier of Brechtian dialectical theatre.[5] Müller manufactures a political theatre in which politics is actively played off against the human subject within the framework of history. The refusal to simplify political decisions and to peddle reductive messages characterizes the tone of the later work. The formation of collective speakers actively challenges our conception of the individual and proposes a new politics.

Yet the introduction brought up a different problem for a political dramatist whose work seemed to correspond with Wilde's dictum of writing either well or badly, regardless of the subject matter. Barnard Turner sums up the problem when asserting that Müller's '"postmodernist" move into boundless interpretive context is checked by the "classicist" view that the texts are unquestionably *about* something'.[6] This 'something' is, naturally, always political. Müller is forced to deal with politics in such a questioning way because of the great historical defeats that socialism has sustained this century. The failure of the Soviet experiment and, more particularly, the GDR has demanded a new political discourse in theatre. Müller is very much interested in the future of Marxism (he is therefore a didactic writer of the Enlightenment school in this sense, just like Brecht) but it is a future which has to submit itself to ruthless (self-)examination in order to have a future. This examination is located in the revolutionary form of his later

5   Superficial links with features of the theatres of Bertolt Brecht abound in Müller. The task of precisely identifying and examining them still remains. We are yet to be presented with a comprehensive thesis that defines the term 'Brechtian' and how it relates to Müller's work. I believe that the fundamentally dialectical view of reality and its representation on stage is probably the most important point of contact.

6   Barnard Turner, 'Müller and Postmodern Classicism: Construction and Theatre', in Gerhard Fischer (ed.), *Heiner Müller. ConTEXTS and HISTORY* (Tübingen: Stauffenberg, 1995), p. 189.

works. Müller's engagement with the problems of emancipation have been undertaken to achieve emancipation; his tenacity towards the difficulties involved acknowledge that emancipation has to confront a series of Herculean challenges if it is to be realized. Müller *is* a committed political writer, yet his commitment is not to a particular party programme; it is a commitment to an aesthetic capable of exploring and testing that programme.

The question arises whether Müller has reached some sort of impasse as a dramatist. Has he solved the problems for which Brechtian dramaturgy is often reproached, such as its perceived reductiveness or naïvety? He has certainly pushed political discourse in the theatre to new limits. Its status as 'Material' within a socio-historical context allows it to be criticized from all sides. In this way it may develop beyond the rigid constraints imposed by theatrical message-mongerers (who try to preserve their 'messages' by pretending there is no breach between text and performance). Critics who have sought to attack Müller have never attempted to criticize the dramaturgy. They have always objected to the socialist, anti-Western impulses in the works. Their objections are either moral or conservative.[7]

The reception of Müller among other writers is also very interesting. Those who show an obvious debt to Müller's style in their work have never really been able to go beyond it.[8] Volker Braun has most consistently aped Müller's textual practices, with the result of reducing the impact of his own work. *Simplex Deutsch* reminds us of *Germania, Transit Europa. Ausflug der Toten* has shades of *Der Auftrag* and the title and organization of *Siegfried Frauenprotokolle Deutscher Furor* imitates *Leben Gundlings* and *Verkommenes Ufer*. Direct reappropriation implies that Braun has ignored the 'necessity' of Müller's innovative techniques (see below). Lothar Trolle and Albert Ostermeier, too, are heavily influenced by Müller. Their work is not so

7   Cf. Horst Domdey/Richard Herzinger, 'Byzanz gegen Rom. Heiner Müllers Manichäismus', in Heinz Ludwig Arnold (ed.), *Literatur in der DDR. Rückblicke* (Munich: Text und Kritik, 1991), pp. 246-57 (or almost any other criticism written by either); Helmut Fuhrmann, 'Der Mythos der Revolution: Heiner Müllers *Der Auftrag*', in *Forum Modernes Theater*, 2/90, 139-54; or Heinz-Dietrich Kittsteiner, 'Und draußen ging die Welt an uns vorbei. Überlegungen zu Heiner Müllers Stück *Wolokolamsker Chaussee*', in Paul Gerhard Klussmann and Heinrich Mohr (eds.), *Jahrbuch zur Literatur der DDR*, vol. 7 (Bonn: Bouvier, 1990), pp. 11-28, for example.

8   Not surprisingly, many have chosen to ignore him. Christoph Hein, Frank Xaver Kroetz and Peter Hacks have pursued a political theatre which is, broadly speaking, post-Brechtian. Their approach, however, has been less experimental than Müller's.

blatantly derivative. Consequently they use the dramaturgy as a tool to mobilize 'Material' whilst combining it with their own ideas. All the same, one cannot assert that any of these writers have pushed political theatre any further than their primary influence. They have not managed to construct a dramaturgy that takes the drama beyond Müller's parameters, which were discussed above. We are left pondering whether Müller represents the end of dialectical drama.

The qualities of Müller's revolutionary practice have been achieved in a highly unschematic way. The playwright's own 'ignorance' is betrayed in his output. One can only posit theories, for example, as to the function of the attribution in *Die Hamletmaschine* because there is no definitive answer to such rationalist questions. Müller's writing technique is based upon notions of sentences and dramatic structures 'hanging together' in a conflict-ridden text, regardless of the perplexing results. His appropriation of dramatic devices from antiquity via Shakespeare to Brecht has always been dependent upon finding points of utility and then problematizing them within his own scheme. Different dramaturgies are able to clash with each other, just like the subject matter, in the plays. The movement away from intention in order to create 'Inseln der Unordnung' has proved to be Müller's strength and has allowed the texts a theatrical vitality unparalleled in the modern theatre.[9] Whether the political theatre can do any more than question and relativize itself is a problem which has not even been formulated in theory. It is still hard to envisage a post-Müllerian theatre.

9   Heiner Müller, 'Mich interessiert der Fall Althusser', in Hörnigk (ed.), p. 28.

Bibliography

Primary Texts by Heiner Müller

Müller, Heiner, *Germania*, tr. by Bernard and Caroline Schütze (New York: Semiotext(e), 1990)
-, *Germania Tod in Berlin* ,Texte 5 (Berlin: Rotbuch, 1977) = G
-, *Gesammelte Irrtümer* (Frankfurt/Main: Verlag der Autoren, 1986)
-, *Gesammelte Irrtümer 2* (Frankfurt/Main: Verlag der Autoren, 1990)
-, *Gesammelte Irrtümer 3* (Frankfurt/Main: Verlag der Autoren, 1994)
-, *Geschichten aus der Produktion 1*, Texte 1 (Berlin: Rotbuch, 1974) = GP1
-, *Geschichten aus der Produktion 2*, Texte 2 (Berlin: Rotbuch, 1974) = GP2
-, *Herzstück*,Texte 7 (Berlin: Rotbuch, 1983) = H
-, *Jenseits der Nation. Heiner Müller im Interview mit Frank M. Raddatz* (Berlin: Rotbuch, 1991)
-, *Krieg ohne Schlacht* (Cologne: Kiepenheuer und Witsch, 1992)
-, *Mauser* ,Texte 6 (Berlin: Rotbuch, 1978) = M
-, *Rotwelsch* (Berlin: Merve, 1982)
-, *Die Schlacht. Wolokolamsker Chaussee*, (Frankfurt/Main: Verlag der Autoren, 1988)
-, *Shakespeare Factory 1* ,Texte 8 (Berlin: Rotbuch, 1985) = SF1
-, *Shakespeare Factory 2* ,Texte 9 (Berlin: Rotbuch, 1989) = SF2
-, *Die Umsiedlerin oder das Leben auf dem Lande*, Texte 3 (Berlin: Rotbuch, 1975)
-, *Zur Lage der Nation. Heiner Müller im Interview mit Frank M. Raddatz* (Berlin: Rotbuch, 1990)

Other Primary and Secondary Literature

Aristotle, *Poetics*, tr. by Leon Golden (New Jersey: Prentice-Hall, 1968)
Barnett, David, '"Ich erfinde gerne Zitate": Interview mit Heiner Müller', *GDR Bulletin*, 2/96, pp. 9-13
-, 'Some Notes on the Difficulties of Operating Heiner Müller's *Die Hamletmaschine*', *German Life and Letters*, 1/95, pp. 75-85
Barthes, Roland, *Image Music Text*, tr. by Stephen Heath (London: Fontana, 1977), pp. 69-78

Bathrick, David, 'The Theatre of the White Revolution is Over', in Reinhold Grimm and Jost Hermand (eds.), *Blacks and German Culture* (Wisconsin: The University of Wisconsin Press, 1986), pp. 135-49

Becker, Thorsten, 'Ewige, umständliche Überlegungen zu Heiner Müllers *Verkommenes Ufer*', *Düsseldorfer Debatte*, 12/85, pp. 45-53

Beckmann, Heinz, 'Heiner Müllers Auswüchse', *Zeitwende*, 1979, pp. 186-7

Bek, Alexander, *Die Wolokolamsker Chaussee. Erzählung* (Berlin: Militärverlag der Deutschen Demokratischen Republik, 1962)

Benjamin, Walter, *Illuminationen*, selected writings vol. 1, ed. by Siegfried Unseld (Frankfurt/Main: Suhrkamp, 1977)

Bergstedt, Alfred, and Morling, Kerstin, 'Zu Anna Seghers Erzählung "Das Duell" (1965) und Heiner Müllers "Wolokolamsker Chaussee III: Das Duell" (1986)', *Wissenschaftliche Zeitschrift der brandenburgischen Landeshochschule*, 5/90, pp. 693-704

Bertram, Christian, 'Machine Morte oder Der entfesselte Wahnsinn. Heiner Müllers *Die Hamletmaschine*', in *Spectaculum 33*, 1980, pp. 308-11

Birringer, Johannes, *Theatre, Theory, Postmodernism* (Bloomington and Indianapolis: 1991, Indiana University Press)

Boal, Augusto, *Theatre of the Oppressed*, tr. by Charles A. and Maria-Odilia Leal-McBride (London: Pluto, 1979)

Bock, Stephan, 'Müller spielen "Brecht" erinnern', in Wolfgang Storch (ed.), *Explosion of a Memory* (Berlin: Hentrich, 1988), pp. 155-7

Brecht, Bertolt, *Große kommentierte Berliner und Frankfurter Ausgabe*, ed. by Werner Hecht, Jan Knopf, Werner Mittenzwei and Klaus-Detlef Müller, *Schriften 1-4*, vols. 21-24 (Berlin, Weimar and Frankfurt/Main: Suhrkamp, 1991-3)

-, *Der Untergang des Egoisten Johann Fatzer* (Leipzig: Suhrkamp, 1994)

Brenner, Eva Elisabeth, '*Hamletmachine* Onstage: a Critical Analysis of Heiner Müller's Play in Production*, unpublished PhD thesis, New York University, 1994

Brook, Peter, *The Shifting Point* (London: Methuen, 1989)

Buck, Theo, 'Von der fortschreitenden Dialektisierung des Dramas. Anmerkung zur Dramaturgie bei Bertolt Brecht und Heiner Müller', *Forum Modernes Theater*, 1/89, pp. 16-28

-, 'Zwei Träume vom deutschen Theater. Anmerkungen zu Heiner Müllers Lessing Tripychon', in Georg Stötzel (ed.), *Germanistik. Forschungsstand und Perspektiven. Vorträge des deutschen Germanistentages in Passau 1984* (Berlin: Walter de Gruyter, 1985), pp. 478-91

Caravjal, Christa, '*Die Hamletmaschine* on two stages: Heiner Müller's allegories and the problem of translation', in Karelisa V. Hartigan (ed.), *Text and Presentation*, vol. 9 (Lanham: University Press of America, 1989), pp. 13-20

Case, Sue Ellen, *Developments in Post-Brechtian Political Theater: The Plays of Heiner Müller* (Ann Arbor: University Microfilms International, 1991)

-, 'From Bertolt Brecht to Heiner Müller', in *Performing Arts Journal*, 1/83, pp. 94-102

Chiarloni, Anna, 'Zu Heiner Müllers "Duell"', in Frank Hörnigk (ed.), *Heiner Müller Material* (Göttingen: Steidl, 1989), pp. 226-35

Dassanowsky-Harris, Robert von, 'The Dream and the Scream: "Die deutsche Misere" and the unrealized GDR in Heiner Müllers *Germania'*, *New German Review*, 5-6/89-90, pp. 15-28

Domdey, Horst, and Herzinger, Richard, 'Byzanz gegen Rom. Heiner Müllers Manichäismus', in Heinz Ludwig Arnold (ed.), *Literatur in der DDR. Rückblicke* (Munich: Text und Kritik, 1991), pp. 246-57

Domdey, Horst, 'Ich lache über den Neger', in Paul Gerhard Klussmann and Heinrich Mohr (eds.), *Jahrbuch zur Literatur in der DDR*, vol. 6 (Bonn: Bouvier, 1987), pp. 220-34

-, 'Mit Nietzsche gegen Utopieverlust. Zur *Hamletmaschine* und Heiner Müllers Rezeption in West und Ost', in Gert-Joachim Glaeßner (ed.), *Die DDR in der Ära Honecker. Politik - Kultur - Gesellschaft* (Opladen: Westdeutscher, 1988)

-, 'Mythos als Phrase oder die Sinnesausstattung des Opfers', *Merkur*, 5/86, pp. 403-13

-, '"Der Tod eine Funktion des Lebens". Stalinmythos in Texten Heiner Müllers', in Paul Gerhard Klussmann and Heinrich Mohr (eds.), *Jahrbuch zur Literatur in der DDR*, vol. 5 (Bonn: Bouvier, 1986), pp. 65-89

Eckardt, Thomas, *Der Herold der Toten. Geschichte und Politik bei Heiner Müller* (Frankfurt/Main: Peter Lang, 1992)

Eisenstein, Sergei, *Das dynamische Quadrat*, tr. by Oksana Bulgakowa and Dietmar Hochmuth (Leipzig: Reclam, 1988)

-, *Towards a Theory of Montage*, tr. by Michael Glenny (London: British Film Institute, 1991)

Eke, Norbert Otto, *Heiner Müller: Apokalypse und Utopie* (Paderborn: Ferdinand Schöningh, 1989)

Elam, Keir, *The Semiotics of Theatre and Drama* (London: Routledge, 1980)

Eliot, T. S., *Collected Poems 1909-1962* (London: Faber and Faber, 1963)

Emmerich, Wolfgang, 'Der Alp der Geschichte. "Preußen" in Heiner Müllers *Leben Gundlings'*, in Paul Gerhard Klussmann and Heinrich Mohr (eds.), *Jahrbuch zur Literatur der DDR*, vol. 2 (Bonn: Bouvier, 1982), pp. 115-58

-, 'Gleichzeitigkeit. Vormoderne, Moderne und Postmoderne in der Literatur der DDR', in Heinz Ludwig Arnold (ed.), *Bestandsaufnahme Gegenwartsliteratur* (Munich: Text und Kritik, 1988), pp. 193-211

-, *Kleine Literaturgeschichte der DDR* (Frankfurt/Main: Luchterhand, 1989)

Fanon, Frantz, *Schwarze Haut, Weiße Maske*, tr. by Eva Moldenhauer (Frankfurt/Main: Suhrkamp, 1985)

-, *The Wretched of the Earth*, tr. by Constance Farrington (London: Penguin, 1967)

Fiebach, Joachim, *Inseln der Unordnung* (Berlin: Henschel, 1990)

Fischborn, Gottfried, Hörnigk, Frank, Streisand, Marianne, and Ullrich, Renate, '*Der Lohndrücker* von Heiner Müller (Für und Wider)', *Weimarer Beiträge*, 7/88, pp. 1180-1194

Fischborn, Gottfried, '"Poesie aus der Zukunft" und künstlerische Subjektivität heute. An einem Beispiel: Heiner Müllers "Wolokolamsker Chaussee I"', *Zeitschrift für Germanistik*, 4/88, pp. 442-8

-, 'Procedio und Oppolonius', in *Neue Deutsche Literatur*, 6/83, 44-57

Fischer-Lichte, Erika, *Semiotik des Theaters*, vol. 3 (Tübingen: Gunter Narr, 1983)

-, 'Was ist eine "werkgetreue" Inszenierung? Überlegungen zum Prozeß der Transformation eines Dramas in eine Aufführung', in Erika Fischer-Lichte (ed.), *Das Drama und seine Inszenierung* (Tübingen: Max Niemeyer, 1985), pp. 37-49

-, 'Zwischen Differenz und Indifferenz. Funktionalisierungen des Montage-Verfahrens bei Heiner Müller', in Erika Fischer-Lichte and Klaus Schwind (eds.), *Avantgarde und Postmoderne* (Tübingen: Stauffenburg, 1991), pp. 231-46

Freud, Sigmund, *Die Traumdeutung* (Frankfurt/Main: Fischer, 1991)

Fuchs, Elinor, 'Presence and the Revenge of Writing. Re-thinking Theater after Derrida', *Performing Arts Journal*, 26-27/85, pp. 163-73

Fuhrmann, Helmut, 'Der Mythos der Revolution: Heiner Müllers *Der Auftrag*', in *Forum Modernes Theater*, 2/90, 139-54

Genet, Jean, *The Balcony*, tr. by Barbara Wright and Terry Hands (London: Faber and Faber, 1991)

Girshausen, Theo, Schmiester, Burkhard, and Weber, Richard, 'Kommunismus oder Barbarei', (a discussion), in Theo Girshausen (ed.), *Die Hamletmaschine*: Heiner Müller's Endspiel (Cologne: Prometh, 1978), pp. 25-45

Theo Girshausen, 'Subjekt und Geschichte in *Die Hamletmaschine*', in Theo Girshausen (ed.), *Die Hamletmaschine*: Heiner Müller's Endspiel (Cologne: Prometh, 1978), pp. 104-27

-, 'Vom Umgang mit Nietzsche in *Der Hamletmaschine*', in Theo Girshausen (ed.), *Die Hamletmaschine: Heiner Müller's Endspiel* (Cologne: Prometh, 1978), pp. 98-103

Goltschnigg, Dietmar, 'Utopie und Revolution', in *Zeitschrift für deutsche Philologie*, 4/90, 571-96

Greiner, Bernhard, '"Einheit (Gleichzeitigkeit) von Beschreibung und Vorgang": Versuch über Heiner Müllers Theater', in Gregor Laschen with Paul Gerhard Klussmann and Heinrich Mohr (eds.), *Jahrbuch zur Literatur in der DDR*, vol. 7 (Bonn: Bouvier, 1990), pp. 69-81

-, 'Explosion einer Erinnerung in einer abgestorbenen dramatischen Struktur: Heiner Müllers "Shakespeare Factory"', in Werner Habicht (ed.), *Jahrbuch der deutschen Shakespeare Gesellschaft West* (Bochum: Ferdinand Kamp, 1989), pp. 88-112

-, 'IM SPIEGEL / DAS FEINDBILD: Heiner Müllers Kriegsrede *Wolokolamsker Chaussee*', *Krieg und Literatur. Internationale Beiträge zur Erforschung der Kriegs- und Antikriegsliteratur*, 2/90, pp. 65-82

-, '"Jetzt will ich sitzen wo gelacht wird": Über das Lachen bei Heiner Müller', in Paul Gerhard Klussmann and Heinrich Mohr (eds.), *Jahrbuch zur Literatur in der DDR*, vol. 5 (Bonn: Bouvier, 1986), pp. 29-63

Grohotolsky, Ernst, *Ästhetik der Negation - Tendenzen des deutschen Gegenwartsdramas* (Königstein: Anton Hain Meisenheim, 1984)

Grotowski, Jerzy, *Towards a Poor Theatre*, tr. by various (London: Methuen, 1975)

Grübel, Rainer, 'Metamorphosen und Umwertungen. Heiner Müllers Dramatisierung von Motiven aus Aleksandr Beks Prosatext *Volokolamskoe Šosse*', in Paul Gerhard Klussmann and Heinrich Mohr (eds.), *Jahrbuch zur Literatur in der DDR*, vol. 7 (Bonn: Bouvier, 1990), pp. 115-46

Gruber, Bettina, *Mythen in den Dramen Heiner Müllers. Zu ihrem Funktionswandel in den Jahren 1958-1982* (Essen: Die blaue Eule, 1989)

Gugnin, Alexander, 'Zur Rezeption von Sowjetliteratur (*Zement* und "Wolokolamsker Chaussee I und II")', in Frank Hörnigk (ed.), *Heiner Müller Material* (Göttingen: Steidl, 1989), pp. 213-25

Guntermann, Georg, 'Heiner Müller: *Die Hamletmaschine*', in Lothar Pikulik, Hajo Kurzenberger and Georg Guntermann (eds.), *Deutsche*

Gegenwartsdramatik, vol. 1 (Göttingen: Vandenhoeck and Ruprecht, 1987), pp. 41-69

Hawkes, Terence, *Structuralism and Semiotics* (London: Routledge, 1977)

Heeg, Günter, 'Das Theater der Auferstehung. Vom Ende der Bilder und von ihrer Notwendigkeit im Theater Heiner Müllers', *TheaterZeitschrift*, 20/87, pp. 61-74

-, 'Der Weg der Panzer. Notizen zu einer geplanten Aufführung von Heiner Müllers *Wolokolamsker Chaussee I-V*', in Wolfgang Storch (ed.), *Explosion of a Memory* (Berlin: Hentrich, 1988), pp. 138-41

Heise, Wolfgang, 'Beispiel einer Lessing-Rezeption: Heiner Müller', in Wolfgang Storch (ed.), *Explosion of a Memory* (Berlin: Hentrich, 1988), pp. 87-9

Hermand, Jost, 'Braut, Mutter oder Hure? Heiner Müllers Germania und ihre Vorgeschichte', in Jost Hermand, *Sieben Arten an Deutschland zu leiden* (Königstein: Athenäum, 1979), pp. 127-41

-, 'Fridericus Rex. Das schwarze Preußen im Drama der DDR', in Ulrich Profitlich (ed.), *Dramatik der DDR* (Frankfurt/Main: Suhrkamp, 1987), pp. 266-96

Herzinger, Richard, *Masken der Lebensrevolution: vitalistische Zivilisations- und Humanismuskritik in Texten Heiner Müllers* (München: Wilhelm Fink, 1992)

Heukenkamp, Ursula, 'Gegen das unheimliche Einverständnis mit dem Untergang', *Weimarer Beiträge*, 4/84, pp. 557-74

Hickethier, Knut, (ed.), *Heiner Müller Inszenieren. Unterhaltung im Theater* (Berlin: Die Dramaturgische Gesellschaft, 1987)

Hitz, Bruno, *Der Streit der Dramaturgien* (Zürich: Amman, 1992)

Hornby, Richard, *Script into Performance. A Structuralist Approach* (New York: Paragon House, 1977)

Hörnigk, Frank, 'Erinnerungen an Revolutionen. Zu Entwicklungstendenzen in der Dramatik Heiner Müllers, Peter Hacks' und Volker Brauns am Ende der siebziger Jahre', in Hans Kaufmann (ed.), *Tendenzen und Beispiele. Zur DDR-Literatur in den siebziger Jahren* (Leipzig: Reclam, 1981), pp. 148-84

- (ed.), *Heiner Müller Material* (Göttingen: Steidl, 1989)

-, 'Zu Heiner Müllers Stück *Der Auftrag*', *Weimarer Beiträge*, 3/81, pp. 114-131

Johansson, Stefan, 'Schweigen und Tanzen. Über die Erfahrung beim Inszenieren von Texten Heiner Müllers in Stockholm', in Wolfgang Storch (ed.), *Explosion of a Memory* (Berlin: Hentrich, 1988), pp. 82-3

Kaufmann, Hans, 'Veränderte Literaturlandschaft', *Weimarer Beiträge*, 3/81, pp. 27-53

Kaufmann, Ulrich, 'Ein noch zu schreibendes Kapitel', *Zeitschrift für Germanistik*, 4/88, pp. 457-63

Keller, Andreas, *Drama und Dramaturgie Heiner Müllers zwischen 1956 - 1988* (Frankfurt/Main: Peter Lang, 1992)

Kittsteiner, Heinz-Dietrich, 'Und draußen ging die Welt an uns vorbei. Überlegungen zu Heiner Müllers Stück *Wolokolamsker Chaussee*', in Paul Gerhard Klussmann and Heinrich Mohr (eds.), *Jahrbuch zur Literatur der DDR*, vol. 7 (Bonn: Bouvier, 1990), pp. 11-28

Kleist, Heinrich von, *Der Findling*, in Heinrich von Kleist, *Erzählungen* (Munich: dtv, 1964), pp. 182-96

Klotz, Günther, 'Shakespeare Adaptionen in der DDR', in *Shakespeare Jahrbuch 1988* (Weimar: Hermann Böhlaus Nachfolger, 1988), pp. 223-34

Klunker, Heinz, 'Vom parasitären Umgang mit einem Gegenwartsstück. Heiner Müllers *Wolokolamsker Chaussee* auf der Bühne', in Paul Gerhard Klussmann and Heinrich Mohr (eds.), *Jahrbuch zur Literatur der DDR*, vol. 7 (Bonn: Bouvier, 1990), pp. 29-44

Klussmann, Paul Gerhard, 'Deutschland-Denkmale: umgestürzt. Zu Heiner Müllers *Germania*', in Paul Gerhard Klussmann and Heinrich Mohr (eds.), *Jahrbuch zur Literatur in der DDR*, vol. 2 (Bonn: Bouvier, 1982), pp. 159-76

Köhn, Lothar, 'Drama aus Zitaten. Text-Montage bei Heiner Müller, Volker Braun und Botho Strauß', in Walter Hinck, Lothar Köhn and Walter Pape (eds.), *Drama der Gegenwart. Themen und Aspekte* (Schwerte: Katholische Akademie Schwerte, 1988), pp. 27-49

Komar and Melamid, catalogue from an exhibition of their work in Edinburgh and Oxford (Edinburgh: The Fruitmarket Gallery, 1985)

Kreuzer, Helmut, '"Ostfront" 1941. Ein dramatisches Thema in drei Variationen von Herbert Reinecke, Johannes R. Becher und Heiner Müller', in Hartmut Eggert, Ulrich Profitilich and Klaus R. Scherpe (eds.), *Geschichte als Literatur. Formen und Grenzen der Repräsentation von Vergangenheit* (Stuttgart: Metzler, 1990), pp. 330-52

Laska, Martin, 'Inszenierungstabelle der Stücke Heiner Müllers', in Heinz Ludwig Arnold (ed.), *Heiner Müller: Text und Kritik*, vol. 73 (Munich: Text und Kritik, 1982), pp. 82-7

Laube, Horst, '(Zerreißung der Fotografie des Autors)', in Horst Laube and Brigitte Landes (eds.), *Theaterbuch*, vol. 1 (Munich: Karl Hanser, 1978), pp. 243-5

Lehmann, Hans-Thies, 'Dramatische Form und Revolution', in Peter von Becker (ed.), *Dantons Tod: Kritische Studienausgabe des Originals mit Quellen, Aufsätze und Materialien* (Frankfurt/Main: Syndikat, 1985), pp. 106-21

-, 'Georg Büchner, Heiner Müller, Georges Bataille: Revolution und Masochismus', in Hermann Gersch, Thomas Michael Mayer and Günter Oesterle (eds.), *Georg Büchner Jahrbuch*, vol. 3 (Frankfurt/Main: Europäische Verlagsanstalt, 1983), pp. 308-29

-, 'Müller/Hamlet/Grüber/Faust: Intertextualität als Problem der Inszenierung', in Christian W. Thomsen (ed.), *Studien zur Ästhetik des Gegenwartstheaters* (Carl Winter, 1985), pp. 33-45

Linzer, Martin, and Ullrich, Peter, (eds.), *Regie: Heiner Müller* (Berlin: Zentrum für Theaterdokumentation und -information, 1993)

McGowan, Moray, 'Marxist - Postmodernist - German: history and dramatic form in the works of Heiner Müller', in Martin Kane (ed.), *Socialism and the Literary Imagination. Essays on East German Writers* (Oxford: Berg, 1991), pp. 125-46

Mitter, Shomit, *Systems of Rehearsal: Stanislavski, Brecht, Grotowski and Brook* (London: Routledge, 1992)

Müry, Andreas, 'Einfach kompliziert', *Theater heute*, 1/86. p. 1

Nägele, Rainer, 'Brecht's Theatre of Cruelty', in Rainer Nägele, *Reading after Freud* (New York: Columbia University Press, 1987), pp. 111-34

Nash, Douglas, 'The Commodification of Opposition: Notes on the Postmodern Image in Heiner Müller's *Die Hamletmaschine*', *Monatshefte*, 3/1989, pp. 298-311

Neumann, Oskar, 'Von Geschichtsbild und Orientierungskraft', *Shakespeare Jahrbuch 1980* (Weimar: Hermann Böhlaus Nachfolger, 1980), pp. 81-4

Perl, Doris, '"A study in Madness". Zu Heiner Müllers Umdeutung der klassischen Charaktere in der *Hamletmaschine*', *Shakespeare Jahrbuch 1992* (Weimar: Hermann Böhlaus Nachfolger, 1992), pp. 157-70

Petersohn, Roland, *Heiner Müllers Shakespeare-Rezeption* (Frankfurt/Main: Peter Lang, 1993)

Raddatz, Frank-Michael, *Dämonen unterm Roten Stern. Zu Geschichtsphilosophie und Ästhetik Heiner Müllers* (Stuttgart: Metzler, 1991)

Reid, J. H., 'Homburg-Maschine. Heiner Müller in the Shadow of Nuclear War', in W.G. Sebald (ed.), *A Radical Stage. Theatre in Germany in the 1970s and 1980s* (Oxford: Berg, 1988), pp. 145-60

-, *Writing without Taboos: the New East German Literature* (New York and London: Oswald Wolf, 1990)

Reinelt, Janelle, 'Approaching the Postmodernist Threshold: Samuel Beckett and Bertolt Brecht', in Ronald Roblin (ed.), *The Aesthetics of the Critical Theorists. Studies on Benjamin, Adorno, Marcuse and Habermas* (Lampeter: Edwin Meller, 1990), pp. 337-358

Rice, John, and Malone, Paul, 'Text or Performance. The Rationalism and Intoxication of Presence in Theatre', in Eitel Timm and Kenneth Mendoza (eds.), *The Poetics of Reading* (Columbia: Camden House, 1993), pp. 104-115

Rischbieter, Henning, 'Zwei Stücke über Deutschland', *Theater heute*, Sonderheft 1977, pp. 92-4

Romero, Christiana Zehl, 'Seghersmaterial in Heiner Müller und Volker Braun', in Margy Gerber (ed.), *Studies in GDR Culture and Society*, vol. 9 (Lanham: University Press of America, 1989), pp. 57-83

Rorrison, Hugh, 'Heiner Müller and Shakespeare', in John Flood (ed.), *Common Currency? Aspects of Anglo-German Literary Relations since 1945. London Symposium* (Stuttgart: Hans-Dieter Heinz, 1991), pp. 151-163

-, 'Küchenschabe und Kanalisation: Montage als Selbstinterpretation bei Heiner Müller', in John Flood (ed.), *Kurz bevor der Vorhang fiel. Zum Theater der DDR. Londoner Symposium* (Amsterdam: Rodopi, 1990), pp. 81-90

Rouse, John, 'Brecht and the Question of the Audience', in Marc Silbermann, John Fuegi Renate Voris and Carl Weber (eds.), *Brecht-Jahrbuch*, vol. 15, pp. 111-123

Schalk, Axel, *Geschichtsmaschinen. Über den Umgang mit der Historie in der Dramatik des technischen Zeitalters. Eine vergleichende Untersuchung* (Heidelberg: Carl Winter, 1989)

Schmid, Herta, 'Das dramatische Werk und seine theatralische Konkretisierung im Lichte der Literaturtheorie Roman Ingardens', in Erika Fischer-Lichte (ed.), *Das Drama und seine Inszenierung* (Tübingen: Max Niemeyer, 1985), pp. 22-36

Schmidt, Ingo, and Vaßen, Florian, *Bibliographie Heiner Müller* (Bielefeld: Aisthesis, 1993)

Schmitt-Sasse, Joachim, 'Die Kunst aufzuhören. Der Nibelungen-Stoff in Heiner Müllers *Germania*', in Joachim Heinzle and Anneliese Waldschmidt (eds.), *Die Nibelungen. Ein deutscher Wahn, ein deutscher Alptraum* (Frankfurt/Main: Suhrkamp, 1991), pp. 370-96

Schelletter, Daniel, 'Die erste Erfahrung ist die Distanz. Schauspielstudenten spielen "Wolokolamsker Chaussee I und III"', *Die deutsche Bühne*, 8/87, p. 45

Schneider, Michael, 'Heiner Müllers "Endspiele"', *Literatur Konkret*, 5/79, pp. 32-7

Schulz, Genia, *Heiner Müller* (Stuttgart: Metzler, 1980)

Genia Schulz and Hans-Thies Lehmann, 'Es ist ein eigentümlicher Apparat', in *Theater heute*, 10/79, pp. 11-14

Genia Schulz, 'Medea. Zu einem Motiv im Werk Heiner Müllers', in Renate Berger and Inge Stephan (eds.), *Weiblichkeit und Tod in der Literatur* (Köln: Böhlau, 1987), pp. 241-64

-, 'Something is rotten in this age of hope', *Merkur*, 5/79, pp. 468-80

-, 'Waste Land / Verkommenes Ufer', in Wolfgang Storch (ed.), *Explosion of a Memory* (Berlin: Hentrich, 1988), pp. 103-4

-, 'Der zersetzte Blick. Sehzwang und Blendung bei Heiner Müller', in Frank Hörnigk (ed.), *Heiner Müller Material* (Göttingen: Steidl, 1989), p. 179.

Schulze-Reimpell, Werner, 'Theater als Laboratorium der sozialen Phantasie: Heiner Müller, Volker Braun, Christoph Hein', in Wilfried Floeck (ed.), *Tendenzen des Gegenwartstheaters* (Tübingen: Franke, 1988), pp. 177-91

Seghers, Anna, 'Das Duell', in Anna Seghers, *Die Kraft der Schwachen* (Berlin: Aufbau, 1994), pp. 99-134

-, *Das Licht auf dem Galgen*, in *Die Hochzeit von Haiti* (Darmstadt: Luchterhand, 1976)

Seibel, Wolfgang, *Die Formenwelt der Fertigteile* (Würzburg: Königshausen und Neumann, 1988)

Shakespeare, William, *Hamlet*, ed. Harold Jenkins (London: Methuen, 1982)

Sheppard, Richard, *Tankred Dorst's "Toller": A Case Study in Reception* (New Alyth: Lochee, 1989)

Silbermann, Marc, *Heiner Müller* (Amsterdam: Rodopi, 1980)

Stanislavski, Constantin, *An Actor's Handbook*, tr. by Elizabeth Reynolds Hapgood (London: Methuen, 1990)

Steiger, Klaus Peter, 'Ein Fetzen Shakespeare', in Klaus Peter Steiger, *Moderne Shakespeare Bearbeitungen* (Stuttgart, Berlin, Cologne: Kohlhammer, 1990), pp. 46-57

Steinbach, Dietrich, 'Heiner Müller: *Germania Tod in Berlin*', in Dietrich Steinbach, *Geschichte und Drama* (Stuttgart: Klett, 1988), pp. 32-47

Steinweg, Rainer, *Das Lehrstück. Brechts Theorie einer politisch-ästhetischen Erziehung*, second, expanded edition (Stuttgart: Metzler, 1976)

Stephan, Erika, 'Erprobung von Spielmodellen. Heiner Müllers *Bau* in Karl-Marx-Stadt und "Wolokolamsker Chaussee I und II" in Potsdam', in

Siegfried Rönisch (ed.), *DDR-Literatur '86 im Gespräch* (Berlin and Weimar: Aufbau, 1987), pp. 297-315

Stillmark, Hans-Christian, 'Entscheidungen um und bei Heiner Müller. Bemerkungen zu "Wolokolamsker Chaussee III-V"', in Werner Biechele (ed.), *Germanistisches Jahrbuch DDR - UVR*, 9/90, pp. 52-62

Streisand, Marianne, '"Mein Platz, wenn mein Drama noch stattfinden würde, wäre auf beiden Seiten der Front, zwischen den Fronten, darüber". Über das Arbeitsprinzip der Gleichzeitigkeit bei Heiner Müller', *Weimarer Beiträge*, 4/91, pp. 485-508

-, 'Das Theater braucht den Widerstand der Literatur', *Weimarer Beiträge*, 7/88, pp. 1156-79

-, 'Theater der sozialen Phantasie und der geschichtlichen Erfahrung', *Sinn und Form*, 5/83, 1058-67

Strindberg, August, *A Dream Play*, in August Strindberg, *Six Plays of Strindberg*, tr. by Elizabeth Sprigge (New York: Anchor, 1955), pp. 185-261

Teichmann, Klaus, *Der verwundete Körper. Zu Texten Heiner Müllers* (Freiburg: Burg, 1986)

Teraoka, Arlene Akiko, '*Der Auftrag* and *Die Maßnahme*: Models of Revolution in Heiner Müller and Bertolt Brecht', *The German Quarterly*, 1/86, 65-84

-, *The Silence of Entropy or Universal Discourse. The Postmodernist Poetics of Heiner Müller* (Frankfurt/Main: Peter Lang, 1985)

Turner, Barnard, 'Müller and Postmodern Classicism: Construction and Theatre', in Gerhard Fischer (ed.), *Heiner Müller. ConTEXTS and HISTORY* (Tübingen: Stauffenberg, 1995), pp. 189-200

Vaßen, Florian, 'Die entfremdete und die fremde Revolution', in Eijiro Iwasaka (ed.), *Akten des VIII Internationalen Germanisten-Kongresses* (Munich: ludicium, 1991), pp. 313-23

Voigt, Peter, 'Zum Film *Wolokolamsker Chaussee IV: Kentauren*', in Wolfgang Storch (ed.), *Explosion of a Memory* (Berlin: Hentrich, 1988), pp. 142-3

Vormweg, Heinrich, 'Sprache - die Heimat der Bilder', in Heinz Ludwig Arnold (ed.), *Heiner Müller: Text und Kritik*, vol. 73 (Munich: Text und Kritik, 1982), pp. 20-31

Was Spielten die Theater? (Darmstadt: Mykenae, 1982-1990)

Weber, Carl, 'Heiner Müller: The Hope and the Despair', *Performing Arts Journal*, 12/80, pp. 135-40

Weber, Manfred, '"Der Mordbericht als Liebeserklärung...". Manfred Weber im Gespräch mit Manfred Karge', in Schauspiel Köln (ed.), *Medea*.

Hans Henny Jahnn. Ein Theaterbuch von Manfred Weber (Berlin: Hentrich, 1989), pp. 177-81

Weber, Richard, 'Ich war, ich bin, ich werde sein', in Theo Girshausen (ed.), *Die Hamletmaschine: Heiner Müller's Endspiel* (Cologne: Prometh, 1978), pp. 86-97

Weigel, Sigrid, 'Das Theater der weißen Revolution', in Inge Stephan and Sigrid Weigel (eds.), *Die Marseillaise der Weiber* (Hamburg: Argument, 1989), pp. 154-74

Wer Spielte Was? (Berlin: Henschel, 1982-1990)

Wer Spielte Was? (Darmstadt: Mykenae, 1991-1994)

Wieghaus, Georg, 'Anmerkungen zu *Germania Tod in Berlin*', *Spectaculum 31* (Frankfurt/Main: Suhrkamp, 1979), pp. 263-6

-, *Zwischen Auftrag und Verrat. Werk und Ästhetik Heiner Müllers* (Frankfurt/Main: Peter Lang, 1984)

Wilde, Oscar, *The Picture of Dorian Gray* (London: Penguin, 1985)

Wittstock, Uwe, 'Die schnellen Wirkungen sind nicht die neuen', in Heinz Ludwig Arnold (ed.), *Heiner Müller: Text und Kritik*, vol. 73 (Munich: Text und Kritik, 1982), pp. 10-19

Wright, Elizabeth, *Postmodern Brecht. A Re-Presentation* (London: Routledge, 1989)

Zurbrugg, Nicholas, 'Postmodernism and the Multimedia Sensibility: Heiner Müller's *Hamletmaschine* and the Art of Robert Wilson', *Modern Drama*, 3/88, pp. 439-53

Interviews Conducted by the Author

Unpublished interview with Sabine Andreas, 23-3-95
Unpublished interview with Regina Fabian, 18-2-95
Unpublished interview with Gabriele Groenewold, 15-11-94
Unpublished interview with Marianne Janietz, 25-5-94
Unpublished interview with Heiner Müller, 20-6-95
Unpublished interview with Christoph Schroth, 8-6-95
Unpublished interview with Wolfgang Schuch, 30-3-95
Unpublished interview with B. K. Tragelehn, 27-3-95

Selected Other Materials, Newspaper Reviews, etc.
Organized by Play and Performance

Der Auftrag

1   Volksbühne, Berlin, 13-11-80

Anon., 'Revolution macht müde', *Süddeutsche Zeitung*, 17-12-80
Beckelmann, Jürgen, 'Heiner Müller unterm Dach', *Frankfurter Rundschau*,
    19-12-80
    -, 'Ein Stück vom Kuchen der Welt', *General-Anzeiger*, 17-12-80
Fischer, Ulrich, 'Theater als Hörspielwerkstatt', *Hessische Allgemeine*, 18-11-
    80
Kerndl, Rainer, 'Erkenntnisweg zwischen Niederlage und Aufbruch', *Neues
    Deutschland*, 18-11-80
Kersten, Heinz, 'Die Revolution als Thema', *Welt der Arbeit*, 27-11-80
Leder, Lily, *Dokumentation zu 'Der Auftrag'* (unpublished documentation
    held in the Zentrum für Theaterdokumentation und -information:
    Berlin, 1981)
Linzer, Martin, '"Der Auftrag bleibt gültig": Heiner Müller - Uraufführung
    im 3. Stock der Volksbühne', *Theater der Zeit*, 1/81, pp. 34-5
Heiner Müllers 'Der Auftrag', programme of the Volksbühne production,
    Berlin, 13-11-80
Rossmann, Andreas, 'Jeder Satz ein Eisberg', *Badische Zeitung*, 20-11-80
    -, 'Das Scheitern von Hoffnungen', *Deutsches Allgemeines Sonntags-
    blatt*, 23-11-80
Seyfarth, Ingrid, *'Der Auftrag'*, *Sonntag*, 7-12-80
Stone, Michael, '"Erinnerung an eine Revolution" vom Pessimismus ge-
    prägt', *Westfälische Rundschau*, 24-11-80
    -, 'Die heimatlose Revolution', *Rheinische Post*, 21-11-80
    -, 'Hoffnungslos in Peru', *Saarbrücker Zeitung*, 2-12-80
    -, 'Die verratene Revolution', *Der Tagesspiegel*, 23-11-80
Wirsing, Sibylle, 'Der Verrat an der Revolution und der Kunst', *Frankfurter
    Allgemeine Zeitung*, 18-11-80
Wirth, Andrzei, 'Erinnerung an eine Revolution: sado-masochistisch',
    Theater heute, 2/81, pp. 6-8

Anon., 'Großes Gequietsche', *Der Spiegel*, 25-5-81

Erdmann, Michael, 'Die Heimlosigkeit der Wollust', *Theater heute*, 7/81, pp. 42-5

Frederiksen, Jens, 'Der Aufstand der Toten auf der Silbersofa', *Rheinische Post*, 23-5-81

Hartmann, Rainer, 'Der Tod ist die Maske der Revolution', *Kölner-Stadt-Anzeiger*, 19-5-81

Hensel, Georg, 'Phantomschmerzen der Revolution', *Frankfurter Allgemeine Zeitung*, 18-5-81

Iden, Peter, 'In Verzweiflung und gegen sie', *Frankfurter Rundschau*, 18-5-81

Klunker, Heinz, 'Ansichten der Revolution', *Deutsches Allgemeines Sonntagsblatt*, 7-6-81

Krämer-Badoni, Rudolf, 'Wie man eine Revolution wiederrufen kann', *Die Welt*, 18-5-81

Schödel, Helmut, 'Meine Rede ist das Schweigen', *Die Zeit*, 22-5-81

Schulze-Reimpell, Werner, 'Szenische Gleichnisse', *Hessische Allgemeine*, 4-6-81

Stadelmaier, Gerhard, 'Revolution kaputt', *Stuttgarter Zeitung*, 18-5-81

Wendland, Jens, 'Revolution im Krebsgang', *Süddeutsche Zeitung*, 22-5-81

3   Schauspielhaus, Bochum, 13-2-82

Anon., '*Der Auftrag*', *Westfalenspiegel*, 3/82

Busch, Frank, '*Der Auftrag*: Theater voll sinnlicher Reflexion', *Westfälische Rundschau*, 15-2-82

Girshausen, Theo, 'Ohne Bedeutung', *Stuttgarter Zeitung*, 16-2-82

Henrichs, Benjamin, 'Die Reise ins Licht', *Die Zeit*, 19-2-82

Jenny, Urs, 'Das Fleisch und die Wörter', *Der Spiegel*, 19-4-82

Klunker, Heinz, 'Die Ästhetik des Verrats', *Deutsches Allgemeines Sonntagsblatt*, 21-2-82

Laroche, Johann, 'Immer bleiben die Engel aus am Ende', *guckloch*, 3/82

Plunien, Eo, 'Hier haben die Verräter gute Zeit', *Die Welt*, 15-2-82

Rischbieter, Henning, 'Die Wörter und die Zeichen', *Theater heute*, 4/82, pp. 7-12

Rossmann, Andreas, 'Die Ästhetik des Verrats', *Rheinische Post*, 7-2-82
   -, 'Fragen nach Freiheit und Unterdrückung', *Badische Zeitung*, 17-2-82

Schmidt, Jochen, 'Die Sprache und die Bilder', *Frankfurter Allgemeine Zeitung*, 17-2-82
Schmidt, Konrad, 'Beklemmung statt Spannung', *Ruhr-Nachrichten*, 15-2-82
Schreiber, Ulrich, 'Texte, die auf Geschichte warten', *Magazin*, 3/82
-, 'Utopische Hoffnungen und Untergangs-Träume', *Handelsblatt*, 19/20-2-82
-, 'Vom Sprachfraß der Bilder', *Frankfurter Rundschau*, 17-2-82
Schulze-Reimpell, Werner, 'Als Regisseur entdeckt', *Hessische Allgemeine*, 19-2-82
-, 'Revolution in der Maske des Todes', *Saarbrücker Zeitung*, 18-2-82
Vormweg, Heinrich, 'Faszinierend wahnwitzige Wahrheit', *Süddeutsche Zeitung*, 17-2-82
Wanzelius, Rainer, 'Die Masken des Verrats', *Westdeutsche Allgemeine Zeitung*, 15-2-82

4   Theater, Anklam, 2-7-83

Linzer, Martin, 'Variante Drei', *Theater der Zeit*, 9/83, p. 50
Heiner Müllers 'Der Auftrag', programme of the Theater Anklam production, Anklam, 2-7-83
Heiner Müllers 'Der Auftrag', video of the Theater Anklam production, Anklam, 2-7-83 (held in the Zentrum für Theaterdokumentation und -information: Berlin, 1983)
Wilzopolski, Siegfried, *Das Associative im Theaterspiel* (unpublished documentation held in the Zentrum für Theaterdokumentation und -information: Berlin, 1985)

5   neues theater, Halle, 2-2-85

Heiner Müllers 'Der Auftrag', programme of the neues theater production, Halle, 2-2-85

6   Freie Kammerspiele, Magdeburg, 22-11-87

Janietz, Marianne, *Konzeptionelle Überlegungen* (unpublished documentation, property of Janietz)
Heiner Müllers 'Der Auftrag', programme of the Freie Kammerspiele production, Magdeburg, 22-11-87
Heiner Müllers 'Der Auftrag', video of the Freie Kammerspiele production, Magdeburg, 22-11-87, in-house copy

7   Schauspielhaus, Düsseldorf, 9-89 (also at the Ruhrfestspiele, Reckling-
         hausen, 4-5-89)

Anon., 'Spröde Abhandlung', *Rheinische Post*, 30-9-89
aro, 'Brechts Erbe', *Frankfurter Allgemeine Zeitung*, 13-10-89
Heuer, Otto, 'Der Fahrstuhl läuft am Schienenstrang', *Rheinische Post*, 6-5-
         89
Jansen, Hans, 'Die Masken des Todes', *Westdeutsche Allgemeine Zeitung*, 6-
         5-89
Reinke, Klaus U., 'Denk-Anstöße', *Handelsblatt*, 12/13-5-89
Schreiber, Ulrich, 'Der Autor als Zensor', *Frankfurter Rundschau*, 23-10-89
Schulze-Reimpell, Werner, 'Die Ruhrfestspiele in einer Krise?', *Kölner-
         Stadt-Anzeiger*, 9-5-89
Steiner, Irene, '*Der Auftrag*: Viel Pomp, wenig Tiefe', *Ruhr-Nachrichten*, 6-5-
         89
Wohlgemuth, Johann, 'Müllers blutlose Texte über alle Revolutionen',
         Westfälische Rundschau, 6-5-89

8   Schlosserei, Cologne, 14-3-92

Hartmann, Rainer, 'Denkspiel kommt auf den Laufsteg', *Kölner-Stadt-An-
         zeiger*, 23-3-92
Hennecke, Günther, 'Die verlorene Revolution', *Neue Züricher Zeitung
         (Fernausgabe)*, 25-3-92
Kill, Rainhard, 'Disput mit den Toten', *Rheinische Post*, 27-3-92
Löhndorf, Marion, 'Schwanengesang der Revolution', *General-Anzeiger*, 31-3-
         92
Preußer, Gerhard, 'Heiliger Heiner', *Die Tageszeitung*, 24-3-92
Rossmann, Andreas, 'Auf schmalem Steg in die Gegenwart', *Frankfurter All-
         gemeine Zeitung*, 25-3-92
Schreiber, Ulrich, 'Freizeit, Gleichheit, Brüderlichkeit', *Der Tagesspiegel*, 23-
         3-92
         -, 'Gleichheit, Brüderlichkeit, Freizeit', *Frankfurter Rundschau*, 3-4-92
Tschapke, Reinhard, 'Die Revolution geht in Rente', *Die Welt*, 23-3-92

1   Münchner Kammerspiele, Munich, 20-4-78

B., E., 'Der Autor und sein Publikum', *Süddeutsche Zeitung*, 2-11-78
Becker, Peter von, 'Schlachthauspostille und Tanz der deutschen Vampire', *Süddeutsche Zeitung*, 22/23-4-78
Beckmann, Heinz, 'Germania Ragout', *Rheinischer Merkur/Christ und Welt*, 28-4-78
Colberg, Klaus, 'Deutschland - eine Dauerkarambolage', *Westdeutsche Allgemeine Zeitung*, 22-4-78
Dultz, Michael, 'Trauer um deutsche Utopien', *Die deutsche Bühne*, 6/78, p. 22
Hensel, Georg, 'Schlacht-Szenen aus der DDR', *Frankfurter Allgemeine Zeitung*, 22-4-78
Iden, Peter, 'Schrecken aus Deutschland', *Die Zeit*, 28-4-78
Krämer-Badoni, Rudolf, 'Wenn der Agitprop kannibalisch wird', *Die Welt*, 22-4-78
Michaelis, Rolf, 'Deutschland, ein Nachtstück', *Die Weltwoche*, 26-4-78
Heiner Müllers 'Germania Tod in Berlin', programme for the Kammerspiele production, Munich, 20-4-78
Heiner Müllers 'Germania Tod in Berlin', prompter's script of the Kammerspiele production, Munich, 20-4-78
Schmidt, Dietmar N., 'Brüder, zur Sonne? Zur Schlachtbank!', *Deutsches Allgemeines Sonntagsblatt*, 30-4-78
-, 'Der Terror kommt aus Deutschland', *Vorwärts*, 4-5-78
-, 'Trauer zu spät oder Hoffnung in der Agonie', *Frankfurter Rundschau*, 24-4-78
Stadelmaier, Gerhard, 'Revue vom deutschen Totentanz', *Stuttgarter Zeitung*, 22-4-78
Ude, Karl, 'Eine deutsch-deutsche Politrevue', *Süddeutsche Zeitung*, 20-4-78

2   Kleines Haus, Mannheim, 25-6-88

Anon., 'Das Vaterland ist ein Monster', *Mannheimer Morgen*, 24-6-88
Buselmeier, Michael, '*Germania Tod in Berlin*', *Theater heute*, 8/88, p.50
Frederiksen, Jens, 'Heino und der blutige Ernst der Geschichte', *Die Welt*, 27-6-88
Koch, Gerhard, 'Witz, blutgeschwängert', *Frankfurter Allgemeine Zeitung*, 1-7-88

Schmidt, Dietmar N., 'Hechelnd überstrengt', *Frankfurter Rundschau*, 1-7-88

Schönfeldt, Heinz, 'Narrenhaus Deutschland. Schlachthaus Welt', *Mann-heimer Morgen*, 27-6-88

3   Schauspielhaus, Bochum, 8-10-88 (and its 'Gastspiel'in Moscow, 1990)

Anon., '*Germania Tod in Berlin*', *Prinz*, 11/88

-, 'Wie eine Sexorgie die Moskowiter erregte', *Hannoversche Allge-meine Zeitung*, 25-1-89

Berke, Bernd, 'Manege frei für die blutige Geschichte der Deutschen', *West-fälische Rundschau*, 10-10-88

Busch, Frank, 'Der Nibelungen Not', *Süddeutsche Zeitung*, 24-10-88

Hartmann, Rainer, 'Benzin saufen im Führerbunker', *Kölner-Stadt-Anzeiger*, 15/16-10-88

Jansen, Hans, 'Auftakt in Bochum: Totentanz der Geschichte', *Westdeutsche Allgemeine Zeitung*, 10-10-88

Kill, Reinhard, 'Die Nibelungen im Kessel von Stalingrad', *Rheinische Post*, 15-10-89

Kunker, Heinz, 'Jubel, Trubel, Sparsamkeit', *Deutsches Allgemeines Sonntags-blatt*, 23-10-88

Heiner Müllers 'Germania Tod in Berlin', programme of the Schauspielhaus production, Bochum, 8-10-88

Heiner Müllers 'Germania Tod in Berlin', video of the Schauspielhaus produc-tion, Bochum, 8-10-88, in-house copy

Pizzini, Duglore, 'Ein blutiger Comic-Strip', *Die Presse*, 31-5-90

Rischbieter, Henning, 'Zu spät? Zu spät!', *Theater heute*, 3/89, pp. 26-9

Rossmann, Andreas, 'Geschichte ohne Gesichter', *Frankfurter Allgemeine Zeitung*, 14-1-89

Schmidt, Konrad, 'Steckel inszenierte Müllers *Germania* - Nacht über Deut-schland und kein Morgen', *Ruhr-Nachrichten*, 11-10-88

Schreiber, Ulrich, 'Deutsche Tragödien', *Handelsblatt*, 14/15-10-88

-, 'Irrwege zu einem Schlachthaus', *Frankfurter Rundschau*, 15-10-88

Siegl, Elfie, 'Moskauer durch *Germania* aus Bochum verunsichert', *West-deutsche Allgemeine Zeitung*, 20-1-89

-, 'Unvermittelt. Steckels falsche Töne in Moskau', *Frankfurter Rund-schau*, 21-1-89

Steckel, Frank-Patrick, unpublished letter to Andreas Rossman, 23-1-89 (held in the Schauspielhaus archive, Bochum)

4   Berliner Ensemble, East Berlin, 20-1-89

Anon., 'Germania Tod in Berlin', Neue Züricher Zeitung (Fernausgabe), 10-2-89
Beckelmann, Jürgen, 'Es war nicht Rosa Luxemburg oder: Die Brüder im Gefängnis', Frankfurter Rundschau, 26-1-89
    -, 'Koteletts Sieg übern Kaviar', Stuttgarter Zeitung, 4-2-89
    -, 'Lieber kaltes Kotelett als Kaviar', General-Anzeiger, 7-2-89
    -, 'Staatsfeiertag, Süßer', Süddeutsche Zeitung, 4/5-2-89
Ebert, Gerhard, 'Szenen, die zu einem Panorama deutscher Geschichte werden', Neues Deutschland, 26-1-89
Isreal, Torsten, Notate zum Proben und zum Probeprozeß (unpublished documentation held in the archive of the Berliner Ensemble, undated)
Linzer, Martin, 'Geschichtslektion?', Theater der Zeit, 4/89, pp. 22-3
Müller, Heiner, unpublished sections of text from Germania (used in rehearsal but not in the final production, held in the archive of the Berliner Ensemble)
Heiner Müllers 'Germania Tod in Berlin', programme of the Berliner Ensemble production, East Berlin, 20-1-89
Heiner Müllers 'Germania Tod in Berlin', video of the Berliner Ensemble production, East Berlin, 20-1-89, in-house copy
Nöldechen, Peter, 'Brisantes über 17. Juni als trockenes Lehrstück', Westfälische Rundschau, 25-1-89
Rischbieter, Henning, 'Zu spät? Zu spät!', Theater heute, 3/89, pp. 26-9
Seyfarth, Ingrid, 'Fragmentarisierung', Sonntag, 5-2-89
Stone, Michael, 'Geschichte in der Zirkus-Manege', Rheinische Post, 28-1-89
    -, 'Heiterkeit statt Moral', Die Presse, 2-2-89
    -, 'Horror Collage', Sonntag, 29-1-89
    -, 'Müllers Geschichtsunterricht', Saarbrücker Zeitung, 26-1-89
Wirsing, Sibylle, 'Deutsches Ungeheuer', Frankfurter Allgemeine Zeitung, 30-1-89
Ziller, Joachim, Probennotate (unpublished documentation held in the archive of the Berliner Ensemble, undated)

5   Wuppertaler Bühnen, Wuppertal, 2-12-89

Anon., 'Aus aktuellem Nachlaß', Wuppertaler Rundschau, 30-11-89
aro, 'Theater Heute. Wuppertal und die Revolution', Frankfurter Allgemeine Zeitung, 6-12-89
Heuer, Otto, 'Wuppertaler Trabbi', Rheinische Post, 6-12-89

Koep, Phillip, 'Rückeroberung der Flexibilität', *Wupper-Nachrichten Magazin*, 24/89

Heiner Müllers 'Germania Tod in Berlin', programme of the Wuppertaler Bühnen production, Wuppertal, 2-12-89

Mohr, Peter, 'Der 9. November auf der Bühne', *Generalanzeiger*, 8-12-89

re, 'Dummes Geschwätz von gestern?', *Wupper-Nachrichten Magazin*, 25/89

Rossmann, Andreas, 'Germania Tod in Berlin', radio report for 'Das Mosaik', *WDR 3*, 5-12-89

sc, 'Die Geschichte holte Müllers Vision ein', *Wuppertaler Zeitung*, 1-12-89

Scurla, Frank, 'Der Verrat der Einheitspartei an der Utopie des Sozialismus', *Wuppertaler Zeitung*, 4-12-89

6   Theater der freien Volksbühne, West Berlin, 30-9-90

Anon., 'Kritische Anmerkungen', *Die Welt*, 24-9-90

-, 'Müllers *Germania* in Berlin', *Ruhr-Nachrichten*, 6-10-90

Beckelmann, Jürgen, 'Die Ausbeutung der Mitläufer', *Stuttgarter Zeitung*, 10-10-90

Heyden, Susanne, 'Ein Ausschneidebogen', *Rheinische Post*, 11-10-90

Köhler, Ingeborg, 'Heiner Müllers Rückblick auf deutsche Geschichte', *Welt am Sonntag*, 7-10-90

Luft, Friedrich, 'Der alte Maurer, die alten Nazis und die Filzliputzlis', *Die Welt*, 2-10-90

Heiner Müllers 'Germania Tod in Berlin', programme of the Theater der Freien Volksbühne production, West Berlin, 30-9-90

Heiner Müllers 'Germania Tod in Berlin', video of the Theater der Freien Volksbühne production, West Berlin, 30-9-90, director's copy

Schaper, Rüdiger, 'Vom Sterben der Sozialisten', *Süddeutsche Zeitung*, 12-10-90

Schnabel, Stefan, 'Das schöne farbige Volkslied von der DDR', *Die Volkszeitung*, 28-9-90

-, 'Totenreich Deutschland', *TheaterZeitschrift*, 33/34, 1993, pp. 45-63

Streisand, Marianne, 'Germania Tod in Berlin', *Sonntag*, 21-10-90

Wiegenstein, Roland H., 'Falsches Märchen und Trauermarsch', *Frankfurter Rundschau*, 5-10-90

Wille, Franz, 'Die Revolution entläßt ihre Stücke', *Theater heute*, 11/90, p. 15-16

Wirsing, Sibylle, 'Von deutscher Revolution', *Frankfurter Allgemeine Zeitung*, 3-10-90

Die Hamletmaschine

1   Théâtre Gérard Phillippe Saint Denis, Paris, 30-1-79

Henry, Ruth, 'Terror und Zauber des poetischen Narziß', *Frankfurter Rundschau*, 27-2-79

Rischbieter, Henning, 'Unter der schwarzen Sonne der Folter', *Theater heute*, 3/79, pp. 35-41

Schlocker, Georges, 'Hamlets Ekel vor Shakespeare', *Deutsches Allgemeines Sonntagsblatt*, 11-3-79

-, 'Unterm Sand der Geschichte', *Stuttgarter Zeitung*, 26-2-79

2   Casa Nova, Essen, 28-4-79

Beckmann, Heinz, 'Hausgemachter Ekel', *Rheinischer Merkur/Christ und Welt*, 4-5-79

Drewes-Merker, Ilse, 'Ein sehenswertes Experiment', *Ruhr-Nachrichten*, 30-4-79

Jansen, Hans, 'Totenklinik der Geschichte', *Westdeutsche Allgemeine Zeitung*, 30-4-79

Schloz, Günther, 'Hamlet darf nicht sterben', *Deutsche Zeitung*, 4-5-79

Schmidt, Hannes, 'Eine Provokation aus tiefster Verzweiflung', *Neue Ruhr Zeitung*, 30-4-79

Schmidt, Jochen, 'Unbehaglicher Platz über den Fronten', *Frankfurter Allgemeine Zeitung*, 4-5-79

Schreiber, Ulrich, 'Durch Enteignung dem Theater gewonnen', *Frankfurter Rundschau*, 11-5-79

Schulze-Reimpell, Werner, 'Aufschrei mit unterdrückter Stimme', *Stuttgarter Zeitung*, 30-4-79

Vielhaber, Gerd, 'Monitoren erobern die Bühne', *Der Tagesspiegel*, 22-7-79

3   Freies Theater, Munich, 3-81

Heiner Müllers 'Die Hamletmaschine', video of the Freies Theater production, Munich, 3-81 (held in the video archive of the Theaterinstitut, Freie Universität, Berlin)

4   Theater Angelus Novus im Semper Depot, Vienna, 23-4-84

Hove, Oliver vom, 'Aufstand und Verweigerung', *Die Presse*, 10-5-84
Kutschera, Waltraud, 'Erinnerungen an *Die Hamletmaschine*. Theater Angelus Novus. Wien 1984', in Wolfgang Storch (ed.), *Explosion of a Memory* (Berlin: Hentrich, 1988), pp. 74-6
Heiner Müllers 'Die Hamletmaschine', programme of the Theater Angelus Novus production, Vienna, 23-4-84

5   Kammerspiele, Munich, 14-11-84 (with Verkommenes Ufer)

Bock, Hans-Bertram, 'Tote Bilder um Treibhaus', *Nürnberger Nachrichten*, 17/18-11-84
Carstensen, Margit, unpublished letter to the author, 17-1-95
Eichholz, Armin, 'Das Abgründige in Hamlet und Medea', *Münchner Morgenzeitung*, 16-11-84
Fischbach, Ute, 'Hamlet zertrümmert den Kopf von Marx', *Münchner Morgenzeitung*, 14-11-84
Kayser, Beate, 'Werkraum quer', *die taz*, 16-11-84
Kr, 'Messer und Wunde, Hals und Strick', *Bayerische Staatszeitung*, 23-11-84
Heiner Müllers 'Verkommenes Ufer', programme of the Münchener Kammerspiele production, Munich, 14-11-84
Nennecke, Charlotte, 'Klassische Figuren in neuer Umgebung', *Süddeutsche Zeitung*, 14-11-84
Reitter, Barbara, 'Heiner Müller: Das Drama findet nicht mehr statt', *Mittelbayerische Zeitung*, 30-11-84
Schödel, Helmut, 'Schlachtbeschreibung', *Die Zeit*, 22-2-85
Schmitz-Burkhardt, Barbara, 'Hamlet sehnt sich nach Väterchen Stalin', *Frankfurter Rundschau*, 23-11-84
Seiler, Manfred, '*Die Hamletmaschine*', *Bayerischer Rundfunk*, 15-11-84
Sucher, C. Bernd, 'Die Gedanken mit den Bildern verloren', *Süddeutsche Zeitung*, 16-11-84

6   Thalia Theater, Hamburg, 4-10-86 (and in New York)

Anon., '*Die Hamletmaschine* in Hamburg', *Die Weltwoche*, 16-10-86
Berndt, Hans, 'Heiner Müllers Wut über die Welt', *Saarbrücker Zeitung*, 8-10-86
-, 'Kalte Schönheit', *Handelsblatt*, 11-10-86

Brenken, Erika, 'Ophelia, auf den schwarzen Lippen Schnee', *Rheinische Post*, 9-10-86

-, 'Welt im Gleichschritt der Verwesung', *Kölner-Stadt-Anzeiger*, 9-11-86

Burkhard, Werner, 'Saison Auftakt vom Rande her', *Süddeutsche Zeitung*, 13-10-86

Fischer, Ulrich, 'Ein souveräner Fehlschlag', *General-Anzeiger*, 8-11-86

Glossner, Herbert, 'Hamlet oder Ein Theater der Stille', *Deutsches Allgemeines Sonntagsblatt*, 12-10-86

Grack, Günther, 'Sinn oder Unsinn', *Der Tagesspiegel*, 9-5-87

Henrichs, Benjamin, 'Sachsen ist nicht Texas', *Die Zeit*, 10-10-86

Honegger, Gitta, 'Wilsonmaschine', *Die Zeit*, 20-6-86

Köpke, Horst, 'Vor den Ruinen Europas', *Frankfurter Rundschau*, 20-11-86

Matussek, Mattias, 'Heiner für alle', *Stern*, 2-10-86, p. 277

Heiner Müllers 'Die Hamletmaschine', programme of the Thalia Theater production, Hamburg, 4-10-86

Heiner Müllers 'Die Hamletmaschine', video of the Thalia Theater production, Hamburg, 4-10-86 (held in the video archive of the Theaterinstitut, Freie Universität, Berlin), NDR version for television

Rischbieter, Henning, 'Deutschland, ein Wilsonmärchen', *Theater heute*, 12/86, pp. 4-6

Rupprecht, Annette, 'Ein höllisches Glaubensbekenntnis?', *Die Tageszeitung*, 10-10-86

Schmidt-Missner, Jürgen, 'Lauter individuelle Endspiele', *Kieler Nachrichten*, 8-10-86

-, 'Strapaziöser Shakespeare', *Stuttgarter Zeitung*, 8-10-86

Schulze-Reimpell, Werner, 'Deutschland ist Hamlet', *Der Tagesspiegel*, 15-10-86

-, 'Geheimnisvolles Ritual über den Lauf der Welt', *Rheinischer Merkur/Christ und Welt*, 10-10-86

Solomon, Alisa, 'Ein Gespräch mit Robert Wilson und Heiner Müller', *Frankfurter Allgemeine Zeitung*, 4-10-86

Wagner, Klaus, 'Ein magisches Quadrat aus lauter letzten Bildern', *Frankfurter Allgemeine Zeitung*, 6-10-86

Warnecke, Kläre, 'Ein Lamento über die verrottete Welt', *Die Welt*, 6-10-86

Wilson, Robert, 'Be Stupid', tr. Guntram Weber, in Wolfgang Storch (ed.), *Explosion of a Memory* (Berlin, Hentrich, 1988), pp. 61-9

-, 'Milk It or Move It', *Theater heute*, 12/86, pp. 4-6

Wolffheim, Elsbeth, '*Hamlet, Hamletmaschine* und anderes', *Neue Züricher Zeitung (Fernausgabe)*, 14-10-86

7   Deutsches Theater, Berlin, 24-3-90

Beckelmann, Jürgen, 'Die DDR im goldenen Gefängnis', *Stuttgarter Zeitung*, 28-3-90
Butter, Martin G., 'Im Wettlauf mit der Geschichte', *Kölner-Stadt-Anzeiger*, 29-3-90
Ebert, Gerhard, 'Müllers *Hamlet* - ein Großmarkt tiefgründiger, flirrender Kunstbilder', *Neues Deutschland*, 27-3-90
Göpfert, Peter Hans, 'Roastbeef bei Shakespeare', *General-Anzeiger*, 28-3-90
Grack, Günther, 'Ein deutscher Totentanz', *Der Tagesspiegel*, 27-3-90
Hacker, Doja, 'Vom Stalinismus zur Deutschen Bank', *Die Weltwoche*, 12-3-90
Henrichs, Benjamin, 'Acht Stunden sind kein Theater', *Die Zeit*, 30-3-90
Kaiser, Ch., 'Müllers *Hamlet* in Berlin: Intellektueller gegen Funktionäre', *Ruhr-Nachrichten*, 26-3-90
Kersten, Heinz, 'Hamlet zwischen Stalin und Kohl', *Die Volkszeitung*, 30-3-90
Krekeler, Elmar, 'Der Däneprinz im Spitzelland', *Die Welt*, 26-3-90
Krug, Hartmut, '"Volk ist immer was Dumpfes"', *Badische Zeitung*, 24/25-3-90
Matussek, Mattias, 'Requiem für einen Staat', *Der Spiegel*, 26-3-90, pp. 290-3
Heiner Müllers 'Die Hamletmaschine', programme of the Deutsches Theater production, Berlin, 24-3-90
Heiner Müllers 'Die Hamletmaschine', video of the Deutsches Theater production, Berlin, 24-3-90 (held in the Zentrum für Theaterdokumentation und -information, Berlin)
Niederdorfer, Hanna, 'Alte und neue Macht', *Handelsblatt*, 30/31-3-90
Petsch, Barbara, 'Heiner Müller. DDR Autor. Material', *Die Presse*, 16/17-6-90
Roelcke, Eckhard, 'Wer ist der Geist?', *Die Zeit*, 16-8-91
Scheffel, Meike, 'Bildschöne Öko-Apokalypse', *Rheinischer Merkur/Christ und Welt*, 30-3-90
Scheller, Bernhard, 'Der Anfang Das Ende. Das Neue Das Alte. *Hamlet/Maschine*', *Sonntag*, 8-4-90
Slevogt, Esther, 'Müllers last game', *Die Tageszeitung*, 28-3-90
Stadelmaier, Gerhard, 'Hamletmaschinenbau', *Frankfurter Allgemeine Zeitung*, 26-3-90

Stone, Michael, 'Der von Ekel gelähmte Mensch im Eiswürfel', *Westfälische Rundschau*, 26-3-90

-, 'Mindestens zwei Stücke pro Abend', *Die Presse*, 29-3-90

-, 'Prinz in der Pfütze', *Rheinische Post*, 28-3-90

Sucher, C. Bernd, 'Heiner Müller, Hamlet und Shakespeare', *Süddeutsche Zeitung*, 26-3-90

-, 'Sein oder Nichtsein - das ist die Frage', *Süddeutsche Zeitung*, 20-8-91

Suschke, Stephan, *Dokumentation zu Heiner Müllers 'Die Hamletmaschine'*, Deutsches Theater, Berlin, 24-3-90 (held in the Zentrum für Theaterdokumentation und -information, Berlin, undated)

Urbaczka, Annett, 'Die Zeit ist aus den Fugen', *Rheinische Post*, 20-8-91

Wenderoth, Horst, 'Im Gleichschritt der Verwesung', *Neue Züricher Zeitung (Fernausgabe)*, 20-4-90

Wiegenstein, Roland H., 'Eine alte Geschichte, wie zum erstenmal erzählt', *Badische Zeitung*, 28-3-90

-, 'Mit dem Gestus des Geschichtsschreibers', *Frankfurter Rundschau*, 28-3-90

Wille, Franz, 'Mühe hat's gemacht', *Theater heute*, 5/90, pp. 25-8

8   Tokio, Japan, 7-92

Anon., 'Heiner Müller zum ersten Mal japanisch', *Die Presse*, 8-7-92

-, 'Heiner Müllers *Hamletmaschine* in Tokio gefeiert', *Westdeutsche Allgemeine Zeitung*, 26-9-92

-, 'Müllers *Hamletmaschine* in Japan', *Westdeutsche Allgemeine Zeitung*, 8-7-92

Schnell, Ralf, 'Ereignis und Eklat', *Zeitschrift für Germanistik*, 2/93, pp. 402-4

Schnell, Ralf, 'Produktivkraft Zeit', *Frankfurter Rundschau*, 20-10-90

9   Mecklenburgisches Staatstheater, Schwerin, 8-10-93[1]

Köpke, Horst, 'Die Macht, die nicht mehr ist', *Frankfurter Rundschau*, no date supplied

Heiner Müllers 'Die Hamletmaschine', programme of the Mecklenburgisches Staatstheater production, Schwerin, 8-10-93

Nümann, Dirk, 'Mein Drama findet nicht meht statt', *Junge Welt*, 12-10-93

---

1   All reviews were supplied by Sabine Andreas and some are unfortunately lacking in certain bibliographical details.

Pätzold, Dietrich, 'Das Zeitalter verendet als starker Theaterabend', no paper title supplied, 11-10-93

Pees, Matthias, 'Was ist hier die Frage?', *Süddeutsche Zeitung*, 12-11-93

Zelt, Manfred, 'Endzeit als unbehagliches Vorspiel', *Schweriner Zeitung*, 13-10-93

Leben Gundlings Friedrich von Preußen Lessings Schlaf Traum Schrei

1   Schauspielhaus, Frankfurt, 26-1-79

Anon., 'Haß auf Preußens Gloria', *Rheinischer Merkur/Christ und Welt*, 2-2-79

Ben, Michael, 'Ich weiß schon, was soll es bedeuten', *Deutsche Volkszeitung*, 8-2-79

Engelhard, Günter, 'Preußen im Abfalleimer', *Deutsche Zeitung*, 2-2-79

Hensel, Georg, 'Müllers Preußen Haß Schmerz Tod', *Frankfurter Allgemeine Zeitung*, 29-1-79

I., P., 'Spekulationen über Preußen', *Frankfurter Rundschau*, 29-1-79

Jansen, Hans, 'Aus Preußens Tollhaus', *Westdeutsche Allgemeine Zeitung*, 29-1-79

Krämer-Badoni, Rudolf, 'Was wollte uns der Dichter sagen?', *Die Welt*, 29-1-79

Heiner Müllers 'Leben Gundlings', programme of the Schauspielhaus production, Frankfurt, 26-1-79

Rischbieter, Henning, 'Unter der schwarzen Sonne der Folter', *Theater heute*, 3/79, pp. 35-41

Schmidt, Dietmar N., 'Preußens Gloria in schwarzer Wanne', *Deutsches Allgemeines Sonntagsblatt*, 4-2-79

-, 'Wut auf die Geschichte', *Vorwärts*, 8-2-79

Schödel, Helmut, 'Vorwärts Preußen, ins Nichts!', *Die Zeit*, 2-2-79

Schönfeld, Heinz, 'Leben Gundlings Friedrich von Preußen Müllers Not Traum Schrei', *Mannheimer Morgen*, 29-1-79

Schultz, Uwe, 'Preußens Aufstieg als zynische Klamotte', *Handelsblatt*, 13-2-79

Stadelmaier, Gerhard, 'Irgendwie daran vorbei', *Stuttgarter Zeitung*, 29-1-79

Wendland, Jens, 'Ins schlechteste Licht gerückt', *Süddeutsche Zeitung*, 29-1-79

Zeis, Renate, 'Kurz-Applaus für langnamiges Stück', *Neue Ruhr Zeitung*, 30-1-79

2   Schauspielhaus, Bochum, 31-3-79

Girshausen, Theo, 'Vom Wahnsinn der Geschichte', *Stuttgarter Zeitung*, 11-4-79
Glauber, Johannes K., 'Über "Preußens Gloria" den Stab gebrochen', *Neue Ruhr Zeitung*, 2-4-79
Hensel, Georg, 'Heiner Müllers Preußen im Raubtierkäfig', *Frankfurter Allgemeine Zeitung*, 6-4-79
Jacobs, Ewald, 'Furioser Zusammenschnitt der preußischen Legende, *Westfälische Rundschau*, 2-4-79
Jansen, Hans, 'Greuelmärchen Preußen', *Westdeutsche Allgemeine Zeitung*, 2-4-79
Heiner Müllers 'Leben Gundlings', programme of the Schauspielhaus production, Bochum, 31-3-79
Heiner Müllers 'Leben Gundlings', prompter's script for the Schauspielhaus production, Bochum, 31-3-79
Schmidt, Konrad, 'Nachtrag zur Preußengeschichte', *Ruhr-Nachrichten*, 2-4-79
Schreiber, Ulrich, 'Ein Greuelmärchen spielbar gemacht', *Frankfurter Rundschau*, 19-4-79
Sucher, C. Bernd, 'Noch einmal Bochum', *Süddeutsche Zeitung*, 2-12-83

3   Schiller-Theater, West Berlin, 2-12-83

Anon., 'Fast ein Tribunal', *Westdeutsche Zeitung*, 6-12-83
     -, 'Heiner Müller sieht reaktionäre Kulturpolitik', *Der Tagesspiegel*, 16-12-83
     -, 'Trost für die Schauspieler', *Der Tagesspiegel*, 14-12-83
Göpfert, Peter Hans, 'Die Mickey Mäuse aus Preußen', *Rhein-Neckar-Zeitung*, 21-12-83
     -, 'Widerwärtigkeiten mit Methode', *General-Anzeiger*, 13-12-83
Grack, Günther, 'Preußen, ein Greuelmärchen', *Der Tagesspiegel*, 5-12-83
Luft, Friedrich, 'Trümmer, Späße, Ferkel', *Die Welt*, 6-12-83
Mommert, Wilfried, 'Derbe Kritik an Preußen sorgt für Tumult im Schiller-Theater', *Westfälische Rundschau*, 5-12-83
Heiner Müllers 'Leben Gundlings', programme of the Schiller-Theater production, West Berlin, 2-12-83
Niehoff, Karena, 'Grausame Aperçus zu einem Mordakt', *Süddeutsche Zeitung*, 28-12-83

Rischbieter, Henning, 'Starke Bilder aus Preußen', *Theater heute*, 2/84, pp. 48-9

Rossmann, Andreas, 'Preußischer Lokal-Termin', *Rheinische Post*, 17-12-83

Wiegenstein, Roland H., 'Preußen allewege', *Frankfurter Rundschau*, 10-12-83

4   Wuppertaler Bühnen, Wuppertal, 2-10-88

Anon., 'Nachdenken über den Verlust an Zielsetzungen', *Die Tageszeitung*, 20/1/89

Berke, Bernd, 'Geisterbahn preußischer Geschichte', *Westfälische Rundschau*, 7-10-88

Busch, Frank, 'Wo holde Ideale schmählich zuschanden gehen', *Süddeutsche Zeitung*, 12-10-88

Hennecke, Günther, 'Von Niebelungentreue und Brudermord', *Neue Züricher Zeitung (Fernausgabe)*, 18-10-88

Jansen, Hans, 'Wuppertal: Greuelmär', *Westdeutsche Allgemeine Zeitung*, 12-10-88

Heiner Müllers 'Leben Gundlings', programme of the Wuppertaler Bühnen production, Wuppertal, 2-10-88

Pfeiffer, Rolf, 'Apo-Revue zwischen Analyse und Parodie', *Westfälische Rundschau*, 12-10-88

Pfister, Eva, 'Jämmerliche deutsche Misere', *Rheinische Post*, 11-10-88

Pohlhausen, Rolf, 'Deutschland, mein Land, unheilig Herz der Völker', *coolibri*, 11/88

Rentsch, Jochen, 'Rückbesinnung auf Hölderlin', *Westfälische Rundschau*, 11-10-88

Schulze-Reimpell, Werner, 'Der Alte Fritz mit Raffzähnen', *Rheinischer Merkur/Christ und Welt*, 14-10-88

-, 'Neue Dringlichkeit', *Theater heute*, 11/88, pp. 26-7

5   Volksbühne, East Berlin, 24-11-88

Anon., 'Greuelmärchen und anderes', *Neue Züricher Zeitung (Fernausgabe)*, 10-1-89

-, *Konzeptionelle Überlegungen* (unpublished documentation held in the archive of the Volksbühne, undated)

-, *Der Probenprozeß 1 und 2* (unpublished documentation held in the archive of the Volksbühne, undated)

Beckelmann, Jürgen, 'Preußens Orangen', *Stuttgarter Zeitung*, 15-12-88

-, 'Schrecken preußischer Geschichte', *Süddeutsche Zeitung*, 22-12-88

-, 'Schrecken preußischer Geschichte', *General-Anzeiger*, 23-12-88

-, 'Tradition der Herrscher - Tradition der Untertanen?', *Frankfurter Rundschau*, 17-12-88

Ebert, Gerhard, 'Wie Theater sich in Metaphern auflöst', *Neues Deutschland*, 8-12-88

Heiner Müllers 'Leben Gundlings', programme and cast list of the Volksbühne production, East Berlin, 24-11-88

Heiner Müllers 'Leben Gundlings', prompter's script for the Volksbühne production, East Berlin, 24-11-88

Stone, Michael, 'Heiner Müllers Preußen-Collage in der DDR', *Westfälische Rundschau*, 7-12-88

-, 'Preußen, ein Greuelmärchen', *Der Tagesspiegel*, 5-12-88

-, 'Preußen, ein Greuelmärchen', *Die Presse*, 4-1-89

6   Maxim-Gorki-Theater, Berlin, 19-12-91

Heyden, Susanne, 'Den Text wie eine Ikone behandelt', *Rheinische Post*, 24-12-91

Kaiser, Ch., '*Gundling*: Zähcs Lebcn in Preußen', *Ruhr-Nachrichten*, 21-12-91

Kramarz, 'Herz König Schwarze Witwe', *Theater Rundschau*, 2/92

Lehme, Jutta, 'Nur ein mäßiger Erfolg für Müller', *Westfälische Rundschau*, 21-12-91

Linzer, Martin, 'Abgesessen?', *Theater der Zeit*, 2/92, p. 27-8

Heiner Müllers 'Leben Gundlings', programme of the Maxim-Gorki-Theater production, Berlin, 19-12-91

Heiner Müllers 'Leben Gundlings', video of the Maxim-Gorki-Theater production, Berlin, 19-12-91, in-house copy

Niederdorfer, Hanna, 'Theater ohne festen Zugriff', *Handelsblatt*, 3/4-1-92

Rauh, Robert, 'Neu am Maxim-Gorki-Theater', *UnAUFGEFORDERT*, 2/92

S, Bv, 'Drei Stunden Langeweile um Preußen-Stück', *Bild*, 21-12-91

Schaper, Rüdiger, 'Naturalismus auf der ganzen Linie', *Süddeutsche Zeitung*, 28/29-12-91

Seifert, Sabine, 'Kleist und Rüben', *Die Tageszeitung*, 23-12-91

W., R. H., 'Klippschul-Lektionen', *Frankfurter Rundschau*, Weihnachten 1991

W., S., 'Das Märchenland liegt anderswo', *Der Tagesspiegel*, 21-12-91

Wenderoth, Horst, 'Instrument der Dialektik', *Neue Züricher Zeitung (Fernausgabe)*, 12-1-92

1   Schauspielhaus, Bochum, 22-4-83

Anon., 'Katastrophen und Tändeleien', *Neue Züricher Zeitung (Fernausgabe)*, 1-5-83
-, *'Verkommenes Ufer Medeamaterial Landschaft mit Argonauten'*, *Bühne und Parkett*, 5/83
-, 'Zusammerarbeit Langhoff-Karge', *guckloch*, 5/83
Bergmann, Kathrin, 'Medea am Swimmingpool', *Die Welt*, 26-4-83
Erdmann, Michael, 'Theatralische Texttransport-Maschine', *Theater heute*, 6/83, pp. 38-43
Grack, Günther, 'Die Welt als Müllkippe', *Der Tagesspiegel*, 23-5-84
Hensel, Georg, 'Zwischen Kolchis und Kassel', *Frankfurter Allgemeine Zeitung*, 25-4-83
Hochhuth, Rolf, 'Wie in einem blinden Spiegel', *Die Weltwoche*, 4-5-83
Ignée, Wolfgang, 'Schlachtfest mit "Material"', *Stuttgarter Zeitung*, 25-4-83
Kill, Reinhard, 'Aerobic in Müll-Landschaft', *Rheinische Post*, 25-4-83
Klunker, Heinz, 'Szenen nach der Katastrophe', *Deutsches Allgemeines Sonntagsblatt*, 1-5-83
Luyken, Sonia, 'Der Rest ist Lyrik', *Rhein-Neckar-Zeitung*, 30-4/1-5-83
Heiner Müllers 'Verkommenes Ufer', programme of the Schauspielhaus production, Bochum, 22-4-83
Heiner Müllers 'Verkommenes Ufer', video of the Schauspielhaus production, Bochum, 22-4-83, in-house copy
Platzek, Ilka, and Ernst, Udo, 'Subjektivität und Phantasie', *guckloch*, 5/83
Platzeck, Wolfgang, 'Die Gespenster der Toten', *Westdeutsche Allgemeine Zeitung*, 25-4-83
Rossmann, Andreas, 'Kot, Tod, Blut, Müll', *Badische Zeitung*, 2-5-83
-, 'Medea - ein zeitloser Mythos der Weiblichkeit', *General-Anzeiger*, 4-5-83
Schödel, Helmut, 'Stunde der Zombies', *Die Zeit*, 29-4-83
Schreiber, Ulrich, 'Der Rest ist Lyrik', *Frankfurter Rundschau*, 25-4-83
-, 'Schluß-Monolog im sportlichen Dauerlauf', *Handelsblatt*, 29/30-4-83
Schulze-Reimpell, Werner, 'Bilder von einer brechenden Beziehung', *Vorwärts*, 5-5-83
-, 'Trümmer der Welt', *Rheinischer Merkur/Christ und Welt*, 29-4-83
-, 'Zauberin übt furchbare Rache', *Kölner-Stadt-Anzeiger*, 3-5-83

Vormweg, Heinrich, 'Immer noch die Argonauten', *Süddeutsche Zeitung*, 28-4-83

Wiltberger, Thomas, 'Endzeitsstimmung und antike Tragödie: Müller Premiere in Bochum', *Ruhr-Nachrichten*, 25-4-83

Wohlgemuth, Johann, 'Kirsten Denes Spiel versöhnt mit Symbolflut', *Westfälische Rundschau*, 25-4-83

2   Schauspielhaus, Vienna, 8-9-83

Friedl, Peter, 'Admiralsjacke und Unterhose', *Theater heute*, 11/83, p. 64

Kathrein, Karin, 'Wie Theater noch attackieren kann', *Die Presse*, 10/11-9-83

3   Kammertheater of the Staatstheater, Stuttgart, 8-12-83

Anon., 'Heiner Müller: *Medeamaterial*', *Süddeutscher Fundfunk*, 9-12-83

Harms, Klaus B., 'Saures von den süßen Jungs aus Texas', *Stuttgarter Nachrichten*, 10-12-83

-, 'Viele verschlüsselte Bilder', *Stuttgarter Nachrichten*, 8-12-83

Koch, Martin Th., 'Das Glück der Schamlippen', *Uni Journal*, 1/84

Ludewig, Wolfgang, 'Medea als Germania', *Südkurier*, 13-12-83

Müller, Christoph, 'Premiere von *Verkommenes Ufer*', *Autoblatt Stuttgart*, 15-12-83

Heiner Müllers 'Verkommenes Ufer', programme of the Staatstheater production, Stuttgart, 8-12-83

petz, 'Medea und die USA', *Stuttgarter Zeitung*, 8-12-83

Schmidt, Hanns-Dietrich, unpublished letter to the author, 14-1-95

Schnabel, Dieter, '*Verkommenes Ufer* Medeamaterial Landschaft mit Argonauten', *Stuttgarter Wochenblatt*, 5-1-84

Stadelmaier, Gerhard, 'Verkommene Show mit Germania: Schmerzensjodler', *Stuttgarter Zeitung*, 10-12-83

4   Münchner Kammerspiele, Munich, 14-11-84

Bock, Hans-Bertram, 'Tote Bilder um Treibhaus', *Nürnberger Nachrichten*, 17/18-11-84

Carstensen, Margit, unpublished letter to the author, 17-1-95

Eichholz, Armin, 'Das Abgründige in Hamlet und Medea', *Münchner Morgenzeitung*, 16-11-84

Fischbach, Ute, 'Hamlet zertrümmert den Kopf von Marx', *Münchner Morgenzeitung*, 14-11-84

Kayser, Beate, 'Werkraum quer', *die taz*, 16-11-84

Kr, 'Messer und Wunde, Hals und Strick', *Bayerische Staatszeitung*, 23-11-84

Heiner Müllers 'Verkommenes Ufer', programme of the Münchener Kammer-
    spiele production, Munich, 14-11-84

Nennecke, Charlotte, 'Klassische Figuren in neuer Umgebung', *Süddeutsche
    Zeitung*, 14-11-84

Reitter, Barbara, 'Heiner Müller: Das Drama findet nicht mehr statt', *Mittel-
    bayerische Zeitung*, 30-11-84

Schödel, Helmut, 'Schlachtbeschreibung', *Die Zeit*, 22-2-85

Schmitz-Burkhardt, Barbara, 'Hamlet sehnt sich nach Väterchen Stalin',
    Frankfurter Rundschau, 23-11-84

Seiler, Manfred, *'Die Hamletmaschine'*, *Bayerischer Rundfunk*, 15-11-84

Sucher, C. Bernd, 'Die Gedanken mit den Bildern verloren', *Süddeutsche
    Zeitung*, 16-11-84

5   Berliner Ensemble, East Berlin, 29-11-87

Gerhardt, Klaus-Peter, 'Drastische Bilder mit sperrigem Text', *Berliner Zeit-
    ung*, 2-10-87

John, Hans Rainer, 'Versachliche Annäherung', *Theater der Zeit*, 3/88, pp.
    3-4

Kühn, Georg-Friedrich, 'Fäden aus den roten Flies', *Frankfurter Rundschau*,
    4-1-88

Heiner Müllers 'Verkommenes Ufer', audio tape of the Berliner Ensemble
    production, East Berlin, 29-11-87 (held in the Zentrum für Theater-
    dokumentation und -information, Berlin)

Heiner Müllers 'Verkommenes Ufer', cast list of the Berliner Ensemble
    production, East Berlin, 29-11-87

Qualmann, Eva, *Dokumentation zu Heiner Müllers 'Verkommenes Ufer'*, East
    Berlin, 29-11-87 (held in the Zentrum für Theaterdokumentation und
    -information, Berlin)

Ullrich, Helmut, 'Medea an einem verkommenen Ufer', *Neue Zeit*, 2-12-87

6   Schauspielhaus, Düsseldorf, 3-6-89

Busch, Frank, 'Teilsieg im Krieg der Geschlechter', *Süddeutsche Zeitung*, 6-
    7-89

Jansen, Hans, 'Das Land der Seele mit dem Körper suchend...', *Westdeut-
    sche Allgemeine Zeitung*, 7-6-89

Kill, Reinhard, 'Kunst-Gewerbe', *Rheinische Post*, 5-6-89

Heiner Müllers 'Verkommenes Ufer', programme of the Schauspielhaus production, Düsseldorf, 3-6-89

Heiner Müllers 'Verkommenes Ufer', video of the Schauspielhaus production, Düsseldorf, 3-6-89, director's copy

Rossmann, Andreas, 'Heiliger Heiner', *Frankfurter Allgemeine Zeitung*, 24-6-89

Tschapke, Reinhard, 'Frauen nach links, Männer nach rechts', *Die Welt*, 5-6-89

7   'Medeamaterial' at the Famagusta, Berlin, 18-2-95

Heiner Müllers 'Medeamaterial', cast list and programme for the Famagusta production, Berlin, 18-2-95

Wolokolamsker Chausee

1   Deutsches Theater, Ostberlin, 8-5-85 ('Russische Eröffnung' with Becker's 'Winterschlacht')

Stone, Michael, 'Moskau 100 Kilometer', *Der Tagesspiegel*, 16-5-85

2   Münchner Kammerspiele, Munich, 20-4-89

Anon., 'Deutsch-deutsche Verhältnisse', *Neue Züricher Zeitung (Fernausgabe)*, 20-4-89

Bauschmidt, Elisabeth, 'Kritik an einem Rätselstück in drei Stufen', *Süddeutsche Zeitung*, 5-5-89

Berger, Jürgen, 'Gefallen an der Front der Dialektik', *Die Tageszeitung*, 25-4-89

Dattenberger, Simone, 'Gefallen an der Front der Dialektik', *Münchner Morgenpost*, 22/3-4-89

Eichholz, Armin, 'Getretene Kreaturen und marxistische Monologe', *Die Welt*, 24-4-89

Göhl, Hans, 'Vor allem Sprache', *Bayern Kurier*, 8-5-89

Grimm, Dieter, 'Ein Dramaturg. Kein Regisseur', *Schwäbische Zeitung*, 27-4-89

Gradinger, Malve, 'Der Zweikampf wird im Gespräch gesucht', *Münchner Morgenzeitung*, 20-4-89

hk, 'Geschichtsphilosophisches Oberseminar', *Applaus*, 6/89

Höbel, Wolfgang, 'Das Leerstück als Lehrstück ernstgenommen', *Handelsblatt*, 22/23-4-89

Iden, Peter, untitled, *Frankfurter Rundschau*, 26-4-89

-, 'Maskenball der toten Avantgarde', *Frankfurter Rundschau*, 13-5-89

Kayser, Beate, 'Nachsitzen in Deutsch', *tageszeitung*, 22/3-4-89

kr, 'Sprödes Sprach- und Denktheater', *Bayerische Staatszeitung*, 28-4-89

Krieger, Hans, 'Kantiges Gestein', *Nürnberger Nachrichten*, 25-4-89

Macher, Hans S., 'Grübeltheater in fünf Stationen', *Trostberger Tageblatt*, 26/7-4-89

Makowsky, Arno, 'Vom Befreiungskampf auf Moskaus Straßen', *Süddeutsche Zeitung*, 20-4-89

Heiner Müllers 'Wolokolamsker Chaussee', programme of the Münchner Kammerspiele production, Munich, 20-4-89

Heiner Müllers 'Wolokolamsker Chaussee', prompter's script of the Münchner Kammerspiele production, Munich, 20-4-89

Nolden, Rainer, 'Getretene Kreaturen und marxistische Monologe', *Die Welt*, 24-4-89

Schostack, Renate, 'Sackgasse Wolokolamsk', *Frankfurter Allgemeine Zeitung*, 28-4-89

Seidenfaden, Ingrid, 'Im Windschatten von Genosse Lenin', *Abendzeitung*, 22/3-4-89

Sucher, C. Bernd, 'Das Theater als Katheder', *Theater heute*, 6/89, p. 52

3   Schlosserei, Cologne, 7-10-89

Hartmann, Rainer, 'Die Furcht vor Panzern bleibt', *Kölner-Stadt-Anzeiger*, 9-10-89

Heuer, Otto, 'Für Aug' und Ohr sinnliche Wortkaskaden', *Rheinische Post*, 17-10-89

Heiner Müllers 'Wolokolamsker Chaussee', programme of the Schlosserei production, Cologne, 7-10-89

Schulze-Reimpell, Werner, 'Erinnerungsarbeit, Überstülpästhetik', *Theater heute*, 12/89, p. 14

Zimmermann, Christoph, 'Dialektik der Verkehrsampel', *Die Welt*, 11-10-89

4   Schauspielhaus, Leipzig, 29-10-89

Ebert, Gerhard, 'Künstlerische Wahrheit, die sich an unserer Wirklichkeit reibt', *Neues Deutschland*, 14-11-89
Heiner Müllers 'Wolokolamsker Chaussee', programme of the Schauspielhaus production, Leipzig, 29-10-89
Heiner Müllers 'Wolokolamsker Chaussee', prompter's script of the Schauspielhaus production, Leipzig, 29-10-89

5   Berliner Ensemble, Berlin, 15-12-89

Beckelmann, Jürgen, 'Von der Zeit überholt', *Stuttgarter Zeitung*, 4-1-90
-, 'Die Wolokolamsker Chausee in ganzer Länge', *General-Anzeiger*, 23/24-12-89
-, 'Zwischen Moskau und Berlin', *Frankfurter Rundschau*, 29-12-89
Kaiser, Ch., 'Von der Wirklichkeit überholt: Müller-Stück in Ostberlin aufgeführt', *Ruhr-Nachrichten*, 20-12-89
Kaiser, Paul, 'Die unbefahrbare Straße', *Die Tageszeitung*, 20-12-89
Heiner Müllers 'Wolokolamsker Chaussee', programme of the Berliner Ensemble production, Berlin, 15-12-89
Heiner Müllers 'Wolokolamsker Chaussee', director's script of the Berliner Ensemble production, Berlin, 15-12-89
Nöldechen, Peter, 'Verkünder der Revolution von der DDR-Wirklichkeit eingeholt', *Westfälische Rundschau*, 19-12-89
Schroth, Christoph, 'Unpublished Notebooks on *Wolokolamsker Chaussee*', property of their author
Wenderoth, Horst, 'Das Recht auf Gedächtnis', *Neue Züricher Zeitung (Fernausgabe)*,5-1-90
Wirsing, Sibylle, 'Auf der langen Straße nach Nirgendwo', *Frankfurter Allgemeine Zeitung*, 28-12-89

6   Thalia Theater, Hamburg, 27-4-90

Anon., 'Lehrstück zur Vergangenheitsbewältigung', *Milwaukee Deutsche Zeitung*, 15-7-90
Bessling, Rainer, 'Auszeit im Vereinigungsprint', *Kreiszeitung für die Landkreise Diepholz und Verden*, 3-5-90
Brachwitz, Christian, 'Reise in die Vergangenheit', *Bergedorfer Zeitung*, 21/22-4-90
Demattia, Oswald, 'Stationen vom Krieg zum Krieg', *Der Standard*, 5/6-5-90

Fürst, Kornelius, 'Beschwerliche Geschichtsreise', *Norddeutsche Nachrichten*, 30-4-90

-, 'Ein Steingrab für Nachkriegs-Träume', *Gießener Anzeiger*, 2-5-90

K., T., 'War das Theater?', *Kieler Nachrichten*, 30-4-90

Kossmann, Julia, 'Parabel vom Krieg mit Wirtschaftlichen Mitteln', *tageszeitung*, 24-4-90

Krieger, Gottfried, 'Fünf kurze Szenen gegen das Vergessen', *Freitag*, 4-5-90

Kronsbein, Joachim, 'Karge Theater-Rohkost', *Hambuger Abendblatt*, 30-4-90

Laages, Michael, 'Gewagte Entwürfe sind immer nötig', *Die Welt*, 27-4-90

-, 'Mehr Bilder braucht das Land', *Hannoverische Allgemeine Zeitung*, 11-5-90

Lange, Mechthild, 'Politische Seminarstunde', *Frankfurter Rundschau*, 8-5-90

Heiner Müllers 'Wolokolamsker Chaussee', programme of the Thalia Theater production, Hamburg, 27-4-90

Heiner Müllers 'Wolokolamsker Chaussee', prompter's script of the Thalia Theater production, Hamburg, 27-4-90

Pees, Matthias, 'Wie Gespenster auf einem Trümmerfeld', *Neue Osnabrücker Zeitung*, 30-4-90

Redetzki, Joachim, 'Müllers Wortfetzen hinterließen Ratlosigkeit', *Stader Tageblatt*, 30-4-90

Rieck, Barbara-Ann, *'Wolokolamsker Chaussee I-V'*, *Print*, 6/90

Riecke, Barbara, *Wolokolamsker Chaussee*, *Die Szene*, 6/90

Sallowsky, Axel M., 'Thalia-Première: Theater zum Abgewöhnen', *Bildzeitung*, 30-4-90

Scheffel, Meike, 'Siegfried Bühr inszeniert *Wolokolamsker Chaussee* von Heiner Müller', *WDR III: 'Feuilleton'*, 28-4-90

Suhl, Rolf, 'Montage-Theater', *Hamburger Rundschau*, 3-5-90

Warnecke, Kläre, 'Ein Eiertanz über den Sozialismus-Abgründen', *Die Welt*, 30-4-90

Wilhelm, Joachim L., 'Theatralische Leichenschändung', *Hamburger Anzeigen und Nachrichten*, 30-4-90

Witzeling, Klaus, 'Ein Erinnern auf Trümmern', *Hamburger Morgenpost*, 30-4-90

-, 'Ich will zum Mitdenken verführen', *Die Morgenpost*, 23-4-90

Goebbels, Heiner, *Hörstücke. Nach Texten von Heiner Müller* (Munich: ECM records, 1452-54, 1994), CD format
Goebbels, Heiner, unpublished letter to the author, 25-5-95
Müller, Heiner, *Heiner Müller liest 'Wolokolamsker Chaussee'* (Frankfurt/Main: Verlag der Autoren, 1990), cassette format

Britische und Irische Studien zur deutschen Sprache und Literatur

Nr. 1 Geoffrey Perkins: Contemporary Theory of Expressionism, 1974. 182 S.

Nr. 2 Paul Kussmaul: Bertolt Brecht und das englische Drama der Renaissance, 1974. 175 S.

Nr. 3 Eudo C. Mason: Hölderlin and Goethe, 1975. 145 S.

Nr. 4 W.E. Yates: Tradition in the German Sonnet, 1981. 98 S.

Nr. 5 Rhys W. Williams: Carl Sternheim. A Critical Study, 1982. 282 S.

Nr. 6 Roger H. Stephenson: Goethe's Wisdom Literature, 1983. 274 S.

Nr. 7 John Hennig: Goethe and the English Speaking World, 1983. 288 S.

Nr. 8 John R.P. McKenzie: Social Comedy in Austria and Germany 1890-1933, 1992. 262 S., 2nd Edition 1996.

Nr. 9 David Basker: Chaos, Control and Consistency: The Narrative Vision of Wolfgang Koeppen, 1993. 352 S.

Nr. 10 John Klapper: Stefan Andres. The Christian Humanist as a Critic of his Times, 1995. 188 S.

Nr. 11 Anthony Grenville: Cockpit of Ideologies. The Literature and Political History of the Weimar Republic, 1995. 394 S.

Nr. 12 T.M. Holmes: The Rehearsal of Revolution. Georg Büchner's Politics and his Drama *Dantons Tod*, 1995. 214 S.

Nr. 13 Andrew Plowman: The Radical Subject. Social Change and the Self in Recent German Autobiography, 1998. 168 S.

Nr. 14 David Barnett: Literature versus Theatre. Textual Problems and Theatrical Realization in the Later Plays of Heiner Müller, 1998. 293 S.

Nr. 15 Stephen Parker: Peter Huchel. A Literary Life in 20th-Century Germany, 1998. 617 S.